C000135988

1 MONTH OF
FREE
READING

at

www.ForgottenBooks.com

By purchasing this book you are eligible for one month membership to ForgottenBooks.com, giving you unlimited access to our entire collection of over 1,000,000 titles via our web site and mobile apps.

To claim your free month visit:

www.forgottenbooks.com/free1305165

ISBN 978-0-428-72560-0
PIBN 11305165

DEPARTMENT OF COMMERCE

BUREAU OF FISHERIES
HENRY O'MALLEY, Commissioner

FISHERY INDUSTRIES OF THE UNITED STATES 1923

By OSCAR E. SETTE
Assistant in Charge, Division of Fishery Industries

APPENDIX IV TO THE REPORT OF THE U. S. COMMISSIONER
OF FISHERIES FOR 1924

Bureau of Fisheries Document No. 976

WASHINGTON
GOVERNMENT PRINTING OFFICE
1925

FISHERY INDUSTRIES OF THE UNITED STATES, 1923 [1]

By Oscar E. Sette

Assistant in Charge, Division of Fishery Industries

CONTENTS

[1] Appendix IV to the Report of the U. S. Commissioner of Fisheries for 1924. B. F. Doc. 976.

INTRODUCTION

In 1923 the fishery industries to a marked degree recovered from the severe depression that existed in 1920 and 1921. This was evidenced by an increased number of landings, a greater amount of fish frozen and canned, and the generally higher prices that prevailed during the year.

The landings by vessels at the principal New England ports substantially exceeded those of previous years. The average price paid the fishermen for all fresh fish landed at Boston was 4.37 cents in 1923, as compared with 3.78 cents per pound in 1922. Although this was a substantial increase, the prices of fish as compared with those of other commodities are still below the pre-war level, though nearly approaching it. A decreased number of landings at Seattle was offset by their increased value, due to the relatively greater salmon catch in Puget Sound. The landings of fresh fish in California also exceeded those of the previous year.

The production of canned fishery products and by-products in 1923 was greater than in 1922, the total value of the former amounting to $72,445,205 and of the latter to $12,702,861. This registers an increase of 19.8 per cent in the value of canned products and of 11.5 per cent in the value of by-products. The Maine sardine and crab packs alone showed a decrease as compared with 1922. The exports of canned fish amounted to 95,365,169 pounds, an increase of 8 per cent over the 88,416,266 pounds exported in 1922.

SUMMARY OF OPERATIONS

During the year statistical canvasses were made of the fisheries of the Mississippi River and its tributaries, the Great Lakes, and the Pacific coast for the calendar year 1922; the shad and alewife fisheries of the Potomac River for 1922 and 1923; and of the canned fishery products and by-products of the United States for 1923. The landings of the vessel fisheries at the ports of Boston and Gloucester, Mass., Portland, Me., and Seattle, Wash., have been collected as heretofore, and published as monthly and annual bulletins. In addition, there have been published monthly bulletins showing the amount of the various species of fish frozen and held in cold storage in the several sections of the country. The results of the canvasses mentioned and summary analyses of the freezing and cold-storage data are embodied in the present report, together with the quantity of fish landed in California in 1923 and the fishery products received at the municipal fish wharf and market, Washington, D. C.

In fisheries technology continued investigation of net preservatives has shown results in commercial practice; the investigation of canning sardines has yielded notable results, and an investigation of the iodine content of fishes has extended our knowledge of the health properties of sea food.

PUBLICATIONS OF THE DIVISION

During the calendar year 1923 the following publications, prepared in this division, were issued. This list does not include the monthly statistical bulletins for Boston and Gloucester, Mass., Portland, Me., and Seattle, Wash., and the monthly publication of the cold-storage holdings of frozen fish.

DOCUMENTS

Trade in fresh and frozen fishery products and related marketing considerations in Boston, Mass.; by L. T. Hopkinson, 8°, 29 pp. 2 figs.   Document No. 939.

Properties and values of certain fish-net preservatives (with bibliography); by Harden F. Taylor and Arthur W. Wells, 8°, 71 pp. 32 figs.   Document No. 947.

Fishery industries of the United States. Report of the Division of Fishery Industries for 1922; by Harden F. Taylor, 8°, 113 pp. 4 figs.   Document No. 954.

STATISTICAL BULLETINS

Statement, by fishing grounds, of the quantities and values of certain fishery products landed at Seattle, Wash.; by American fishing vessels during the calendar year 1922.   Statistical Bulletin No. 558.

Statement, by months, of the quantities and values of certain fishery products landed at Boston and Gloucester, Mass., and Portland, Me., by American fishing vessels during the calendar year 1922.   Statistical Bulletin No. 559.

Statement, by fishing grounds, of the quantities and values of certain fishery products landed at Boston and Gloucester, Mass., and Portland Me., by American fishing vessels during the calendar year 1922.   Statistical Bulletin No. 560.

Fisheries of New York, New Jersey, and Delaware, 1921.   Statistical Bulletin No. 569.

Canned fishery products and by-products of the United States and Alaska, 1922.   Statistical Bulletin No. 570.

TECHNOLOGICAL INVESTIGATIONS

The primary function of the Bureau of Fisheries is to properly conserve the food fishes of the Nation. Conservation should be understood to include more than a simple saying or hoarding of resources. In order that our fisheries may be of greatest value, they must be made to yield the maximum supply of fish food commensurate with their continued productivity. This means that raw materials taken from the sea should be utilized in a manner that will provide the greatest amount of properly prepared food materials to the Nation. The fishing industry is notoriously backward in the adoption of improved methods of preserving and marketing its products, the utilization of its by-products, and in so conducting its business as to furnish a stable supply of products.

Fisheries technology, as practiced by the Bureau of Fisheries, has to do with the improvement of existing and the development of new and better equipment, methods, products, and practices within the different branches of the fishing industry, and with the proper utilization of its wastes and by-products. The accomplishment of these ends calls for the application of science in many forms, and the carrying out of quite widely diversified research, both as to type and purpose. Knowledge of practices thus gained are then presented to the industry and their application thereto urged and directed until they become integral parts of it.

The fisheries industries offer an almost virgin field for work of this nature, and a large amount of such work must be done before they can be placed in the same class with other industries that supply the Nation with food. Well-directed efforts along these lines may be expected to and do yield large returns. The success now being attained with the results of the bureau's net-preservative and sardine-canning investigations bears out this statement.

The policy of the bureau is to carry on such technological investigations as are possible with the limited funds and personnel available for this purpose. Endeavor is made to select broad fundamental studies, which are urgent, promise to be of the greatest value to the largest number, and which the industry itself is least capable of undertaking. In this work direct results are not the only ones obtained. A successful investigation gives general confidence in what science can do for the fishery industries, and leads to independent initiative in fisheries' technology.

CANNING SARDINES

In the bureau's experimental laboratory at San Pedro, Calif., attention to the technology of sardine canning has been continued. This research has been yielding excellent results of evident value to the industry.

An opinion has been prevalent that the method of preparing the fish for canning greatly influences the ability of the canned product to withstand the vicissitudes of storage and shipment. It was shown by the laboratory that the physical condition of the fish themselves at the time of being packed, and not the method of producing that condition, is the determining factor. Since the preparation of fish for canning as sardines is essentially a process of removing excess water from them, any procedure that effectively accomplishes this removal without adding any foreign product to the fish, and at the same time leaves them in good physical condition, gives a good final product.

Partial drying by moving air has so far been an essential step in all successful commerical methods of preparing fish for canning as sardines. Fundamental knowledge of this procedure was needed to enable further effective work upon the development of a new method. This information was therefore obtained, and now, for the first time, data are at hand, which will enable drying equipment in the sardine canning industry to be designed upon a scientific basis. Advantage has already been taken of this fact, with very good results, in the building of new equipment and the improvement of old within the industry. It has been possible to show how fish may be dried for frying in from one-third to one-fifth of the time formerly required. The size of the equipment may be decreased correspondingly.

The real outcome of the drying research and the studies that preceded it has been the development of a new process of preparing fish for canning. This process depends on rapidly moving hot air to cook and dry the fish simultaneously, followed by a period of cooling in a blast of cold air, so that they may be packed immediately. The time required for carrying out this process has finally been shortened to about 40 minutes for the largest California pilchards, and operation can be continuous. In the frying-in-oil method now in use the fish are dried at least 30 minutes, fried 7 to 10 minutes, and allowed to drain and cool over night before being packed. Fish prepared in the new way are not open to the objections to which fried fish are subject.

PRESERVATION OF NETS

The publication during the year 1923 of the results of experiments in the preservation of fish nets has enabled commercial fishermen and the trade to take advantage of the information resulting from the extensive experiments carried on in this field. Manufacturers were quick to see the possibilities and sufficient quantities of copper oleate were produced to meet the demand. Its use as a fish-net preservative has even passed beyond the borders of our own country. The results, on the whole, give very favorable evidence of the usefulness of copper oleate, but for certain fishing gear modifications of application have been found to be necessary.

Further experiments were conducted on the preservation of fish nets, and a large series of tests were made. This series included tests in salt water at Beaufort, N. C.; Boothbay Harbor, Me.; San Pedro, Calif.; and Astoria, Oreg.; and in fresh water at Charlevoix, Mich.; Put in Bay, Ohio; Fairport, Iowa; and Washington, D. C. Previous tests had indicated that copper oleate was possibly slightly too soluble (especially in fresh water) to be entirely satisfactory as a preservative. In an effort to overcome this objection copper oleate was applied in combinations including both raw and boiled linseed oil, paraffin, and coal tar. It was found, however, that although linseed oil decreased the solubility to some extent, this combination does not make as efficient a preservative and anti-fouling agent as copper oleate alone. Evidently a certain degree of solubility is desirable. Tests in the Potomac River demonstrated that it is well to frequently treat with copper oleate twine that is continuously exposed, and it was found that twine treated every 30 days lasted almost twice as long as that given but one treatment.

The experiments as a whole clearly indicated that the use of coal tar with copper oleate preserved the tensile strength of the lines best. Where considerable increase in weight and stiffness is objectionable, such treatment, of course, should not be given.

Other experiments showed that, in general, twine that is periodically submerged will last longer than that continuously submerged. It was also found that there was a marked difference in effectiveness of preservatives in one year as compared with their effectiveness when similarly used in the same waters the following year. It is therefore clearly indicated that the degree of success to be attained with any net preservative in any particular case can not be predicted. It can, however, be said, when all factors are taken into consideration, that copper oleate has proved itself superior to any preservative tested experimentally.

IODINE CONTENT OF SEA FOODS

In recent years a lack of iodine in food and drinking water has been recognized as one of the most important causes of endemic goiter, cretinism, and other disorders of the thyroid gland. Thyroxin, the active principle of the thyroid gland, has been shown to be an iodine compound. Various observers have shown that it is only necessary to have small amounts of iodine in the food or drinking water to enable the thyroid gland to function properly.

Physiologists and physicians recently have called attention to the probability that sea foods might constitute an agreeable and convenient source of iodine for the public at large. In order to supply information on this subject, an investigation of the iodine content of sea foods was made in the fishery products laboratory, and the iodine content of a large number of fresh and salt water fish and shellfish was determined. The work showed that oysters, clams, and lobsters are unusually rich in iodine, containing about 200 times as much as such common foods as beefsteak, milk, eggs, etc. Shrimp contain about 100 times as much, and crabs and most marine fish an average of about 50 times as much. Fresh-water fishes were found to contain very small amounts of iodine, the quantity being about the same as that found in milk, eggs, beefsteak, etc. The results of these determinations have been published for the use of the trade.

PRODUCTION OF CERTAIN FISHERY PRODUCTS IN 1922 AND 1923

The following table has been prepared to show the general trend of the fishing industry in so far as changes can be shown by data available that apply to 1922 and 1923:

Production and value of certain fishery products in 1922 and 1923 compared

Products	1922		1923		Per cent increase (+) or decrease (−)	
	Quantity	*Value*	*Quantity*	*Value*	*Quantity*	*Value*
Fish landed by fishing vessels at Boston and Gloucester, Mass., and Portland, Me_____pounds__	159, 875, 391	$5, 465, 932	174, 941, 469	$7, 051, 154	+9. 4	+29. 0
Trips_____number__	6, 349	----------	6, 535	----------	+2. 9	
Fish landed by fishing and collecting vessels at Seattle, Wash. _____pounds__	26, 415, 440	2, 214, 654	25, 625, 060	2, 630, 318	−2. 9	+18. 7
Trips_____number__	836	----------	919	----------	+9. 9	
Product of fisheries of California _____pounds__	168, 969, 733	----------	230, 830, 942	----------	+36. 6	
Fish received at Washington, D. C., municipal wharf___pounds__	6, 442, 663	----------	5, 678, 157	----------	−11. 9	
Sponges sold at Sponge Exchange, Tarpon Springs, Fla___pounds__	526, 885	699, 092	490, 200	734, 391	−6. 9	+5. 0
Canned salmon:						
Pacific Coast States____cases__	733, 246	8, 633, 524	1, 367, 263	12, 660, 566	+86. 4	+46. 6
Alaska_____do____	4, 501, 652	29, 787, 193	5, 035, 697	32, 873, 007	+11. 9	+10. 4
Total, canned salmon_do____	5, 234, 898	38, 420, 717	6, 402, 960	45, 533, 573	+22. 3	+18. 5
Canned sardines:						
Maine and Massachusetts _____cases__	1, 775, 878	5, 750, 109	1, 219, 675	5, 288, 865	−31. 3	−8. 0
California_____do____	728, 979	3, 361, 480	1, 115, 422	4, 607, 931	+53. 0	+37. 1
Total, canned sardines_do____	2, 504, 857	9, 111, 589	2, 335, 097	9, 896, 796	−6. 8	+8. 6
Canned tuna and tunalike fishes in California_____cases__	629, 920	4, 372, 806	788, 611	6, 914, 760	+25. 2	+58. 1
Canned shrimp_____do____	586, 691	3, 064, 087	691, 339	4, 256, 379	+17. 8	+38. 9
Canned clams, hard, soft, and razor_____cases__	308, 640	1, 716, 365	328, 329	1, 710, 616	+6. 4	−.3
Canned oysters_____do____	522, 549	2, 423, 616	537, 549	2, 720, 073	+2. 9	+12. 2
All canned fishery products_do____	10, 094, 549	60, 464, 947	11, 453, 367	72, 445, 205	+13. 5	+19. 8
Menhaden industry:						
Fish utilized_____number__	1, 212, 450, 669	2, 457, 690	1, 110, 291, 427	4, 430, 463	−8. 4	+80. 3
Fish meal and scrap produced_____tons__	93, 576	3, 221, 758	88, 387	3, 094, 276	−5. 5	−4. 0
Oil_____gallons__	7, 102, 677	2, 904, 833	7, 461, 365	3, 316, 277	+5. 1	+14. 2
Fish oils other than menhaden _____gallons__	1, 185, 651	441, 213	2, 355, 606	996, 033	+98. 7	+125. 7
Fish meal and scrap other than menhaden_____tons__	22, 590	1, 114, 919	25, 498	1, 319, 109	+12. 9	+18. 3
Liquid glue_____gallons__	323, 003	278, 424	465, 814	680, 054	+44. 2	+144. 3
All by-products_____	----------	11, 390, 693	----------	12, 702, 861	----------	+11. 5
Fish, frozen_____pounds__	75, 453, 674	----------	91, 548, 643	----------	+21. 3	----------

CANNED FISHERY PRODUCTS AND BY-PRODUCTS OF THE UNITED STATES AND ALASKA, 1923

The bureau has made a canvass of the canned fishery products and by-products of the United States and Alaska for 1923, and statistics were published and distributed to the trade as Statistical Bulletin No. 608. The total value of canned products in 1923 amounted to $72,445,205 and of by-products $12,702,861. As compared with 1922 there was an increase in the value of canned products of $11,980,258, or 19.81 per cent, and in the value of by-products of $1,312,168, or 11.52 per cent. The canned products consisted principally of canned salmon, sardines, shad, alewives, albacore, tuna, shrimp, crabs, clams, and oysters, and the by-products of fish scrap, meal, and oil, and the crushed shells of oysters, mussels, and clams for poultry food, lime, and stucco. The fish scrap, meal, and oil prepared in the menhaden industry are also included under by-products of the fisheries.

CANNED FISHERY PRODUCTS

SALMON

In 1923 there were 188 plants engaged in canning salmon in the Pacific Coast States and Alaska, as compared with 179 in the previous year. Of this number 130 were operated in Alaska, 35 in Washington, 21 in Oregon, and 2 in California. The pack of canned salmon in 1923, on the basis of 48 one-pound cans to the case, amounted to 6,402,960 cases, valued at $45,533,578.

In the Pacific Coast States the pack amounted to 1,367,263 cases, valued at $12,660,566, as follows: Chinook, 384,705 cases, valued at $5,790,419; sockeye, 105,336 cases, valued at $1,955,549; coho or silver, 245,548 cases, valued at $1,608,627; humpback or pink, 445,175 cases, valued at $2,211,742; chum, 154,342 cases, valued at $769,839; steelhead, 32,157 cases, valued at $324,390; and other salmon products to the value of $122,228.

In Alaska the pack amounted to 5,035,697 cases, valued at $32,-873,007, divided as follows: Chinook, 38,343 cases, valued at $328-270; sockeye, 1,859,496 cases, valued at $17,253,792; coho or silver, 164,107 cases, valued at $943,318; humpback or pink, 2,448,129 cases, valued at $11,899,956; and chum, 525,622 cases, valued at $2,447,671.

Compared with previous years there was an increase of 7 canneries in Alaska, 1 in Washington, and 1 in Oregon. There was an increase in the pack of canned salmon of 1,168,062 cases, or 22 per cent in quantity, and of $7,112,856, or 19 per cent, in value. The Alaska pack increased 534,045 cases, or 12 per cent, in quantity and $3,085,-814, or 10 per cent, in value. This was due to a moderate increase in the pack of king or chinook salmon, and a decided increase in humpbacks. The sockeyes, cohoes, and chums were packed in lesser quantities than in 1922. In the Pacific Coast States there was an increase of 634,017 cases, or 86 per cent, in quantity and $4,027,042, or 47 per cent, in value. An increase occurred in all the species, but was particularly noticeable in the humpbacks and chums.

Pack of canned salmon, 1923

Products	Pacific Coast States						Alaska	
	Washington		Oregon and California		Total		Southeast	
	Cases	Value	Cases	Value	Cases	Value	Cases	Value
King, chinook, or spring:								
1-pound tall	42,773	$452,609	5,913	$58,338	48,686	$510,947	4,090	$33,361
1-pound flat	42,572	637,719	86,045	1,255,263	128,617	1,892,982	4,093	40,074
1-pound oval	4,918	108,196	5,719	125,818	10,637	234,014		
½-pound flat	57,362	901,180	138,225	2,218,312	195,587	3,119,492	4,865	50,330
½-pound oval	167	4,676	1,011	28,308	1,178	32,984		
Total	147,792	2,104,380	236,913	3,686,039	384,705	5,790,419	13,048	123,765
Red or sockeye:								
1-pound tall	1,781	30,989	4,022	69,983	5,803	100,972	99,098	881,486
1-pound flat	19,783	336,311	85	1,445	19,868	337,756	35,313	370,994
½-pound flat	55,449	1,055,749	24,216	461,072	79,065	1,516,821	43,914	560,555
Total	77,013	1,423,049	28,323	532,500	105,336	1,955,549	178,325	1,813,035
Coho or silver:								
1-pound tall	77,162	447,540	34,317	199,039	111,479	646,579	112,276	611,535
1-pound flat	67,125	456,450	35,457	241,107	102,582	697,557	8,128	56,215
½-pound flat	11,514	96,718	19,973	167,773	31,487	264,491	9,947	82,486
Total	155,801	1,000,708	89,747	607,919	245,548	1,608,627	130,351	750,236
Humpback or pink:								
1-pound tall	395,732	1,915,343	489	2,367	396,221	1,917,710	2,218,495	10,753,740
1-pound flat	28,099	149,487	1,322	7,033	29,421	156,520	6,988	37,382
½-pound flat	19,282	135,745	251	1,767	19,533	137,512	26,536	174,552
Total	443,113	2,200,575	2,062	11,167	445,175	2,211,742	2,252,019	10,965,674
Chum or keta:								
1-pound tall	134,392	645,082	4,865	23,352	139,257	668,434	427,210	1,999,026
1-pound flat	553	2,721	71	349	624	3,070	16	76
½-pound flat	5,964	40,555	8,497	57,780	14,461	98,335	6,150	38,144
Total	140,909	688,358	13,433	81,481	154,342	769,839	433,376	2,037,246
Steelhead:								
1-pound tall	1,216	15,808			1,216	15,808		
1-pound flat	3,323	21,932	13,234	87,344	16,557	109,276		
½-pound flat	6,641	78,629	7,743	120,677	14,384	199,306		
Total	11,180	116,369	20,977	208,021	32,157	324,390		
Grand total	975,808	7,533,439	391,455	5,127,127	1,367,263	12,660,566	3,007,119	15,689,956

Pack of canned salmon, 1923—Continued

Products	Alaska—continued						Grand total	
	Central		Western		Total			
	Cases	*Value*	*Cases*	*Value*	*Cases*	*Value*	*Cases*	*Value*
King, chinook, or spring:								
1-pound tall_____	6,914	$53,343	14,592	$108,041	25,596	$194,745	74,282	$705,692
1-pound flat_____	3,188	34,930			7,281	75,004	135,898	1,967,986
1-pound oval_____							10,637	234,014
½-pound flat_____	601	8,191			5,466	58,521	201,053	3,178,013
½-pound oval_____							1,178	32,984
Total_____	10,703	96,464	14,592	108,041	38,343	328,270	423,048	6,118,689
Red or sockeye:								
1-pound tall_____	294,912	2,639,812	1,184,440	10,539,114	1,578,450	14,060,412	1,584,253	14,161,384
1-pound flat_____	68,799	687,154	55,159	541,029	159,271	1,599,177	179,139	1,936,933
½-pound flat_____	67,621	898,129	10,240	135,519	121,775	1,594,203	201,440	3,111,024
Total_____	431,332	4,225,095	1,249,839	11,215,662	1,859,496	17,253,792	1,964,832	19,209,341
Coho or silver:								
1-pound tall_____	27,017	146,557	797	4,381	140,090	762,473	251,569	1,409,052
1-pound flat_____	2,023	12,947			10,151	69,162	112,733	766,719
½-pound flat_____	3,891	28,051	28	246	13,866	111,683	45,353	376,174
Total_____	32,931	188,455	825	4,627	164,107	943,318	409,655	2,551,945
Humpback or pink:								
1-pound tall_____	190,843	903,395			2,409,338	11,657,135	2,805,559	13,574,845
1-pound flat_____	2,440	11,712			9,428	49,094	38,849	205,614
½-pound flat_____	2,827	19,175			29,363	193,727	48,896	331,239
Total_____	196,110	934,282			2,448,129	11,899,956	2,893,304	14,111,698
Chum or keta:								
1-pound tall_____	72,358	320,492	19,682	88,533	519,250	2,408,051	658,507	3,076,485
1-pound flat_____					16	76	640	3,146
½-pound flat_____	206	1,400			6,356	39,544	20,817	137,879
Total_____	72,564	321,892	19,682	88,533	525,622	2,447,671	679,964	3,217,510
Steelhead:								
1-pound tall_____							1,216	15,808
1-pound flat_____							16,557	109,276
½-pound flat_____							14,384	199,306
Total_____							32,157	324,390
Grand total_____	743,640	5,766,188	1,284,938	11,416,863	5,035,697	32,873,007	6,402,960	45,533,573

SARDINES

In 1923 there was a marked increase in the California pack of sardines and a decrease in the Maine pack. In Maine 29 plants were engaged in the canning of sardines and in Massachusetts there was 1. These produced 1,219,675 cases, valued at $5,288,865. Most of the pack was in quarter-pound cans, 100 to the case. When the entire pack is converted to this standard and the 1922 pack is similarly treated, the total amounts are 1,272,277 and 1,869,719 cases, respectively, which shows a decrease in 1923 of 597,442 cases, or 32 per cent. The decrease in value was $461,244, or 8 per cent. This indicates a substantial increase in prices.

In California 22 plants were engaged in the canning of sardines, producing 1,115,422 cases, valued at $4,607,931. These were packed mostly in 1-pound cans, 48 to the case. When the entire pack is converted to this standard and the 1922 pack similarly treated, we find that the total amounts in these two years were 1,100,162 and 715,364 cases respectively, which shows an increase in 1923 of 384,798 cases, or 54 per cent. The value increased $1,246,451, or 37 per cent, indicating a lower price for this product in 1923.

Pack of sardines, 1923

Sardines (herring)	Maine and Massachusetts		Sardines (pilchard)	California	
	Cases	Value		Cases	Value
In olive oil: Quarters(100 cans)	38,704	$243,783	½-pound oval (48 cans) [1]	6,431	$21,788
In other oils: Quarters (100 cans)	964,261	4,143,461	1-pound oval (48 cans): In tomato sauce	888,541	3,553,080
In mustard:			In mustard	136,828	547,278
Quarters (100 cans)	87,463	378,578	Soused	38,751	154,977
Three-quarters (48 cans)	119,549	479,329	In other sauces	17,294	74,248
In other sauces: Quarters (100 cans) [1]	9,698	43,714	¼-pound square (100 cans) [2]	25,342	227,347
			½-pound square (100 cans) [2]	[3] 2,235	29,213
Total	1,219,675	5,288,865	Total	1,115,422	4,607,931

[1] Largely in tomato sauce.
[2] Largely in oil.
[3] Includes a few cases of 48 cans each which have been converted to a basis of 100 cans to the case.

SHAD AND ALEWIVES

The canning of shad and shad roe is carried on solely in the Pacific Coast States. In 1923 there were 6 plants in Washington and 8 plants in Oregon engaged in canning these products. The total production amounted to 3,409 cases, valued at $53,483 in 1923, and is a substantial increase over the 1922 production, both in amount and value.

The pack of alewives and alewife roe was prepared in Maryland, Virginia, and North Carolina, where there were 9, 21, and 2 plants, respectively, making a total of 32 plants engaged in this business. The production in 1923 was 43,920 cases, valued at $171,350, consisting mostly of alewife roe. This is an increase both in amount and value, as compared with the previous year.

Pack of shad and alewives, 1923

Shad	Washington and Oregon		Alewives	Maryland, Virginia, and North Carolina	
	Cases	Value		Cases	Value
½-pound flat (48 cans)	350	$2,800	No. 2 (24 cans)	1,145	$1,915
1-pound flat (48 cans)	[1] 706	16,944	Roe:		
1-pound tall (48 cans)	1,281	17,421	No. ½ and No. 1 (48 cans)	[2] 2,266	10,499
Roe:			No. 2 (24 cans)	40,509	158,936
½-pound flat (48 cans)	376	3,760	Total	43,920	171,350
½-pound oval (48 cans)	696	12,528			
Total	3,409	53,483			

[1] Includes a few cases of 1-pound oval.
[2] The No. ½ cans have been converted to a basis of No. 1 cans, 48 to a case.

TUNA AND TUNALIKE FISHES

The canning of these fishes is confined to the State of California, where, in 1923, there were 19 plants operating in this business. The total pack, including "tonno," bonito, and yellowtail, amounted to 788,611 cases, valued at $6,914,760, as compared with 654,183 cases, valued at $4,511,873, packed the previous year.

Most of the tunas are packed in half-pound cans, 48 to the case. In the following comparisons the entire pack is converted to this standard. The total amount packed in 1923 was 817,836 cases; as compared with 672,321 cases the previous year. This is an increase of 145,515 cases, or 22 per cent, in amount. The value increased 53 per cent. The pack of the highly prized white-meated tuna (albacore), however, does not show such a distinct increase. In 1923 there were 310,037 cases packed, as compared with 296,210 in 1922, representing an increase of only 5 per cent. The pack of bluefin, yellowfin, and striped tuna, "tonno," and bonito amounted to 497,740 cases, as compared with 371,393 cases in 1922, an increase of 126,347 cases, or 34 per cent. This increase was to a large extent accomplished by extending fishing operations into Mexican waters.

A development worthy of note is the "tonno" pack. This consists of a highly seasoned pack in oil, prepared after the Italian method. A recent ruling of the Bureau of Chemistry permits canning of the striped tuna, or skipjack, as well as the yellowfin and bluefin tunas under this name. In 1921 this pack consisted of only 1,256 standard cases, valued at $1,953; in 1923 this product attained the amount of 124,420 standard cases, valued at $1,136,184.

The pack of tuna and tunalike fishes, 1923

Sizes	Albacore		Yellowfin		Bluefin		Tuna, bluefin and yellowfin	
	Cases	*Value*	*Cases*	*Value*	*Cases*	*Value*	*Cases*	*Value*
¼-pound round (48 cans)	27,264	$170,402	10,058	$47,777	3,328	$15,810		
¼-pound round (100 cans)							1,299	$12,665
½-pound round (48 cans)	240,159	2,401,590	149,552	1,121,643	57,910	434,327	7,525	56,438
1-pound round (48 cans)	28,123	534,337	11,149	156,086	5,157	72,198	2,001	28,014
4-pound round (12 cans)			1,061	14,854				
Total	295,546	3,106,329	171,820	1,340,360	66,395	522,335	10,825	97,117

Sizes	Tuna, striped		"Tonno"		Bonito		Yellowtail		Total	
	Cases	*Value*	*Cases*	*Value*	*Cases*	*Value*	*Cases*	*Value*	*Cases*	*Value*
¼-pound round (48 cans)	4,846	$18,339	21,504	$118,275					67,000	$370,603
¼-pound round (100 cans)	3,368	25,260	[1] 12,882	153,129	458	$4,988			18,007	196,042
½-pound round (48 cans)	72,838	437,404	[2] 95,435	829,816	13,828	69,140	5,349	$29,740	642,596	5,380,098
1-pound round (48 cans)	8,841	97,251			397	3,778	2,355	25,905	58,023	917,569
4-pound round (12 cans)									1,061	14,854
5-pound round (12 cans)			1,924	35,594					1,924	35,594
Total	89,893	578,254	131,745	1,136,814	14,683	77,906	7,704	55,645	788,611	6,914,760

[1] Includes a few cases packed 50 cans to the case which have been converted to the equivalent of 100 cans to the case.

[2] Includes a few cases packed 50 cans to the case which have been converted to the equivalent of 48 cans to the case.

SHRIMP AND CRABS

In 1923 there were 8 shrimp canneries operated in Georgia, 1 in North Carolina, 9 in Florida, 7 in Alabama, 28 in Mississippi, 23 in Louisiana, and 2 in Texas, making a total of 78 plants engaged in this business. The production of canned shrimp in tins amounted to 691,339 cases, valued at $4,256,379. In addition to this, there were packed in 5½ and 14 ounce glass jars in Florida and Mississippi 29,166 cases, valued at $125,155. When the entire pack is converted to the basis of No. 1 cans, 48 to the case, the total amount is 700,429 cases, valued at $4,381,534, which, compared to 1922 on the same basis, represents an increase of 120,632 standard cases, or 21 per cent, in amount, and $1,317,447, or 43 per cent, in value.

Crabs were canned at 2 plants in Alaska, 1 in Maine, 3 in Maryland, 1 in Mississippi, and 2 in Virginia. The total pack amounted to 4,138 cases, valued at $47,023, as compared with 9,111 cases, valued at $104,171, in 1922.

Pack of shrimp and crabs, 1923

SHRIMP

States	No. 1 cans (4 dozen)		No. 1½ cans (2 dozen)		Total	
	Cases	Value	Cases	Value	Cases	Value
Georgia and North Carolina	81,858	$488,954	6,601	$35,080	88,459	$524,034
Florida	71,367	446,238	4,322	27,320	75,689	473,558
Alabama	57,830	361,246	3,800	23,372	61,630	384,618
Mississippi	163,200	1,005,460	5,832	35,950	169,032	1,041,410
Louisiana and Texas	281,110	1,737,743	15,419	95,016	296,529	1,832,759
Total	655,365	4,039,641	35,974	216,738	691,339	4,256,379

CRABS

States	7½, 8, 9, and 12 ounce cans (4 dozen)		15 and 16 ounce cans (2 dozen)		Total	
Alaska, Maine, Maryland, Mississippi, and Virginia	Cases	Value	Cases	Value	Cases	Value
	[1] 2,993	$33,390	[2] 1,145	$13,633	4,138	$47,023

[1] The 8, 9, and 12 ounce cans have been converted to the equivalent of 7½-ounce cans, 4 dozen to the case.
[2] The 16-ounce cans have been converted to the equivalent of 15-ounce cans, 4 dozen to the case.

CLAMS

In 1923 razor clams were canned at 24 plants in Washington, 3 in Oregon, and 12 in Alaska; hard clams at 2 plants in Florida, 1 in Rhode Island, and 2 in Washington; and soft clams at 19 plants in Maine and 2 in Massachusetts; making a total of 65 canneries engaged in this business. The total production amounted to 328,229 cases, valued at $1,710,616, as compared with 308,640 cases, valued at $1,716,365, in 1922.

Pack of clams, 1923

RAZOR CLAMS

Sizes	Washington		Oregon		Alaska		Total	
	Cases	Value	Cases	Value	Cases	Value	Cases	Value
Whole:								
½-pound flat (4 dozen)	251	$1,355					251	$1,355
No. 2 (2 dozen)	75	450					75	450
1-pound (4 dozen)	4,601	47,030			4,795	$48,004	9,396	95,034
20-ounce (2 dozen)					788	3,546	788	3,546
5-pound (1 dozen)					495	2,722	495	2,722
Minced:								
½-pound flat (4 dozen)	29,206	160,048	66	$362	49,269	314,613	78,541	475,023
No. 1 (4 dozen)	16,975	120,862	962	6,849	16,256	129,084	34,193	256,795
No. 2 (2 dozen)	605	3,751	180	1,116			785	4,867
1-pound (4 dozen)	55	583			5,679	43,160	5,734	43,743
Juice: No. 2 (2 dozen)	130	299			1	10	131	309
Total	51,898	334,378	1,208	8,327	77,283	541,139	130,389	883,844

HARD CLAMS

Sizes	Florida, Rhode Island, and Washington		Sizes	Florida, Rhode Island, and Washington	
	Cases	Value		Cases	Value
Whole:			Chowder and soup:		
½-pound flat (4 dozen)	300	$405	No. 1 (4 dozen)	12,473	$60,272
1-pound (4 dozen)	1,202	9,135	No. 1½ (4 dozen)	9,709	40,000
No. 1 (4 dozen)	7,846	60,926	No. 2 (2 dozen)	26	104
No. 2 (2 dozen)	14,649	77,891	No. 3 (2 dozen)	14,052	64,260
No. 10 (½ dozen)	3,255	21,968	No. 10 (½ dozen)	287	1,866
Minced:			Bouillon, juice, and broth:		
No. 1 (4 dozen)	2,764	16,113	1½ and 3 ounce bottles	1,246	6,286
No. 2 (2 dozen)	1,671	7,823	7 and 14 ounce bottles (2 dozen)	3,284	18,163
No. 10 (½ dozen)	96	676	No. 1 (4 dozen)	77	291
			No. 2 (2 dozen)	979	3,045
			No. 10 (½ dozen)	180	910
			Total	74,096	390,134

Pack of claims, 1923—Continued

SOFT CLAMS

Sizes	Maine and Massachusetts		Sizes	Maine and Massachusetts	
	Cases	*Value*	Chowder:	*Cases*	*Value*
Whole:			10-ounce (2 dozen)	14,792	$17,841
4-ounce (4 dozen)	740	$4,685	10½-ounce (2 dozen)	31,928	51,468
5-ounce (4 dozen)	35,752	168,416	32 and 34 ounce (2 dozen)	[1]15,227	55,070
6-ounce (2 dozen)	2,260	12,814	1-gallon (½ dozen)	1,034	2,965
8-ounce (4 dozen)	8,871	54,954	Bouillon and juice:		
8½-ounce (2 dozen)	627	3,070	8-ounce (2 dozen)	296	296
10-ounce (4 dozen)	7,887	46,391	10-ounce (4 dozen)	37	113
15-ounce (4 dozen)	1,084	7,480	14 ounce (4 dozen)	50	220
18-ounce (2 dozen)	3,084	10,750	No. 2 (2 dozen)	75	105
			Total	123,744	436,638

[1] The 34-ounce cans have been converted to equivalent of 32-ounce cans, 2 dozen to the case.

OYSTERS

Oysters were canned at 12 plants in Maryland, 4 in North Carolina, 10 in South Carolina, 7 in Georgia, 5 in Florida, 6 in Alabama, 3 in Louisiana, and 21 in Mississippi, the total pack amounting to 537,549 cases, valued at $2,720,073. Most of the pack was in No. 1 5-ounce cans, 48 to the case. When the entire pack is converted to this standard and the 1922 pack is similarly treated, the total amounts are 524,544 and 505,973 cases, respectively, which shows an increase in 1923 of 4 per cent. The value increased $296,457, or 12 per cent.

Pack of oysters, 1923

Sizes	Maryland		North Carolina		South Carolina		Georgia	
	Cases	*Value*	*Cases*	*Value*	*Cases*	*Value*	*Cases*	*Value*
4-ounce (4 dozen)	8,886	$48,000	600	$2,760	[1] 5,058	$19,890		
5-ounce (4 dozen)	42,041	240,248	49,370	228,388	83,338	337,719	16,250	$75,939
6-ounce (4 dozen)	19,181	196,429			157	737	99	891
8-ounce (2 dozen)	2,883	14,140	800	3,200	957	3,775		
10-ounce (2 dozen)	16,264	89,553	7,000	36,075	20,443	88,174		
12-ounce (2 dozen)	1,901	18,603					24	192
Total	91,156	606,973	57,770	270,423	109,953	490,295	16,373	77,022

Sizes	Florida		Alabama		Louisiana and Mississippi		Total	
	Cases	*Value*	*Cases*	*Value*	*Cases*	*Value*	*Cases*	*Value*
4-ounce (4 dozen)	1,068	$5,340	673	$2,906	43,176	$196,126	59,461	$275,022
5-ounce (4 dozen)	9,800	48,772	41,222	201,222	100,515	499,352	342,536	1,671,640
6-ounce (4 dozen)					1,242	11,136	20,679	209,193
8-ounce (2 dozen)	120	456	525	1,785	22,983	106,537	28,268	129,893
10-ounce (2 dozen)	86	344	11,356	54,428	29,431	145,356	84,580	413,930
12-ounce (2 dozen)					100	1,600	2,025	20,395
Total	11,074	54,912	53,776	260,341	197,447	960,107	537,549	2,720,073

[1] Includes pack of 3-ounce cans converted to equivalent of 4-ounce cans, 4 dozen to the case.

MISCELLANEOUS CANNED FISHERY PRODUCTS

In addition to the products shown above, there were packed in Maine, Massachusetts, New York, New Jersey, Maryland, and Wisconsin, 254,562 cases of miscellaneous fishery products, valued at $658,583, and in California, 34,387 cases of tuna flakes, abalone, barracuda, mackerel, and squid, valued at $235,186.

EXPORTS OF CANNED FISHERY PRODUCTS IN 1923

Statistics of the quantity of canned fish exported from the United States during the calendar year 1923, collected and compiled by the Bureau of Foreign and Domestic Commerce, are given in the following table:

Domestic exports of canned fish from the United States, by countries, 1923

Countries	Salmon		Sardines		Tuna		Other canned fish	
	Lbs.	*Dolls.*	*Lbs.*	*Dolls.*	*Lbs.*	*Dolls.*	*Lbs.*	*Dolls.*
Belgium	814, 367	91, 817	627, 520	58, 945			13, 750	1, 200
Denmark	6, 000	635					7, 214	2, 537
France	57, 700	6, 049	33, 560	3, 757			1, 540	482
Germany	82, 918	11, 478	1, 089	223	63	23	107	48
Greece	120, 041	14, 534	23, 245	2, 645			33, 812	8, 306
Italy	194, 800	19, 210			121	15	725	283
Netherlands	479, 836	76, 799	80, 055	7, 420				
Norway	45, 192	10, 855	157	19	85	27	719	204
Russia in Europe	45, 000	3, 675	344	75				
Spain	1, 008	119					9, 000	1, 950
Sweden	20, 041	3, 739					11, 400	4, 038
Turkey in Europe	12, 560	1, 581					108	53
Ukraine	572	157	51, 320	8, 543			1, 360	192
England	31, 090, 188	5, 685, 074	543, 940	53, 664	36	11	64, 440	25, 660
Scotland	637, 768	125, 416	7, 200	612				
Ireland	40, 800	7, 700						
Canada:								
Maritime Provinces	13, 742	1, 667	272, 964	23, 351			2, 536	459
Quebec and Ontario	245, 809	29, 848	1, 779	267	27, 495	7, 726	24, 223	5, 556
Prairie Provinces	23, 560	3, 665			1, 740	548	1, 997	601
British Columbia and Yukon	1, 073, 172	137, 562	10, 369	1, 042	20, 045	6, 107	16, 302	3, 830
British Honduras	36, 375	3, 926	40, 064	4, 430			220	27
Costa Rica	87, 393	9, 353	137, 459	13, 670	216	89	1, 137	333
Guatemala	51, 066	5, 605	121, 094	12, 982	531	185	1, 426	429
Honduras	69, 266	8, 753	126, 391	17, 176	445	193	4, 356	816
Nicaragua	89, 027	9, 553	99, 814	11, 965	363	126	503	171
Panama	220, 927	29, 459	112, 453	13, 442	3, 799	1, 216	11, 168	2, 968
Salvador	16, 800	1, 807	96, 863	9, 427	32	17	1, 579	277
Mexico	1, 654, 380	143, 263	2, 373, 308	231, 359	1, 606	566	132, 736	25, 403
Newfoundland and Labrador			12	5	126	37	211	68
Bermuda	41, 326	8, 134	17, 696	2, 770	642	234	1, 702	502
Barbados	118, 346	16, 008	575	49	94	54	61	43
Jamaica	86, 171	15, 592	97, 190	10, 270			1, 450	548
Trinidad and Tobago	139, 119	22, 499	12, 613	1, 672	412	202	571	152
Other British West Indies	67, 570	12, 107	30, 356	4, 267	60	15	2, 101	514
Cuba	844, 877	82, 169	1, 801, 671	155, 519	3, 444	1, 127	472, 675	36, 336
Dominican Republic	190, 885	20, 271	231, 320	30, 617	495	174	3, 881	1, 183
Dutch West Indies	39, 942	6, 902	12, 683	1, 433	188	61	649	175
Haiti	4, 084	575	1, 838	326	100	42	25, 621	1, 399
French West Indies	700	82						
Virgin Islands of the U. S	30, 454	3, 829	10, 824	2, 072	21	13	1, 827	224
Argentina	1, 021, 474	116, 777	1, 489, 799	126, 017			49, 345	3, 944
Bolivia	65, 676	6, 154	255, 162	18, 696			4, 065	954
Brazil	3, 491	741					801	419
Chile	216, 696	23, 299	548, 018	45, 336	60	28	5, 636	1, 311
Colombia	414, 017	47, 561	115, 449	13, 573	4, 286	1, 672	9, 807	3, 278
Ecuador	117, 542	10, 832	224, 646	19, 984			92	33
British Guiana	212, 694	37, 525	101, 177	11, 214			3, 970	1, 019
Dutch Guiana	32, 497	3, 594	22, 757	3, 126	130	81	1, 432	413
French Guiana	9, 948	1, 164						
Paraguay	840	105						
Peru	426, 163	45, 684	487, 880	43, 717	206	127	2, 434	1, 136
Uruguay	8, 096	1, 404	7, 200	586			4, 459	1, 574
Venezuela	577, 041	58, 614	86, 430	8, 889	2, 473	882	9, 718	2, 018
Aden	480	60						
British India	205, 472	30, 766	197, 931	23, 227	565	227	7, 967	1, 076
Ceylon	54, 931	8, 607	15, 670	1, 936	306	128	3, 626	468
Straits Settlements	115, 750	19, 431	6, 053, 497	503, 511	96	27	229, 574	13, 746
Other British East Indies	2, 736	350	2, 700	270			144	18
China	51, 357	8, 295	334, 050	33, 359	2, 741	870	17, 004	1, 343
Chosen	5, 610	635	96	10	72	30	146	41
Java and Madura	249, 343	27, 207	2, 126, 161	197, 514	66	35	13, 942	1, 207
Other Dutch East Indies	115, 724	11, 961	435, 173	42, 381				
Far Eastern Republic			820	162			2, 000	276
French Indo-China	240	51	108, 260	11, 070			15, 440	1, 308
Hongkong	24, 710	4, 307	442, 598	37, 885	54	22	22, 210	4, 405
Japan	1, 577, 926	150, 328	62, 528	6, 227	470	160	152, 163	16, 753
Kwangtung, leased territory	144	32	84, 712	7, 342			192	24

Domestic exports of canned fish from the United States, by countries, 1923—Con.

Countries	Salmon		Sardines		Tuna		Other canned fish	
	Lbs.	*Dolls.*	*Lbs.*	*Dolls.*	*Lbs.*	*Dolls.*	*Lbs.*	*Dolls.*
Palestine and Syria	31, 588	3, 676	1, 690	117			744	159
Philippine Islands	7, 055, 041	667, 713	13, 225, 126	1, 051, 186	1, 521	640	586, 671	37, 255
Russia in Asia	1, 491	159	5, 760	449				
Siam	2, 916	794	71, 516	4, 570	24	11		
Turkey in Asia	19, 200	2, 280						
Other Asia	336	29						
Australia	6, 142, 166	999, 702	15, 463	2, 911	1, 044	211	5, 425	1, 759
British Oceania	27, 317	3, 871	7, 953	833			75	31
French Oceania	190, 548	21, 263	75, 785	9, 878			116	69
New Zealand	153, 854	28, 405	1, 491	158	21	13	218	74
Other Oceania	33, 893	3, 688	1, 778	296			138	37
Belgian Kongo	1, 498	216					143	59
British West Africa	34, 778	3, 631	6, 470	826			88	22
British South Africa	1, 495, 449	160, 324	33, 020	4, 127			23, 455	4, 605
British East Africa	450	97						
Canary Islands	8, 202	742						
Egypt	41, 755	5, 572	295	54				
Other French Africa	384	54						
Liberia	1, 684	195					95	10
Morocco	1, 353	186	910	105	36	13		
Portuguese East Africa	46, 095	5, 150	33, 200	4, 211			64	36
Other Portuguese Africa	44	13			12	7	6, 962	1, 124
Total	59, 594, 422	9, 154, 711	33, 660, 937	2, 919, 767	76, 342	23, 992	2, 033, 468	228, 971

BY-PRODUCTS OF THE FISHERIES

Although the value of the by-products does not make an impressive total, as compared to the value of canned products, their production is of importance in offsetting excessive overhead costs and salvaging valuable materials that would otherwise be completely lost. Principal among the by-products are the fish oils, fish scrap, crushed shells, and fish glue. Including the oil and scrap produced in the menhaden industry, the by-products in 1923 had a total value of $12,702,861, as compared with $11,390,693 in 1922.

FISH OILS

The fish-oil production in the United States and Alaska in 1923 amounted to 9,590,875 gallons, valued at $4,228,592. This does not include the production of whale oil, which in 1923 was 1,346,356 gallons, valued at $701,731, nor sperm oil, which was 210,474 gallons, valued at $90,153. The largest item of fish oil was menhaden oil, of which 7,461,365 gallons were produced, valued at $3,316,277. In 1922 the total production of fish oil was 8,288,328 gallons, valued at $3,346,046. There was thus in 1923 an increase of 16 per cent in the total quantity of fish oils (exclusive of whale and sperm) and 26 per cent in value.

FISH SCRAP AND MEAL

The total value of all fish scrap and meal, green and dry, including that prepared from shrimp and menhaden, was, in 1923, $4,413,385, as compared with $4,336,677 the previous year, an increase of 24 per cent. There was a relatively greater production of the crude or green scrap this year than last.

LIQUID FISH GLUE

In 1923 the production of liquid fish glue was 465,814 gallons, valued at $680,054, an increase of 44 per cent in quantity and 145 per cent in value over the production of 1922, which was 323,003 gallons, valued at $278,424.

SHELL BY-PRODUCTS

The principal source of shells is the oyster industry, which in 1923 furnished the material for the production of 224,983 tons of crushed shells for poultry food and 83,808 tons of oyster-shell lime, both together having a value of $2,358,535, as compared with $2,437,051 in 1922. The shell by-products of the pearl-button industry in the interior United States consisted of 6,830 tons of crushed mussel shells, 510 tons of lime dust, and 1,417 tons of stucco, valued altogether at $68,271.

Production of various by-products of the fisheries, 1923

Products	Maine, Massachusetts, and New York		Maryland and Virginia		North Carolina, Georgia, and Florida		Alabama, Mississippi, and Louisiana	
	Quantity	Value	Quantity	Value	Quantity	Value	Quantity	Value
Fish scrap and meal:								
Dried _____tons__	3,233	$192,519	2,203	$69,062	--------	--------	--------	--------
Crude or green _____do____	1,593	13,721	--------	--------	--------	--------	--------	--------
Shrimp bran _____do____					325	$17,475	944	$30,815
Oil:								
Herring _____gallons__	49,579	15,861	--------	--------	--------	--------	--------	--------
Sperm _____do____	93,505	46,753	--------	--------	--------	--------	--------	--------
Cod-liver, crude [1] _____do____	94,394	49,166	--------	--------	--------	--------	--------	--------
Miscellaneous _____do____	5,099	1,772	22,250	7,438	1,320	876	--------	--------
Liquid glue _____do____	465,814	680,054	--------	--------	--------	--------	--------	--------
Miscellaneous by-products [2] _____pounds__	624,666	56,920	40,000	2,800	63,324	13,498	--------	--------
Total _____	--------	996,766	--------	79,300	--------	31,849	--------	30,815

Products	Alaska, Washington, Oregon, and California		Indiana, Pennsylvania, and Wisconsin		Total	
	Quantity	Value	Quantity	Value	Quantity	Value
Fish scrap and meal:						
Dried _____tons__	17,200	$1,055,517	--------	--------	22,636	$1,257,098
Crude or green _____do____	--------	--------	--------	--------	1,593	13,721
Shrimp bran _____do____	--------	--------	--------	--------	1,269	48,290
Oil:						
Salmon _____gallons__	78,861	33,178	--------	--------	78,861	33,178
Sardine _____do____	966,247	424,103	--------	--------	966,247	424,103
Tuna _____do____	44,584	21,815	--------	--------	44,584	21,815
Herring _____do____	895,845	368,192	--------	--------	945,424	384,053
Whale _____do____	1,346,356	701,731	--------	--------	1,346,356	701,731
Sperm _____do____	116,969	43,400	--------	--------	210,474	90,153
Cod-liver, crude [1] _____do____	--------	--------	--------	--------	94,394	49,166
Miscellaneous _____do____	167,707	59,337	29,720	$14,295	226,096	83,718
Liquid glue _____do____	--------	--------	--------	--------	465,814	680,054
Miscellaneous by-products [2] _pounds__	3,280	2,604	--------	--------	731,270	75,822
Total _____	--------	2,709,877	--------	14,295	--------	3,862,902

[1] Includes about 5,000 gallons refined for medicinal use.
[2] Includes shark hides and fins, herring skins and scales, pearl or fish-scale essence, and whalebone.

Production of shell by-products, 1923.

States	Crushed oyster shells (for poultry)		Oyster-shell lime		Total	
	Tons	Value	Tons	Value	Tons	Value
Rhode Island, New York, New Jersey, and Pennsylvania	18,063	$211,982	5,402	$20,026	23,465	$232,008
Maryland	81,862	726,226	36,319	95,694	118,181	821,920
Virginia	19,682	201,488	31,341	215,506	51,023	416,994
North Carolina, South Carolina, and Georgia	5,818	61,218	5,300	30,500	11,118	91,718
Alabama and Florida	19,693	165,272	999	3,775	20,692	169,047
Mississippi	32,789	278,031	2,285	2,285	35,074	280,316
Louisiana and Texas	47,076	342,032	2,162	4,500	49,238	346,532
Total	224,983	1,986,249	83,808	372,286	308,791	2,358,535

States	Crushed fresh-water mussel shells (for poultry)	
	Tons	Value
Iowa	5,072	$38,642
Illinois	590	4,588
Indiana, Kentucky, and Ohio	412	3,146
Kansas and Missouri	225	1,804
Wisconsin	531	3,746
Total	6,830	51,826

NOTE.—In addition to the above there were produced elsewhere 217 tons crushed marine clam shells, valued at $2,600, and in Iowa, Illinois, Kentucky, Missouri, Ohio, and Wisconsin 510 tons of lime dust, valued at $1,522, and 1,417 tons of stucco, valued at $14,923.

MENHADEN INDUSTRY

In 1923 there were 52 factories engaged in the manufacture of fish oil, scrap, and meal from menhaden, distributed as follows: Massachusetts, 1; Connecticut, 1; New York, 2; New Jersey, 3; Delaware, 3; Virginia, 18; North Carolina, 17; Georgia, 1; Florida, 4; and Texas, 2. This is an increase of 7 plants as compared with 1922.

The number of fish utilized was 1,110,291,427, or 666,174,873 pounds, as compared with 1,212,450,669 fish, or 747,470,402 pounds, in 1922. The production of dry scrap and meal was 43,452 tons, valued at $2,029,406, and of wet or acidulated scrap 44,935 tons, valued at $1,064,870, as compared with 67,821 tons, valued at $2,665,441, and 25,712 tons, valued at $555,973, respectively, in 1922. The production of menhaden oil amounted to 7,461,365 gallons, valued at $3,316,277, as compared with 7,102,677, valued at $2,904,833, in 1922. The total value of menhaden products in 1923 amounted to $6,410,553, as compared with $6,126,591 in the previous year.

Products of the menhaden industry, 1923

Products	Massachusetts, Connecticut, and New York		New Jersey and Delaware		Virginia	
Fish utilized: Menhaden _____number..	*Quantity* 270, 688, 228	*Value* $1, 083, 007	*Quantity* 142, 774, 000	*Value* $598, 584	*Quantity* 390, 377, 144	*Value* $1, 523, 064
Manufactured products:						
Dry scrap and fish meal_tons..	1, 730	34, 300	852	38, 340	28, 944	1, 402, 303
Acidulated scrap_____do..	21, 250	494, 250	11, 445	261, 563	_____	_____
Total_____	22, 980	528, 550	12, 297	299, 903	28, 944	1, 402, 303
Oil_____gallons..	2, 479, 235	1, 097, 127	909, 050	411, 805	2, 717, 922	1, 206, 757
Grand total_____	_____	1, 625, 677	_____	711, 708	_____	2, 609, 060

Products	North Carolina		Georgia, Florida, and Texas		Total	
Fish utilized: Menhaden _____number..	*Quantity* 132, 665, 178	*Value* $530, 660	*Quantity* 173, 786, 907	*Value* $695, 148	*Quantity* [1] 1, 110, 291, 427	*Value* $4, 430, 463
Manufactured products:						
Dry scrap and fish meal _____tons..	4, 596	196, 672	7, 330	357, 791	[2] 43, 452	2, 029, 406
Acidulated scrap _____do..	7, 068	178, 785	5, 172	130, 272	44, 935	1, 064, 870
Total_____	11, 664	375, 457	12, 502	488, 063	88, 387	3, 094, 276
Oil_____gallons..	777, 829	349, 245	577, 329	251, 343	7, 461, 365	3, 316, 277
Grand total_____	_____	724, 702	_____	739, 406	_____	6, 410, 553

[1] 666,174,873 pounds.
[2] Of this quantity 10,004 tons, valued at $357,178, were reported as fish meal.

COLD-STORAGE HOLDINGS OF FROZEN FISH IN 1923

The statistics of the cold-storage holdings of frozen fish and the quantity of fish frozen are collected by the Bureau of Agricultural Economics, Department of Agriculture. These statistics were collected by the Bureau of Markets and Crop Estimates, Department of Agriculture, from October, 1916, to June, 1922. The reports give the holdings on the 15th of each month. Through the courtesy of that bureau arrangements were made in December, 1921, for the Bureau of Fisheries to publish and disseminate this information. beginning with the returns for January 15, 1922, in the form of a monthly statistical bulletin. This bulletin gives the holdings by species and sections, total holdings for the current month and for the same month the previous year, the 5-year average, holdings for the previous month, and the quantity of each species frozen during the month and during the same month the previous year.

In 1923 the cold-storage holdings of fish, as compared with 1922, were smaller from January to June and larger from July to December being smallest in April and largest in December.

The following table gives the total holdings of all the freezers in 1923 which were devoted wholly or in part to the cold storage of fish, together with the totals for the years 1917 to 1922, inclusive. for comparison:

Monthly holdings of frozen fish in the United States in 1923, by species, and in 1917 to 1922, by totals

Species	Month ended					
	Jan. 15	Feb. 15	Mar. 15	Apr. 15	May 15	June 15
	Pounds	*Pounds*	*Pounds*	*Pounds*	*Pounds*	*Pounds*
Bluefish (all trade sizes)	584, 272	353, 467	164, 225	77, 095	47, 518	64, 102
Butterfish (all trade sizes)	459, 800	218, 224	137, 786	84, 233	25, 083	146, 548
Catfish	431, 262	363, 682	244, 264	158, 877	165, 206	115, 365
Ciscoes (including bluefin, blackfin, chub, lake herring, etc.)	5, 035, 408	2, 881, 589	1, 405, 389	725, 489	270, 788	184, 625
Ciscoes (tullibees)	861, 644	778, 923	552, 997	322, 554	227, 515	195, 809
Cod, haddock, hake, pollock	325, 654	153, 731	125, 286	191, 596	354, 031	472, 220
Croaker	4, 210	2, 863	653	114, 563	211, 873	488, 593
Flounders	259, 541	120, 551	91, 925	94, 035	200, 796	576, 312
Halibut (all trade sizes)	3, 779, 318	2, 296, 364	711, 655	381, 868	1, 284, 648	2, 641, 059
Herring, sea (including alewives and bluebacks)	2, 484, 139	1, 518, 641	1, 172, 046	936, 217	1, 647, 713	2, 050, 867
Lake trout	1, 441, 352	836, 531	285, 443	49, 776	43, 211	195, 577
Mackerel (except Spanish)	4, 652, 764	3, 440, 104	2, 696, 475	1, 705, 987	1, 474, 894	1, 721, 709
Pike perches and pike or pickerel	2, 015, 425	1, 317, 595	829, 767	329, 358	695, 255	1, 499, 231
Sablefish (black cod)	393, 824	257, 757	142, 851	59, 441	60, 428	129, 487
Salmon, silver and fall	2, 785, 545	2, 563, 165	1, 671, 868	998, 567	518, 714	310, 641
Salmon, steelhead trout	679, 824	342, 985	67, 439	50, 866	62, 106	54, 351
Salmon, all other	3, 309, 030	1, 739, 652	1, 111, 900	771, 933	589, 057	634, 392
Scup (porgies)	1, 549, 700	1, 199, 858	1, 090, 364	1, 027, 904	909, 940	953, 293
Shad and shad roe	229, 507	136, 998	43, 733	35, 396	151, 205	260, 150
Shellfish	428, 465	268, 764	182, 663	214, 020	230, 015	231, 872
Smelts, eulachon, etc	236, 845	166, 662	283, 371	91, 771	85, 617	74, 341
Squeteagues or "sea trout"	352, 049	55, 197	11, 592	9, 582	204, 603	348, 784
Squid	233, 037	99, 331	83, 647	40, 129	37, 900	951, 828
Sturgeon and spoonbill cat	445, 895	410, 407	310, 267	265, 154	214, 425	232, 965
Suckers	17, 569	3, 109	10, 176	4, 703	18, 330	22, 918
Whitefish	1, 561, 553	1, 220, 814	852, 204	256, 260	146, 902	175, 675
Whiting	2, 395, 008	1, 144, 828	729, 262	380, 563	165, 410	159, 040
Miscellaneous frozen fish	3, 311, 051	2, 627, 328	1, 884, 916	1, 216, 773	1, 881, 890	2, 787, 373
Total, 1923	40, 263, 691	26, 519, 120	16, 894, 164	10, 594, 710	11, 925, 073	17, 679, 127
Total, 1922	48, 320, 212	37, 742, 262	25, 474, 714	17, 484, 975	17, 075, 917	20, 821, 345
Total, 1921	53, 851, 000	42, 116, 000	33, 404, 000	28, 440, 000	26, 346, 000	32, 311, 000
Total, 1920	61, 510, 357	47, 904, 057	29, 958, 132	20, 632, 834	19, 803, 817	27, 779, 230
Total, 1919	80, 683, 761	67, 617, 473	50, 036, 475	37, 110, 856	37, 174, 104	48, 840, 359
Total, 1918	51, 116, 037	35, 907, 071	28, 457, 301	26, 548, 272	31, 403, 425	50, 298, 027
Total, 1917	32, 234, 530	14, 727, 099	13, 374, 429	9, 516, 217	14, 040, 024	27, 791, 047

Monthly holdings of frozen fish in the United States in 1923, by species, and in 1917 to 1922, by totals—Continued

Species	Month ended					
	July 15	Aug. 15	Sept. 15	Oct. 15	Nov. 15	Dec. 15
	Pounds	*Pounds*	*Pounds*	*Pounds*	*Pounds*	*Pounds*
Bluefish (all trade sizes)	260,079	281,548	330,373	503,004	465,986	474,180
Butterfish (all trade sizes)	235,730	383,557	409,358	496,165	605,085	518,635
Catfish	114,715	176,516	164,553	315,077	381,606	340,389
Ciscoes (including bluefin, blackfin, chub, lake herring, etc.)	440,389	4,011,074	8,347,401	10,317,394	9,590,272	12,110,876
Ciscoes (tullibees)	193,353	215,417	309,435	444,941	545,396	657,852
Cod, haddock, hake, pollock	537,661	875,276	1,019,013	1,243,287	1,450,754	1,541,771
Croaker	363,266	351,850	● 339,445	392,356	348,064	327,493
Flounders	640,948	690,650	593,838	735,933	702,963	653,863
Halibut (all trade sizes)	4,500,103	5,788,723	7,574,946	7,191,619	6,870,307	6,287,017
Herring, sea (including alewives and bluebacks)	2,818,420	3,435,332	3,484,113	3,830,883	4,118,240	3,385,846
Lake trout	281,412	370,868	383,122	576,372	1,191,235	1,611,529
Mackerel (except Spanish)	2,698,169	2,934,802	5,322,185	6,755,510	6,253,804	5,505,332
Pike perches and pike or pickerel	1,368,776	1,193,426	1,126,067	1,477,014	1,955,150	3,326,939
Sablefish (black cod)	864,023	1,438,279	1,912,926	2,126,880	2,234,092	2,123,445
Salmon, silver and fall	713,120	981,622	1,828,089	3,505,965	3,832,490	3,251,575
Salmon, steelhead trout	290,023	571,714	845,094	889,762	986,485	879,119
Salmon, all other	2,138,638	3,345,629	4,725,535	4,908,772	4,684,777	3,787,517
Scup (porgies)	1,124,537	1,154,520	1,222,977	1,155,134	1,036,881	836,085
Shad and shad roe	306,481	419,169	439,940	470,886	466,951	565,195
Shellfish	249,381	345,290	376,845	625,364	666,308	932,481
Smelts, eulachon, etc	68,606	75,560	78,703	109,638	145,565	244,103
Squeteagues or "sea trout"	578,527	643,656	726,573	1,698,677	1,538,208	1,211,522
Squid	1,343,477	1,403,842	1,284,967	1,159,907	925,792	774,103
Sturgeon and spoonbill cat	277,193	318,391	336,828	333,916	388,052	343,985
Suckers	24,918	19,077	18,054	17,353	20,744	17,357
Whitefish	257,771	568,127	677,003	833,469	1,124,697	1,688,948
Whiting	1,343,637	3,187,652	4,697,684	5,058,395	5,087,778	4,507,470
Miscellaneous frozen fish	3,288,013	3,855,408	4,622,371	5,570,808	5,840,229	6,386,962
Total, 1923	27,321,366	39,036,975	53,197,438	62,744,481	63,457,884	64,291,589
Total, 1922	25,620,042	32,226,170	41,141,144	54,756,783	54,502,283	48,689,830
Total, 1921	40,160,000	47,431,000	54,469,000	58,899,000	61,228,000	59,125,646
Total, 1920	36,617,706	47,140,132	56,295,975	64,730,531	67,549,377	65,841,000
Total, 1919	59,674,301	65,145,234	69,580,555	76,763,253	78,769,101	74,202,339
Total, 1918	64,864,532	82,554,798	89,203,946	93,811,909	99,631,789	96,600,247
Total, 1917	38,431,221	44,024,666	47,197,660	60,676,722	70,938,957	69,986,671

QUANTITIES OF FISH FROZEN IN 1923

The total quantity of fish frozen during the year ended December 15, 1923, was 91,548,643 pounds, an increase of 16,094,969 pounds, or 21.3 per cent, over the previous year. The principal species frozen during the year were ciscoes, 16,101,224 pounds; salmon, 11,043,424 pounds; halibut, 10,211,251 pounds; whiting, 8,664,680 pounds; mackerel, 7,248,381 pounds; herring, 5,748,228 pounds; and pike perches and pike or pickerel, 4,283,697 pounds. The following table gives the quantity of fish frozen in the United States in 1923, by months, with totals for 1920 to 1922, inclusive, for comparison:

Fish frozen monthly in 1923, by species, and in 1920 to 1922, by totals

Species	Month ended						
	Jan. 15	Feb. 15	Mar. 15	Apr. 15	May 15	June 15	July 15
	Pounds	*Pounds*	*Pounds*	*Pounds*	*Pounds*	*Pounds*	*Pounds*
Bluefish (all trade sizes)	3,056	259	240	50	1,000	24,910	204,275
Butterfish (all trade sizes)	330	295	35	3,500	7,782	154,457	105,946
Catfish	214,550	12,407	14,497	18,136	39,621	10,108	22,808
Ciscoes (including bluefin, blackfin, chub, lake herring, etc.)	921,082	76,765	66,249	24,352	15,863	72,640	397,146
Ciscoes (tullibees)	139,217	26,944	30,051	13,660	----	3,725	2,253
Cod, haddock, hake, pollock	33,604	31,507	28,150	40,194	214,780	166,401	145,733
Croaker	----	----	----	114,244	105,783	18,052	52,668
Flounders	4,372	23,255	10,725	32,237	147,592	413,179	78,578
Halibut (all trade sizes)	160,895	142,996	81,301	182,762	1,209,749	1,432,445	2,244,047
Herring, sea (including alewives and bluebacks)	58,425	131,759	104,820	514,440	982,782	701,399	667,523
Lake trout	26,204	10,747	2,172	5,837	3,919	166,209	85,724
Mackerel (except Spanish)	191,297	185,010	216,052	24,211	207,812	451,799	1,041,630
Pike perches and pike or pickerel	43,074	25,942	33,187	14,523	449,123	961,693	185,504
Sablefish (black cod)	17,243	27,130	17,732	18,781	33,633	77,974	757,041
Salmon, silver and fall	93,203	95,437	8,808	19,541	51,159	55,582	493,093
Salmon, steelhead trout	2,485	----	----	480	856	20,213	255,365
Salmon, all other	26,490	74,686	28,929	11,103	203,264	245,445	1,749,376
Scup (porgies)	782	----	----	----	----	137,500	214,241
Shad and shad roe	1,009	257	20	16,638	126,390	142,120	31,996
Shellfish	123,762	109,570	42,283	100,574	95,250	97,963	95,614
Smelts, eulachon, etc.	28,200	28,357	13,372	11,570	17,635	110	15
Squeteagues or "sea trout"	2,275	----	----	2,432	200,415	52,265	237,833
Squid	----	3,091	----	----	21,964	928,905	463,277
Sturgeon and spoonbill cat	3,550	13,986	30	10,607	63,447	71,679	61,512
Suckers	833	----	----	----	11,411	13,020	----
Whitefish	80,463	73,823	21,417	41,952	2,843	41,197	86,046
Whiting	231,886	129,270	468,078	4,434	----	121,568	1,518,104
Miscellaneous frozen fish	333,251	438,642	224,342	173,820	812,815	1,088,569	674,297
Total frozen fish, 1923	2,741,538	1,662,135	1,412,490	1,400,078	5,026,888	7,671,127	11,871,645
Total frozen fish, 1922	1,452,801	1,363,942	1,496,538	1,980,435	5,849,537	7,376,237	9,121,160
Total frozen fish, 1921	2,843,000	1,770,000	2,413,000	2,698,000	9,624,000	10,151,000	9,845,000
Total frozen fish, 1920	2,273,744	2,630,482	2,465,375	3,687,538	10,094,367	12,761,791	13,620,232

Species	Month ended					Total
	Aug. 15	Sept. 15	Oct. 15	Nov. 15	Dec. 15	
	Pounds	*Pounds*	*Pounds*	*Pounds*	*Pounds*	*Pounds*
Bluefish (all trade sizes)	43,017	44,463	197,203	22,811	59,127	600,411
Butterfish (all trade sizes)	154,344	46,689	117,263	176,142	26,438	793,221
Catfish	59,468	28,139	135,469	70,727	25,290	651,220
Ciscoes (including bluefin, blackfin, chub, lake herring, etc.)	3,583,530	5,194,742	2,004,259	678,663	3,065,933	16,101,224
Ciscoes (tullibees)	1,526	27,710	26,404	5,300	113,781	390,571
Cod, haddock, hake, pollock	418,164	239,808	337,984	344,835	221,517	2,222,677
Croaker	6,296	7,316	61,541	14,000	----	379,900
Flounders	97,707	27,286	161,512	45,554	45,188	1,087,185
Halibut (all trade sizes)	1,574,852	1,797,756	401,152	569,229	414,067	10,211,251
Herring, sea (including alewives and bluebacks)	914,347	367,819	563,179	528,471	213,204	5,748,228
Lake trout	106,801	64,594	124,374	614,453	609,094	1,820,128
Mackerel (except Spanish)	340,610	2,521,194	1,770,455	178,640	119,671	7,248,381
Pike perches and pike or pickerel	21,621	128,079	434,203	450,639	1,536,109	4,283,697
Sablefish (black cod)	569,913	378,032	281,027	240,210	73,108	2,491,824
Salmon, silver and fall	249,946	612,052	1,685,185	977,257	132,225	4,473,488
Salmon, steelhead trout	283,456	279,591	182,203	29,574	14,134	1,068,357
Salmon, all other	1,200,689	1,138,630	473,132	203,534	146,301	5,501,579
Scup (porgies)	71,780	82,867	8,313	74	----	515,557
Shad and shad roe	8,705	2,861	1,932	281	3,837	336,046
Shellfish	67,193	155,492	275,271	162,544	351,296	1,676,812
Smelts, eulachon, etc.	1,373	2,203	30,432	38,467	23,243	194,977
Squeteagues or "sea trout"	142,953	150,645	976,592	5,741	12,853	1,784,004
Squid	198,468	21,401	37,862	10,020	9,302	1,694,290
Sturgeon and spoonbill cat	77,557	48,443	22,649	74,661	33,950	482,071
Suckers	350	4,454	1,707	4,066	3,799	39,640
Whitefish	303,401	83,694	52,597	210,259	602,223	1,599,915
Whiting	2,546,912	1,845,098	1,032,249	414,998	352,083	8,664,680
Miscellaneous frozen fish	898,999	1,116,074	1,115,417	880,489	1,730,554	9,487,309
Total frozen fish, 1923	13,943,978	16,417,132	12,511,606	6,951,639	9,938,387	91,548,643
Total frozen fish, 1922	10,826,942	16,830,080	9,344,469	7,069,995	2,741,538	75,453,074
Total frozen fish, 1921	9,356,000	9,990,000	9,869,000	8,173,000	2,441,892	79,173,892
Total frozen fish, 1920	11,803,606	11,168,810	9,711,800	9,750,844	4,005,000	93,973,589

NEW ENGLAND VESSEL FISHERIES

GENERAL STATISTICS

The vessel fisheries centering at Boston and Gloucester, Mass., and Portland, Me., were more productive in 1923 than in either of the two previous years. There was an increase of 2.93 per cent in the number of trips, and of 9.42 per cent in the quantity and 29 per cent in the value of the products as compared with 1922. The increase in the number of trips and in the quantity of the products was all at Boston, but there was an increase in the value of the products at each of the three ports. The increase in the number of trips at Boston was 16.42 per cent, with a decrease at Gloucester of 4.48 per cent, and at Portland of 11.92 per cent. At Boston the increase in the products landed amounted to 16.97 per cent in quantity and 35.16 per cent in value; at Gloucester there was a decrease of 7.21 per cent in quantity, with an increase of 11.97 per cent in value; and at Portland a decrease of 1.49 per cent in quantity, with an increase of 11.73 per cent in value. Statistics of the fisheries have been collected by the local agents and published in monthly bulletins, showing by species and fishing grounds the quantities and values of fishery products landed by American fishing vessels during the year at these ports. Two annual bulletins have been issued, one showing the catch by months and the other by fishing grounds.

The fishing fleet at these ports during the calendar year 1923, numbered 306 sail, steam, and gasoline vessels, including 33 steam trawlers. These vessels landed at Boston 3,368 trips, aggregating 124,215,034 pounds of fish, valued at $5,433,731; at Gloucester, 1,579 trips, aggregating 35,029,848 pounds, valued at $910,739; and at Portland, 1,588 trips, aggregating 15,696,587 pounds, valued at $706,684. The total for the three ports amounted to 6,535 trips, aggregating 174,941,469 pounds of fresh and salted fish, having a value to the fishermen of $7,051,154.

Compared with the previous year there was an increase of 186 trips, or 2.93 per cent, in the total number landed at Boston, Gloucester, and Portland, and an increase of 15,066,078 pounds, or 9.42 per cent, in the quantity, and of $1,585,222, or 29 per cent, in the value of the products landed. There was an increase in both the quantity and value of cod, haddock, hake, cusk, and mackerel, and a decrease in quantity with an increase in value of pollock, halibut, and swordfish. In the herring catch there was a decrease in both quantity and value. The catch of cod increased 7,475,109 pounds, or 13.55 per cent, in quantity and $548,862, or 33.56 per cent, in value; haddock increased 3,565,525 pounds, or 5.08 per cent, in quantity and $613,777, or 33.92 per cent, in value; hake increased 963,530 pounds, or 17.93 per cent, in quantity and $31,036, or 27.88 per cent, in value; cusk increased 750,756 pounds or 33.40 per cent in quantity and $27,176, or 78.65 per cent in value; and mackerel increased 6,838,481 pounds or 144.68 per cent in quantity and $211,138 or 76.36 per cent in value. The catch of pollock decreased 292,759 pounds or 5.74 per cent in quantity and increased $34,183, or 28.97 per cent, in value; halibut decreased 749,645 pounds, or 13.33 per cent, in quantity and increased $138,597, or 17.68 per cent, in value; and swordfish decreased 826,329 pounds, or 25.18 per cent, in quantity and increased $1,103, or 0.25 per cent, in value. The herring catch decreased 1,161,514 pounds, or 43.92 per cent, in quantity and $36,636, or 45.14 per cent, in value. The Newfoundland herring catch decreased from 2,302,420 pounds, valued at $76,855 in 1922, to 1,219,300 pounds, valued at $40,861 in 1923. In the various other species combined there was a decrease of 1,497,076 pounds, or 27.20 per cent, in quantity and an increase of $15,986, or 9.48 per cent, in value.

The catch of scrod cod landed at these ports decreased from 815,371 pounds, valued at $9,200, in 1922, to 414,659 pounds, valued at $6,447, in 1923, and the catch of scrod haddock increased from 253,283 pounds, valued at $4,261, in 1922, to 4,845,695 pounds, valued at $94,481, in 1923. The small quantity of these grades landed, as compared with other grades of these species, is said to be due to the fact that the price is so low that the fishermen do not save all that are caught.

The following tables present in detail, by fishing grounds and also by months, the fishery products landed at Boston and Gloucester, Mass., and Portland, Me., by American fishing vessels for the calendar year 1923. The weights of fresh and salted fish given in these statistics represent the fish as landed from the vessels, and the values are those received by the fishermen. The grades, or sizes, given for certain species are those recognized in the trade.

Statement, by fishing grounds, of quantities and values of certain fishery products landed at Boston and Gloucester, Mass., and Portland, Me., by American fishing vessels during the calendar year 1923

	Cod							
Fishing grounds	Large (10 pounds and over)				Market (under 10 and over 2½ pounds)			
	Fresh		Salted		Fresh		Salted	
	Pounds	Value	Pounds	Value	Pounds	Value	Pounds	Value
LANDED AT BOSTON								
East of 66° W. longitude								
La Have Bank	454,892	$17,034			96,602	$2,703		
Western Bank	2,768,700	112,060	17,500	$700	1,747,385	43,497		
Quereau Bank	38,975	1,434	2,375	112	1,500	30		
Grand Bank	1,670	50						
St. Peters Bank	6,900	233			400	10		
Cape Shore	20,650	1,745			24,820	1,008		
The Gully	2,450	98			170	3		
West of 66° W. longitude								
Browns Bank	2,331,581	117,416			2,165,542	56,551		
Georges Bank	11,711,036	501,490	8,000	360	4,016,222	113,517		
Cashes Bank	40,950	3,629			24,707	1,206		
Clark Bank	25,510	766			4,260	93		
Fippenies Bank	50,365	1,909			40,645	846		
Middle Bank	164,575	10,579			111,020	4,869		
Jeffreys Ledge	177,587	10,889			127,525	4,328		
Ipswich Bay	5,520	386						
South Channel	3,624,559	185,277			4,228,715	106,777		
Nantucket Shoals	555,124	27,144			1,045,400	23,600		
Off Highland Light	9,160	275			7,160	179		
Off Chatham	239,098	9,918			267,545	6,664		
Seal Island	76,065	4,134			102,860	3,177		
Shore, general	1,209,402	57,415	2,065	81	354,777	10,654		
Total	23,514,769	1,063,881	29,940	1,253	14,367,255	379,712		

Statement, by fishing-grounds, of quantities and values of certain fishery products landed at Boston and Gloucester, Mass., and Portland, Me., by American fishing vessels during the calendar year 1923—Continued

Fishing grounds	Cod—Continued							
	Large (10 pounds and over)				Market (under 10 and over 2½ pounds)			
	Fresh		Salted		Fresh		Salted	
	Pounds	Value	Pounds	Value	Pounds	Value	Pounds	Value
LANDED AT GLOUCESTER								
East of 66° W. longitude								
La Have Bank	188,905	$4,643	12,720	$615	148,505	$2,519	2,815	$112
Western Bank	4,538,430	101,533	920,099	43,415	3,429,460	59,448	864,407	32,066
Quereau Bank	372,439	8,597	662,185	31,537	346,030	6,246	207,230	9,258
Misaine Bank	13,245	331			670	13		
Grand Bank	104,890	2,298	475,455	22,702	7,362	108	65,545	2,545
St. Peters Bank	154,345	3,515	248,160	12,291	13,515	255	88,630	3,407
The Gully	86,710	1,927	72,355	3,448	5,955	107	9,055	341
West of 66° W. longitude								
Browns Bank	260,765	6,498	19,865	947	260,640	4,985	4,144	156
Georges Bank	1,790,395	44,219	241,060	11,735	1,499,385	29,211	40,665	1,492
Jeffreys Ledge					120	2		
South Channel	123,250	3,087			429,410	8,352		
Nantucket Shoals					130	3		
Shore, general	2,008,756	101,819	160	8	7,460	149		
Total	9,642,130	278,467	2,652,059	126,698	6,148,642	111,398	1,282,491	49,377
LANDED AT PORTLAND								
East of 66° W. longitude								
La Have Bank	2,460	74	27,015	1,370	145	3	7,325	307
Western Bank	1,432,455	30,259	60,400	2,978	130,260	4,516	13,215	395
Quereau Bank	5,840	263	8,800	418	1,410	28	1,600	60
Green Bank			15,150	847			700	35
Grand Bank	22,645	1,023	79,210	3,793	1,125	42	5,680	218
St. Peters Bank	11,625	610	14,410	684			320	12
The Gully	10,230	256	9,840	467	500	10	290	11
West of 66° W. longitude								
Browns Bank	24,780	1,206	33,827	1,798	31,370	725	12,140	592
Georges Bank	22,355	889	21,397	1,008	17,325	454	6,375	225
Cashes Bank	140,481	5,401	3,500	175	114,073	2,529	535	19
Fippenies Bank	8,178	348			7,345	248		
Platts Bank	99,495	5,120			61,380	1,803		
Jeffreys Ledge	235,980	14,131	4,420	221	157,055	5,872	950	38
Seal Island	2,570	167			4,070	116		
Shore, general	1,387,042	64,622	17,677	762	321,164	9,560	5,195	200
Total	3,406,136	124,369	295,646	14,521	847,222	25,906	54,325	2,112
Grand total	36,563,035	1,466,717	2,977,645	142,472	21,363,119	517,016	1,336,816	51,489

NOTE.—The items under "Miscellaneous" includes bluebacks, 44,740 pounds, value $368; butterfish, 19,209 pounds, value $2,678; flounders, 3,436,820 pounds, value $163,683; herring, fresh, 263,540 pounds, value $3,657; herring, salted, 1,219,300 pounds, value $40,861; rosefish, 15,260 pounds, value $334; salmon, 41 pounds, value $10; scup, 600 pounds, value $30; shad, 4,747 pounds, value $289; sharks, 12,407 pounds, value $234; skates, 9,705 pounds, value $110; smelt, 1,217 pounds, value $139; sturgeon, 1,413 pounds, value $260; swordfish, 2,455,419 pounds, value $448,119; tuna, 822 pounds, value $57; wolffish, 195,414 pounds, value $4,666; lobster, 69 pounds, value $24; squid, 110 pounds, value $6; scallops, 72 pounds, value $23; livers, 125,375 pounds, value $2,453; spawn, fresh, 129,376 pounds, value $8,972; spawn, salted, 8,600 pounds, value $258; and tongues, 375 pounds, value $30.

Statement, by fishing grounds, of quantities and values of certain fishery products landed at Boston and Gloucester, Mass., and Portland, Me., by American fishing vessels during the calendar year 1923—Continued

Fishing grounds	Cod—Continued				Haddock			
	Scrod (1 to 2½ pounds)				Large (over 2½ pounds)			
	Fresh		Salted		Fresh		Salted	
	Pounds	Value	Pounds	Value	Pounds	Value	Pounds	Value
LANDED AT BOSTON								
East of 66° W. longitude								
La Have Bank					272,210	$6,062		
Western Bank	8,450	$125			4,763,420	129,316		
Cape Shore	2,900	23			83,400	3,510		
West of 66° W. longitude								
Browns Bank	26,130	265			7,788,227	293,053		
Georges Bank	11,260	192			14,262,805	553,120		
Cashes Bank					22,665	1,440		
Clark Bank					136,400	4,787		
Fippenies Bank	3,140	21			24,505	613		
Middle Bank	18,670	340			1,137,814	66,866		
Jeffreys Ledge	8,270	151			736,257	39,296		
South Channel	30,065	440			24,131,326	845,296		
Nantucket Shoals	2,040	35			1,151,715	34,272		
Off Highland Light	360	4			5,750	460		
Off Chatham	6,865	69			1,067,780	52,621		
Seal Island	700	7			323,275	9,623		
Shore, general	11,305	165			216,829	11,786		
Total	130,155	1,837			56,124,378	2,052,121		
LANDED AT GLOUCESTER								
East of 66° W. longitude								
La Have Bank	640	4			107,225	1,072		
Western Bank	20,890	160	86,010	$2,568	2,869,060	29,389	40,250	$895
Quereau Bank	1,105	8	8,325	156	123,475	1,235	1,360	27
Grand Bank			500	12				
St. Peters Bank			13,570	465	150	2		
The Gully			490	18	100	1		
West of 66° W. longitude								
Browns Bank	3,110	25			419,365	4,194		
Georges Bank	5,990	46			2,567,265	27,154		
Middle Bank	730	5						
Jeffreys Ledge	600	5						
South Channel	650	6			1,137,230	11,135		
Nantucket Shoals					60,410	1,812		
Seal Island					59,000	1,475		
Shore, general	400	3			368,711	20,942		
Total	34,115	262	108,895	3,219	7,711,991	98,411	41,610	922
LANDED AT PORTLAND								
East of 66° W. longitude								
La Have Bank			7,160	128				
Western Bank	2,225	23	723	18	3,231,035	64,396		
Quereau Bank			5,200	94				
West of 66° W. longitude								
Browns Bank	2,975	15	1,200	27	85,100	3,216		
Georges Bank	925	5	550	11	101,660	3,951		
Cashes Bank	9,840	58			118,555	5,600		
Fippenies Bank	620	3			4,085	270		
Platts Bank	9,390	54			65,894	4,004		
Jeffreys Ledge	33,829	182			773,728	54,685		
Seal Island	165	1			6,610	446		
Shore, general	61,467	357	5,225	153	651,182	40,674		
Total	121,436	698	20,058	431	5,037,849	177,242		
Grand total	285,706	2,797	128,953	3,650	68,874,218	2,327,774	41,610	922

Statement, by fishing grounds, of quantities and values of certain fishery products landed at Boston and Gloucester, Mass., and Portland, Me., by American fishing vessels during the calendar year 1923—Continued

Fishing grounds	Haddock—Continued				Hake			
	Scrod (1 to 2½ pounds)				Large (6 pounds and over)			
	Fresh		Salted		Fresh		Salted	
	Pounds	Value	Pounds	Value	Pounds	Value	Pounds	Value
LANDED AT BOSTON								
East of 66° W. longitude								
La Have Bank	1,200	$24						
Western Bank	38,950	550						
Cape Shore	600	9						
West of 66° W. longitude								
Browns Bank	7,600	85						
Georges Bank	674,350	21,878			700	$49		
Cashes Bank	475	5			600	12		
Fippenies Bank	67,625	684						
Middle Bank	229,629	5,363			50,974	3,201		
Jeffreys Ledge	182,735	4,075			26,135	1,507		
South Channel	2,923,999	52,914			38,920	1,056		
Nantucket Shoals	171,180	3,154						
Off Highland Light	470	19						
Off Chatham	68,785	1,015			2,300	69		
Seal Island	2,625	45						
Shore, general	46,045	906	1,975	$35	3,015	168		
Total	4,416,268	90,726	1,975	35	122,644	6,062		
LANDED AT GLOUCESTER								
East of 66° W. longitude								
La Have Bank					4,985	50		
Western Bank	37,030	244			40,880	410	270	$5
Quereau Bank					9,885	104	3,415	60
Grand Bank					18,595	196	10,125	175
St. Peters Bank					4,425	45	1,825	34
The Gully							70	1
West of 66° W. longitude								
Browns Bank	10,160	102			53,050	660		
Georges Bank	24,790	130			11,835	121	550	9
Middle Bank	3,000	15			147,675	1,846		
Jeffreys Ledge	4,900	25			25,510	319		
South Channel	1,770	35			57,395	621		
Nantucket Shoals	9,560	72			460	6		
Seal Island	1,760	9						
Shore, general	7,615	38			197,290	4,369		
Total	100,585	670			571,985	8,747	16,255	284
LANDED AT PORTLAND								
East of 66° W. longitude								
La Have Bank					3,895	49		
Western Bank	1,340	7						
Quereau Bank					6,900	86	1,135	23
West of 66° W. longitude								
Browns Bank	4,700	41						
Georges Bank	4,075	46						
Cashes Bank	25,652	201			345	14		
Fippenies Bank	3,155	23						
Platts Bank	14,845	193			3,715	185		
Jeffreys Ledge	152,361	1,364			20,315	345		
Seal Island	910	5						
Shore, general	119,829	1,170			3,625	127	49	2
Total	326,867	3,050			38,795	806	1,184	25
Grand total	4,843,720	94,446	1,975	35	733,424	15,615	17,439	309

Statement, by fishing grounds, of quantities and values of certain fishery products landed at Boston and Gloucester, Mass., and Portland, Me., by American fishing vessels during the calendar year 1923—Continued

Fishing grounds	Hake—Continued				Pollock			
	Small (under 6 pounds)							
	Fresh		Salted		Fresh		Salted	
	Pounds	Value	Lbs.	Value	Pounds	Value	Pounds	Value
LANDED AT BOSTON								
East of 66° W. longitude								
La Have Bank	13,202	$209			3,495	$63		
Western Bank	29,425	604			498,020	14,532		
Quereau Bank	3,900	29						
Cape Shore					1,140	25		
The Gully	300	6			50	1		
West of 66° W. longitude								
Browns Bank	44,775	1,568			213,265	6,928		
Georges Bank	115,046	3,269			626,200	21,633		
Cashes Bank	44,920	891			5,380	180		
Clark Bank					500	20		
Fippenies Bank	960	35			12,910	206		
Middle Bank	400,210	12,416			104,090	4,083		
Jeffreys Ledge	417,499	12,994			79,010	2,601		
South Channel	3,092,908	55,211			966,302	36,736		
Nantucket Shoals	28,735	414			82,205	2,312		
Off Highland Light	1,700	51			500	25		
Off Chatham	52,665	1,783			46,825	1,448		
Seal Island	16,140	259			2,420	58		
Shore, general	114,760	2,262	1,500	$24	434,359	13,274		
Total	4,377,145	92,001	1,500	24	3,076,671	104,125		
LANDED AT GLOUCESTER								
East of 66° W. longitude								
La Have Bank					6,060	61		
Western Bank					97,650	1,022	24,335	$508
Quereau Bank					6,570	65	6,760	134
Grand Bank							80	2
St. Peters Bank							2,675	78
The Gully							40	1
West of 66° W. longitude								
Browns Bank					8,470	84	375	8
Georges Bank					89,225	907	2,080	33
South Channel					14,680	148		
Shore, general					899,707	33,105		
Total					1,122,362	35,392	36,345	764
LANDED AT PORTLAND								
East of 66° W. longitude								
La Have Bank	1,220	15			910	14	225	5
Western Bank	580	9	1,900	38	67,740	959		
Quereau Bank					200	4	265	5
Grand Bank	8,125	85					215	6
Cape Shore							750	11
West of 66° W. longitude								
Browns Bank	4,455	55			860	11	795	19
Georges Bank	2,260	23	220	4	1,095	21		
Cashes Bank	145,716	1,876			50,815	593		
Fippenies Bank	2,700	215			4,113	88		
Platts Bank	83,575	2,213			29,147	666		
Jeffreys Ledge	408,324	15,371			145,210	4,346		
Seal Island	1,195	23			320	6		
Shore, general	546,691	14,465	1,308	26	266,198	5,152	90	2
Total	1,204,841	34,350	3,428	68	566,608	11,860	2,340	48
Grand total	5,581,986	126,351	4,928	92	4,765,641	151,377	38,685	812

Statement, by fishing grounds, of quantities and values of certain fishery products landed at Boston and Gloucester, Mass., and Portland, Me., by American fishing vessels during the calendar year 1923—Continued

Fishing grounds	Cusk				Halibut			
	Fresh		Salted		Fresh		Salted	
	Pounds	Value	Pounds	Value	Pounds	Value	Lbs.	Value
LANDED AT BOSTON								
East of 66° W. longitude								
La Have Bank	43,960	$633	23,000	$690	222,881	$46,171		
Western Bank	20,560	384			401,857	79,440		
Quereau Bank	21,075	239			452,857	81,786		
Green Bank					198,243	31,280		
Grand Bank	3,000	60			904,252	138,257		
St. Peters Bank					239,047	43,792		
Cape Shore	5,480	66						
The Gully	2,725	55			192,597	38,158		
West of 66° W. longitude								
Browns Bank	614,694	11,660			244,617	53,898		
Georges Bank	56,460	1,393			577,990	135,920		
Cashes Bank	60,485	1,288			239	90		
Clark Bank					490	132		
Fippenies Bank	74,950	1,016			1,052	319		
Middle Bank	221,520	6,348			3,436	816		
Jeffreys Ledge	166,175	3,641			3,387	982		
South Channel	125,905	2,487			99,213	23,793		
Nantucket Shoals					3,389	784		
Off Highland Light					289	47		
Off Chatham	19,065	659			6,549	1,404		
Seal Island	61,180	875			3,420	1,154		
Shore, general	19,735	604			4,570	1,036		
Total	1,516,969	31,408	23,000	690	3,560,375	679,259		
LANDED AT GLOUCESTER								
East of 66° W. longitude								
La Have Bank	30,990	399						
Western Bank	43,480	508	7,755	156	15,180	3,230	510	$36
Quereau Bank	35,055	479	7,740	123				
Grand Bank	4,210	56	5,220	100	8,980	1,239	220	18
St. Peters Bank	26,670	319	6,605	167				
The Gully	760	10	1,060	23	69,890	14,906		
West of 66° W. longitude								
Browns Bank	49,985	534	1,575	35				
Georges Bank	81,875	1,010	7,615	139	12,834	2,738	780	54
Middle Bank	8,270	99						
Jeffreys Ledge	6,530	101						
South Channel	1,800	23						
Shore, general	485	7						
Total	290,110	3,545	37,570	743	106,884	22,113	1,510	108
LANDED AT PORTLAND								
East of 66° W. longitude								
La Have Bank	14,015	206	12,920	355	82,159	13,984		
Western Bank	87,105	982	4,125	103	306,781	62,624		
Quereau Bank	8,195	110			127,503	23,176		
Green Bank					44,863	10,840		
Grand Bank	2,165	23	450	11	276,926	38,937		
St. Peters Bank					65,818	9,514		
Gulf of St. Lawrence					23,939	5,179		
The Gully			335	10	8,916	1,579		
West of 66° W. longitude								
Browns Bank	83,415	1,044	8,730	194	209,591	44,041		
Georges Bank	18,100	250			31,047	6,359		
Cashes Bank	185,942	2,670			6,113	997		
Fippenies Bank	3,970	148			1,107	202		
Platts Bank	103,585	2,465			1,262	286		
Jeffreys Ledge	312,015	9,499			4,941	826		
Seal Island	735	22						
Shore, general	284,575	7,248	180	2	14,769	2,630		
Total	1,103,817	24,667	26,740	675	1,205,735	221,174		
Grand total	2,910,896	59,620	87,310	2,108	4,872,994	922,546	1,510	108

Statement, by fishing grounds, of quantities and values of certain fishery products landed at Boston and Gloucester, Mass., and Portland, Me., by American fishing vessels during the calendar year 1923—Continued

Fishing grounds	Mackerel				Miscellaneous			
	Fresh		Salted		Fresh		Salted	
	Pounds	Value	Pounds	Value	Pounds	Value	Pounds	Value
LANDED AT BOSTON								
East of 66° W. longitude								
La Have Bank					6,016	$1,003		
Western Bank					92,081	4,333		
Quereau Bank					2,830	494		
Grand Bank					2,886	580		
Cape Shore	857,017	$63,049			30,126	6,015		
West of 66° W. longitude								
Browns Bank					112,938	10,685		
Georges Bank	16,794	2,861			2,786,424	404,926		
Middle Bank	904,089	42,739			20,210	1,996		
Jeffreys Ledge	100,959	22,683			21,433	1,450		
South Channel	30	2			1,037,288	57,050	8,600	$258
Nantucket Shoals	175,690	5,148			547,619	29,026		
Off Highland Light					300	6		
Off Chatham	6,700	402			13,649	823		
Shore, general	4,518,787	179,605	187,600	$12,719	1,501,924	82,744		
Total	6,580,066	316,489	187,600	12,719	6,175,724	601,131	8,600	258
LANDED AT GLOUCESTER								
East of 66° W. longitude								
Off Newfoundland							1,219,300	40,861
Cape Shore	3,180	254	10,000	550				
West of 66° W. longitude								
Shore, general	3,184,083	85,170	611,800	38,284	95,946	4,500		
Total	3,187,263	85,424	621,800	38,834	95,946	4,500	1,219,300	40,861
LANDED AT PORTLAND								
East of 66° W. longitude								
Western Bank					1,190	16		
Quereau Bank					1,789	244		
Cape Shore	113,345	9,304	6,275	344				
Gulf of St. Lawrence					170	14		
West of 66° W. longitude								
Browns Bank					4,244	687		
Georges Bank					137,578	23,520		
Cashes Bank					417	7		
Fippenies Bank					125	1		
Platts Bank					300	19		
Jeffreys Ledge					26,918	1,571		
Shore, general	803,749	22,578	65,130	1,945	272,330	4,432		
Total	917,094	31,882	71,405	2,289	445,061	30,511		
Grand total	10,684,423	433,795	880,805	53,842	6,716,731	636,142	1,227,900	41,119

Statement, by fishing grounds, of quantities and values of certain fishery products landed at Boston and Gloucester, Mass., and Portland, Me., by American fishing vessels during the calendar year 1923—Continued

Fishing grounds	Number of trips	Total Fresh Pounds	Total Fresh Value	Total Salted Pounds	Total Salted Value	Grand total Pounds	Grand total Value
LANDED AT BOSTON							
East of 66° W. longitude							
La Have Bank	29	1,114,458	$73,902	23,000	$690	1,137,458	$74,592
Western Bank	162	10,368,848	384,841	17,500	700	10,386,348	385,541
Quereau Bank	17	521,137	84,012	2,375	112	523,512	84,124
Green Bank	7	198,243	31,280			198,243	31,280
Grand Bank	27	911,808	138,947			911,808	138,947
St. Peters Bank	8	246,347	44,035			246,347	44,035
Cape Shore	26	1,026,133	75,450			1,026,133	75,450
The Gully	8	198,292	38,321			198,292	38,321
West of 66° W. longitude							
Browns Bank	240	13,549,369	552,109			13,549,369	552,109
Georges Bank	773	34,855,287	1,760,248	8,000	360	34,863,287	1,760,608
Cashes Bank	7	200,421	8,741			200,421	8,741
Clark Bank	3	167,160	5,798			167,160	5,798
Fippenies Bank	6	276,152	5,649			276,152	5,649
Middle Bank	231	3,366,237	159,616			3,366,237	159,616
Jeffreys Ledge	124	2,046,972	104,597			2,046,972	104,597
Ipswich Bay	1	5,520	386			5,520	386
South Channel	727	40,299,230	1,367,039	8,600	258	40,307,830	1,367,297
Nantucket Shoals	103	3,763,097	125,889			3,763,097	125,889
Off Highland Light	1	25,689	1,066			25,689	1,066
Off Chatham	66	1,797,826	76,875			1,797,826	76,875
Seal Island	14	588,685	19,332			588,685	19,332
Shore, general	788	8,435,508	360,619	193,140	12,859	8,628,648	373,478
Total	3,368	123,962,419	5,418,752	252,615	14,979	124,215,034	5,433,731
LANDED AT GLOUCESTER							
East of 66° W. longitude							
La Have Bank	8	487,310	8,748	15,535	727	502,845	9,475
Western Bank	103	11,092,060	195,944	1,943,636	79,649	13,035,696	275,593
Quereau Bank	39	894,559	16,734	897,015	41,295	1,791,574	58,029
Misaine Bank	1	13,915	344			13,915	344
Grand Bank	42	144,037	3,897	557,145	25,554	701,182	29,451
St. Peters Bank	14	199,105	4,136	361,465	16,442	560,570	20,578
Off Newfoundland	5			1,219,300	40,861	1,219,300	40,861
Cape Shore	2	3,180	254	10,000	550	13,180	804
The Gully	11	163,415	16,951	83,070	3,832	246,485	20,783
West of 66° W. longitude							
Browns Bank	26	1,065,545	17,082	25,959	1,146	1,091,504	18,228
Georges Bank	135	6,083,594	105,536	292,750	13,462	6,376,344	118,998
Middle Bank	12	159,675	1,965			159,675	1,965
Jeffreys Ledge	3	37,660	452			37,660	452
South Channel	23	1,766,185	23,407			1,766,185	23,407
Nantucket Shoals	2	70,560	1,893			70,560	1,893
Seal Island	1	60,760	1,484			60,760	1,484
Shore, general	1,152	6,770,453	250,102	611,960	38,292	7,382,413	288,394
Total	1,579	29,012,013	648,929	6,017,835	261,810	35,029,848	910,739
LANDED AT PORTLAND							
East of 66° W. longitude							
La Have Bank	4	104,804	14,345	54,645	2,165	159,449	16,510
Western Bank	39	5,260,711	163,791	80,363	3,532	5,341,074	167,323
Quereau Bank	5	151,837	23,911	17,000	600	168,837	24,511
Green Bank	2	44,863	10,840	15,850	882	60,713	11,722
Grand Bank	13	310,986	40,110	85,555	4,028	396,541	44,138
St. Peters Bank	2	77,443	10,124	14,730	696	92,173	10,820
Cape Shore	6	113,345	9,304	7,025	355	120,370	9,659
Gulf of St. Lawrence	1	24,109	5,193			24,109	5,193
The Gully	1	19,646	1,845	10,465	488	30,111	2,333
West of 66° W. longitude							
Browns Bank	14	451,490	51,041	56,692	2,630	508,182	53,671
Georges Bank	21	336,420	35,518	28,542	1,248	364,962	36,766
Cashes Bank	52	797,949	19,946	4,035	194	801,984	20,140
Fippenies Bank	4	35,398	1,546			35,398	1,546
Platts Bank	45	472,588	17,008			472,588	17,008
Jeffreys Ledge	239	2,270,676	108,192	5,370	259	2,276,046	108,451
Seal Island	1	16,575	786			16,575	786
Shore, general	1,139	4,732,621	173,015	94,854	3,092	4,827,475	176,107
Total	1,588	15,221,461	686,515	475,126	20,169	15,696,587	706,684
Grand total	6,535	168,195,893	6,754,196	6,745,576	296,958	174,941,469	7,051,154

Statement by months, of quantities and values of certain fishery products landed at Boston and Gloucester, Mass., and Portland, Me., by American fishing vessels during the calendar year 1923

Months	Cod							
	Large (10 pounds and over)				Market (under 10 and over 2½ pounds)			
	Fresh		Salted		Fresh		Salted	
	Pounds	Value	Pounds	Value	Pounds	Value	Pounds	Value
LANDED AT BOSTON								
January	881,997	$74,776			613,131	$28,367		
February	3,783,925	176,072			572,178	34,464		
March	3,773,046	144,759	2,065	$81	590,173	20,411		
April	2,230,831	77,487	12,000	480	678,595	16,515		
May	2,177,229	75,617	8,000	360	1,518,761	29,530		
June	1,478,264	64,582			1,429,875	29,720		
July	1,848,295	80,873	2,375	112	1,777,758	35,954		
August	1,686,499	79,845			1,802,850	36,282		
September	1,555,695	66,306	5,500	220	1,539,915	34,726		
October	1,534,847	80,470			1,598,017	45,969		
November	1,627,113	75,271			1,291,655	33,003		
December	937,028	67,823			954,347	34,771		
Total	23,514,769	1,063,881	29,940	1,253	14,367,255	379,712		
LANDED AT GLOUCESTER								
January	47,355	3,025	9,870	420	412	8	2,210	$83
February	5,450	307	4,340	211			395	17
March	791,756	24,038	23,525	1,237	16,105	311	3,820	184
April	1,182,575	38,309	94,465	4,430	206,295	3,881	13,650	499
May	1,240,699	31,083	357,475	16,798	721,845	13,481	114,640	4,187
June	1,265,545	28,099	509,647	23,593	1,360,440	23,781	516,255	18,929
July	2,049,755	45,933	171,565	8,254	1,509,780	26,249	25,475	700
August	1,140,365	25,833	813,485	38,634	1,152,755	20,928	287,162	10,704
September	591,350	14,904	397,745	19,898	590,450	11,383	237,315	9,455
October	762,980	32,115	248,337	12,138	478,890	9,220	77,605	4,448
November	384,635	23,493	19,240	962	51,755	993	1,500	60
December	179,665	11,328	2,365	123	59,915	1,163	2,464	111
Total	9,642,130	278,467	2,652,059	126,698	6,148,642	111,398	1,282,491	49,377
LANDED AT PORTLAND								
January	81,330	6,609			88,155	4,181		
February	78,057	4,157			72,239	2,973		
March	186,054	6,534	20,672	1,164	40,007	1,756	6,785	384
April	421,688	10,260	27,585	1,472	74,059	1,937	4,410	190
May	920,624	19,743	33,260	1,586	43,286	903	10,270	263
June	327,629	10,248	32,230	1,566	24,959	607	7,085	267
July	251,109	11,509	67,737	3,185	34,488	822	4,435	171
August	192,315	9,985	90,852	4,295	28,255	843	13,630	513
September	222,160	11,411	22,845	1,229	38,378	1,101	7,210	303
October	263,091	10,965	465	24	143,951	3,426	500	21
November	187,577	9,849			110,065	2,757		
December	274,502	13,099			149,380	4,600		
Total	3,406,136	124,369	295,646	14,521	847,222	25,906	54,325	2,112
Grand total	36,563,035	1,466,717	2,977,645	142,472	21,363,119	517,016	1,336,816	51,489
Grounds east of 66° W. long	10,238,456	287,983	2,625,674	125,377	5,955,814	120,546	1,266,812	48,767
Grounds west of 66° W. long	26,324,579	1,178,734	351,971	17,095	15,407,305	396,470	70,004	2,722
Landed at Boston in 1922	17,718,297	719,118	47,750	1,671	12,859,415	285,623		
Landed at Gloucester in 1922	8,705,914	193,243	3,081,385	122,244	6,416,904	94,757	1,645,358	56,565
Landed at Portland in 1922	3,173,273	132,183	123,385	5,199	580,603	14,991	12,510	485

Statement, by months, of quantities and values of certain fishery products landed at Boston and Gloucester, Mass., and Portland, Me., by American fishing vessels during the calendar year 1923—Continued

Months	Cod—Continued				Haddock			
	Scrod (1 to 2½ pounds)				Large (over 2½ pounds)			
	Fresh		Salted		Fresh		Salted	
	Pounds	Value	Pounds	Value	Pounds	Value	Pounds	Value
LANDED AT BOSTON								
January	19,630	$355			4,038,944	$244,078		
February	12,200	279			5,592,545	335,735		
March	5,420	91			6,855,125	256,801		
April	1,600	13			5,196,830	135,091		
May	5,910	87			4,339,415	152,319		
June	4,070	24			3,181,967	94,087		
July	2,675	16			3,091,502	103,719		
August	10,690	81			4,003,687	91,732		
September	8,645	80			4,054,888	96,458		
October	20,775	313			5,240,585	157,971		
November	16,985	231			5,352,980	197,640		
December	21,555	267			5,175,910	186,490		
Total	130,155	1,837			56,124,378	2,052,121		
LANDED AT GLOUCESTER								
January					39,573	3,354		
February					45,925	3,688		
March			330	$8	363,115	11,495		
April	100	1			910,060	12,123		
May	3,880	29	1,410	36	536,435	5,637	1,360	$27
June	7,120	50	49,465	1,514	951,350	9,408		
July	11,670	88	70	2	1,382,730	13,660		
August	7,940	68	21,435	541	1,367,840	13,566	36,885	827
September	380	3	29,020	984	1,049,125	10,492	3,135	63
October	1,000	8	7,145	133	644,905	6,796		
November	720	6			112,990	3,247		
December	1,305	9	20	1	307,943	4,945	230	5
Total	34,115	262	108,895	3,219	7,711,991	98,411	41,610	922
LANDED AT PORTLAND								
January	10,200	59			258,786	18,015		
February	9,600	52			251,422	19,457		
March	5,289	31			369,752	16,982		
April	8,452	49			1,220,651	26,609		
May	2,683	16	420	9	1,265,565	28,356		
June	3,648	19	5,175	152	593,869	13,174		
July	5,682	38	330	7	65,056	3,529		
August	3,026	19	12,883	235	38,210	2,038		
September	5,510	30	600	15	43,490	2,493		
October	18,286	109	650	13	182,871	8,840		
November	21,425	119			332,246	16,839		
December	27,635	157			415,931	20,910		
Total	121,436	698	20,058	431	5,037,849	177,242		
Grand total	285,706	2,797	128,953	3,650	68,874,218	2,327,774	41,610	922
Grounds east of 66° W. long	36,210	343	121,978	3,459	11,450,075	234,983	41,610	922
Grounds west of 66° W. long	249,496	2,454	6,975	191	57,424,143	2,092,791		
Landed at Boston in 1922	494,095	5,428			52,664,489	1,501,570		
Landed at Gloucester in 1922	38,652	364	94,812	2,364	12,453,416	162,922	131,385	2,736
Landed at Portland in 1922	186,842	1,020	970	24	4,693,425	137,911		

Statement, by months, of quantities and values of certain fishery products landed at Boston and Gloucester, Mass., and Portland, Me., by American fishing vessels during the calendar year 1923—Continued

Months	Haddock—Continued				Hake			
	Scrod (1 to 2½ pounds)				Large (6 pounds and over)			
	Fresh		Salted		Fresh		Salted	
	Pounds	Value	Pounds	Value	Pounds	Value	Pounds	Value
LANDED AT BOSTON								
January	344,145	$15,884			22,081	$1,716		
February	464,620	18,647			30,948	2,281		
March	520,085	11,479			1,800	126		
April	174,060	2,178						
May	85,850	1,627			500	10		
June	138,905	1,454			75	2		
July	174,550	1,643						
August	177,380	1,161	1,975	$35				
September	142,360	1,372						
October	467,415	7,253			4,130	48		
November	919,104	12,552			47,515	1,267		
December	807,794	15,476			15,595	612		
Total	4,416,268	90,726	1,975	35	122,644	6,062		
LANDED AT GLOUCESTER								
January					440	4		
March	360	3					1,620	$45
April							135	2
May					2,425	24	1,065	16
June					1,700	19	5,230	79
July					24,900	249	965	14
August	8,540	69			21,460	216	3,845	62
September	7,500	38			38,860	397	630	12
October	31,140	215			91,390	1,622	2,335	45
November	24,620	199			267,090	3,737	430	9
December	28,425	146			123,720	2,479		
Total	100,585	670			571,985	8,747	16,255	284
LANDED AT PORTLAND								
January	17,509	130			405	30		
February	33,516	309			160	10		
March	21,530	418			1,730	112		
April	10,741	171			2,620	115		
May	2,370	29						
June	5,382	55						
July	23,267	285						
August	9,287	88			8,135	116	1,135	23
September	15,405	151			3,975	51		
October	42,305	380			20,270	342	49	2
November	77,391	579						
December	68,164	455			1,500	30		
Total	326,867	3,050			38,795	806	1,184	25
Grand total	4,843,720	94,446	1,975	35	733,424	15,615	17,439	309
Grounds east of 66° W. long	79,120	834			89,565	940	16,840	298
Grounds west of 66° W. long	4,764,600	93,612	1,975	35	643,859	14,675	599	11
Landed at Boston in 1922	198,425	3,855			97,810	3,330		
Landed at Gloucester in 1922	675	7			838,655	20,556	21,950	342
Landed at Portland in 1922	54,183	399			40,200	1,162	300	5

Statement, by months, of quantities and values of certain fishery products landed at Boston and Gloucester, Mass., and Portland, Me., by American fishing vessels during the calendar year 1923—Continued

Months	Hake—Continued				Pollock			
	Small (under 6 pounds)							
	Fresh		Salted		Fresh		Salted	
	Pounds	Value	Lbs.	Value	Pounds	Value	Pounds	Value
LANDED AT BOSTON								
January	89,064	$6,625			177,905	$11,672		
February	150,916	8,962			81,635	5,207		
March	75,040	4,522			131,434	6,345		
April	57,995	2,658			142,118	6,756		
May	37,485	1,685			255,120	7,114		
June	82,804	2,007			192,469	5,323		
July	490,954	6,784	500	$9	221,793	8,971		
August	419,000	8,327			290,678	11,874		
September	530,630	8,863			391,460	10,340		
October	826,188	15,307	1,000	15	402,858	10,569		
November	1,088,240	12,858			493,131	9,422		
December	528,829	13,403			296,070	10,532		
Total	4,377,145	92,001	1,500	24	3,076,671	104,125		
LANDED AT GLOUCESTER								
January					163,912	11,574		
February					10,105	577		
March					16,115	1,009		
April					28,315	1,102	325	$7
May					18,545	213	3,265	65
June					36,660	368	9,040	182
July					36,905	363	995	16
August					21,340	246	8,875	197
September					49,125	492	5,645	134
October					186,520	4,938	7,800	155
November					238,250	5,320		
December					316,570	9,190	400	8
Total					1,122,362	35,392	36,345	764
LANDED AT PORTLAND								
January	84,352	5,067			37,413	1,863		
February	106,044	5,645			27,645	1,320		
March	104,141	4,943			18,358	731	225	6
April	119,040	4,703			29,864	737	250	7
May	82,747	1,543	220	4	39,867	384	215	6
June	56,832	1,101	1,308	26	37,436	395	840	13
July	40,109	517			54,669	846		
August	29,776	363	1,900	38	39,135	858	490	10
September	30,970	642			48,279	700		
October	189,736	2,395			105,198	1,345	320	6
November	190,702	2,763			64,242	978		
December	170,392	4,668			64,502	1,703		
Total	1,204,841	34,350	3,428	68	566,608	11,860	2,340	48
Grand total	5,581,986	126,351	4,928	92	4,765,641	151,377	38,685	812
Grounds east of 66° W. long	56,752	957	1,900	38	681,835	16,746	35,345	750
Grounds west of 66° W. long	5,525,234	125,394	3,028	54	4,083,806	134,631	3,340	62
Landed at Boston in 1922	3,420,536	68,107	1,200	36	3,415,801	78,657	250	5
Landed at Gloucester in 1922					1,058,725	27,181	49,005	932
Landed at Portland in 1922	944,136	17,621	9,460	172	573,259	11,230	45	1

Statement, by months, of quantities and values of certain fishery products landed at Boston and Gloucester, Mass., and Portland, Me., by American fishing vessels during the calendar year 1923—Continued

Months	Cusk				Halibut			
	Fresh		Salted		Fresh		Salted	
	Pounds	*Value*	*Pounds*	*Value*	*Pounds*	*Value*	*Pounds*	*Value*
LANDED AT BOSTON								
January	133,705	$4,595			29,955	$9,815		
February	142,995	5,322			90,447	21,430		
March	128,795	3,547			157,971	39,167		
April	54,480	1,093			284,435	58,720		
May	171,405	2,366			496,344	101,019		
June	52,295	776			675,207	100,426		
July	71,215	1,073	23,000	$690	467,496	77,964		
August	36,900	678			518,030	93,551		
September	47,305	654			366,205	72,342		
October	191,605	3,071			382,451	77,109		
November	200,774	3,187			55,449	16,077		
December	285,495	5,046			36,385	11,639		
Total	1,516,969	31,408	23,000	690	3,560,375	679,259		
LANDED AT GLOUCESTER								
February					5,192	1,126		
March	630	8			59,730	12,924		
April	23,335	217	1,160	25	7,160	1,202		
May	36,440	362	7,460	113	25,642	5,611		
June	15,260	215	3,525	82	7,080	1,133	220	$18
July	39,675	559	2,990	59	1,900	106	780	54
August	46,065	583	8,810	195			100	4
September	57,580	700	11,705	230			410	32
October	27,940	350	1,855	38	180	11		
November	18,950	222	65	1				
December	24,235	329						
Total	290,110	3,545	37,570	743	106,884	22,113	1,510	108
LANDED AT PORTLAND								
January	74,329	3,265			1,108	220		
February	112,182	3,907			68	8		
March	111,706	3,584	4,670	93	109,186	27,246		
April	177,099	3,590	300	9	244,217	48,736		
May	136,651	1,899			172,497	35,392		
June	15,316	418	450	11	218,625	32,157		
July	23,460	488	335	10	146,545	23,556		
August	33,542	520	17,045	458	188,763	28,897		
September	59,985	1,020	2,200	61	86,140	17,367		
October	179,918	2,483	1,740	33	32,035	6,465		
November	95,410	1,618			4,269	717		
December	84,219	1,875			2,282	413		
Total	1,103,817	24,667	26,740	675	1,205,735	221,174		
Grand total	2,910,896	59,620	87,310	2,108	4,872,994	922,546	1,510	108
Grounds east of 66° W. long	349,445	4,529	69,210	1,738	3,642,689	644,092	730	54
Grounds west of 66° W. long	2,561,451	55,091	18,100	370	1,230,305	278,454	780	54
Landed at Boston in 1922	1,196,932	18,417			3,948,456	550,735		
Landed at Gloucester in 1922	465,779	4,698	53,030	1,196	42,352	6,781	15,706	915
Landed at Portland in 1922	531,304	10,233	405	8	1,617,635	225,626		

Statement, by months, of quantities and values of certain fishery products landed at Boston and Gloucester, Mass., and Portland, Me., by American fishing vessels during the calendar year 1923—Continued

Months	ackerel				Miscellaneous [1]			
	Fresh		Salted		Fresh		Salted	
	Pounds	Value	Pounds	Value	Pounds	Value	Pounds	Value
LANDED AT BOSTON								
January					279, 166	$17, 100		
February					302, 303	17, 934		
March					384, 143	24, 483	8, 600	$258
April					556, 000	23, 088		
May	167, 770	$27, 832			603, 946	15, 109		
June	917, 736	67, 285			214, 387	11, 119		
July	621, 143	27, 004			1, 276, 994	194, 874		
August	911, 387	43, 642			1, 102, 120	180, 923		
September	2, 387, 595	65, 960	38, 400	$2, 678	570, 416	65, 397		
October	1, 161, 516	50, 140	149, 200	10, 041	365, 682	18, 248		
November	342, 414	18, 362			227, 266	13, 260		
December	70, 505	16, 264			293, 301	19, 596		
Total	6, 580, 066	316, 489	187, 600	12, 719	6, 175, 724	601, 131	8, 600	258
LANDED AT GLOUCESTER								
January					718	72		
February					28, 748	3, 454		
March					2, 480	174		
May							339, 100	10, 836
June	4, 340	347	10, 400	574				
July	8, 137	244	74, 800	4, 686				
August	14, 298	450						
September	2, 304, 995	41, 741	308, 200	16, 685	18, 000	225		
October	695, 615	14, 894	211, 800	15, 644	46, 000	575		
November	84, 655	10, 878	16, 600	1, 245			114, 400	4, 004
December	75, 223	16, 870					765, 800	26, 021
Total	3, 187, 263	85, 424	621, 800	38, 834	95, 946	4, 500	1, 219, 300	40, 861
LANDED AT PORTLAND								
January					7, 081	487		
February					14, 097	814		
March					7, 823	423		
April					4, 246	130		
May	2, 563	408			1, 770	43		
June	121, 363	9, 867	6, 275	344	157, 996	2, 454		
July	28, 476	1, 942	390	39	40, 348	4, 558		
August	1, 728	222			120, 718	16, 699		
September	687, 517	16, 521	43, 870	1, 025	27, 911	3, 994		
October	75, 249	2, 888	20, 870	881	57, 800	764		
November	198	34			4, 294	104		
December					977	41		
Total	917, 094	31, 882	71, 405	2, 289	445, 061	30, 511		
Grand total	10, 684, 423	433, 795	880, 805	53, 842	6, 716, 731	636, 142	1, 227, 900	41, 119
Grounds east of 66° W. long	973, 542	72, 607	16, 275	894	137, 088	12, 699		
Grounds west of 66° W. long	9, 710, 881	361, 188	864, 530	52, 948	6, 579, 643	623, 443	8, 600	258
Landed at Boston in 1922	2, 871, 000	181, 962	65, 400	4, 109	7, 146, 947	596, 409	43, 600	1, 073
Landed at Gloucester in 1922	374, 545	27, 166	370, 555	32, 029			1, 892, 420	56, 355
Landed at Portland in 1922	1, 020, 822	29, 983	24, 425	1, 250	2, 346, 088	42, 930	495	41

[1] Includes herring from Newfoundland, 1,219,300 pounds salted, value $40,861.

Statement, by months, of quantities and values of certain fishery products landed at Boston and Gloucester, Mass., and Portland, Me., by American fishing vessels during the calendar year 1923—Continued

Months	Number of trips	Total				Grand total	
		Fresh		Salted			
		Pounds	*Value*	*Pounds*	*Value*	*Pounds*	*Value*
LANDED AT BOSTON							
January	175	6,629,723	$414,983			6,629,723	$414,983
February	250	11,224,712	626,333			11,224,712	626,333
March	251	12,623,032	511,731	10,665	$339	12,633,697	512,070
April	228	9,376,944	323,599	12,000	480	9,388,944	324,079
May	289	9,859,735	414,315	8,000	360	9,867,735	414,675
June	228	8,368,054	376,805			8,368,054	376,805
July	362	10,044,375	538,875	25,875	811	10,070,250	539,686
August	394	10,959,221	548,096	1,975	35	10,961,196	548,131
September	324	11,595,114	422,498	43,900	2,898	11,639,014	425,396
October	345	12,196,069	466,468	150,200	10,056	12,346,269	476,524
November	276	11,662,626	393,130			11,662,626	393,130
December	246	9,422,814	381,919			9,422,814	381,919
Total	3,368	123,962,419	5,418,752	252,615	14,979	124,215,034	5,433,731
LANDED AT GLOUCESTER							
January	94	252,410	18,037	12,080	503	264,490	18,540
February	52	95,420	9,152	4,735	228	100,155	9,380
March	162	1,250,291	49,962	29,295	1,474	1,279,586	51,436
April	276	2,357,840	56,835	109,735	4,963	2,467,575	61,798
May	108	2,585,911	56,440	825,775	32,078	3,411,686	88,518
June	59	3,649,495	63,420	1,103,782	44,971	4,753,277	108,391
July	64	5,065,452	87,451	277,640	13,785	5,343,092	101,236
August	72	3,780,603	61,959	1,180,597	51,164	4,961,200	113,123
September	146	4,707,365	80,375	993,805	47,493	5,701,170	127,868
October	235	2,966,560	70,744	556,877	32,601	3,523,437	103,345
November	168	1,183,665	48,095	152,235	6,281	1,335,900	54,376
December	143	1,117,001	46,459	771,279	26,269	1,888,280	72,728
Total	1,579	29,012,013	648,929	6,017,835	261,810	35,029,848	910,739
LANDED AT PORTLAND							
January	90	660,668	39,926			660,668	39,926
February	90	705,030	38,652			705,030	38,652
March	117	975,576	62,760	32,352	1,647	1,007,928	64,407
April	147	2,312,677	97,037	32,545	1,678	2,345,222	98,715
May	165	2,670,623	88,716	44,385	1,868	2,715,008	90,584
June	154	1,563,055	70,495	53,363	2,379	1,616,418	72,874
July	164	713,209	48,090	73,227	3,412	786,436	51,502
August	126	692,890	60,648	137,935	5,572	830,825	66,220
September	163	1,269,720	55,481	76,725	2,633	1,346,445	58,114
October	148	1,310,710	40,402	24,594	980	1,335,304	41,382
November	119	1,087,819	36,357			1,087,819	36,357
December	105	1,259,484	47,951			1,259,484	47,951
Total	1,588	15,221,461	686,515	475,126	20,169	15,696,587	706,684
Grand total	6,535	168,195,893	6,754,196	6,745,576	296,958	174,941,469	7,051,154
Grounds east of 66° W. long	582	33,690,591	1,397,259	5,415,674	223,158	39,106,265	1,620,417
Grounds west of 66° W. long	5,953	134,505,302	5,356,937	1,329,902	73,800	135,835,204	5,430,737
Landed at Boston in 1922	2,893	106,032,203	4,013,211	158,200	6,894	106,190,403	4,020,105
Landed at Gloucester in 1922	1,653	30,395,617	537,675	7,355,606	275,678	37,751,223	813,353
Landed at Portland in 1922	1,803	15,761,770	625,289	171,995	7,185	15,933,765	632,474

The fishery products landed at Boston and Gloucester, Mass., and Portland, Me., by fishing vessels each year are taken chiefly from fishing grounds off the coast of the United States. In the calendar year 1923, 77.26 per cent of the quantity and 76.71 per cent of the value landed by fishing vessels were from these grounds; 2.51 per cent of the quantity and 5.27 per cent of the value, consisting mostly of cod, halibut, and herring, were from fishing banks off the coast of Newfoundland; and 20.23 per cent of the quantity and 18.01 per cent of the value were from fishing grounds off the Canadian Provinces. There was some decrease compared with the previous year in the percentage of products from grounds off the United States and Newfoundland and a small increase in the percentage from grounds off the Canadian Provinces. Newfoundland herring constituted less than 1 per cent of the quantity and value of fishery products landed at these ports during the year. The herring were taken from the treaty coast of Newfoundland, and the cod, haddock, hake, halibut, and other species from that region were obtained from fishing banks on the high seas. All fish caught by American fishing vessels off the coast of the Canadian Provinces were from offshore fishing grounds. The catch from each of these regions is given in detail in the following table:

Quantity and value of fish landed by American fishing vessels at Boston and Gloucester, Mass., and Portland, Me., in 1923, from fishing grounds off the coast of the United States, Newfoundland, and Canadian Provinces

Species	United States		Newfoundland		Canadian Provinces		Total	
	Pounds	Value	Pounds	Value	Pounds	Value	Pounds	Value
Cod:								
Fresh	41,794,950	$1,570,056	324,477	$8,144	16,092,433	$408,330	58,211,860	$1,986,530
Salted	428,950	20,008	1,007,330	47,011	3,007,134	130,592	4,443,414	197,611
Haddock:								
Fresh	61,794,563	2,174,800	150	2	11,923,225	247,418	73,717,938	2,422,220
Salted	1,975	35			41,610	922	43,585	957
Hake:								
Fresh	6,151,758	139,787	31,145	326	132,507	1,853	6,315,410	141,966
Salted	3,627	65	11,950	209	6,790	127	22,367	401
Pollock:								
Fresh	4,081,066	134,567			684,575	16,810	4,765,641	151,377
Salted	3,340	62	2,970	86	32,375	664	38,685	812
Cusk:								
Fresh	2,499,536	54,194	36,045	458	375,315	4,968	2,910,896	59,620
Salted	18,100	370	12,275	278	56,935	1,460	87,310	2,108
Halibut:								
Fresh	1,226,885	277,300	1,738,129	273,859	1,907,980	371,387	4,872,994	922,546
Salted	780	54	220	18	510	36	1,510	108
Mackerel:								
Fresh	9,710,881	361,188			973,542	72,607	10,684,423	433,795
Salted	864,530	52,948			16,275	894	880,805	53,842
Herring:								
Fresh	263,540	3,657					263,540	3,657
Salted			1,219,300	40,861			1,219,300	40,861
Swordfish: Fresh	2,407,541	438,896	2,886	580	44,992	8,643	2,455,419	448,119
Miscellaneous:								
Fresh	3,908,562	180,890			89,210	3,476	3,997,772	184,366
Salted	8,600	258					8,600	258
Total	135,169,184	5,409,135	4,386,877	371,832	35,385,408	1,270,187	174,941,469	7,051,154

SPECIES

COD

In 1923 there was a decrease of 32 vessels in the fishing fleet landing fish at Boston, Gloucester, and Portland, as compared with 1922. There were 7 vessels in the salt-bank fishery, as compared with 17 in 1922, and 108 in the market fishery, or 14 more than in 1922. These vessels landed their fares of cod and other ground fish at these ports during the year, and large quantities were also landed by vessels fishing on the shore grounds. The catch of cod landed at these ports during the year was 62,655,274 pounds, valued at $2,184,171, of which 58,211,860 pounds, valued at $1,986,530, were landed fresh, and 4,443,414 pounds, valued at $197,611, were landed salted. Cod ranked second in both quantity and value among the various species landed.

HADDOCK

Haddock ranked first in both quantity and value, the catch exceeding that of cod by 11,106,249 pounds in quantity and $239,036 in value. The quantity of haddock landed at these ports by fishing vessels during the year was 73,761,523 pounds, valued at $2,423,177, all landed fresh except 43,585 pounds, valued at $957, landed salted. These fish were taken chiefly from Western Bank, Browns Bank, Georges Bank, and South Channel, and about 48 per cent of the quantity and nearly 42 per cent of the value were taken in the otter-trawl fishery. The greater part of the catch, or 60,542,621 pounds, valued at $2,142,882, was landed at Boston.

HAKE

The catch of hake amounted to 6,337,777 pounds, valued at $142,367, all landed fresh except 22,367 pounds salted, valued at $401. Of this catch, 4,501,289 pounds, valued at $98,087, were landed at Boston, 588,240 pounds, valued at $9,031, at Gloucester, and 1,248,248 pounds, valued at $35,249, at Portland. About half of the catch was taken in South Channel, and about 71 per cent was landed at Boston.

POLLOCK

The catch of pollock amounted to 4,804,326 pounds, valued at $152,189, all landed fresh except 38,685 pounds salted, valued at $812. The greater part of the catch, or 3,076,671 pounds, valued at $104,125, was landed at Boston. The catch was obtained largely from Browns Bank, Georges Bank, South Channel, and shore grounds.

CUSK

The catch of cusk amounted to 2,998,206 pounds, valued at $61,728, all landed fresh except 87,310 pounds salted, valued at $2,108. More than half of the catch was landed at Boston. There was an increase in the catch of cusk of 750,756 pounds in quantity and $27,176 in value as compared with 1922.

HALIBUT

The catch of halibut amounted to 4,874,504 pounds, valued at $922,654, all landed fresh except 1,510 pounds salted, valued at $108. There was a considerable decrease in the quantity, but an increase in the value, as compared with 1922. The quantity landed at Boston was 3,560,375 pounds, valued at $679,259; at Gloucester, 108,394 pounds, valued at $22,221; and at Portland, 1,205,735 pounds, valued at $221,174.

MACKEREL

The total catch of fresh mackerel taken by the American fishing fleet in 1923 was 121,982 barrels, compared with 53,703 barrels in 1922, an increase of 68,279 barrels. The total catch of salted mackerel was 18,864 barrels, compared with 2,749 barrels in 1922, an increase of 16,115 barrels. The quantity of mackerel landed at Boston, Gloucester, and Portland during the year was 11,565,228 pounds, valued at $487,637, of which 10,684,423 pounds, valued at $433,795, were fresh, and 880,805 pounds, valued at $53,842, were salted. There was an increase in the total catch of mackerel landed by fishing vessels at these ports of 6,838,481 pounds in quantity and of $211,138 in value, as compared with 1922.

In 1923 the total catch of mackerel up to July 1 was 22,866 barrels fresh and 217 barrels salted, compared with 25,090 barrels fresh and 2,344 barrels salted for the same period in 1922. The southern mackerel fleet numbered about 25 purse-seine vessels and 136 gill-net vessels. Both seiners and netters had poor success on account of windy weather and scarcity of fish during the spring months. The first catch was landed at Norfolk on April 9, and consisted of 300 pounds of large mackerel, which sold at 75 cents per pound in New York. This was three days earlier than the landing of the first catch the previous year. A considerable quantity of tinker mackerel scattered in small schools was reported in the south. The first catch of mackerel from Cape Shore was landed at Yarmouth, Nova Scotia, on May 29, and consisted of 4,000 pounds of large fish, which were shipped to Boston. The first arrival at Boston, direct from the fleet, was on June 7, and consisted of 20,000 pounds of large fish, which sold at 6½ cents per pound. Fresh mackerel sold during the season at from 6½ to 40 cents per pound, according to market conditions, and salted mackerel from Cape Shore sold at $11 per barrel.

SWORDFISH

The catch of swordfish amounted to 2,455,419 pounds, valued at $448,119. There were 52 vessels engaged in this fishery, or 2 more than in the previous year. There was, however, a decrease in the catch of 25.17 per cent in the quantity, but a slight increase of about a quarter of 1 per cent in the value.

FLOUNDERS

The catch of flounders taken in the vessel fisheries amounted to 3,436,820 pounds, valued at $163,683, an increase of 155,493 pounds, or 4.73 per cent, in quantity and of $28,934, or 21.47, per cent, in value. The catch taken by boats under 5 tons net tonnage is not included in these statistics.

HERRING

The catch of herring amounted to 1,482,840 pounds, valued at $44,518. Of this quantity 263,540 pounds, valued at $3,657, were taken off the coast of the United States and landed fresh, and the remainder, consisting of 1,219,300 pounds salted, valued at $40,861, were Newfoundland herring.

OTTER-TRAWL FISHERY

In 1923 there were 665 trips landed at Boston, Gloucester, and Portland by 33 otter-trawl vessels, amounting to 54,298,289 pounds of fish, valued at $1,696,321, or 31.03 per cent of the quantity and 24.05 per cent of the value of the total catch landed by fishing vessels at these ports during the year. The catch included cod, 14,961,590 pounds, valued at $485,799; haddock, 35,527,297 pounds, valued at $1,011,810; hake, 471,660 pounds, valued at $12,280; pollock, 1,229,361 pounds, valued at $43,312; cusk, 13,195 pounds, valued at $402; halibut, 148,668 pounds, valued at $34,829; mackerel, 59,500 pounds, valued at $5,205; and other species, 1,887,018 pounds, valued at $102,684. The catch by otter trawls consists principally of haddock, which in 1923 amounted to 48.16 per cent of the quantity and 41.75 per cent of the value of the entire catch of this species landed. The catch by otter trawls was taken chiefly from Western Bank, Georges Bank, and South Channel.

The following tables give, by fishing grounds and by months, the catch landed by otter trawlers at these ports in 1923, and also the catch of cod, haddock, and hake landed by them in various years:

Fishery products landed at Boston and Gloucester, Mass., and Portland, Me., by otter trawlers in 1923

	Cod		Haddock		Hake	
BY FISHING GROUNDS						
East of 66° W. Longitude	*Pounds*	*Value*	*Pounds*	*Value*	*Pounds*	*Value*
Western Bank	7,836,102	$218,512	10,321,517	$215,246	33,615	$484
Cape Shore						
West of 66° W. Longitude						
Browns Bank	51,380	1,129	444,425	12,693		
Georges Bank	4,348,143	164,113	9,295,985	321,240	49,886	1,581
Middle Bank	4,280	193	17,200	494	8,100	81
South Channel	2,594,460	97,394	14,162,865	423,388	352,679	9,785
Nantucket Shoals	115,120	3,991	1,198,075	34,532	24,810	308
Off Chatham	12,105	467	87,230	4,217	2,570	41
Total	14,961,590	485,799	35,527,297	1,011,810	471,660	12,280
BY MONTHS						
January	666,115	40,706	2,112,180	122,111	21,454	1,816
February	1,526,985	76,400	2,764,410	154,997	6,251	397
March	1,073,020	39,582	3,883,785	129,481	16,270	1,085
April	1,195,008	33,402	4,21,635	91,031	37,405	1,817
May	1,690,995	38,044	3,72,410	91,032	6,210	181
June	1,094,050	24,639	2,015,445	55,138	28,995	702
July	1,363,190	30,803	2,814,515	47,032	21,155	284
August	1,295,180	30,455	2,402,699	36,983	32,870	383
September	941,916	24,517	2,725,183	33,538	54,690	945
October	1,582,540	52,418	2,850,655	63,848	71,140	1,158
November	1,755,103	57,562	2,893,500	81,999	86,745	965
December	777,488	37,271	3,460,880	104,620	88,475	2,547
Total	14,961,590	485,799	35,527,297	1,011,810	471,660	12,280

Fishery products landed at Boston and Gloucester, Mass., and Portland, Me., by otter trawlers in 1923—Continued

	Pollock		Cusk		Halibut	
BY FISHING GROUNDS						
East of 66° W. Longitude	*Pounds*	*Value*	*Pounds*	*Value*	*Pounds*	*Value*
Western Bank	615,940	$15,765	2,545	$50	43,042	$9,598
West of 66° W. Longitude						
Browns Bank	5,630	169			1,970	427
Georges Bank	167,470	7,952	4,100	156	55,108	13,387
Middle Bank	1,100	22	3,875	78		
South Channel	411,501	18,837	2,040	99	46,711	10,942
Nantucket Shoals	24,585	487			1,777	466
Off Chatham	3,135	80	635	19	60	9
Total	1,229,361	43,312	13,195	402	148,668	34,829
BY MONTHS						
January	125,735	8,493			7,196	2,140
February	39,500	2,536			14,598	3,805
March	96,924	4,918	735	24	16,182	4,155
April	97,770	4,696	5,320	202	9,067	2,152
May	157,087	3,863			18,357	3,844
June	47,550	901			9,053	1,869
July	37,695	838			12,049	2,487
August	32,525	895	2,275	46	9,699	1,814
September	76,545	1,787	175	2	10,367	2,239
October	78,360	2,346	560	43	20,053	4,666
November	231,180	3,774	4,040	81	15,422	3,957
December	208,490	8,265	90	4	6,625	1,701
Total	1,229,361	43,312	13,195	402	148,668	34,829

	Mackerel		Miscellaneous		Number of trips	Total	
BY FISHING GROUNDS							
East of 66° W. Longitude	*Pounds*	*Value*	*Pounds*	*Value*		*Pounds*	*Value*
Western Bank			87,835	$3,431	187	18,940,596	$463,086
Cape Shore	59,500	$5,205			1	59,500	5,205
West of 66° W. Longitude							
Browns Bank			17,925	244	4	521,330	14,662
Georges Bank			646,905	37,499	183	14,567,597	545,928
Middle Bank					1	34,555	868
South Channel			934,894	52,846	268	18,505,150	613,291
Nantucket Shoals			192,079	8,221	18	1,556,446	48,005
Off Chatham			7,380	443	3	113,115	5,276
Total	59,500	5,205	1,887,018	102,684	665	54,298,289	1,696,321
BY MONTHS							
January			37,676	5,704	55	2,970,356	180,970
February			70,262	7,012	57	4,422,006	245,147
March			117,253	10,438	62	5,204,169	189,683
April			282,195	14,311	58	5,648,400	147,611
May			327,295	8,773	59	5,672,354	145,737
June	59,500	5,205	85,445	3,279	48	4,240,038	91,733
July			48,793	1,753	46	4,097,397	83,197
August			147,932	5,934	53	3,923,180	76,510
September			167,455	6,921	45	3,386,331	69,949
October			276,821	13,694	58	4,880,129	138,173
November			184,710	10,777	57	5,170,700	159,115
December			141,181	14,088	67	4,683,229	168,496
Total	59,500	5,205	1,887,018	102,684	665	54,298,289	1,696,321

Cod, haddock, and hake landed at Boston and Gloucester, Mass., and Portland, Me.,
by otter trawlers in various years, 1908 to 1923

Year	Trips	Cod	Haddock	Hake	Year	Trips	Cod	Haddock	Hake
	No.	Pounds	Pounds	Pounds		No.	Pounds	Pounds	Pounds
1908	44	209,800	1,542,000	46,600	1914	387	1,149,595	15,383,550	259,913
1909	47	159,800	1,719,000	74,400	1920	646	6,311,389	51,962,457	
1910	59	125,850	2,775,000	46,600	1921	346	2,482,833	26,734,893	241,650
1911	178	564,500	7,367,100	151,700	1922	578	11,161,947	35,878,524	576,370
1912	295	1,952,950	12,966,700	105,500	1923	665	14,961,590	35,527,297	471,660
1913	326	1,667,806	12,488,992	209,485					

VESSEL FISHERIES AT SEATTLE, WASH.

In the vessel fisheries at Seattle, Wash., there was a decrease, as compared with 1922, in the quantity but an increase in the value of products landed by the fishing fleet and an increase in both the quantity and value of products landed by collecting vessels, which was due chiefly to an increase in the landings of salmon. Statistics of the vessel fisheries at Seattle have been collected by the local agent and published as monthly and annual statistical bulletins, giving the quantity and value of fishery products landed by American fishing and collecting vessels at that port.

In 1923 the fishing fleet at Seattle landed 919 trips, amounting to 10,237,590 pounds of fish, having a value to the fishermen of $1,321,587. The catch was taken chiefly from fishing grounds along the coast from Oregon to Yakutat grounds, Alaska. The fishing areas from which the largest quantities of fish were taken were Flattery Banks, west coast of Vancouver Island, and Hecate Strait. The products included halibut, 7,804,990 pounds, valued at $1,188,878; sablefish, 2,108,600 pounds, valued at $123,514; "lingcod," 194,100 pounds, valued at $4,355; and rockfishes, 129,900 pounds, valued at $4,840. Compared with 1922 there was an increase of 83 trips by fishing vessels but a decrease of 1,094,460 pounds, or 9.66 per cent, in the quantity, and an increase of $71,765, or 5.74 per cent, in the value of the products landed. There was a decrease in the catch of halibut of 2,133,160 pounds, or 21.46 per cent, in quantity, and of $7,512, or 0.63 per cent, in value. There was an increase in the catch of sablefish of 1,094,500 pounds, or 107.93 per cent, in quantity and of $76,862, or 164.76 per cent, in value. The catch of "lingcod" decreased 64,100 pounds, or 24.82 per cent, in quantity, and $154, or 3.42 per cent, in value; and the catch of rockfishes increased 8,300 pounds, or 6.82 per cent, in quantity, and $2,569, or 113.12 per cent, in value.

The fishery products taken in Puget Sound and landed at Seattle by collecting vessels during the year amounted to 17,387,478 pounds, valued at $1,308,731. The products included salmon, 15,711,200 pounds, valued at $1,209,855; herring, 218,000 pounds, valued at $1,900; sturgeon, 5,000 pounds, valued at $500; steelhead trout, 185,400 pounds, valued at $15,020; smelt, 229,500 pounds, valued at $22,284; perch, 60,900 pounds, valued at $4,113; rockfishes, 88,700 pounds, valued at $4,694; "lingcod," 47,300 pounds, valued at $2,998; flounders, 70,500 pounds, valued at $1,556; sole, 231,700 pounds, valued at $8,443; and crabs, 539,278 pounds, valued at $37,368. Compared with 1922 there was an increase in the products landed by collecting vessels of 2,304,088 pounds, or 15.28 per cent, in quantity, and $343,899, or 35.64 per cent, in value.

Statement, by fishing grounds and months, of quantities and values of certain fishery products landed at Seattle, Wash., by American fishing vessels, 1923

	Halibut		Sablefish		"Lingcod"	
	Fresh		Fresh		Fresh	
BY FISHING GROUNDS	*Pounds*	*Value*	*Pounds*	*Value*	*Pounds*	*Value*
Oregon Coast	25,000	$3,944	5,000	$250		
Flattery Banks	1,457,780	241,755	1,292,900	75,376	96,300	$1,97
West Coast, Vancouver Island	1,383,400	234,850	386,600	22,675	71,900	1,85
Cape Scott Grounds	76,000	11,131	500	50	3,000	6
Queen Charlotte Islands Grounds	27,000	4,500	16,500	825		
Hecate Strait	4,601,810	660,168	329,100	20,058	22,900	4
Forrester Island Grounds	4,000	520	40,000	2,000		
Coronation Island	65,000	9,285	38,000	2,280		
Yakutat Grounds	165,000	22,725				
Total	7,804,990	1,188,878	2,108,600	123,514	194,100	
BY MONTHS						
January	104,500	15,601	14,300	805		
February	240,600	39,620	51,900	2,665	10,000	2
March	424,300	82,734	52,500	4,165	24,300	92
April	618,700	94,543	50,200	4,110	85,700	1,75
May	1,347,800	186,145	22,000	1,850	30,100	60
June	969,910	144,794	316,400	21,552	17,000	34
July	1,427,850	196,934	635,900	35,530	3,000	2
August	1,006,600	128,859	303,300	15,815	4,000	8
September	788,400	128,841	222,700	12,700	1,000	2
October	520,100	105,036	307,000	16,125	16,000	35
November	259,500	49,422	113,200	7,100	3,000	6
December	96,730	16,349	19,200	1,097		
Total	7,804,990	1,188,878	2,108,600	123,514	194,100	

	Rockfishes		Number of trips	Total	
	Fresh			Fresh	
BY FISHING GROUNDS	*Pounds*	*Value*		*Pounds*	*Value*
Oregon Coast			2	30,000	$4,19
Flattery Banks	55,500	$2,650	335	2,902,480	321,75
West Coast, Vancouver Island	26,900	1,060	219	1,868,800	260,44
Cape Scott Grounds			8	79,500	11,24
Queen Charlotte Islands Grounds	7,000	140	2	50,500	5,46
Hecate Strait	40,500	990	344	4,994,310	681,67
Forrester Island Grounds			1	44,000	2,52
Coronation Island			4	103,000	11,56
Yakutat Grounds			4	165,000	22,72
Total	129,900	4,840	919	10,237,590	1,321,58
BY MONTHS					
January			6	118,800	16,40
February	12,500	250	36	315,000	42,73
March	5,900	260	68	507,000	88,08
April			93	754,600	100,41
May	15,800	556	133	1,415,700	189,15
June	21,500	430	134	1,324,810	167,11
July	9,000	450	124	2,075,750	232,93
August	17,200	729	92	1,331,100	145,48
September	41,500	2,015	86	1,053,600	143,57
October	3,500	90	84	846,600	121,60
November	3,000	60	50	378,700	56,64
December			13	115,930	17,44
Total	129,900	4,840	919	10,237,590	1,321,58

Fishery products, by months, taken in Puget Sound and landed at Seattle, Wash., by collecting vessels, 1923

Species	January Pounds	January Value	February Pounds	February Value	March Pounds	March Value	April Pounds	April Value	May Pounds	May Value
Sturgeon									1,400	$140
Herring	24,000	$600	34,000	$340	32,000	$320	128,000	$640		
Salmon:										
King or spring									420,000	50,400
Sockeye or red									4,000	400
Trout: Steelhead									64,000	2,880
Smelt	35,500	4,200			2,750	2,750	16,000	1,600		
Perch	6,000	360	9,500	665	8,200	492	11,800	690	12,600	882
Rockfishes	5,000	400	4,100	328	7,000	420	6,400	512	6,000	120
"Lingcod"	28,000	1,960	16,300	978						
Flounders	2,600	78	4,000	80	4,100	82	5,000	100		
Sole	24,500	980	17,800	712	26,000	780	32,000	1,280	21,000	840
Crabs	98,000	7,760	68,640	4,680	57,200	3,900	118,804	7,623	20,284	1,333
Total	223,600	16,338	154,340	7,783	162,000	8,744	318,004	12,445	549,284	56,995

Species	June Pounds	June Value	July Pounds	July Value	August Pounds	August Value	September Pounds	September Value
Sturgeon					3,600	$360		
Salmon:								
Humpback or pink			27,000	$1,080	1,633,400	65,336	86,000	$3,440
Chum or keta			16,300	326	271,200	8,136	22,000	660
King or spring	2,235,200	$268,224	2,777,800	277,780	1,620,000	162,000	237,500	23,750
Coho or silver	88,300	4,415	178,000	8,900	1,015,000	50,750	1,230,000	73,800
Sockeye or red	24,900	2,998	26,400	1,320	36,800	3,680		
Trout: Steelhead	65,500	6,560	19,000	1,900	28,800	2,880		
Smelt			18,400	2,208			31,600	1,476
Rockfishes	8,200	164	8,600	602	8,700	696	7,400	144
"Lingcod"	3,000	60						
Flounders	10,500	210	13,400	268	6,000	120	6,000	120
Sole	6,300	252	7,000	245	20,600	824	12,500	490
Crabs	19,140	1,305						
Total	2,461,140	284,188	3,091,900	294,629	4,644,100	294,782	1,633,000	103,880

Species	October Pounds	October Value	November Pounds	November Value	December Pounds	December Value	Total Pounds	Total Value
Sturgeon							5,000	$500
Herring							218,000	1,900
Salmon:								
Humpback or pink							1,746,400	69,856
Chum or keta	898,000	$35,920	410,000	$16,400			1,617,500	61,442
King or spring	41,400	4,140	32,000	3,200			7,363,900	789,494
Coho or silver	1,620,000	97,200	760,000	45,600			4,891,300	280,665
Sockeye or red							92,100	8,398
Trout: Steelhead	8,000	800					185,400	15,020
Smelt	17,500	1,750	18,000	1,800	65,000	$6,500	229,500	22,284
Perch					12,800	1,024	60,900	4,113
Rockfishes	6,500	520	11,500	230	9,300	558	88,700	4,694
"Lingcod"							47,300	2,998
Flounders	4,000	80	6,000	240	8,900	178	70,500	1,556
Sole	12,000	480	6,000	180	46,000	1,380	231,700	8,443
Crabs	26,950	1,837	68,000	4,635	62,260	4,295	1 539,278	37,368
Total	2,634,350	142,727	1,311,500	72,285	204,260	13,935	17,387,478	1,308,731

1 23,459 dozen.

FISHERIES OF CALIFORNIA, 1923

Through the courtesy of the California Fish and Game Commission the bureau has received copies of its monthly sheets showing the catch of fish, by species and by counties, for California, and also the quantity of fish imported into California from Mexico, during the calendar year 1923. These statistics have been compiled by species and by months, as shown in the appended tables.

In 1923 the catch of fish taken in the waters of California amounted to 230,830,942 pounds, an increase of 61,861,209 pounds, or 37 per cent, over the catch of 1922. The species taken in largest quantities were p lchar , 159,197,006 pounds; albacore and tuna, 16,562,351 pounds; flou ders, 10,485,431 pounds; barracuda, 5,135,824 pounds;

Statement, by fishing grounds and ·months, of quantities, and values of certain fishery products landed at Seattle, ·Wash., by American fishing vessels, 1923

	Halibut		Sablefish		"Lingcod"	
	Fresh		Fresh		Fresh	
BY FISHING GROUNDS	*Pounds*	*Value*	*Pounds*	*Value*	*Pounds*	*Value*
Oregon Coast	25,000	$3,944	5,000	$250		
Flattery Banks	1,457,780	241,755	1,292,900	75,376	96,300	$1,978
West Coast, Vancouver Island	1,383,400	234,850	386,600	22,675	71,900	1,859
Cape Scott Grounds	76,000	11,131	500	50	3,000	60
Queen Charlotte Islands Grounds	27,000	4,500	16,500	825		
Hecate Strait	4,601,810	660,168	329,100	20,058	22,900	458
Forrester Island Grounds	4,000	520	40,000	2,000		
Coronation Island	65,000	9,285	38,000	2,280		
Yakutat Grounds	165,000	22,725				
Total	7,804,990	1,188,878	2,108,600	123,514	194,100	4,355
BY MONTHS						
January	104,500	15,601	14,300	805		
February	240,600	39,620	51,900	2,665	10,000	200
March	424,300	82,734	52,500	4,165	24,300	926
April	618,700	94,543	50,200	4,110	85,700	1,757
May	1,347,800	186,145	22,000	1,850	30,100	602
June	969,910	144,794	316,400	21,552	17,000	340
July	1,427,850	196,934	635,900	35,530	3,000	20
August	1,006,600	128,859	303,300	15,815	4,000	80
September	788,400	128,841	222,700	2,700	1,000	20
October	520,100	105,036	307,000	6,125	16,000	350
November	259,500	49,422	113,200	7,100	3,000	60
December	96,730	16,349	19,200	1,097		
Total	7,804,990	1,188,878	2,108,600	123,514	194,100	4,355

	Rockfishes		Number of trips	Total	
	Fresh			Fresh	
BY FISHING GROUNDS	*Pounds*	*Value*		*Pounds*	*Value*
Oregon Coast			2	30,000	$4,194
Flattery Banks	55,500	$2,650	335	2,902,480	321,759
West Coast, Vancouver Island	26,900	1,060	219	1,868,800	260,444
Cape Scott Grounds			8	79,500	11,241
Queen Charlotte Islands Grounds	7,000	140	2	50,500	5,465
Hecate Strait	40,500	990	344	4,994,310	681,674
Forrester Island Grounds			1	44,000	2,520
Coronation Island			4	103,000	11,565
Yakutat Grounds			4	165,000	22,725
Total	129,900	4,840	919	10,237,590	1,321,587
BY MONTHS					
January			6	118,800	16,406
February	12,500	250	36	315,000	42,735
March	5,900	260	68	507,000	88,085
April			93	754,600	100,410
May	15,800	556	133	1,415,700	189,153
June	21,500	430	134	1,324,810	167,116
July	9,000	450	124	2,075,750	232,934
August	17,200	729	92	1,331,100	145,483
September	41,500	2,015	86	1,053,600	143,576
October	3,500	90	84	846,600	121,601
November	3,000	60	50	378,700	56,642
December			13	115,930	17,446
Total	129,900	4,840	919	10,237,590	1,321,587

Fishery products, by months, taken in Puget Sound and landed at Seattle, Wash., by collecting vessels, 1923

Species	January		February		March		April		May	
	Pounds	Value	Pounds	Value	Pounds	Value	Pounds	Value	Pounds	Value
Sturgeon									1,400	$140
Herring	24,000	$600	34,000	$340	32,000	$320	128,000	$640		
Salmon:										
King or spring									420,000	50,400
Sockeye or red									4,000	400
Trout: Steelhead									64,000	2,880
Smelt	35,500	4,200			2,750	2,750	16,000	1,600		
Perch	6,000	360	9,500	665	8,200	492	11,800	690	12,600	882
Rockfishes	5,000	400	4,100	328	7,000	420	6,400	512	6,000	120
"Lingcod"	28,000	1,960	16,300	978						
Flounders	2,600	78	4,000	80	4,100	82	5,000	100		
Sole	24,500	980	17,800	712	26,000	780	32,000	1,280	21,000	840
Crabs	98,000	7,760	68,640	4,680	57,200	3,900	118,804	7,623	20,284	1,333
Total	223,600	16,338	154,340	7,783	162,000	8,744	318,004	12,445	549,284	56,995

Species	June		July		August		September	
	Pounds		Pounds	Value	Pounds	Value	Pounds	Value
Sturgeon					3,600	$360		
Salmon:								
Humpback or pink			27,000	$1,060	1,633,400	65,336	86,000	$3,440
Chum or keta			16,300	326	271,200	8,136	22,000	660
King or spring	2,235,200	$268,224	2,777,800	277,780	1,620,000	162,000	237,500	23,750
Coho or silver	88,300	4,415	178,000	8,900	1,015,000	50,750	1,230,000	73,800
Sockeye or red	24,900	2,998	26,400	1,320	36,800	3,680		
Trout: Steelhead	65,600	6,560	19,000	1,900	28,800	2,880		
Smelt			18,400	2,208			31,600	1,476
Rockfishes	8,200	164	8,600	602	8,700	696	7,400	144
"Lingcod"	3,000	60						
Flounders	10,500	210	13,400	268	6,000	120	6,000	120
Sole	6,300	252	7,000	245	20,600	824	12,500	490
Crabs	19,140	1,305						
Total	2,461,140	284,188	3,091,900	294,629	4,644,100	294,782	1,633,000	103,880

Species	October		November		December		Total	
	Pounds	Value	Pounds	Value	Pounds	Value	Pounds	Value
Sturgeon							5,000	$500
Herring							218,000	1,900
Salmon:								
Humpback or pink							1,746,400	69,856
Chum or keta	898,000	$35,920	410,000	$16,400			1,617,500	61,442
King or spring	41,400	4,140	32,000	3,200			7,363,900	789,494
Coho or silver	1,620,000	97,200	760,000	45,600			4,891,300	280,665
Sockeye or red							92,100	8,398
Trout: Steelhead	8,000	800					185,400	15,020
Smelt	17,500	1,750	18,000	1,800	65,000	$6,500	229,500	22,284
Perch					12,800	1,024	60,900	4,113
Rockfishes	6,500	520	11,500	230	9,300	558	88,700	4,694
"Lingcod"							47,300	2,998
Flounders	4,000	80	6,000	240	8,900	178	70,500	1,556
Sole	12,000	480	6,000	180	46,000	1,380	231,700	8,443
Crabs	26,950	1,837	68,000	4,635	62,260	4,295	1 539,278	37,368
Total	2,634,350	142,727	1,311,500	72,285	204,260	13,935	17,387,478	1,308,731

1 23,459 dozen.

FISHERIES OF CALIFORNIA, 1923

Through the courtesy of the California Fish and Game Commission the bureau has received copies of its monthly sheets showing the catch of fish, by species and by counties, for California, and also the quantity of fish imported into California from Mexico, during the calendar year 1923. These statistics have been compiled by species and by months, as shown in the appended tables.

In 1923 the catch of fish taken in the waters of California amounted to 230,830,942 pounds, an increase of 61,861,209 pounds, or 37 per cent, over the catch of 1922. The species taken in largest quantities were pilchard, 159,197,006 pounds; albacore and tuna, 16,562,351 pounds; flounders, 10,485,431 pounds; barracuda, 5,135,824 pounds;

bonito or skipjack, 5,057,848 pounds; salmon, 7,090,260 pounds; rockfishes, 4,932,350 pounds; mackerel, 3,553,954 pounds; yellow-tail, 2,968,596 pounds; white sea bass ors queteague, 1,782,008 pounds; shad, 1,285,383 pounds; crabs, 1,075,800 pounds; shrimp, 1,113,358 pounds; abalones, 1,555,134 pounds; and squid, 1,176,065 pounds.

The imports of fresh fish from Mexico in 1923 amounted to 23,956,962 pounds, an increase of 11,810,896 pounds, or 97 per cent, as compared with 1922. The principal species imported during the year were albacore and tuna, 10,752,864 pounds; bonito or skipjack, 7,519,191 pounds; barracuda, 2,064,751 pounds; yellowtail, 1,011,015 pounds; flounders, 883,263 pounds; white sea bass or squeteague, 591,877 pounds; and sea crawfish or spiny lobster, 708,477 pounds. These products are caught by fishermen having their home ports in California and fishing in Mexican waters a portion of the year.

Products, in pounds, of the fisheries of California, 1923

Species	January	February	March	April	May	June	July
Albacore and tuna	1,064		27,580	8,339	131,467	1,595,647	3,617,461
Anchovies	14,347	1,015	475	6,250	465	6,448	24,743
Barracuda	16,435	37,271	127,466	765,298	1,473,143	966,696	608,849
Bluefish, California, or sque-teague	986	1,343	1,631	3,567	4,840	5,160	3,025
Bonito or skipjack	16,645	631	14,168	1,163	3,876	4,123	33,054
Carp	8,739	12,280	14,303	21,509	16,177	7,426	3,133
Catfish	11,121	11,279	15,380	19,197	9,540		
Eels			18,116		53	64	
Flounders	840,277	1,122,805	986,002	686,337	941,997	860,741	860,788
"Hake"	1,250		40	8,631	6,363	8,875	7,800
Hardhead	2,995	2,613					
Herring	118,779	117,774	31,230	800		330	
Kingfish	38,216	27,634	58,564	74,073	49,809	13,667	15,251
"Lingcod"	28,227	55,402	55,306	15,421	16,660	12,436	28,447
Mackerel	212,682	244,445	189,439	184,843	248,237	208,054	249,943
Mullet		5,746	1,411	2,850			
"Perches," surf	14,376	17,151	74,256	28,746	15,601	17,144	38,403
Pike, Sacramento	1,797	233	90	81	122	232	127
Pilchard	21,402,901	36,811,099	16,757,293	5,791,332	928,054	2,136,721	4,909,163
Pompano, California	99	972	1,312	1,206	2,475	3,183	6,501
Rockfishes	557,490	644,820	879,178	462,798	256,467	270,119	299,981
Sablefish	9,105	22,117	27,687	13,604	53,035	49,073	27,126
Salmon	23,849	322,509	50,384	314,994	766,799	1,474,866	1,276,202
Sculpin	3,305	3,020	9,522	8,339	8,215	2,970	300
Sea bass, black	6,244	7,382	3,995	3,458	6,375	15,163	11,690
Sea basses, or "rock bass"	2,438	19,257	22,684	13,137	31,880	73,113	65,505
Sea bass, white or squeteague	40,359	21,670	25,153	178,328	445,564	261,768	197,695
Shad	1,694	822	98,788	637,026	535,419	748	
Sharks	57,535	35,177	30,390	30,695	28,244	19,593	8,392
Sheepshead	9,032	8,042	4,415	1,275	644	53	
Skates	25,042	13,193	15,891	7,372	12,293	3,645	4,268
"Smelt"	57,578	40,804	93,044	67,387	45,290	27,770	39,735
Split-tail	5,380	5,916	1,804	20			
Stingaree or stingary	365						
Striped bass	88,708	41,537	128,507	216,652	197,732	524	69
Suckers	90	183					
Swordfish							2,234
Tomcod	4,727	6,233	2,271			2,573	4,150
Whitebait	320	867	2,750	3,688	12,	22,181	12,573
Whitefish	3,323	2,825	1,998	1,743	2,	775	1,795
Yellowtail	23,871	3,756	87,322	150,623	94,	593,288	427,488
Other fish	15,789	35,091	16,895	10,794	16,384	18,627	14,045
Crabs	145,584	100,416	206,496	67,368	68,600	31,392	34,176
Sea crawfish or spiny lobster	65,154	60,233					
Shrimp	72,365	67,509	92,553	60,746	64,691	82,693	136,319
Abalones	2,439		85,603	153,700	241,	154,370	193,005
Clams	43,992	42,528	45,730	41,341	46,	43,535	50,338
Cockles	6,169	5,473	5,665	6,416	4,509	2,279	1,877
Mussels	812	1,305	1,383	8,695	4,860	10,310	8,675
Oysters, eastern	60,134	81,354	68,746	51,700	42,735	38,214	29,700
Octopus	9,258	15,213	17,827	8,519	6,203	8,552	11,754
Squid	165	14,830	62,680	103,647	429,369	356,970	78,360
Terrapins						72	336
Turtles							960
Total	24,073,252	40,093,775	20,463,423	10,243,698	7,272,026	9,412,183	13,345,437

Products, in pounds, of the fisheries of California, 1923—Continued

Species	August	September	October	November	December	Total
Albacore and tuna	9,965,354	844,069	146,554	224,361	455	16,562,351
Anchovies	70,811	54,055	81,758	45,310	1,397	307,074
Barracuda	324,214	260,946	484,469	53,079	17,958	5,135,824
Bluefish, California, or squeteague	3,486	2,491	45,370	37,447	37,032	146,378
Bonito or skipjack	229,237	4,625,133	80,741	29,324	19,753	5,057,848
Carp	4,023	805	24,757	16,560	18,895	148,607
Catfish	7,843	15,149	10,559	17,030	12,188	129,286
Eels			16			18,249
Flounders	855,740	820,651	974,339	804,167	731,587	10,485,431
"Hake"	5,600	10,150	16,625	8,460	5,175	78,969
Hardhead		34	1,516	806	1,599	9,563
Herring			50	224	114,763	383,950
Kingfish	11,467	14,308	30,757	27,895	41,794	403,435
"Lingcod"	60,060	82,710	37,594	39,197	35,840	467,300
Mackerel	239,541	231,625	699,246	517,274	328,625	3,553,954
Mullet						10,007
"Perches," surf	27,378	14,854	33,403	17,406	27,331	326,049
Pike, Sacramento	465	136	6	113	1,222	4,624
Pilchard	5,118,255	18,767,887	14,640,205	13,516,474	18,417,622	159,197,006
Pompano, California	1,175	565	436	836	1,020	19,780
Rockfishes	185,376	240,769	241,853	454,721	438,778	4,932,350
Sablefish	35,242	56,484	71,664	84,036	89,119	538,292
Salmon	1,451,935	1,083,229	74,405	221,776	29,312	7,090,260
Sculpin	417	2,764	7,267	7,836	6,521	60,466
Sea bass, black	6,099	3,300	3,844	6,210	1,979	75,740
Sea basses, or "rock bass"	45,700	10,602	16,620	16,026	11,077	328,039
Sea bass, white or squeteague	364,963	102,850	67,147	54,057	22,454	1,782,008
Shad	3,075	682		4,393	2,736	1,285,383
Sharks	7,870	12,330	39,260	34,838	56,039	360,363
Sheepshead	50	350	1,081	3,861	2,308	31,111
Skates	8,400	7,100	4,310	11,158	21,316	133,988
"Smelt"	48,698	94,059	105,780	104,012	74,683	798,840
Split-tail	600	200			36	13,956
Steelhead trout	2,675	100	14	222		3,011
Stingaree or stingary						365
Striped bass	89,996	41,617		43,480	60,751	909,573
Suckers				20	49	342
Swordfish	4,160	2,706	561	1,395		11,056
Tomcod	11,636	2,391	3,972	867	2,563	41,767
Whitebait	7,222	3,557	1,351	282	135	67,818
Whitefish	110	4,608	5,029	2,996	7,111	34,503
Yellowtail	303,231	529,623	554,112	198,722	1,563	2,968,596
Other fish	10,231	6,747	13,263	6,021	5,893	170,045
Crabs				147,096	275,184	1,075,800
Sea crawfish or spiny lobster			59,789	126,967	72,238	384,381
Shrimp	120,296	146,419	130,366	81,144	58,257	1,113,358
Abalones	191,350	172,934	88,092	158,704	113,428	1,555,134
Clams	51,427	48,565	44,500	46,223	41,312	546,091
Cockles	1,673	636	341	321	584	36,117
Mussels	12,603	4,540	3,136	2,164	2,203	60,026
Oysters, eastern	29,601	58,784	59,119	73,238	94,778	688,103
Octopus	6,327	2,376	4,456	8,178	11,559	110,222
Squid	51,123	6,218	5,389	625	66,689	1,176,065
Terrapins	552	72	96			1,128
Turtles						960
Total	19,977,287	28,392,180	18,915,218	17,257,552	21,384,911	230,830,942

Mexican fishery products, in pounds, imported into California, 1923

Species	January	February	March	April	May	June	July
Albacore and tuna	8,640	198	90,982	104,862	210,414	105,810	----
Barracuda	405,924	160,640	390,676	122,189	----	205	1,517
Bluefish, California, or squeteague						730	
Bonito or skipjack	26,581	20,128	10,862				
Flounders	34,464	41,825	82,929	12,710	27,710	74,561	155,699
Kingfish	70	187	----	5,900	1,820	----	57
"Lingcod"	10		21				
Mackerel	8,741	18,845	5,665	200	125	130	
Mullet	5,173	10,686	8,951	5,885	3,918	----	
"Perches," surf	7,160	15,442	677				
Pompano, California	215	2,361	4,792				
Rockfishes	3,800	5,249	----		160	5,582	145
Sea bass, black	24,071	25,857	30,295	875	5,580	1,670	1,409
Sea basses or "rock bass"	5,302	1,819	4,181	2,488	----	20	
Sea bass, white or squeteague	18,806	50,682	61,476	59,895	11,654	18,716	75,617
Sheepshead	40	----	35				
"Smelt"	1,100	820	25	80			85
Swordfish			70				
Whitefish	1,276	1,180	----	118			
Yellowtail	101,314	86,271	66,633	11,527	2,283	903	2,371
Other fish	1,486	2,292	1,260	140	2,225	795	286
Sea crawfish or spiny lobster	93,057	115,909	158,087	66,693			
Abalones					2,430	5,145	6,650
Clams		797					
Squid		----	4,381				
Turtles	1,050	785					
Total	748,280	561,973	921,998	393,562	268,319	214,267	243,236

Species	August	September	October	November	December	Total
Albacore and tuna	37,456	1,532,320	6,047,814	2,550,922	63,446	10,752,864
Barracuda	24,433	48,061	346,908	338,033	216,165	2,064,751
Bluefish, California, or squeteague						730
Bonito or skipjack	27,191	29,800	2,629,321	3,951,665	823,643	7,519,191
Flounders	171,503	132,566	52,223	50,931	46,742	883,263
Kingfish	----				95	8,129
"Lingcod"				16		47
Mackerel	45	2,344	690	665	1,045	38,495
Mullet			8,435	8,740	12,430	64,218
"Perches," surf				1,835	8,519	33,633
Pompano, California			140		5,630	13,138
Rockfishes			1,260	1,070	628	17,894
Sea bass, black	1,386	1,040	10,684	18,656	29,732	151,255
Sea basses or "rock bass"	363	1,172	213	2,397	11,275	29,230
Sea bass, white or squeteague	142,322	68,848	36,016	32,200	15,645	591,877
Sheepshead			145	297		517
"Smelt"	174	366	277	718	3,895	7,540
Swordfish			565			635
Whitefish				2,681	150	5,405
Yellowtail	12,040	36,071	31,373	294,869	365,360	1,011,015
Other fish	404		397		4,499	13,784
Sea crawfish or spiny lobster			47,464	115,256	112,011	708,477
Abalones	11,954				6,420	32,599
Clams						797
Squid						4,381
Turtles		142			1,120	3,097
Total	429,271	1,852,730	9,223,925	7,370,951	1,728,450	23,956,962

FISHERY PRODUCTS RECEIVED AT MUNICIPAL FISH WHARF AND MARKET, WASHINGTON, D. C.[2]

The receipts of fishery products at the municipal fish wharf and market, Washington, D. C., in 1923 amounted to 5,678,157 pounds, a decrease of 764,506 pounds, or 12 per cent, as compared with 1922. The most important products in quantity were squeteagues or "sea trout," 1,162,927 pounds; oysters, 804,266 pounds; croaker, 645,376 pounds; river herring, 545,845 pounds; and crabs, including crab meat, 327,017 pounds. The species ranking next in importance include bass, butterfish, carp, catfish, flounders, haddock, hake, halibut, mackerel, perch, shad, spot, and striped bass.

Fishery products, in pounds, received at municipal fish wharf and market, Washington, D. C., 1923

Species	January	February	March	April	May	June	July
Bass, black or sea	26,429	5,641	9,895		3,000	13,900	6,950
Bluefish				1,000	2,200	1,812	3,200
Butterfish				1,000	10,200	32,800	30,100
Carp	5,203	3,477	7,834	5,090	17,955	20,712	4,507
Catfish	8,914	4,660	20,667	14,456	14,493	6,172	4,429
Cod	4,700	4,100	3,300			1,800	4,800
Croaker		1,500	74,380	81,500	60,800	81,620	219,828
Eels	625		462	797	72	30	80
Flounders	5,250	4,975	6,315	3,010	9,400	15,900	15,180
Gizzard shad	4,000	11,870	5,100				60
Haddock	9,430	13,675	25,470	13,000	1,500	1,200	5,300
Hake	2,000						500
Halibut	15,050	9,350	4,100	3,400	4,800	6,250	7,000
Herring, river	1,782	10,685	92,738	158,990	279,240	1,200	
Hickory shad or "jacks"	600		6,082	2,907	600		
Kingfish		2,100					
Mackerel	10,700	14,500	9,200	1,150	4,000	9,220	4,250
Mullet	144	1,176	140				
Perch	12,148	10,143	42,221	21,735	13,080	2,065	3,247
Pike or pickerel	1,722	706	2,481	217			
Pollock							1,650
Redfish or red drum					600	200	1,440
Red snapper		400	1,000				
Salmon	3,350			150		150	3,000
Scup or porgy						400	3,700
Shad	600	600	18,300	100,942	72,170	700	
Sheepshead		600					
Smelt	300	450					
Spot				11,800	2,900	650	3,930
Squeteagues or "sea trout"	28,030	21,090	9,380	10,600	63,500	118,500	124,000
Squid							1,200
Striped bass	151	531	32,099	26,858	10,500	5,041	10,262
Sturgeon						69	
Swordfish							300
Tilefish	400	200	1,000	400	1,600	2,100	
Clams	1,728	1,024	544	1,696	1,408	5,888	8,896
Oysters:							
In the shell	46,690	18,200	19,215	3,290	175	98	91
Opened	57,659	35,483	51,356	4,084			
Scallops	400						
Crabs				165	3,300	36,492	128,511
Crab meat	275	275	50	150	6,625	31,560	14,405
Lobster						100	50
Shrimp		1,450	200			400	725
Turtles			205				
Frogs				24			
Total	248,280	178,861	443,734	468,411	584,118	397,029	611,591

Note.—The clams have been reduced to pounds on the basis of 8 pounds of meat to a bushel; the oysters on a basis of 7 pounds of meat to a bushel and 8¾ pounds to a gallon.

[2] Daily reports of the quantity of fishery products received at this market are received by the bureau for tabulation through the courtesy of the health department of the District of Columbia.

Fishery products, in pounds, received at municipal fish wharf and market, Washington, D. C., 1923—Continued

Species	August	September	October	November	December	Total
Bass, black or sea	3,200	4,700	6,100	21,000	17,405	118,220
Bluefish	8,572	19,300	16,100	800	710	53,694
Butterfish	27,860	31,000	12,900	7,100	1,000	153,960
Carp	6,140	5,300	9,630	5,175	10,580	101,603
Catfish	4,198	11,895	27,950	26,300	12,150	156,284
Ciscoes				300		300
Cod	3,300	6,100	10,200	4,000	4,000	46,300
Croaker	42,548	43,400	14,800	16,900	8,100	645,376
Eels	25	100	975	1,800	1,560	6,526
Flounders	5,250	6,157	19,400	9,600	10,500	110,937
Gizzard shad	200	1,300	4,	10,400	8,430	45,860
Haddock	9,350	17,170	20,	33,000	26,060	175,635
Hake			125	1,500	62,400	34,001
Halibut	4,350	4,100	7,480	66,000	4,100	136,300
Herring:						
River		100	680	430		545,845
Sea				1,500		1,500
Hickory shad or "jacks"						10,189
Kingfish				1,000	1,400	4,500
Mackerel	5,200	15,550	15,800	4,700	19,900	114,170
Mullet			2,200	900	350	4,910
Perch	1,995	1,960	5,800	16,300	15,400	146,094
Pike or pickerel		400	875	3,800	2,360	12,561
Pollock	800	4,900	16,100	12,201	1,200	36,851
Pompano		250	200			450
Redfish or red drum		200	3,084	1,000		6,524
Red snapper					1,400	2,800
Salmon	4,150	2,300	5,800	10,500	1,000	30,400
Scup or porgy	1,200	400	800		200	6,700
Shad				1,000		194,312
Sheepshead			200	50		850
Smelt					2,080	2,830
Spot	16,275	18,050	48,300	2,500		104,405
Squeteagues or "sea trout"	157,727	282,300	236,900	78,000	32,900	1,162,927
Squid						1,200
Striped bass	28,455	9,745	52,650	34,400	9,900	220,592
Sturgeon			346			415
Swordfish	350					650
Tilefish		500	1,350	2,000	800	10,350
Whitefish			200	600		800
Whiting			1,400	11,800	3,700	16,900
Clams	4,448	4,960	4,000	3,072	2,624	[1]40,288
Oysters:						
In the shell	308	21,210	127,204	168,602	98,322	[2]503,405
Opened	297	10,288	43,544	48,914	49,236	[3]300,861
Scallops			80	160	320	600
Crabs	47,325	32,304	8,850		300	257,247
Crab meat	6,355	6,445	2,410		1,220	69,770
Lobster		50		50	50	300
Shrimp	900	2,100	3,600	2,088	975	12,438
Terrapin					598	598
Turtles	200	95	20			520
Frogs						24
Total	390,978	564,834	734,708	670,502	385,111	5,678,157

[1] 5,036 bushels   [2] 71,915 bushels.   [3] 36,468 gallons.

FLORIDA SPONGE FISHERY

The quantity of sponges sold at the Tarpon Springs Exchange in Florida, in 1923, was 490,200 pounds, valued at $734,391. This total included large wool sponges, 243,230 pounds, valued at $604,343; small wool, 54,292 pounds, valued at $59,721; yellow, 87,878 pounds, valued at $46,868; grass, 88,772 pounds, valued at $15,979; wire, 16,028 pounds, valued at $7,480. It is estimated that sponges to the value of $50,000 were sold at Tarpon Springs outside of the exchange.

SHAD AND ALEWIFE FISHERY OF THE POTOMAC RIVER, 1922 AND 1923

The shad and alewife fishery of the Potomac River was canvassed for the calendar years 1922 and 1923. The statistics show that in 1922 this fishery employed 832 fishermen, with a total investment of $190,532, and produced 884,176 shad weighing 3,115,571 pounds, valued at $420,022, and 11,367,000 alewives weighing 4,546,800 pounds, valued at $38,342. The same fishery in 1923 employed 888 fishermen, with an investment of $240,832 and produced 351,546 shad weighing 1,187,382 pounds, valued at $198,619, and 11,428,569 alewives weighing 4,570,828 pounds, valued at $49,421.

Comparing these data with the average for the three previous years (1919, 1920, and 1921), we find that in 1922 there were fewer fishermen by 1 per cent, with an increase of 79 per cent in the number of shad and 22 per cent in the number of alewives caught; and in 1923, with a 5 per cent increase over the three-year average of fishermen employed, there was a 29 per cent decrease in the number of shad and a 23 per cent increase in the number of alewives caught.

The following tables give the detailed statistics of this fishery in 1922 and 1923:

Shad and alewife fishery of the Potomac River, 1922

Items	Maryland			Virginia			Total		
	Number	Pounds	Value	Number	Pounds	Value	Number	Pounds	Value
Fishermen	292			540			832		
Rowboats	118		$4,550	162		$4,500	280		$9,050
Gasoline boats	46		12,490	186		58,025	232		70,515
Pound nets	82		12,085	216		65,850	298		77,935
Gill nets	114		7,260	135		18,252	249		25,512
Seines	4		720				4		720
Shore and accessory property			2,600			4,200			6,800
Total			39,705			150,827			190,532
Shad caught:									
With pound nets	31,555	110,387	15,154	387,035	1,385,209	188,313	418,590	1,495,596	203,467
With gill nets	168,427	583,664	78,354	293,459	1,023,861	136,569	461,886	1,607,525	214,923
With seines	3,700	12,450	1,632				3,700	12,450	1,632
Total	203,682	706,501	95,140	680,494	2,409,070	324,882	884,176	3,115,571	420,022
Alewives caught:									
With pound nets	1,275,000	510,000	3,613	9,934,500	3,973,800	33,902	11,209,500	4,483,800	37,515
With gill nets	7,000	3,000	37	140,000	56,000	740	147,500	59,000	777
With seines	10,000	4,000	50				10,000	4,000	50
Total	1,292,002	517,000	3,700	10,074,500	4,029,800	34,642	11,367,000	4,546,800	38,342

Shad and alewife fishery of the Potomac River, 1923

Items	Maryland			Virginia			Total		
	Number	Pounds	Value	Number	Pounds	Value	Number	Pounds	Value
Fishermen	283			605			888		
Rowboats	124		$4,810	208		$7,250	332		$12,060
Gasoline boats	50		12,475	229		70,460	279		82,935
Pound nets	89		12,425	293		102,210	382		114,635
Gill nets	114		10,580	139		12,782	253		23,362
Seines	4		1,200				4		1,200
Shore and accessory property			2,725			3,915			6,640
Total			44,215			196,617			240,832
Shad caught:									
With pound nets	6,936	21,932	3,623	170,389	580,856	95,379	177,325	602,788	99,002
With gill nets	76,183	259,484	44,754	87,538	297,797	50,323	163,721	557,281	95,077
With seines	10,500	27,313	4,540				10,500	27,313	4,540
Total	93,619	308,729	52,917	257,927	878,653	145,702	351,546	1,187,382	198,619
Alewives caught:									
With pound nets	2,009,787	803,916	8,214	8,827,532	3,530,412	37,055	10,837,319	4,334,328	45,269
With gill nets				481,250	192,500	3,602	481,250	192,500	3,602
With seines	110,000	44,000	550				110,000	44,000	550
Total	2,119,787	847,916	8,764	9,308,782	3,722,912	40,657	11,428,569	4,570,828	49,421

PEARL-BUTTON INDUSTRY, 1922

The canvassing of the Mississippi River and tributaries and of the Great Lakes in 1922 permits of a statistical summary of the pearl-button industry of the interior United States.

The fresh-water mussel, which furnishes the raw materials for this industry occurs mainly in the Mississippi River and tributaries, the yield of mussel shells in this region amounting to 51,768,173 pounds valued at $1,050,592, to which may be added 6,245,975 pounds, valued at $218,148, coming from rivers tributary to Lake Michigan and Lake Erie, making a total of 58,014,148 pounds, valued at $1,268,740 in 1922.

The manufacture of pearl buttons takes place principally in the Mississippi River region, Muscatine, Iowa, being the center of the industry, especially in the manufacture of the complete button. There are many factories, scattered over the entire Mississippi Valley, engaged in making button blanks only. Many of these are merely branches of Muscatine or eastern button factories, while others work under contract with these firms or sell the blanks on the open market. One button factory, one blank factory, and one crusher, located in Michigan, are the only establishments in the interior United States outside of the Mississippi region.

Including these and one factory engaged in finishing and grading only, there were, in 1922, 16 factories, with a value of $1,362,280, in the interior United States engaged in making the complete button, and 100 factories, valued at $697,039, engaged in cutting blanks only. Of the above factories 34 had crushers attached, valued at $46,744, for grinding shells into a product sold mainly as poultry grit. There were also four independent crushers, not attached to button or button-blank factories. The total number of persons connected with this industry in 1922 was 4,984, and the amount of wages paid was $3,277,136, which included that paid in the manufacture of button blanks shipped to button factories in the east. The total output of buttons in 1922 was 12,413,984 gross, with a value of $4,725,242. Several million gross of button blanks manufactured in this region were shipped east for use in making the finished button. Among the by-products from shells were 18,276 tons of poultry grit, valued at $146,142, and 2,335 tons of stucco, valued at $33,975.

The following table shows the detailed statistics of this industry. In addition, there were two firms in Muscatine, Iowa, engaged in the manufacture of novelties, not shown below.

Pearl-button industry of the Mississippi River, its tributaries, and the Great Lakes, 1922

Items	Arkansas		Illinois		Indiana and Missouri		Iowa	
	Number	Value	Number	Value	Number	Value	Number	Value
Persons engaged	209		455		740		2,922	
Wages paid		$86,178		$266,611		$444,746		$2,078,243
Classification of plants:								
Complete button manufacture					3	85,251	[1] 10	1,152,555
Cutting only	5	17,194	[2] 15	92,121	16	103,475	48	360,074
Crushers connected with factories	1	500	3	4,900	6	3,400	14	23,874
Independent crushers			1	1,000			3	28,300
Total separate plants	5	17,694	16	98,021	19	192,126	61	1,564,803
Products manufactured:								
Buttons_____gross					573,246	188,484	10,712,597	4,086,100
Button blanks [3]____do	664,667	141,847	2,156,863	454,613	2,985,086	669,716	7,070,850	1,681,599
By-products—								
Poultry grit____tons	9	45	431	3,544	889	7,069	15,200	121,738
Stucco_____do					30	300	2,305	33,675
Lime and dust__do			250	250	138	177	2,000	2,000
Waste shells sold_____do	1,450	2,300			625	1,200	6,728	16,572

Items	Kansas, Kentucky, and Minnesota		Ohio, Tennessee, and West Virginia		Wisconsin [4]		Total	
	Number	Value	Number	Value	Number	Value	Number	Value
Persons engaged	177		196		285		4,984	
Wages paid		$141,765		$129,042		$130,551		$3,277,136
Classification of plants:								
Complete button manufacture					3	124,474	16	1,362,280
Cutting only	7	48,144	4	49,710	5	26,321	100	697,039
Crushers connected with factories	3	3,200	3	5,400	4	5,500	34	46,774
Independent crushers							4	29,300
Total separate plants	7	51,344	4	55,110	8	156,295	120	2,135,393
Products manufactured:								
Buttons_____gross					1,128,141	450,658	12,413,984	4,725,242
Button blanks [3]__do	1,177,820	252,066	1,143,702	269,358	504,236	110,559	15,703,224	3,579,758
By-products—								
Poultry grit__tons	243	2,191	902	6,582	602	4,973	18,276	146,142
Stucco_____do							2,335	33,975
Lime and dust____tons	23	210	150	600	54	264	2,615	3,501
Waste shells sold_____do	498	274	56	140			9,357	20,486

[1] Includes one plant engaged in finishing and grading only.
[2] Includes one plant engaged in grading only.
[3] Includes all blanks except those made at factories where both blanks and complete buttons are manufactured.
[4] Includes one button factory, one blank factory, and one crusher in Michigan.

FISHERIES OF THE MISSISSIPPI RIVER AND TRIBUTARIES, 1922

The statistics of the fisheries of the Mississippi River and tributaries, presented in this report, are for the calendar year 1922. Excepting for the inclusion of the Atchafalaya River in the canvass for 1922, the area covered and the method of taking the data were so arranged as to make the statistics comparable with those of 1899 and 1903. A summary of these statistics has already been published as Statistical Bulletin No. 607, but the detailed statistics are published herewith for the first time.

COMMON AND SCIENTIFIC NAMES OF FISHES

Following is a list of the common and scientific names of the fishes referred to in the tables and discussions in this report:

Black bass	*Micropterus salmoides.*
Bowfin	*Amiatus calvus.*
Buffalofish	*Ictiobus cyprinella.*
Carp, German	*Cyprinus carpio.*
Catfish and bullheads	{*Ameiurus* (species). *Ictalurus* (species).}
Crappie	{*Pomoxis annularis.* *Pomoxis sparoides.*}
Drum, fresh-water, or sheepshead	*Aplodinotus grunniens.*
Eels	*Anguilla chrysypa.*
Moon-eye, or toothed herring	Hiodon (species).
Paddlefish, or spoonbill cat	*Polyodon spathula.*
Pike and pickerel	Esox (species).
Pike perch (sauger)	{*Stizostedion canadense griseum.* *Stizostedoin canadense.*}
Pike perch (wall-eyed)	*Stizostedion vitreum.*
Quillback, or American carp	*Carpiodes velifer.*
Rock bass	*Ambloplites rupestris.*
Sturgeon, lake	*Acipenser rubicundus.*
Sturgeon, shovelnose	*Scaphirhynchus platorhynchus.*
Suckers	Catostomidæ (species).
Sunfish	Centrarchidæ (species).
White bass	*Roccus chrysops.*
Yellow bass	*Morone interrupta.*
Yellow perch	*Perca flavescens.*

GENERAL STATISTICS

The number of persons engaged in the fisheries in this entire region in 1922 was 19,122, as compared with 13,377 in 1903, the year covered by the last canvass of this bureau. Nearly one-third of those engaged were connected either with the pearl-button industry or the wholesale fish trade. The total investment of the entire region amounted to $7,345,034 as compared with $3,555,540 in 1903. As in the case of persons engaged, a large part of the investment was in the pearl-button industry and wholesale fish trade. Other items contributing to the investment were the boats and gear operated by the fishermen. The fyke net was the most widely distributed, except lines, of any form of apparatus, occurring in all States except Pennsylvania and West Virginia. Slightly over one-half the entire number was used in Illinois and Louisiana. Haul seines occurred in all but seven States. Trammel nets and gill nets were not generally used, although in Iowa trammel nets were quite common. Shrimp traps were used only in Louisiana and Mississippi.

The total production of the fisheries of this region in 1922 amounted to 105,733,734 pounds, valued at $4,503,521, as compared with 93,374,159 pounds, valued at $1,841,168, taken in 1903, or an increase of 13 per cent in quantity and 145 per cent in value. The most important product, in terms of value and amount, was mussel shells, of which there were 51,768,173 pounds, valued at $1,050,592, together with $101,504 worth of pearls and slugs found in the mussels. These were taken in all of the States of this region except Louisiana, Mississippi, Texas, and Nebraska. Other important products were buffalo fish, $17,267,177 pounds, valued at $1,013,692; carp, 18,338,371 pounds, valued at $872,128; catfish and bullheads, 8,092,690 pounds, valued at $713,461; drum or sheepshead, 5,260,892 pounds, valued at $290,480; paddlefish or spoonbill cat, 1,398,991 pounds, valued at $132,545; to which might be added 12,398 pounds of caviar worth $29,546. The spoonbill cat, as this species is most commonly known, is in great demand in New York City, the fishermen sometimes receiving as high as 45 cents per pound for it. The caviar usually nets the shipper $3 a pound. The meat is used mainly in smoking. Among other important species might be mentioned suckers, quillback or American carp, and crappie, the combined value of these species being $171,587.

Along the lower portion of the Mississippi Valley the buffalofish is a predominating species and comprises about one-half of the catch taken, while the carp occurs irregularly or not at all in many portions of this region. From the Ohio River northward, however, the proportion of carp to buffalofish steadily increases. In Illinois we find two and one-half times as much carp as buffalofish, and in Wisconsin six times as much carp. In these two States the carp are practically all taken from the Illinois and Mississippi Rivers.

The output of the Mississippi River proper, including a few minor tributaries too unimportant to be shown separately, in 1922 amounted to 28,266,157 pounds, valued at $1,410,265, or about 27 per cent in quantity and 31 per cent in value of that of the Mississippi River and all of its tributaries. Fishing is prosecuted on this river from its mouth to Minneapolis. Mussels, however, are not taken to any extent commercially south of the mouth of the Missouri River, but are taken in some of the minor tributaries 200 miles or more north of Minneapolis. This river has probably been worked longer and more steadily than any other mussel-bearing stream.

The Illinois River was the most important tributary of the Mississippi River. In 1922 the number of persons engaged in the fisheries or related industries of this river and a few minor tributaries was 927. The total investment, including boats, apparatus, shore property, and cash capital, amounted to $332,367, and the entire output was 12,660,512 pounds, valued to the fishermen at $617,254. Carp and buffalo were the leading species making up this total, the catch of the two combined being equal in value to more than two-thirds that of the entire catch.

The White River and tributaries, in Arkansas and Missouri, rank next to the Illinois River. In 1922 there were 1,997 persons engaged in its fisheries or related industries. Its total investment was $190,327. Of this amount $105,060 was invested in boats, $47,470 in apparatus, $36,797 in shore property, and $1,000 in cash capital.

The total output of the White River and tributaries in 1922 amounted to 14,662,413 pounds, valued at $405,860. Buffalofish and catfish were far in the lead in value of catch among the fish, that of the two combined amounting to $95,477. Paddlefish and drum or sheepshead were also important, but the value of all of these species combined was less than one-half of that realized by the fishermen from mussel shells. Included with the White River, as a tributary, is the Black River, which is quite an important mussel stream.

The Ohio and minor tributaries follow the White River and tributaries in importance. The persons engaged numbered 1,720, and the investment was $656,212. The wholesale fish trade of Cincinnati contributed materially to this investment. The total production of this river in 1922 was 7,458,157 pounds, having a value of $379,089. Among the more valuable species, in the order of their importance, were catfish, carp, drum or sheepshead, suckers, quillback, and buffalofish. The total value of these species is about 72 per cent of the river's entire output. The value of the mussel shells, including pearls and slugs, amounted to $97,773, and was greater than that of any single species of fish.

Among other tributaries of the Mississippi River worthy of mention were the Wabash, with an output of 9,112,600 pounds, valued at $275,835, made up mainly both in quantity and value of mussel shells; and the Red River in Arkansas and Louisiana, with a total output in 1922 of 3,286,860 pounds, valued at $152,143, buffalofish contributing more than one-half of this value.

The Atchafalaya River, in Louisiana, was canvassed in 1922 for the first time since 1894. Though not strictly a tributary of the Mississippi, this river was found to have substantial communication with the latter and forms a part of the Mississippi River system. Its products in 1922 amounted to 4,579,220 pounds, valued at $254,651. Catfish and bullheads were the most important contributors to this total, followed in order by buffalofish, drum, and frogs.

Summaries of the statistics, by principal tributaries and by States, are shown in the following tables:

Persons engaged, investment, and products of the fisheries of the Mississippi River and tributaries in 1922, by tributaries

Items	Arkansas River		Atcháfalaya River		Cumberland River	
	Number	Value	Number	Value	Number	Value
Persons engaged	451		1,012		94	
Gasoline boats	66	$7,770	672	$85,300	— 12	$1,450
Rowboats and scows	334	3,723	1,046	21,160	94	924
House boats	32	6,875	679	64,600		
Fyke nets	1,248	12,041	8,150	119,000	192	1,940
Lines		785		7,300		114
Haul seines	14	1,790	15	4,075		
Trammel nets	8	575				
Crowfoot bars (pairs)					51	690
Forks, tongs, rakes, and dredges	25	80			22	230
Other apparatus				1,373		
Shore and accessory property		29,780		147,820		405
Cash capital		1,000		35,700		
Totál		64,419		486,328		5,753
PRODUCTS						
	Pounds	Value	Pounds	Value	Pounds	Value
Black bass	2,568	$205				
Buffalofish	655,225	47,368	1,778,412	$85,910	21,850	$2,397
Carp, German	208,948	17,693			6,850	693
Catfish and bullheads	246,834	28,066	1,829,665	121,161	23,200	3,219
Crappie	13,740	845				
Drum, fresh-water, or sheepshead	443,266	34,679	721,727	25,852	10,250	1,041
Paddlefish or spoonbill cat	18,333	1,506			1,500	163
Paddlefish caviar	10	30				
Quillback or "American carp"	6,100	275				
Rock bass	500	40				
Sturgeon, shovelnose					1,400	120
Suckers					7,400	740
White bass	5,300	398				
Crawfish			7,265	509		
Frogs			216,912	17,376		
Turtles			12,867	1,940		
Alligator hides			12,372	1,912		
Mussel shells	432,860	4,962			656,000	5,965
Pearls						50
Slugs		222				289
Total	2,033,684	136,289	4,579,220	254,651	728,450	14,677

Persons engaged, investment, and products of the fisheries of the Mississippi River and tributaries, in 1922, by tributaries—Continued

Items	Illinois River and tributaries		Mississippi River and minor tributaries			
			Mississippi River [1]		Reelfoot Lake	
	Number	Value	Number	Value	Number	Value
Persons engaged	927		7,964		146	
Gasoline boats	261	$45,681	1,386	$274,470	6	$825
Rowboats and scows	617	20,205	2,139	43,001	156	2,865
House boats	64	24,950	217	42,823		
Fyke nets	9,004	79,130	15,339	182,430	2,223	15,650
Lines		3,259		6,690		838
Haul seines	91	32,175	386	110,457		
Trammel nets			224	17,656	20	2,360
Gill nets	3	900	803	12,348		
Pound nets			3	160		
Crowfoot bars (pairs)	139	2,625	407	4,170		
Forks, tongs, rakes, and dredges	21	73	83	225		
Shrimp traps			4,360	4,163		
Other apparatus		150		1,413		23
Shore and accessory property		105,319		3,409,555		17,970
Cash capital		17,900		196,000		4,600
Total		332,367		4,305,561		44,931

PRODUCTS	Pounds	Value	Pounds	Value	Pounds	Value
Black bass			6,674	$723	33,962	$6,105
Bowfin	102,065	$4,543	43,135	1,038	4,873	97
Buffalofish	2,336,033	150,532	5,842,828	357,352	206,366	16,509
Carp, German	6,434,539	290,144	9,374,073	392,286	55,111	2,204
Catfish and bullheads	392,844	55,458	3,095,732	280,473	97,360	7,789
Crappie	108,135	8,729	133,630	10,776	84,018	12,603
Drum, fresh-water, or sheepshead	80,710	5,400	2,066,591	100,478	71,294	1,426
Eels	6,500	325	8,482	672	578	35
Paddlefish or spoonbill cat	21,200	1,640	508,076	50,279	1,888	142
Paddlefish caviar			2,338	6,024		
Pike and pickerel			20,100	1,850		
Pike perch (sauger)			2,280	274		
Pike perch (wall-eyed)			15,975	2,280		
Quillback or "American carp"			309,617	10,098		
Rock bass			775	83	863	129
Sturgeon, lake			6,773	1,034		
Sturgeon, shovelnose	2,000	200	122,900	9,834		
Sturgeon, shovelnose, caviar			1,580	2,165		
Sturgeon, shovelnose, eggs			449	764		
Suckers	77,000	3,465	124,886	5,394		
Sunfish	165,117	13,453	69,850	4,285	134,191	6,709
White bass	26,800	2,363	25,004	2,204	1,968	98
Yellow bass	6,100	488	1,400	112		
Yellow perch	18,250	1,584	4,000	320		
Other fish	61,240	3,497	10,000	960		
Shrimp, fresh-water			147,482	14,570		
Frogs	3,289	496	1,830	276	6,000	1,800
Turtles	59,550	444	22,157	345		
Alligator hides			3,244	761		
Mussel shells	2,759,140	68,541	6,294,296	128,029		
Pearls		2,790		11,944		
Slugs		3,162		12,582		
Total	12,660,512	617,254	28,266,157	1,410,265	698,472	55,646

[1] Includes all tributaries not shown separately.

Persons engaged, investment, and products of the fisheries of the Mississippi River and tributaries in 1922, by tributaries—Continued

Items	Mississippi River and minor tributaries—Continued					
	Des Moines River and minor tributaries		Rock River and tributaries		Total	
	Number	Value	Number	Value	Number	Value
Persons engaged	200		249		8,559	
Gasoline boats	5	$1,450	201	,$24,300	1,598	$300,845
Rowboats and scows	72	840	83	1,220	2,450	47,926
House boats					217	42,823
Fyke nets					17,562	198,080
Lines		134				7,662
Haul seines	6	5,125			392	115,582
Trammel nets					244	20,016
Gill nets					803	12,348
Pound nets					3	160
Crowfoot bars (pairs)	5	55	248	2,480	660	6,705
Forks, tongs, rakes, and dredges	39	194			122	419
Shrimp traps					4,360	4,163
Other apparatus						1,436
Shore and accessory property		9,865		940		3,438,330
Cash capital						200,600
Total		17,663		28,940		4,397,095
PRODUCTS	Pounds	Value	Pounds	Value	Pounds	Value
Black bass	750	$142			41,386	$6,970
Bowfin					48,008	1,135
Buffalofish	116,024	8,290			6,165,218	382,151
Carp, German	721,506	36,058			10,150,690	430,548
Catfish and bullheads	11,200	2,340			3,204,292	290,602
Crappie	1,550	177			219,198	23,556
Drum, fresh-water, or sheepshead					2,137,885	101,904
Eels					9,060	707
Paddlefish or spoonbill cat					509,964	50,421
Paddlefish caviar					2,338	6,024
Pike and pickerel					20,100	1,850
Pike perch (sauger)					2,280	274
Pike perch (wall-eyed)	750	81			16,725	2,361
Quillback or "American carp"					309,617	10,098
Rock bass					1,638	212
Sturgeon, lake					6,773	1,034
Sturgeon, shovelnose					122,900	9,834
Sturgeon, shovelnose, caviar					1,580	2,165
Sturgeon, shovelnose, eggs					449	764
Suckers	141	8			125,027	5,402
Sunfish					204,041	10,994
White bass	100	12			27,072	2,314
Yellow bass					1,400	112
Yellow perch					4,000	320
Other fish					10,000	960
Shrimp, fresh-water					147,482	14,570
Frogs					7,830	2,076
Turtles					22,157	345
Alligator hides					3,244	761
Mussel shells	943,900	10,716	3,184,000	$108,910	10,422,196	247,655
Pearls		76		1,990		14,010
Slugs		3,564		6,997		23,143
Total	1,795,921	61,464	3,184,090	117,897	33,944,550	1,645,272

Persons engaged, investment, and products of the fisheries of the Mississippi River and tributaries in 1922, by tributaries—Continued

Items	Missouri River and tributaries		Ohio River and minor tributaries		Red River and tributaries			
					Red River [1]		Ouachita River and minor tributaries	
	Number	Value	Number	Value	Number	Value	Number	Value
Persons engaged	557		1,720		409		419	
Gasoline boats	33	$4,095	391	$42,720	95	$20,955	109	$16,570
Rowboats and scows	254	5,434	795	11,878	289	4,037	353	3,531.
House boats	17	3,865	81	8,725	54	16,325	59	12,230
Fyke nets	914	7,532	2,649	27,193	2,061	19,301	1,458	12,063.
Lines		986		2,545		998		2,764
Haul seines	40	5,449	18	1,775	25	4,060	15	3,290
Trammel nets	144	5,805			22	910	4	230
Gill nets	6	230			20	1,065	22	1,026
Pound nets					5	125		
Crowfoot bars (pairs)			726	14,410			2	8.
Forks, tongs, rakes, and dredges	16	29	8	10			67	370
Other apparatus						1		
Shore and accessory property		548,686		495,956		28,610		15,920
Cash capital		36,000		51,000		5,000		500.
Total		618,111		656,212		101,387		68,602

PRODUCTS	Pounds	Value	Pounds	Value	Pounds	Value	Pounds	Value
Black bass	125	$25	65	$11	11,078	$1,317	6,250	$1,072
Buffalofish	271,206	22,895	318,130	35,370	1,668,188	81,702	876,766	48,310
Carp, German	512,583	45,872	482,898	53,298	27,922	1,908	1,200	36
Catfish and bullheads	143,831	24,824	455,938	54,016	320,267	19,476	294,284	24,188.
Crappie	3,225	473	480	40	55,136	6,542	20,650	2,726
Drum, fresh-water, or sheepshead	12,675	1,133	388,578	46,976	385,938	19,809	175,083	8,922
Mooneye or toothed herring	2,450	116						
Paddlefish or spoonbill cat	31,500	2,091	3,835	536	99,288	8,411	145,879	21,510
Paddlefish caviar			150	225	1,399	3,657	4,737	10,422.
Pike perch (sauger)			2,465	494				
Pike perch (wall-eyed)	200	40	5,625	1,019				
Quillback or "American carp"	35,372	3,775	347,800	40,209				
Sturgeon, lake	3,600	250	580	85				
Sturgeon, shovelnose			52,475	5,239				
Sturgeon, shovelnose, caviar			300	450				
Suckers	4,490	437	373,642	43,247	400	28	5,000	498.
Sunfish	50	8	25	4			1,000	200.
White bass			171	37				
Other fish	1,000	400			845	9	25	1
Crawfish	625	250						
Frogs					230	26		
Turtles					169	3		
Mussel shells	208,610	2,505	5,025,000	88,162	716,000	8,990	790,000	10,664.
Pearls		50		2,180		65		25.
Slugs		80		7,431		200		61
Total	1,231,542	105,224	7,458,157	379,089	3,286,860	152,143	2,320,874	128,635.

[1] Includes all tributaries not shown separately.

Persons engaged, investment, and products of the fisheries of the Mississippi River and tributaries in 1922, by tributaries—Continued

Items	Red River and tributaries—Con.				St. Francis River and tributaries		Tennessee River and tributaries	
	Black River (La.)		Total					
	Number	*Value*	*Number*	*Value*	*Number*	*Value*	*Number*	*Value*
Persons engaged	140		968		510		253	
Gasoline boats	37	$5,050	241	$42,575	89	$9,595	79	$8,985
Rowboats and scows	109	1,655	751	9,323	364	3,549	240	2,711
House boats	13	4,400	104	32,955	57	11,775	42	4,885
Fyke nets	684	5,610	4,203	36,974	1,189	11,327	615	5,370
Lines		487		4,249		528		627
Haul seines	8	1,900	48	9,250	28	4,054		
Trammel nets			26	1,140	8	442		
Gill nets			42	2,091	1	40		
Pound nets			5	125	3	193		
Crowfoot bars (pairs)					77	780	127	1,268
Forks, tongs, rakes, and dredges					160	704		
Other apparatus				1		33		
Shore and accessory property		10,410		54,940		54,805		29,030
Cash capital		4,000		9,500		1,000		
Total		33,512		203,123		98,825		52,876
PRODUCTS	*Pounds*	*Value*	*Pounds*	*Value*	*Pounds*	*Value*	*Pounds*	*Value*
Black bass			17,328	$2,389	3,150	$457		
Bowfin					40,000	400		
Buffalofish	489,804	$16,416	3,034,758	146,428	544,157	35,398	17,350	$2,339
Carp, German			29,122	1,944	99,850	3,227	23,100	2,741
Catfish and bullheads	182,764	9,210	797,315	52,874	123,671	10,579	125,800	17,255
Crappie			75,786	9,268	3,150	382		
Drum, fresh-water, or sheepshead	166,252	3,323	727,273	32,054	129,840	5,420	88,600	10,179
Eels					500	25		
Mooneye or toothed herring					1,000	50		
Paddlefish or spoonbill cat	229,054	12,079	474,221	42,000	81,769	6,254	730	102
Paddlefish caviar	1,019	2,736	7,155	16,815	3	9		
Pike perch (wall-eyed)					500	40		
Quillback or "American carp"							4,000	458
Rock bass					600	60		
Sturgeon, shovelnose							640	96
Suckers			5,400	526			48,250	5,148
Sunfish			1,000	200	3,600	230		
White bass					750	75		
Other fish			870	10				
Frogs			230	26	3,500	445		
Turtles			169	3	2,000	40		
Mussel shells			1,506,000	19,654	2,646,000	44,761	4,682,000	57,933
Pearls				90		200		550
Slugs				261		850		1,499
Total	1,068,893	43,764	6,676,627	324,542	3,684,040	108,902	4,990,470	98,300

Persons engaged, investment, and products of the fisheries of the Mississippi River and tributaries in 1922, by tributaries—Continued

Items	Wabash River and tributaries					
	Wabash River [1]		White River, including East Fork and West Fork		Total	
	Number	Value	Number	Value	Number	Value
Persons engaged	1,457		508		1,965	
Gasoline boats	574	$43,925	115	$11,500	689	$55,425
Rowboats and scows	918	9,770	362	3,620	1,280	13,390
House boats	18	1,750	3	300	21	2,050
Fyke nets	805	8,050			805	8,050
Lines		976		217		1,193
Crowfoot bars (pairs)	967	19,340	254	5,080	1,221	24,420
Forks, tongs, rakes, and dredges	615	2,421	254	1,270	869	3,691
Shore and accessory property		48,780		30,156		78,936
Total		135,012		52,143		187,155
PRODUCTS						
	Pounds	Value	Pounds	Value	Pounds	Value
Buffalofish	108,300	$8,246	15,600	$1,720	123,900	$9,966
Carp, German	210,200	17,266	28,600	3,080	238,800	20,346
Catfish and bullheads	173,600	13,816	28,400	3,200	202,000	17,016
Drum, fresh-water, or sheepshead	119,000	9,366	17,800	1,940	136,800	11,306
Quillback or "American carp"	62,500	4,346			62,500	4,346
Sturgeon, shovelnose	38,000	2,932	4,550	519	42,550	3,451
Suckers	55,300	3,832			55,300	3,832
Sunfish	700	66			700	66
Mussel shells	8,345,000	199,635	2,855,000	63,120	11,200,000	262,755
Pearls		7,134		5,370		12,504
Slugs		9,196		3,049		12,245
Total	9,112,600	275,835	2,949,950	81,998	12,062,550	357,833

[1] Includes all tributaries not shown separately.

Persons engaged, investment, and products of the fisheries of the Mississippi River and tributaries in 1922, by tributaries—Continued

Items	White River (Mo. and Ark.) and tributaries		Yazoo River		Grand total	
	Number	*Value*	*Number*	*Value*	*Number*	*Value*
Persons engaged	1,997		109		19,122	
Gasoline boats	419	$58,770	60	$8,670	[1] 4,610	$671,881
Rowboats and scows	1,011	9,075	72	1,151	9,308	150,449
House boats	262	37,215	35	9,240	1,633	249,958
Fyke nets	1,641	25,302	1,480	14,675	49,652	546,614
Lines		3,301		1,654		34,203
Haul seines	45	10,836	17	5,115	708	190,101
Trammel nets	29	1,771			459	29,749
Gill nets	8	280	3	295	866	16,184
Pound nets					11	478
Crowfoot bars (pairs)	487	2,930			3,490	53,836
Forks, tongs, rakes, and dredges	500	3,050			1,810	8,656
Shrimp traps					4,310	4,163
Other apparatus						2,993
Shore and accessory property		36,797		8,965		5,029,769
Cash capital		1,000		2,300		356,000
Total		190,327		52,065		7,345,034

PRODUCTS	*Pounds*	*Value*	*Pounds*	*Value*	*Pounds*	*Value*
Black bass	8,812	$805	120	$12	73,554	$10,874
Bowfin					190,073	6,078
Buffalofish	1,331,918	64,003	669,020	28,935	17,267,177	1,013,692
Carp, German	148,806	5,551	2,185	71	18,338,371	872,128
Catfish and bullheads	429,743	31,474	117,557	6,917	8,092,690	713,461
Crappie	80,130	5,445	8,579	600	512,423	49,338
Drum, fresh-water, or sheepshead	285,535	10,942	97,753	3,594	5,260,892	290,480
Eels					16,060	1,057
Mooneye or toothed herring					3,450	166
Paddlefish or spoonbill cat	135,370	14,360	120,569	13,472	1,398,991	132,545
Paddlefish caviar	1,637	4,722	1,105	1,721	12,398	29,546
Pike and pickerel					20,100	1,850
Pike perch (sauger)					4,745	768
Pike perch (wall-eyed)	1,600	290			24,650	3,750
Quillback or "American carp"					765,389	59,221
Rock bass					2,738	312
Sturgeon, lake					10,953	1,369
Sturgeon, shovelnose	5,100	380	300	3	227,365	19,323
Sturgeon, shovelnose, caviar					1,880	2,615
Sturgeon, shovelnose, eggs					449	764
Suckers	3,030	231			699,539	63,028
Sunfish					374,533	24,955
White bass	200	10	4,331	303	64,624	5,500
Yellow bass					7,500	600
Yellow perch					22,250	1,904
Other fish	165	50			73,275	4,917
Shrimp, fresh-water					147,482	14,570
Crawfish					7,890	759
Frogs					231,761	20,410
Turtles					96,743	2,772
Alligator hides					15,616	2,673
Mussel shells	12,230,367	247,699			51,768,173	1,050,592
Pearls		13,700				46,124
Slugs		6,198				55,380
Total	14,662,413	405,860	1,021,519	55,628	105,733,734	4,503,521

[1] Includes 13 transporting vessels of 214 net tons, valued at $35,200.

Persons engaged and investment in the fisheries of the Mississippi River and tributaries, by States, in 1922.

States	Persons engaged	Gasoline boats		Rowboats and scows		House boats		Fyke nets	
	Number	Number	Value	Number	Value	Number	Value	Number	Value
Alabama	101	30	$4,085	95	$1,030	23	$2,960	362	$2,820
Arkansas	3,153	645	84,755	1,903	18,593	369	56,940	4,556	54,284
Illinois	2,484	948	118,693	1,277	32,697	103	31,700	14,552	130,418
Indiana	2,189	675	55,725	1,375	15,190	27	2,625	1,149	11,780
Iowa	3,930	328	59,223	529	10,652	48	9,085	5,342	66,916
Kansas	180	2	135	101	1,425	4	175	288	2,623
Kentucky	496	109	16,300	307	4,540	34	3,550	1,488	15,805
Louisiana	2,252	909	149,765	1,958	33,864	816	100,685	11,946	151,970
Minnesota	[1] 736	132	28,675	258	5,729	1	150	354	5,225
Mississippi	434	186	39,725	232	4,587	101	16,763	2,962	29,619
Missouri	1,023	78	11,215	235	4,255	23	5,515	1,422	12,248
Nebraska	89	5	510	40	1,084	----	----	44	369
Ohio	252	17	4,945	72	1,173	12	1,675	110	1,228
Oklahoma	109	10	1,050	106	1,170	15	3,400	465	4,350
Pennsylvania	40	----	----	2	25	----	----	----	----
South Dakota	17	2	200	13	265	1	600	55	434
Tennessee	562	113	17,525	437	6,480	48	12,775	3,182	30,075
Texas	57	10	2,250	45	855	----	----	275	2,750
West Virginia	129	8	850	51	700	6	625	----	----
Wisconsin	889	343	76,255	272	6,135	2	735	1,100	23,700
Total	19,122	[2] 4,610	671,881	9,308	150,449	1,633	249,958	49,652	546,614

States	Haul seines		Trammel nets		Gill nets		Pound nets		Crowfoot bars (pairs)	
	Number	Value	Number	Value	Number	Value	Number	Value	Number	Value
Alabama									42	$418
Arkansas	90	$19,615	88	$6,016	38	$2,136	3	$193	566	3,718
Illinois	124	36,235	9	860	238	3,250	----	----	830	13,765
Indiana	8	775	----	----	----	----	----	----	1,296	25,820
Iowa	76	16,753	181	13,863	----	----	----	----	109	963
Kansas	18	992	12	378	6	230	----	----	----	----
Kentucky	12	1,200	----	----	----	----	----	----	156	2,955
Louisiana	102	19,008	----	----	----	----	----	----	----	----
Minnesota	99	43,580	----	----	24	1,840	3	160	67	745
Mississippi	42	15,960	10	583	26	1,058	----	----	----	----
Missouri	37	3,238	85	3,630	----	----	----	----	1	7
Nebraska	3	314	35	1,269	----	----	----	----	----	----
Ohio	----	----	----	----	----	----	----	----	47	930
Pennsylvania	----	----	----	----	----	----	----	----	2	40
South Dakota	----	----	3	95	----	----	----	----	----	----
Tennessee	10	3,556	22	2,495	----	----	----	----	117	1,325
Texas	----	----	14	560	16	740	5	125	----	----
West Virginia	----	----	----	----	----	----	----	----	8	160
Wisconsin	87	28,875	----	----	518	6,930	----	----	249	2,990
Total	708	190,101	459	29,749	866	16,184	11	478	3,490	53,836

States	Forks, tongs, rakes, and dredges		Shrimp traps		Lines	Other apparatus	Shore and accessory property	Cash capital	Total investment
	Number	Value	Number	Value	Value	Value	Value	Value	Value
Alabama	----	----	----	----	$500	----	$1,070	----	$12,883
Arkansas	717	$4,104	----	----	5,955	$36	133,457	$3,500	393,302
Illinois	160	761	----	----	5,438	150	223,244	20,900	618,111
Indiana	732	3,006	----	----	1,662	----	96,117	----	212,700
Iowa	84	266	----	----	203	12	1,781,834	21,800	1,981,570
Kansas	25	80	----	----	250	----	19,505	----	25,793
Kentucky	9	90	----	----	1,214	----	185,792	19,000	250,446
Louisiana	----	----	4,060	$3,963	12,116	2,755	193,445	47,500	715,071
Minnesota	9	21	----	----	155	----	386,436	73,000	[3] 545,716
Mississippi	----	----	300	200	3,315	----	75,676	15,800	203,286
Missouri	40	159	----	----	1,186	----	1,027,754	82,800	1,152,007
Nebraska	----	----	----	----	3	----	171,115	10,000	184,664
Ohio	8	10	----	----	105	----	148,580	15,000	173,646
Oklahoma	1	3	----	----	278	----	2,010	----	12,261
Pennsylvania	----	----	----	----	----	----	109,315	17,000	126,380
South Dakota	12	16	----	----	46	----	545	----	2,201
Tennessee	13	140	----	----	1,311	23	174,407	18,600	268,712
Texas	----	----	----	----	32	----	3,350	1,000	11,662
West Virginia	----	----	----	----	145	----	9,193	----	11,673
Wisconsin	----	----	----	----	289	17	286,924	10,100	442,920
Total	1,810	8,656	4,360	4,163	34,203	2,993	5,029,769	356,000	7,345,034

[1] Includes 17 men connected with the wholesale fishery trade of North Dakota.
[2] Includes 13 transporting vessels, with a net tonnage of 214 and value of $35,200.
[3] Includes $5,000 cash capital and $23,300 worth of shore property connected with the wholesale fishery trade of North Dakota.

Yield of the fisheries of the Mississippi River and tributaries, by States, in 1922

States	Black bass Pounds	Value	Bowfin Pounds	Value	Buffalofish Pounds	Value	Carp Pounds	Value
Alabama					11,100	$1,680	9,200	$1,329
Arkansas	20,980	$2,566	40,000	$400	3,452,873	199,693	538,096	27,326
Illinois	4,800	480	107,165	4,797	3,051,608	215,261	7,734,264	367,554
Indiana					174,650	17,841	356,700	37,654
Iowa	1,150	194	4,000	80	834,556	59,474	2,001,171	92,530
Kansas					48,967	4,831	79,852	7,754
Kentucky	60	10			278,765	26,972	298,203	25,033
Louisiana					4,938,777	222,944	41,630	2,555
Minnesota			15,799	422	761,370	46,748	2,948,230	122,881
Mississippi	767	92			2,096,288	105,188	23,110	1,275
Missouri	802	123			287,474	21,536	551,536	35,160
Nebraska					16,445	1,551	82,300	8,258
Ohio	5	1			11,045	2,017	9,805	1,849
Oklahoma					86,550	7,723	61,050	5,646
South Dakota					5,675	568	5,875	587
Tennessee	33,962	6,105	5,373	127	561,138	38,232	200,261	9,653
Texas	11,028	1,309			57,145	4,421	8,100	486
West Virginia					3,370	650	2,790	526
Wisconsin			17,736	252	589,381	36,362	3,386,198	124,072
Total	73,554	10,874	190,073	6,078	17,267,177	1,013,692	18,338,371	872,128

States	Catfish and bullheads Pounds	Value	Crappie Pounds	Value	Drum, fresh-water, or sheepshead Pounds	Value	Eels Pounds	Value
Alabama	42,400	$6,380			26,500	$3,915		
Arkansas	1,014,621	88,637	135,770	$11,458	934,135	52,472		
Illinois	959,399	116,467	123,710	10,056	504,760	39,296	10,500	$540
Indiana	284,700	30,519			233,700	26,204		
Iowa	768,142	78,685	54,995	3,669	332,143	16,331		
Kansas	33,447	6,213			990	118		
Kentucky	293,528	33,639	475	39	269,528	24,605		
Louisiana	3,229,056	207,350			1,439,368	52,633	1,100	100
Minnesota	84,351	10,158			204,235	7,877	540	48
Mississippi	448,690	27,566	51,589	4,141	329,109	11,636	29	2
Missouri	194,371	24,745	4,725	593	82,888	5,950	3,000	325
Nebraska	25,395	4,728			100	10		
Ohio	17,420	3,154	5	1	18,320	3,226		
Oklahoma	55,425	7,172			110,725	10,076		
South Dakota	9,900	2,120						
Tennessee	302,910	30,536	86,018	12,839	265,066	14,409	578	35
Texas	16,361	1,780	55,136	6,542	9,369	628		
West Virginia	32,490	4,880			6,030	1,200		
Wisconsin	280,084	28,732			493,926	19,894	313	7
Total	8,092,690	713,461	512,423	49,338	5,260,892	290,480	16,060	1,057

States	Garfish Pounds	Value	Minnows Pounds	Value	Mooneye, or toothed herring Pounds	Value	Paddlefish, or spoonbill cat Pounds	Value	Paddlefish caviar Pounds	Value
Alabama							500	$75		
Arkansas							338,612	31,594	4,077	$10,603
Illinois							61,700	5,185		
Indiana							1,500	195		
Iowa							48,930	3,136		
Kentucky							15,015	1,176	150	225
Louisiana	3,370	$60					422,478	36,560	5,908	13,956
Mississippi							352,260	36,672	1,563	3,037
Missouri			1,165	$450	3,450	$166	36,850	2,133		
Nebraska							10,800	890		
Oklahoma							550	55		
Tennessee			500	500			54,015	10,929	200	600
Texas							26,310	2,256	500	1,125
Wisconsin							29,471	1,689		
Total	3,370	60	1,665	950	3,450	166	1,398,991	132,545	12,398	29,546

Yield of the fisheries of the Mississippi River and tributaries, by States, in 1922—Continued

States	Pike and pickerel		Pike perch, sauger		Pike perch, wall-eyed		Quillback, or American carp		Rock bass	
	Pounds	Value	Pounds	Value	Pounds	Value	Pounds	Value	Pounds	Value
Alabama							400	$80		
Arkansas					1,100	$165	2,100	115	1,600	$150
Illinois					500	25	90,800	7,216		
Indiana							178,000	20,675		
Iowa	20,100	$1,850	2,280	$274	16,150	2,331	127,700	3,683		
Kansas							14,880	1,891		
Kentucky			1,765	329	5,395	962	123,450	13,467		
Minnesota							19,080	758		
Missouri					1,275	210	20,492	1,884	275	33
Ohio			700	165	230	57	20,450	3,515		
Oklahoma							4,000	160		
Tennessee							23,500	1,003	863	129
Wisconsin							140,537	4,774		
Total	20,100	1,850	4,745	768	24,650	3,750	765,389	59,221	2,738	312

States	Sturgeon, lake		Sturgeon, shovelnose		Sturgeon, shovelnose, caviar		Sturgeon, shovelnose, eggs	
	Pounds	Value	Pounds	Value	Pounds	Value	Pounds	Value
Alabama			640	$96				
Arkansas			5,750	413				
Illinois			91,000	7,224	95	$185	449	$764
Indiana			47,250	4,508	250	375		
Iowa			31,100	2,340	795	905		
Kentucky	580	$85	14,250	1,458	50	75		
Louisiana			280	25				
Minnesota	6,173	983	3,255	448				
Mississippi			1,411	92				
Missouri	4,200	301	30,504	2,519	690	1,075		
Ohio			460	70				
Tennessee			1,400	120				
West Virginia			65	10				
Total	10,953	1,369	227,365	19,323	1,880	2,615	449	764

States	Suckers		Sunfish		White bass		Yellow bass		Yellow perch	
	Pounds	Value	Pounds	Value	Pounds	Value	Pounds	Value	Pounds	Value
Alabama	5,800	$895								
Arkansas	6,530	579	4,100	$485	6,250	$483				
Illinois	210,900	13,929	176,817	14,463	31,700	2,737	7,500	$600	22,250	$1,904
Indiana	156,100	18,050	200	16						
Iowa			57,650	3,225	6,800	677				
Kentucky	142,847	16,646	25	4	133	26				
Louisiana	400	28								
Minnesota	45,261	1,222								
Mississippi					16,085	1,301				
Missouri	10,790	989	1,550	53						
Nebraska	400	40								
Ohio	26,345	4,114			38	11				
Tennessee	47,900	4,770	134,191	6,709	3,618	265				
Wisconsin	46,266	1,766								
Total	699,539	63,028	374,533	24,955	64,624	5,500	7,500	600	22,250	1,904

States	Other fish		Shrimp		Crawfish		Frogs		Turtles	
	Pounds	Value	Pounds	Value	Pounds	Value	Pounds	Value	Pounds	Value
Arkansas							5,100	$695	300	$6
Illinois	68,240	$3,907					3,289	496	71,550	484
Louisiana			142,182	$13,870	7,265	$509	217,372	17,419	20,786	2,181
Minnesota									65	2
Mississippi			5,000	400					1,600	47
Missouri					625	250			2,000	40
Tennessee			300	300			6,000	1,800		
Wisconsin									442	12
Total	68,240	3,907	147,482	14,570	7,890	759	231,761	20,410	96,743	2,772

Yield of the fisheries of the Mississippi River and tributaries, by States, in 1922—
Continued

States	Alligator hides		Mussel shells		Pearls	Slugs	Total	
	Pounds	Value	Pounds	Value	Value	Value	Pounds	Value
Alabama			1,146,000	$12,898	$100	$181	1,242,540	$27,629
Arkansas			16,282,367	310,614	13,990	7,309	22,794,361	759,747
Illinois			9,265,000	237,597	10,895	15,903	22,597,996	1,077,965
Indiana			11,144,000	260,116	9,849	11,409	12,577,050	437,411
Iowa			2,453,000	44,895	3,931	7,967	6,760,662	326,177
Kansas			437,100	5,033		222	615,236	26,062
Kentucky			1,449,000	21,312	95	1,202	2,893,219	167,360
Louisiana	15,616	$2,673					10,485,588	572,863
Minnesota			1,571,196	36,427	1,456	995	5,659,555	230,425
Mississippi							3,327,501	191,449
Missouri			327,500	4,042	368	810	1,566,162	103,755
Nebraska							135,440	15,477
Ohio			597,500	10,765	380	795	702,323	30,120
Oklahoma			44,870	359		24	363,170	31,215
Pennsylvania			49,000	1,593	5	160	49,000	1,758
South Dakota			80,000	1,080	50	6	101,450	4,411
Tennessee			3,766,000	46,455	500	1,545	5,493,793	187,561
Texas							183,949	18,547
West Virginia			50,500	631		68	£5,245	7,965
Wisconsin			3,105,140	56,775	4,505	6,784	8,089,494	285,624
Total	15,616	2,673	51,768,173	1,050,592	46,124	55,380	105,733,734	4,503,521

PRODUCTS BY APPARATUS

The most important forms of apparatus employed in the fisheries of the Mississippi River and tributaries, as determined by the value of the products secured, are fyke nets, haul seines, and the crowfoot bars, forks, tongs, etc., used in the capture of mussels. The yield of fyke nets totaled 18,668,868 pounds, valued at $1,205,421, and haul seines brought in 22,877,569 pounds, valued at $1,195,776. The following table shows the production of each of the various types of apparatus by species:

Yield of the fisheries of the Mississippi River and tributaries in 1922, by apparatus and species

Species	Fyke nets		Haul seines		Crowfoot bars	
	Pounds	Value	Pounds	Value	Pounds	Value
Black bass	11,335	$1,188	5,207	$468		
Bowfin	55,436	1,156	125,614	4,774		
Buffalofish	8,235,022	487,036	7,199,078	402,229		
Carp, German	4,539,155	248,050	11,517,073	497,275		
Catfish and bullheads	1,545,071	167,211	1,004,237	96,452		
Crappie	181,688	16,332	185,060	14,196		
Drum, fresh-water, or sheepshead	2,646,066	150,706	1,406,006	60,147		
Eels	2,336	277	283	8		
Mooneye, or toothed herring	200	16	1,200	81		
Paddlefish, or spoonbill cat	120,485	9,649	725,103	626,121		
Paddlefish caviar	659	1,749	4,704	11,956		
Pike and pickerel			15,000	1,380		
Pike perch (sauger)	2,865	542	150	18		
Pike perch (wall-eyed)	6,865	1,211	13,400	1,865		
Quillback, or American carp	476,030	45,305	225,059	11,823		
Rock bass	2,063	219	275	33		
Sturgeon, lake	5,851	907	708	106		
Sturgeon, shovelnose	79,241	6,565	9,000	927		
Sturgeon, shovelnose, caviar	345	560	340	510		
Sturgeon, shovelnose, eggs	449	764				
Suckers	508,040	49,850	141,399	9,756		
Sunfish	177,463	10,947	128,667	10,301		
White bass	25,253	2,201	36,550	3,104		
Yellow bass	3,600	288	3,900	312		
Yellow perch	10,600	911	11,600	988		
Other fish	29,000	1,685	43,535	3,180		
Shrimp			300	300		
Crawfish			625	250		
Frogs			560	224		
Turtles	3,750	96	72,936	501		
Mussel shells					31,546,966	$631,338
Pearls						27,306
Slugs						37,454
Total	18,668,868	1,205,421	22,877,569	1,195,776	31,546,966	696,098

Yield of the fisheries of the Mississippi River and tributaries in 1922, by apparatus and species—Continued

Species	Lines		Forks, tongs, rakes, dredges, etc.		Trammel nets		Gill nets	
	Pounds	*Value*	*Pounds*	*Value*	*Pounds*	*Value*	*Pounds*	*Value*
Black bass	55,550	$9,067			1,462	$151		
Bowfin	5,600	69			1,873	37	1,150	$30
Buffalofish	514,967	39,372			895,102	57,619	384,799	24,881
Carp, German	668,399	49,484			799,897	43,255	770,430	32,426
Catfish and bullheads	5,128,590	406,394			376,489	40,633	35,506	2,509
Crappie	113,110	15,754			32,145	3,011	420	45
Drum, fresh-water, or sheepshead	887,783	66,955			155,189	7,248	157,603	5,033
Eels	13,441	772						
Mooneye, or toothed herring					2,050	69		
Paddlefish, or spoonbill cat	441,763	50,679			44,318	3,010	65,686	6,533
Paddlefish caviar	5,020	11,242			223	546	1,792	4,053
Pike and pickerel					5,100	470		
Pike perch (sauger)	30	4			1,700	204		
Pike perch (wall-eyed)	1,310	219			3,075	455		
Quillback, or American carp	2,495	207			32,205	1,164	29,600	722
Rock bass	400	60						
Sturgeon, lake	1,294	121			2,300	123	800	112
Sturgeon, shovelnose	89,324	7,780			49,800	4,051		
Sturgeon, shovelnose, caviar					1,195	1,545		
Suckers	23,350	2,388			565	56	15,735	447
Sunfish	47,183	2,559			21,020	1,128	200	20
White bass	2,200	143			300	15	321	37
Yellow perch							50	5
Other fish	600	42					140	10
Frogs			2,729	$272				
Turtles	17,342	523					75	2
Alligator hides	1,242	291						
Mussel shells			20,221,207	419,254				
Pearls				18,818				
Slugs				17,926				
Total	8,020,993	664,125	20,223,936	456,270	2,426,008	164,790	1,464,307	76,865

Species	Shrimp traps		Pound nets		Other apparatus		Total	
	Pounds	*Value*	*Pounds*	*Value*	*Pounds*	*Value*	*Pounds*	*Value*
Black bass							73,554	$10,874
Bowfin			400	$12			190,073	6,078
Buffalofish			29,810	1,839	8,399	$716	17,267,177	1,013,692
Carp, German			16,825	761	26,592	877	18,338,371	872,128
Catfish and bullheads			2,200	210	597	52	8,092,690	713,461
Crappie							512,423	49,338
Drum, fresh-water, or sheepshead			7,600	365	645	26	5,260,892	290,480
Eels							16,060	1,057
Mooneye, or toothed herring							3,450	166
Paddlefish, or spoonbill cat			1,000	30	636	32	1,398,991	132,545
Paddlefish caviar							12,398	29,546
Pike and pickerel							20,100	1,850
Pike perch (sauger)							4,745	768
Pike perch (wall-eyed)							24,650	3,750
Quillback, or American carp							765,389	59,221
Rock bass							2,738	312
Sturgeon, lake							10,953	1,369
Sturgeon, shovelnose							227,365	19,323
Sturgeon, shovelnose, caviar							1,880	2,615
Sturgeon, shovelnose, eggs							449	764
Suckers					10,450	531	699,539	63,028
Sunfish							374,533	24,955
White bass							64,624	5,500
Yellow bass							7,500	600
Yellow perch							22,250	1,904
Other fish							73,275	4,917
Shrimp	147,182	$14,270					147,482	14,570
Crawfish							7,890	759
Frogs					228,472	19,914	231,761	20,410
Turtles					2,640	1,650	96,743	2,772
Alligator hides					14,374	2,382	15,616	2,673
Mussel shells							51,768,173	1,050,592
Pearls								46,124
Slugs								55,380
Total	147,182	14,270	57,835	3,217	300,070	26,689	105,733,734	4,503,521

COMPARISON WITH PREVIOUS STATISTICS

The literature does not provide many references from which to draw material for the comparison of the present industry with that of past years. A canvass of interior waters for 1894[3] provides material on the Mississippi River and tributaries, but the published compilations are so arranged as to make it impossible to clearly separate the statistics of this river system from those of other interior waters. The separation was attempted, however, and it is believed that the resulting figures, though not strictly comparable, give at least an approximately correct summary of the production in 1894. For the year 1899 there is a canvass of the Mississippi River and tributaries,[4] which is believed to be entirely comparable to the 1922 canvass, as is also the canvass for 1903. The latter has been published only as a summary in Bureau of Fisheries Statistical Bulletin No. 175. Figures for 1908 were the result of a canvass of fisheries made by the Bureau of the Census in cooperation with the Bureau of Fisheries.[5] The scheme of collection and compilations differed somewhat from the other canvasses, and therefore may be only approximately comparable to the 1922 figures.

The following table shows the yield of the fisheries by species. As pointed out above, the figures for 1899, 1903, and 1922 are probably strictly comparable; the others are only approximately so.

Products of the fisheries of the Mississippi River and tributaries for various years, 1894 to 1922

Products	1894	1899	1903	1908	1922
	Pounds	Pounds	Pounds	Pounds	Pounds
Fishes:					
Bass, black	754, 219	948, 184	431, 170	1, 459, 000	73, 554
Bass, rock, yellow and white	510, 763	278, 457	104, 557	83, 000	74, 862
Bowfin	173, 330	811, 000	1, 105, 250	1, 449, 000	190, 073
Buffalofish	15, 924, 810	14, 215, 975	11, 491, 663	15, 040, 000	15, 488, 765
Carp	1, 294, 843	11, 868, 840	12, 270, 346	30, 670, 000	18, 338, 371
Catfish and bullheads	9, 689, 034	7, 648, 179	5, 191, 850	8, 073, 000	6, 2 3, 025
Crappie	814, 859	1, 318, 832	1, 118, 770	2, 563, 000	512, 423
Drum, fresh-water, or sheepshead	4, 478, 620	3, 149, 232	2, 748, 743	4, 737, 000	4, 539, 165
Eels	133, 223	93, 905	74, 210	61, 000	16, 060
Mooneye, or toothed herring	60, 021	17, 366	8, 850		3, 450
Paddlefish, or spoonbill cat	1, 028, 445	2, 473, 250	1, 421, 086	1, 439, 000	1, 398, 991
Pike and pickerel	354, 063	216, 952	707, 093	367, 000	20, 100
Pike perch, wall-eyed and sauger	910, 075	249, 435	398, 668	133, 000	29, 395
Quillback					765, 389
Sturgeon, lake and shovelnose	1, 015, 009	945, 838	941, 497	845, 000	238, 318
Suckers	2, 178, 608	2, 243, 934	1, 109, 276	892, 000	699, 539
Sunfish	445, 119	910, 963	1, 221, 752	2, 821, 000	374, 533
Yellow perch	177, 909	65, 006	73, 447	36, 000	22, 250
Other fish	37, 005	193, 750	84, 011	70, 900	73, 275
Total	39, 979, 955	47, 649, 098	40, 502, 239	70, 738, 900	49, 121, 538
Miscellaneous:					
Caviar		70, 700	11, 171	25, 000	14, 727
Shrimp, fresh-water	90, 562	200, 058	190, 884	306, 000	147, 482
Crawfish	6, 700			9, 400	625
Frogs	237, 718	440, 996	336, 049	193, 000	14, 849
Turtles and terrapin	360, 704	782, 015	477, 370	713, 000	83, 876
Alligator hides	[1] 25, 397	4, 950			3, 244
Other hides	[1] 850	1, 620	16	[1] 32, 000	
Mussel shells	[1] 195, 500	47, 648, 000	51, 856, 430	76, 266, 000	51, 768, 173

[1] Represents the number of hides instead of weight of hides.

NOTE.—The above figures do not include the statistics for the Atchafalaya River.

[3] Hugh M. Smith, Statistics of the Fisheries of the Interior Waters of the United States. Appendix 11 to the Report of the Commissioner for the year ended June 30, 1896 (1898).
[4] C. H. Townsend. Statistics of the Mississippi River and Tributaries. Appendix 15 to Report of the Commissioner of Fisheries for 1901 (1902).
[5] Fisheries of the United States, 1908. Special Report of the Bureau of the Census, 1911.

From the above table it may be seen that the buffalofish and paddlefish are the only species of which the total catch is being maintained, as compared to former years. Carp, catfish, and drum are being taken in considerably lesser amounts than formerly, though still approaching their former importance. The commercial catch of all other species has declined in no uncertain fashion.

The appearance of quillback in the statistics of 1922 for the first time does not necessarily indicate the beginning of a new fishery for this species. It may have been reported previously under a different name, most probably among the suckers.

FISHERIES OF LAKE PEPIN AND LAKE KEOKUK

In view of the rather extensive biological and ecological experiments and investigations to which the aquatic life of Lake Pepin and Lake Keokuk has been subjected in recent years, especial significance is attached to the statistics of the fisheries of these lakes. There are presented herewith the detailed statistics for the year 1922 and comparative statistics for the years 1914, 1917, and 1922.

Fisheries of Lake Pepin and Lake Keokuk, 1922

Items	Lake Pepin		Lake Keokuk	
	Number	*Value*	*Number*	*Value*
Fishermen	219		122	
Gasoline boats	109	$25, 110	58	$6, 218
Rowboats	134	3, 530	102	2, 180
House boats	2	735	9	1, 950
Fyke nets	95	15, 300	1, 301	12, 250
Seines	33	24, 100	2	650
Set gill nets	351	4, 340	235	2, 350
Trammel nets			17	1, 620
Dip nets			1	12
Spears	7	17		
Trot and hand lines		82		280
Shore and accessory property		39, 220		4, 190
Total		112, 434		31, 700
PRODUCTS				
With seines:	*Pounds*	*Value*	*Pounds*	*Value*
Bowfin	14, 650	$199		
Buffalofish	198, 324	8, 474	225	$18
Carp, German	1, 869, 386	60, 006	3, 700	285
Catfish and bullheads	55, 292	4, 776	8, 600	872
Crappie			100	10
Drum, freshwater, or sheepshead	182, 126	5, 907	4, 850	243
Eels	263	6		
Paddlefish, or spoonbill cat	15, 585	597	5, 625	332
Pike perch, sauger			150	18
Quillback, or American carp	11, 957	254		
Sturgeon, lake	108	11		
Sturgeon, shovelnose	1, 080	129	400	40
Suckers	22, 351	762		
Turtles	367	10		
Total	2, 371, 489	81, 131	23, 650	1, 818
With fyke nets:				
Black bass			5, 400	452
Bowfin	736	11		
Buffalofish	68, 059	3, 190	83, 396	6, 993
Carp, German	255, 414	9, 527	199, 341	7, 647
Catfish and bullheads	14, 440	1, 116	111, 349	10, 277
Crappie			11, 720	937
Drum, freshwater, or sheepshead	81, 504	2, 551	34, 820	1, 744
Eels	136	18		
Paddlefish, or spoonbill cat	100	3	13, 680	748
Pike perch, sauger			400	48
Quillback, or American carp	14, 000	215		
Sturgeon, lake	3, 471	649		
Sturgeon, shovelnose			100	10
Suckers	8, 250	181		
Sunfish			10, 590	756
Total	446, 110	17, 461	470, 796	29, 612

Fisheries of Lake Pepin and Lake Keokuk, 1922—Continued

Items	Lake Pepin		Lake Keokuk	
	Pounds	*Value*	*Pounds*	*Value*
With set gill nets:				
Bowfin	750	$10		
Buffalofish	70,441	3,166	18,000	$2,700
Carp, German	420,105	14,707	12,000	1,320
Catfish and bullheads	11,100	311		
Drum, freshwater, or sheepshead	129,143	3,656		
Paddlefish, or spoonbill cat	250	7		
Quillback, or American carp	21,300	324		
Sturgeon, lake	800	112		
Suckers	12,635	279		
Turtles	75	2		
Total	666,599	22,574	30,000	4,020
With trammel nets:				
Buffalofish			7,025	561
Carp, German			37,890	1,771
Catfish and bullheads			26,470	2,749
Crappie			1,150	72
Drum, freshwater, or sheepshead			19,070	941
Paddlefish, or spoonbill cat			7,300	390
Pike perch, sauger			1,700	204
Sunfish			500	20
Total			101,105	6,708
With dip nets:				
Carp, German			1,500	75
Catfish and bullheads			250	30
Drum, freshwater, or sheepshead			150	8
Paddlefish, or spoonbill cat			600	30
Total			2,500	143
With spears:				
Buffalofish	1,399	46		
Carp, German	25,092	802		
Catfish and bullheads	347	22		
Drum, freshwater, or sheepshead	495	18		
Paddlefish, or spoonbill cat	36	2		
Suckers	50	3		
Total	27,419	893		
With trot and hand lines:				
Black bass			800	80
Buffalofish	2,086	94	5,300	432
Carp, German	8,919	290	22,000	705
Catfish and bullheads	46,205	4,980	37,250	3,660
Crappie			800	80
Drum, freshwater, or sheepshead	2,324	80	6,150	355
Eels	142	12		
Paddlefish, or spoonbill cat			200	10
Pike perch, sauger			30	4
Quillback, or American carp	120	4		
Sturgeon, lake	874	71		
Sturgeon, shovelnose			100	10
Suckers	180	12		
Sunfish			500	50
Total	60,850	5,543	73,130	5,386
Products, by species:				
Black bass			6,200	532
Bowfin	16,136	220		
Buffalofish	340,309	14,970	113,946	10,704
Carp, German	2,578,916	85,332	276,431	11,803
Catfish and bullheads	127,384	11,205	183,919	17,588
Crappie			13,770	1,099
Drum, freshwater, or sheepshead	395,592	12,212	65,040	3,291
Eels	541	36		
Paddlefish, or spoonbill cat	15,971	609	27,405	1,510
Pike perch, sauger			2,280	274
Quillback, or American carp	47,377	797		
Sturgeon, lake	5,253	843		
Sturgeon, shovelnose	1,080	129	600	60
Suckers	43,466	1,237		
Sunfish			11,590	826
Turtles	442	12		
Total	3,572,467	127,602	701,181	47,687

Comparative statistics of the fisheries of Lakes Pepin and Keokuk for the years 1914, 1917, and 1922

LAKE PEPIN

Items	1914		1917		1922	
PERSONS ENGAGED	*Number*	*Value*	*Number*	*Value*	*Number*	*Value*
Fishermen	135		126		219	
Shoresmen	2		5			
Total	137		131		219	
INVESTMENT						
Gasoline boats	28	$7,625	35	$6,810	109	$25,110
Rowboats and barges [1]	53	1,300	52	1,395	134	3,530
House boats	1	100	3	250	2	735
Fyke nets	295	24,995	262	37,472	95	15,300
Seines	14	3,340	17	6,460	33	24,100
Anchored gill nets	664	4,421	371	2,350	351	4,340
Trap nets	8	480	14	450		
Spears					7	17
Trot and hand lines		3		[2] 13		82
Shore and accessory property		1,335		3,851		39,220
Total		43,599		59,051		112,434
PRODUCTS	*Pounds*	*Value*	*Pounds*	*Value*	*Pounds*	*Value*
Bowfin	1,534	$16	24,021	$342	16,136	$220
Buffalofish	261,250	19,728	300,808	25,009	340,309	14,970
Carp, German	237,517	7,623	467,588	23,277	2,578,916	85,332
Catfish and bullheads	26,830	1,745	254,249	24,437	127,384	11,205
Eels					541	36
Fresh-water drum or sheepshead	131,785	2,450	118,304	3,508	395,592	12,212
Mooneye, fresh	9,300	88	7,656	77		
Mooneye, smoked	1,465	70	7,250	855		
Pike	50	5				
Quillback or American carp	60,605	864	14,238	259	47,377	797
Spoonbill cat or paddlefish	8,877	557	2,923	215	15,971	609
Sturgeon lake	1,067	129	512	104	5,253	843
Sturgeon, shovelnose					1,080	129
Suckers	18,340	439	15,260	472	43,466	1,237
Sunfish	50	5				
Turtles					442	12
Total	758,670	33,719	1,212,809	78,555	3,572,467	127,602

LAKE KEOKUK

	1914		1917		1922	
PERSONS ENGAGED	*Number*	*Value*	*Number*	*Value*	*Number*	*Value*
Fishermen	105		118		122	
INVESTMENT						
Gasoline boats	36	$3,870	52	$4,730	58	$6,218
Rowboats	84	1,250	64	810	102	2,180
House boats	10	1,075	16	3,975	9	1,950
Fyke nets	1,378	5,693	1,368	8,929	1,301	12,250
Seines			1	800	2	650
Anchored gill nets			12	180	235	2,350
Trammel nets	14	304	17	472	17	1,620
Trap nets			81	221		
Dip nets					1	12
Trot and hand lines		153		[2] 132		280
Shore and accessory property		3,845		1,630		4,190
Total		16,190		21,879		31,700
PRODUCTS	*Pounds*	*Value*	*Pounds*	*Value*	*Pounds*	*Value*
Black bass	15	$1	4,163	$418	6,200	$532
Bowfin			26,000	390		
Buffalofish	249,900	9,252	696,543	40,563	113,946	10,704
Carp, German	302,365	7,823	762,259	28,800	276,431	11,803
Catfish and bullheads	71,535	4,855	109,904	8,192	183,919	17,588
Crappie	70	4	17,560	1,103	13,770	1,099
Eels	3,800	250	2,087	318		
Fresh-water drum or sheepshead	26,860	827	160,554	8,130	65,040	3,291
Pike			20	3		
Pike perch, sauger					2,280	274
Quillback or American carp			5,936	244		
Spoonbill cat or paddlefish			927	68	27,405	1,510
Sturgeon, sand [3]	1,900	121	454	37		
Sturgeon, shovelnose					600	60
Suckers	4,640	164	700	38		
Sunfish	50	3	13,879	813	11,590	826
Total	661,135	23,300	1,800,986	89,117	701,181	47,687

[1] No barges were reported in 1914 and 1922.   [3] Reported as lake sturgeon in 1914.
[2] No hand lines were reported for 1917.

WHOLESALE FISH TRADE

In the region of the Missisipi River and tributaries there were 142 establishments engaged in the wholesale fish trade. These employed 1,216 persons and represented an investment of $3,956,072. The distribution of this business among the several States may be seen from the following table:

Wholesale fish trade

State	Establishments		Persons engaged		Cash capital	Total investment
	Number	Value	Number	Wages paid		
Arkansas	4	$45,025	14	$3,903	$3,500	$52,428
Illinois	16	68,038	90	45,868	20,900	134,806
Iowa	16	135,337	120	59,395	15,800	210,532
Kentucky	8	148,300	72	78,900	17,000	2 4,200
Louisiana and Texas	30	138,135	150	105,300	48,500	291,935
Missouri	23	888,651	331	381,727	82,800	1,353,178
Minnesota	12	323,874	140	162,294	73,000	559,168
Mississippi	9	69,014	47	39,711	15,800	124,525
Nebraska and North Dakota	3	192,665	54	70,386	15,000	278,051
Ohio and Pennsylvania	7	221,300	113	148,364	32,000	401,664
Tennessee	7	135,352	63	47,091	18,600	201,043
Wisconsin	7	83,100	22	11,342	10,100	104,542
Total	142	2,448,791	1,216	1,154,281	353,000	3,956,072

SMOKED-FISH INDUSTRY

The smoking of fish is not extensively practiced in the Mississippi River region and consists largely of the smoking of fish that have been shipped there from the Great Lakes region and elsewhere. In 1922 there were 10 establishments engaged in this business, located as follows: Iowa, 5; Missouri, 2; Minnesota, 1; Pennsylvania, 1; Ohio, 1. The total number of persons engaged was 183; the capital invested, including wages paid, amounted to $667,097. Since most of these plants also engage in the wholesale fresh fish business, the figures on persons engaged and investment are not accurately indicative of the importance of the smoking industry. The products in 1922 amounted to 695,283 pounds, valued at $141,067. Most of these were ciscoes, the sturgeon being next in importance. The following table presents the statistics of this business:

Smoked-fish industry

Items	Number	Value	Items	Pounds	Value
Establishments	10	$386,937	Smoked fish—Continued.		
Persons engaged	183		Ciscoes	451,283	$79,442
Wages paid		208,460	Sablefish	10,000	1,000
Cash capital		71,700	Salmon, kippered	18,000	4,800
			Salmon, mild-cured	45,000	18,000
	Pounds	Value	Sturgeon	147,000	29,590
			Trout	1,000	360
Smoked fish:			Whitefish	500	130
Buffalofish	11,500	3,875			
Carp, German	10,000	3,600	Total	695,283	141,067
Catfish	1,000	270			

ALABAMA

The commercial fisheries of Alabama, connected with the Miss issippi River and its tributaries, are confined entirely to the Tennesse River. In 1922 101 persons, including 4 shoresmen, were engaged The total investment, including boats, apparatus, and shore property amounted to $12,883. The mussel fishery was the most important the value of the output, including pearls and slugs, amounting t $13,179; the output of fish proper amounted to 96,540 pounds valued at $14,450, the most important species being catfish and drum or sheepshead.

Persons engaged and investment in the fisheries of Alabama, 1922

Items	Number	Value	Items	Number	
Persons engaged:			Investment—Continued.		
Fishermen	97		House boats	23	$2, 96
Shoresmen	4		Crowfoot bars (pairs)	42	41
			Fyke nets	362	2, 82
Total	101		Set lines	220	50
			Shore property		1, 07
Investment:					
Gasoline boats	30	$4, 085	Total		
Rowboats	95	1, 030			

Yield, by apparatus, of the fisheries o

Species	Crowfoot bars		Fyke nets		Set lines			
	Pounds	Value	Pounds	Value	Pounds	Value	Pounds	Valu
Buffalofish			9, 300	$1, 395	1, 800	$285	11, 100	$1, 6
Carp			7, 300	1, 065	1, 900	264	9, 200	1, 3
Catfish			15, 100	2, 235	27, 300	4, 145	42, 400	6, 3
Drum, fresh-water, or sheepshead			21, 700	3, 190	4, 800	725	26, 500	3, 91
Paddlefish or spoonbill cat			500	75			500	7
Quillback or American carp			400	80			400	8
Sturgeon, shovelnose			640	96			640	9
Suckers			4, 800	745	1, 000	150	5, 800	89
Mussel shells	1, 146, 000	$12, 898					1, 146, 000	12, 89
Pearls		100						1
Slugs		181						1
Total	1, 146, 000	13, 179	59, 740	8, 881	36, 800	5, 569	1, 242, 540	

ARKANSAS

The fisheries of Arkansas are confined entirely to the Mississipp River and its tributaries. The White River ranks first in importance due to its extensive mussel fisheries. Beginning near Brandon Mo., shells are taken at intervals along the entire length of this rive to within a few miles of its mouth, where fishing proper prevails The fish in the latter region are purchased by "buy-boats" fro Rosedale, Miss., which make regular trips for a distance of 75 mile up the river from its mouth two or three times weekly. Amon other important streams contributing to the output of Arkansa were the Arkansas, St. Francis, Ouachita, Black, and Mississipp Rivers. Of these, the St. Francis, Black, and Ouachita Rive supported important mussel fisheries, but no shells were taken fro the Arkansas and Mississippi Rivers.

In 1922 Arkansas ranked second among the Mississippi River States in the total value of its fishery products and first in the value of its mussel-shell yield. During that year 2,493 fishermen, 650 shoresmen, and 10 men on transporting vessels were engaged. The total investment, including boats, apparatus, shore property, and cash capital, amounted to $393,302, with a yield in fishery products amounting to 22,794,361 pounds, having a value to the fishermen of $759,747, of which mussels contributed 16,282,367 pounds, valued at $331,913, including the pearls and slugs. The most important species of true fish taken in the State was the buffalofish, with a total catch of 3,452,873 pounds, valued at $199,693, followed by the catfish, with a catch of 1,014,621 pounds, valued at $88,637, and the drum, or sheepshead, with a catch of 934,135 pounds, valued at $52,472. The paddlefish, with an output of 338,612 pounds, valued at $31,594, together with 4,077 pounds of caviar worth $10,603, are also worthy of notice. Fyke nets, set lines, and haul seines were most important in the capture of the above fish; the first two named are usually found in every fishing locality.

In the following tables are shown the detailed statistics of the fisheries of this State:

Persons engaged and investment in the fisheries of Arkansas, 1922

Waters	Persons engaged			Gasoline boats		Rowboats		House boats		Fyke nets	
	Fishermen	Shoresmen	Total								
	No.	No.	No.	No.	Val.	No.	Val.	No.	Val.	No.	Val.
Arkansas River	228	2	230	55	$6,570	180	$2,035	16	$3,350	747	$7,377
Black River	209	180	389	71	9,415	192	2,483	45	6,775	114	963
Cache River	30	2	32	8	675	25	208	3	425	106	850
Little River and Big Lake	113	6	119	20	1,985	90	773	12	2,975	305	4,376
Mississippi River	106		106	28	4,380	85	768	10	1,800	383	4,084
Ouachita River	173	8	181	34	3,615	164	1,209	18	1,900	350	2,484
Red River	18	1	19			12	130			58	580
St. Francis River	312	25	337	63	6,835	229	2,373	42	8,475	609	5,634
White River	1,047	425	1 1,482	1 337	48,155	735	5,940	212	29,790	1,327	22,745
Horseshoe Lake	37		37	3	325	28	1,195				
Miscellaneous waters	220	1	221	26	2,800	163	1,479	11	1,450	557	5,191
Total	2,493	650	3,153	645	84,755	1,903	18,593	369	56,940	4,556	54,284

Waters	Set lines		Haul seines			Trammel nets			Gill nets			Pound nets		Hand lines
	No.	Val.	No	Yds.	Val.	No.	Yds.	Val.	No.	Yds.	Val.	No.	Val.	Val.
Arkansas River	462	$423	9	2,800	$1,625	4	570	$175						
Black River	136	456	3	350	216	3	270	136						$6
Cache River	18	31				2	200	120						
Little River and Big Lake	101	97	7	950	670	3	250	170	1	100	$40			7
Mississippi River	267	341	4	700	400	16	2,650	1,121						10
Ouachita River	295	828				4	425	230	18	2,050	798			53
Red River			2	650	225	5	425	230	3	625	285			
St. Francis River	126	345	13	2,640	2,249	5	480	272				3	$193	24
White River	630	2,427	40	13,535	10,615	23	2,725	1,465	8	830	280			1
Horseshoe Lake	25	75	1	800	1,500	13	2,950	1,455	3	950	465			
Miscellaneous waters	165	692	11	2,720	2,115	10	1,290	642	5	500	268			139
Total	2,225	5,715	90	25,145	19,615	88	12,235	6,016	38	5,055	2,136	3	193	240

[1] Includes 10 men on 5 transporting vessels.
[2] Includes 5 transporting vessels with a net tonnage of 22 and value of $16,000.

Persons engaged and investment in the fisheries of Arkansas, 1922—Continued

Waters	Gigs		Crowfoot bars, pairs		Tongs		Rakes		Forks		Dredges		Shore property	Cash capital	Total investment
	No.	Val.	No.	Val.	No.	Val.	No.	Val.	No.	Val.	No.	Val.	Val.	Val.	Val.
Arkansas River	----	----	----	----	----	----	----	----	----	----	----	----	$12,030	$1,000	$34,585
Black River	----	----	35	$325	105	$655	30	$100	----	----	1	$100	12,510	------	34,140
Cache River	----	----	8	80	4	27	----	----	----	----	----	----	873	------	3,289
Little River and Big Lake	----	----	1	20	18	110	----	----	36	$95	----	----	3,175	------	14,493
Mississippi River	5	$3	----	----	----	----	----	----	----	----	----	----	1,095	------	14,002
Ouachita River	----	----	2	8	31	258	8	15	28	97	----	----	9,195	500	21,190
Red River	----	----	----	----	----	----	----	----	----	----	----	----	905	------	2,355
St. Francis River	22	33	76	760	58	364	----	----	36	100	----	----	49,890	1,000	78,547
White River	----	----	444	2,525	210	1,811	----	----	120	287	----	----	21,974	1,000	149,015
Horseshoe Lake	----	----	----	----	----	----	----	----	----	----	----	----	12,445	------	17,460
Miscellaneous waters	----	----	----	----	----	----	----	----	32	85	----	----	9,365	------	24,226
Total	27	36	566	3,718	426	3,225	38	115	252	664	1	100	133,457	3,500	393,302

Yield, by apparatus and waters, of the fisheries of Arkansas, 1922

Apparatus and species	Arkansas River		Black River		Cache River		Little River and Big Lake	
	Pounds	Value	Pounds	Value	Pounds	Value	Pounds	Value
Fyke nets:								
Black bass	2,000	$160	--------	--------	150	$23	1,000	$150
Bowfin							35,000	350
Buffalofish	386,450	24,871	22,525	$1,897	12,905	1,084	65,000	4,340
Carp, German	37,898	2,933	4,091	372	100	8	29,000	1,030
Catfish and bullheads	48,600	5,577	1,585	172	250	26	8,100	653
Crappie	13,440	818			150	22		
Drum, fresh-water	179,605	11,991	6,720	489	4,475	374	15,000	450
Paddlefish or spoonbill cat	3,250	252	50	3	--------	--------		
Quillback or American carp	2,100	115						
Rock bass	500	40						
Suckers			200	16				
Sunfish							500	25
White bass	4,600	351						
Total	678,443	47,108	35,171	2,949	18,030	1,537	153,600	6,998
Set lines:								
Black bass	568	45						
Bowfin							5,000	50
Buffalofish	37,735	3,142	3,625	367	100	10	--------	--------
Carp, German	30,550	2,456						
Catfish and bullheads	83,877	7,796	20,363	2,203	2,770	285	28,150	1,952
Drum, fresh-water	63,501	5,435	14,100	1,349	1,225	102	7,200	205
Paddlefish or spoonbill cat	1,033	102	5,000	500				
Paddlefish caviar	10	30	50	125				
White bass	400	32	--------	--------				
Total	217,674	19,038	43,138	4,544	4,095	397	40,350	2,225
Haul seines:								
Buffalofish	96,000	7,410	14,250	1,130			19,335	1,300
Carp, German	51,600	4,112	4,750	380			20,670	515
Catfish and bullheads	42,400	5,050	550	55				
Drum, fresh-water	75,400	6,020	550	44			1,665	25
Paddlefish or spoonbill cat	13,500	1,097	2,000	80				
White bass	300	15						
Total	279,200	23,704	22,100	1,689	--------	--------	41,670	1,840
Trammel nets:								
Buffalofish	6,700	446	7,125	570	5,625	450	6,000	480
Carp, German	400	26	4,250	340			5,000	250
Catfish and bullheads	1,100	80	250	25				
Crappie	300	27	--------	--------				
Drum, fresh-water	--------	--------	400	32	835	50	2,000	100
Paddlefish or spoonbill cat	--------	--------	500	25				
Total	8,500	579	12,525	992	6,460	500	13,000	830

Yield, by apparatus and waters, of the fisheries of Arkansas, 1922—Continued

Apparatus and species	Arkansas River		Black River		Cache River		Little River and Big Lake	
	Pounds	Value	Pounds	Value	Pounds	Value	Pounds	Value
Hand lines:								
Black bass			402	$57				
Drum, fresh-water			650	100				
Total			1,052	157				
Crowfoot bars:								
Mussel shells			560,000	11,480	120,000	$1,800		
Pearls				1,000		30		
Slugs				400		30		
Total			560,000	12,880	120,000	1,860		
Tongs, rakes, forks, etc.:								
Mussel shells			948,000	18,627	21,000	325		
Pearls				3,000		5		
Slugs				1,140		8		
Total			948,000	22,767	21,000	338		
Total by species:								
Black bass	2,568	$205	402	57	150	23	1,000	$150
Bowfin							40,000	400
Buffalofish	526,885	35,869	47,525	3,964	18,630	1,544	90,335	6,120
Carp, German	120,448	9,527	13,091	1,092	100	8	54,670	1,795
Catfish and bullheads	175,977	18,503	22,748	2,455	3,020	311	36,250	2,578
Crappie	13,740	845			150	22		
Drum, fresh-water	318,506	23,446	22,420	2,014	6,535	526	25,865	825
Paddlefish or spoonbill cat	17,783	1,451	7,550	608				
Paddlefish caviar	10	30	50	125				
Quillback or American carp	2,100	115						
Rock bass	500	40						
Suckers			200	16				
Sunfish							500	25
White bass	5,300	398						
Mussel shells			1,508,000	30,107	141,000	2,125		
Pearls				4,000		35		
Slugs				1,540		38		
Total	1,183,817	90,429	1,621,986	45,978	169,585	4,632	248,620	11,983

Yield, by apparatus and waters, of the fisheries of Arkansas, 1922—Continued

Apparatus and species	Mississippi River		Ouachita River		Red River		St. Francis River	
	Pounds	Value	Pounds	Value	Pounds	Value	Pounds	Value
Fyke nets:								
Black bass							800	$112
Buffalofish	113,750	$8,391	162,000	$9,051	25,900	$1,675	244,610	16,752
Carp, German	93,800	4,737			1,900	109	8,260	525
Catfish and bullheads	8,150	603	20,750	1,706	1,000	103	27,915	2,515
Crappie	200	30	50	8			1,400	217
Drum, fresh-water	25,975	1,430	36,300	1,813	4,400	254	41,085	1,794
Paddlefish or spoonbill cat	4,000	140	2,900	220	3,400	358	150	7
Paddlefish caviar			181	403	88	282		
Rock bass	500	50					600	60
Suckers			4,100	410				
Sunfish	500	50					1,600	160
Turtles	300	6						
Total	247,175	15,437	226,281	13,611	36,688	2,781	326,420	22,142
Set lines:								
Buffalofish	5,175	311	200	22			4,247	345
Catfish and bullheads	86,275	8,661	79,200	8,063			35,296	3,386
Drum, fresh-water	13,750	590	31,650	2,928			23,010	1,276
Paddlefish or spoonbill cat	20,000	1,000	4,600	925			18,224	1,910
Paddlefish caviar	100	150	260	775			3	9
Sturgeon, shovelnose	650	33						
Total	125,950	10,745	115,910	12,713			80,780	6,926
Haul seines:								
Black bass	100	15						
Buffalofish	14,000	770			13,000	1,280	113,435	5,770
Carp, German	7,000	200			500	32	9,740	216
Catfish and bullheads	3,000	380			950	110	3,000	240
Crappie	500	75						
Drum, fresh-water	6,500	195			800	50	15,580	305
Paddlefish or spoonbill cat	10,800	440			4,000	500	55,360	3,805
Paddlefish caviar	50	75			55	150		
Total	41,950	2,150			19,305	2,122	197,115	10,336
Trammel nets:								
Buffalofish	93,400	4,309	11,700	816	12,300	890	18,000	1,160
Carp, German	17,000	658			1,700	131		
Catfish and bullheads	7,950	608			600	62	2,000	200
Drum, fresh-water	3,600	192			1,850	130	200	6
Paddlefish or spoonbill cat	400	24			400	50		
Paddlefish caviar					5	13		
Total	122,350	5,791	11,700	816	16,855	1,276	20,200	1,366
Gill nets:								
Buffalofish			41,500	2,235	13,000	960		
Carp, German					1,000	62		
Catfish and bullheads			200	26	150	18		
Drum, fresh-water			200	25	850	53		
Paddlefish or spoonbill cat			23,900	2,503				
Paddlefish caviar			1,250	2,625				
Suckers			100	13				
Total			67,150	7,427	15,000	1,093		
Pound nets:								
Buffalofish							1,560	105
Carp, German							200	16
Catfish and bullheads							200	30
Drum, fresh-water							3,550	120
Total							5,510	271
Hand lines:								
Black bass	350	53	1,250	186			850	120
Crappie	3,700	555	12,900	1,603			50	5
Sunfish	500	50						
Total	4,550	658	14,150	1,789			900	125
Gigs: Frogs	1,600	250					3,500	445
Crowfoot bars:								
Mussel shells							1,200,000	21,000
Pearls								150
Slugs								420
Total							1,200,000	21,570

Yield, by apparatus and waters, of the fisheries of Arkansas, 1922—Continued

Apparatus and species	Mississippi River		Ouachita River		Red River		St. Francis River	
	Pounds	*Value*	*Pounds*	*Value*	*Pounds*	*Value*	*Pounds*	*Value*
Tongs, rakes, forks, etc.:								
Mussel shells			790, 000	$10, 664			1, 286, 000	$21, 761
Pearls				25				50
Slugs				61				390
Total			790, 000	10, 750			1, 286, 000	22, 201
Total by species:								
Black bass	450	$68	1, 250	186			1, 650	232
Buffalofish	226, 325	13, 781	215, 400	12, 124	64, 200	$4, 805	381, 852	24, 132
Carp, German	117, 800	5, 595			5, 100	334	18, 200	757
Catfish and bullheads	105, 375	10, 252	100, 150	9, 795	2, 700	293	68, 411	6, 371
Crappie	4, 400	660	12, 950	1, 611			1, 450	222
Drum, fresh-water	49, 825	2, 407	68, 150	4, 766	7, 900	487	83, 425	3, 501
Paddlefish or spoonbill cat	35, 200	1, 604	31, 400	3, 648	7, 800	908	73, 734	5, 722
Paddlefish caviar	150	225	1, 691	3, 803	148	445	3	9
Rock bass	500	50					600	60
Sturgeon, shovelnose	650	33						
Suckers			4, 200	423				
Sunfish	1, 000	100					1, 600	160
Frogs	1, 600	250					3, 500	445
Turtles	300	6						
Mussel shells			790, 000	10, 664			2, 486, 000	42, 761
Pearls				25				200
Slugs				61				810
Total	543, 575	35, 031	1, 225, 191	47, 106	87, 848	7, 272	3, 120, 425	85, 382

*Yield, by apparatus and waters, of the fisheries of Arkansas, 1922—*Continued

Apparatus and species	White River		Horseshoe Lake		Miscellaneous waters		Total	
	Pounds	*Value*	*Pounds*	*Value*	*Pounds*	*Value*	*Pounds*	*Value*
Fyke nets:								
Black bass	2,200	$180			120	$15	6,270	$640
Bowfin							35,000	350
Buffalofish	741,700	32,645			222,108	15,491	1,996,948	116,197
Carp, German	73,310	2,552			16,312	1,105	264,671	13,371
Catfish and bullheads	32,700	2,337			20,715	2,254	169,765	15,946
Crappie	17,800	1,100			360	60	33,400	2,255
Drum, fresh-water	106,050	2,905			58,279	3,939	477,889	25,439
Paddlefish or spoonbill cat	2,400	274			17,190	1,746	33,340	3,000
Paddlefish caviar	26	78			144	470	439	1,233
Pike perch, wall-eyed					1,100	165	1,100	165
Quillback or American carp							2,100	115
Rock bass							1,600	150
Suckers	500	15			1,630	125	6,430	566
Sunfish							2,600	235
White bass					750	75	5,350	426
Turtles							300	6
Total	976,686	42,086			338,708	25,445	3,037,202	180,094
Set lines:								
Black bass	200	16					768	61
Bowfin							5,000	50
Buffalofish	26,913	1,541	9,650	$519	4,250	346	91,895	6,603
Carp, German	10,070	323					40,620	2,779
Catfish and bullheads	312,275	22,132	13,150	1,048	45,880	4,926	707,236	60,425
Crappie	100	6					100	6
Drum, fresh-water	32,200	1,447			19,670	1,793	206,306	15,170
Paddlefish or spoonbill cat	88,980	10,374			17,300	2,028	155,137	16,839
Paddlefish caviar	858	2,504			475	1,420	1,756	5,013
Sturgeon, shovelnose	5,100	380					5,750	413
White bass							400	32
Total	476,696	38,723	22,800	1,567	87,575	10,513	1,214,968	107,391
Haul seines:								
Black bass	4,200	340			200	20	4,500	375
Buffalofish	332,400	16,184	60,000	3,000	131,875	8,020	794,295	44,864
Carp, German	27,900	827	16,625	500	1,400	56	140,185	6,838
Catfish and bullheads	35,570	2,264	1,500	225	5,500	430	92,470	8,754
Crappie	55,600	3,566	15,000	1,500	2,000	20	71,300	5,161
Drum, fresh-water	78,725	2,023	5,000	85	7,600	261	191,820	9,008
Paddlefish or spoonbill cat	9,300	602			11,335	845	106,295	7,369
Paddlefish caviar	121	361					226	586
White bass	200	10					500	25
Total	544,016	26,177	98,125	5,310	158,110	9,652	1,401,591	82,980
Trammel nets:								
Black bass	1,300	124					1,300	124
Buffalofish	114,350	5,080	111,800	6,318	39,675	2,860	426,675	23,379
Carp, German	13,000	407	15,475	710	13,945	1,053	70,770	3,575
Catfish and bullheads	13,900	997	7,800	546	4,900	482	38,500	3,000
Crappie	5,600	581					5,900	608
Drum, fresh-water	20,985	558	6,650	399	11,650	920	48,170	2,387
Paddlefish or spoonbill cat	1,540	79			3,000	300	5,840	478
Paddlefish caviar	50	150					55	163
Total	170,725	7,976	141,725	7,973	73,170	5,615	597,210	33,714
Gill nets:								
Buffalofish	38,000	2,020	19,000	950	30,000	2,380	141,500	8,545
Carp, German	11,000	325	8,650	300	1,000	60	21,650	747
Catfish and bullheads	5,000	330			100	8	5,450	382
Drum, fresh-water	3,650	108			600	40	5,300	226
Paddlefish or spoonbill cat	13,100	1,305			1,000	100	38,000	3,908
Paddlefish caviar	298	824			53	159	1,601	3,608
Suckers							100	13
Total	71,048	4,912	27,650	1,250	32,753	2,747	213,601	17,429

Yield, by apparatus and waters, of the fisheries of Arkansas, 1922—Continued

Apparatus and species	White River		Horseshoe Lake		Miscellaneous waters		Total	
	Pounds	*Value*	*Pounds*	*Value*	*Pounds*	*Value*	*Pounds*	*Value*
Pound nets:								
Buffalofish							1,560	$105
Carp, German							200	16
Catfish and bullheads							200	30
Drum, fresh-water							3,550	120
Total							5,510	271
Hand lines:								
Black bass	240	$50			5,050	$894	8,142	1,060
Catfish and bullheads					1,000	100	1,000	100
Crappie	720	150			7,700	1,115	25,070	3,428
Drum, fresh-water					450	22	1,100	122
Sunfish					1,000	200	1,500	250
Total	960	200			15,200	2,331	36,812	5,260
Gigs :Frogs							5,100	695
Crowfoot bars:								
Mussel shells	5,880,000	116,605			20,000	150	7,780,000	151,035
Pearls		5,320						6,500
Slugs		3,980				25		4,855
Total	5,880,000	125,905			20,000	175	7,780,000	162,390
Tongs, rakes, forks, etc.:								
Mussel shells	4,528,667	96,190			928,700	12,012	8,502,367	159,579
Pearls		4,220				190		7,490
Slugs		620				235		2,454
Total	4,528,667	101,030			928,700	12,437	8,502,367	169,523
Total by species:								
Black bass	8,140	710			5,370	929	20,980	2,560
Bowfin							40,000	400
Buffalofish	1,253,363	57,	200,450	$10,787	427,908	29,097	3,452,873	199,693
Carp, German	135,280	4,	40,750	1,510	32,657	2,274	538,096	27,326
Catfish and bullheads	399,445	28,	22,450	1,819	78,095	8,200	1,014,621	88,637
Crappie	79,820	5,470	15,000	1,500	8,260	1,195	135,770	11,458
Drum, fresh-water	241,610	7,660	11,650	484	98,249	6,975	934,135	52,472
Paddlefish or spoonbill cat	115,320	12,634			49,825	5,019	338,612	31,594
Paddlefish caviar	1,353	3,917			672	2,049	4,077	10,603
Pike perch, wall-eyed					1,100	165	1,100	165
Quillback or American carp							2,100	115
Rock bass							1,600	150
Sturgeon, shovelnose	5,100	380					5,750	413
Suckers	500	15			1,630	125	6,530	579
Sunfish					1,000	200	4,100	485
White bass	200	10			750	75	6,250	483
Frogs							5,100	695
Turtles							300	6
Mussel shells	10,408,667	212,795			948,700	12,162	16,282,367	310,614
Pearls		9,540				190		13,990
Slugs		4,600				260		7,309
Total	12,648,798	347,009	290,300	16,100	1,654,216	68,915	22,794,361	759,747

ILLINOIS

Illinois ranks first among the Mississippi River States in the extent of its fisheries on the Mississippi River and tributaries. In 1922 there were 1,905 fishermen and 575 shoresmen engaged, most of the latter being connected either with the mussel fishery or in factories where button blanks were made. The total investment in boats, apparatus, shore property, and cash capital amounted to $618,111. There were 948 gasoline boats, with a value of $118,693; 1,277 row-boats and scows, valued at $32,697; and 103 houseboats, worth $31,700. The most important forms of apparatus were haul seines and fyke nets, there being 124 of the former, valued at $38,065;

and 14,552 of the latter, valued at $130,418. Set lines were also quite commonly used. The products of Illinois amounted to 22,597,996 pounds, valued at $1,077,965. Of these mussel shells contributed 9,265,000 pounds, valued at (including pearls and slugs) $264,395, giving Illinois third rank among mussel-producing States. Among the fish proper, carp was the most valuable species, with a catch of 7,734,264 pounds, valued at $367,554; other important species were buffalofish, 3,051,608 pounds, valued at $215,261; catfish and bullheads, 919,399 pounds, worth $113,267; and drum or sheepshead, 504,760 pounds, valued at $39,296.

The Illinois River, with its valuable carp and buffalofish, ranks first among the rivers of the State. Its total output in 1922 amounted to 10,607,372 pounds, valued at $551,013. The Mississippi River ranks second, with a catch of 3,033,524 pounds, valued at $212,574. The Rock River ranks next in importance, with a total output of 2,872,000 pounds, valued at $109,820, consisting entirely of mussel shells, pearls, and slugs. It is one of the most prolific mussel streams in the country. Both the Wabash and the Ohio Rivers contribute considerably to the value of the fishery resources of the State, mussel shells, pearls, and slugs furnishing about one-half of the value of their products.

The following tables give the detailed statistics of the fisheries of this State in 1922:

Persons engaged and investment in the fisheries of Illinois, 1922

Waters	Persons engaged			Gasoline boats		Rowboats, etc.		House boats		Haul seines		
	Fishermen	Shoresmen	Total	No.	Val.	No.	Val.	No.	Val.	No.	Yds.	Val.
Big Muddy River	3		3			3	$35					
Embarras River	10		10	1	$100	10	110					
Fox River	119		119			119	1,890					
Illinois River	478	159	1 641	2 235	43,236	367	16,830	64	$24,950	91	32,890	$32,175
Iroquois River	15		15			15	150					
Kankakee River	93		93			93	930					
Kaskaskia River	23	2	25	1	150	20	225					
Little Vermillion River	3		3			3	30					
Little Wabash River	8		8			8	80					
Mississippi River	387	301	688	220	27,782	250	7,147	14	4,250	33	5,175	4,060
Ohio River	329	31	360	182	14,175	159	2,145	14	1,400			
Pecatonica River	28		28	27	4,050	10	150					
Rock River	214		214	170	19,650	71	1,030					
Wabash River	195	82	277	112	9,550	149	1,945	11	1,100			
Total	1,905	575	2,484	948	118,693	1,277	32,697	103	31,700	124	38,065	36,235

Waters	Fyke nets		Crowfoot bars, pairs		Set lines		Gill nets			Forks	
	No.	Val.	No.	Val.	No.	Val.	No.	Yds.	Val.	No.	Val.
Big Muddy River	15	$150			16	$16					
Embarras River	8	80	2	$40	6	6				2	$10
Fox River	20	60	34	680						16	48
Illinois River	8,984	79,070	57	1,140	448	3,259	3	1,500	$900		
Kaskaskia River	72	550									
Mississippi River	4,301	39,308	41	395	620	1,311	235	11,750	2,350	2	3
Ohio River	618	5,860	280	5,600	492	492					
Pecatonica River			27	270							
Rock River			214	2,140							
Wabash River	534	5,340	175	3,500	340	340				135	675
Total	14,552	130,418	830	13,765	1,922	5,424	238	13,250	3,250	155	736

[1] Includes 4 men on two transporting vessels.
[2] Includes two transporting vessels with a net tonnage of 18 and a value of $4,200.

Persons engaged and investment in the fisheries of Illinois, 1922—Continued

Waters	Trammel nets			Dredges		Dip nets		Hand lines	Shore prop- erty	Cash capital	Total invest- ment
	No.	Yds.	Val.	No.	Val.	No.	Val.	Val.	Val.	Val.	Val.
Big Muddy River									$35		$236
Embarras River									200		546
Fox River									1,570		4,248
Illinois River				5	$25	15	$150		98,239	$17,900	317,874
Iroquois River									300		450
Kankakee River									1,860		2,790
Kaskaskia River								$14	520		1,459
Little Vermillion River									60		90
Little Wabash River									160		240
Mississippi River	9	900	$860						93,245	3,000	183,711
Ohio River									10,915		40,587
Pecatonica River									125		4,595
Rock River									800		23,620
Wabash River									15,215		37,665
Total	9	900	860	5	25	15	150	14	223,244	20,900	618,111

Yield, by apparatus and waters, of the fisheries of Illinois, 1922

Apparatus and waters	Black bass		Bowfin		Buffalofish		Carp	
	Pounds	Value	Pounds	Value	Pounds	Value	Pounds	Value
Haul seines:								
Illinois River			85,965	$3,808	1,764,103	$113,988	4,976,939	$224,314
Mississippi River			5,100	254	102,000	9,600	249,000	15,080
Total			91,065	4,062	1,866,103	123,588	5,225,939	239,394
Fykes:								
Big Muddy River					4,500	450	7,000	420
Embarras River					800	80	2,000	200
Illinois River			15,700	715	469,330	29,812	1,166,600	52,330
Kaskaskia River					7,700	840	7,900	865
Mississippi River	4,000	$400			424,275	38,381	737,100	40,344
Ohio River					46,300	4,174	55,500	5,050
Wabash River					38,500	2,634	43,000	2,932
Total	4,000	400	15,700	715	991,405	76,371	2,019,100	102,141
Set lines:								
Embarras River					400	40	1,000	100
Illinois River					36,600	2,112	93,000	3,600
Mississippi River	800	80			32,200	2,684	88,400	4,102
Ohio River					15,400	1,344	39,700	3,590
Wabash River					16,800	1,148	37,400	2,546
Total	800	80			101,400	7,328	259,500	13,938
Gill nets:								
Illinois River			400	20	65,000	4,550	198,000	9,900
Mississippi River					18,000	2,700	12,000	1,320
Total			400	20	83,000	7,250	210,000	11,220
Trammel nets: Mississippi River					8,200	594	19,025	791
Dip nets: Illinois River					1,000	70		
Hand lines: Kaskaskia River					500	60	700	70
Total by waters:								
Big Muddy River					4,500	450	7,000	420
Embarras River					1,200	120	3,000	300
Illinois River			102,065	4,543	2,336,033	150,532	6,434,539	290,144
Kaskaskia River					8,200	900	8,600	935
Mississippi River	4,800	480	5,100	254	584,675	53,959	1,105,525	61,637
Ohio River					61,700	5,518	95,200	8,640
Wabash River					55,300	3,782	80,400	5,478
Total	4,800	480	107,165	4,797	3,051,608	215,261	7,734,264	367,554

Yield, by apparatus and waters, of the fisheries of Illinois, 1922—Continued

Apparatus and waters	Catfish and bullheads		Crappie		Drum, fresh-water, or sheepshead		Eels	
	Pounds	Value	Pounds	Value	Pounds	Value	Pounds	Value
Haul seines:								
Illinois River	205,344	$30,948	57,248	$4,731	40,800	$2,771		
Mississippi River	24,000	3,170	5,000	440	30,000	2,690		
Total	229,344	34,118	62,248	5,171	70,800	5,461		
Fykes:								
Big Muddy River					2,000	120		
Embarras River	2,000	200			1,000	100		
Illinois River	140,500	19,490	50,767	3,974	28,100	1,880		
Kaskaskia River	6,800	1,120			5,100	620		
Mississippi River	142,700	16,865	8,700	742	187,900	14,958		
Ohio River	42,500	3,860			40,300	3,594		
Wabash River	36,800	2,508			29,800	2,044		
Total	371,300	44,043	59,467	4,716	294,200	23,316		
Set lines:								
Big Muddy River	6,000	825			2,000	120		
Embarras River	1,000	100			1,000	100		
Illinois River	45,000	4,820			11,600	735	6,500	$325
Mississippi River	202,300	23,748	800	80	70,400	5,462	4,000	215
Ohio River	43,000	3,870			24,100	2,108		
Wabash River	42,000	2,922			25,100	1,740		
Total	339,300	36,285	800	80	134,200	10,265	10,500	540
Gill nets: Illinois River	2,000	200	120	24	210	14		
Trammel nets: Mississippi River	16,955	1,696	1,075	65	5,250	220		
Hand lines: Kaskaskia River	500	125			100	20		
Total by waters:								
Big Muddy River	6,000	825			4,000	240		
Embarras River	3,000	300			2,000			
Illinois River	352,844	52,258	108,135	8,729	80,710	5,	6,500	325
Kaskaskia River	7,300	1,245			5,200			
Mississippi River	385,955	45,479	15,575	1,327	293,550		4,000	215
Ohio River	85,500	7,730			64,400	200		
Wabash River	78,800	5,430			54,900	23,564		
Total	919,399	113,267	123,710	10,056	504,760	39,296	10,500	540

Apparatus and waters	Paddlefish or spoonbill cat		Pike perch, wall-eyed		Quillback, or American carp		Sturgeon, shovelnose	
	Pounds	Value	Pounds	Value	Pounds	Value	Pounds	Value
Haul seines:								
Illinois River	21,200	$1,640						
Mississippi River	29,500	2,715	500	$25			2,000	$100
Total	50,700	4,355	500	25			2,000	100
Fykes:								
Embarras River					1,000	$100		
Mississippi River	11,000	830					48,000	3,680
Ohio River					49,500	4,390	4,800	432
Wabash River					40,300	2,726		
Total	11,000	830			90,800	7,216	52,800	4,112
Set lines:								
Embarras River							100	10
Illinois River							2,000	200
Mississippi River							6,000	600
Ohio River							10,200	974
Wabash River							17,900	1,228
Total							36,200	3,012
Total by waters:								
Embarras River					1,000	100	100	10
Illinois River	61,200	4,840					2,000	200
Mississippi River	40,500	3,545	500	25			56,000	4,380
Ohio River					49,500	4,390	15,000	1,406
Wabash River					40,300	2,726	17,900	1,228
Total	101,700	8,385	500	25	90,800	7,216	91,000	7,224

Yield, by apparatus and waters, of the fisheries of Illinois, 1922—Continued

Apparatus and waters	Sturgeon, shovelnose, caviar		Sturgeon, shovelnose, eggs		Suckers		Sunfish	
	Pounds	*Value*	*Pounds*	*Value*	*Pounds*	*Value*	*Pounds*	*Value*
Haul seines:								
Illinois River					38, 500	$1, 710	100, 217	$8, 542
Mississippi River					9, 000	620	2, 500	200
Total					47, 500	2, 330	102, 717	8, 742
Fykes:								
Embarras River					2, 000	200		
Illinois River					26, 500	1, 155	64, 700	4, 891
Mississippi River	95	$185	449	$764	19, 300	1, 352	8, 175	734
Ohio River					54, 200	4, 824		
Wabash River					35, 600	2, 412		
Total	95	185	449	764	137, 600	9, 943	72, 875	5, 625
Set lines:								
Ohio River					9, 000	720		
Wabash River					4, 800	336	500	50
Total					13, 800	1, 056	500	50
Gill nets: Illinois River					2, 000	100	200	20
Trammel nets: Mississippi River							525	26
Dip nets: Illinois River					10, 000	500		
Total by waters:								
Embarras River					2, 000	200		
Illinois River					77, 000	3, 465	165, 117	13, 453
Mississippi River	95	185	449	764	28, 300	1, 972	11, 200	960
Ohio River					63, 200	5, 544		
Wabash River					40, 400	2, 748	500	50
Total	95	185	449	764	210, 900	13, 929	176, 817	14, 463

Apparatus and waters	White bass		Yellow bass		Yellow perch		Other fish		Frogs	
	Pounds	*Value*	*Pounds*	*Value*	*Pounds*	*Value*	*Pounds*	*Value*	*Pounds*	*Value*
Haul seines:										
Illinois River	14, 100	$1, 240	3, 200	$256	9, 100	$788	38, 000	$2, 050	560	$224
Mississippi River	2, 900	214	700	56	2, 500	200	3, 000	170		
Total	17, 000	1, 454	3, 900	312	11, 600	988	41, 000	2, 220	560	224
Fykes:										
Illinois River	12, 600	1, 113	2, 900	232	9, 100	791	22, 500	1, 395		
Mississippi River	2, 000	160	700	56	1, 500	120	4, 000	240		
Total	14, 600	1, 273	3, 600	288	10, 600	911	26, 500	1, 635		
Set lines: Illinois River							600	42		
Gill nets: Illinois River	100	10			50	5	140	10		
Forks, dredges, etc.: Illinois River									2, 729	272
Total by waters:										
Illinois River	26, 800	2, 363	6, 100	488	18, 250	1, 584	61, 240	3, 497	3, 289	496
Mississippi River	4, 900	374	1, 400	112	4, 000	320	7, 000	410		
Total	31, 700	2, 737	7, 500	600	22, 250	1, 904	68, 240	3, 907	3, 289	496

Yield, by apparatus and waters, of the fisheries of Illinois, 1922—Continued

Apparatus and waters	Turtles		Mussel shells		Pearls	Slugs	Total	
	Pounds	Value	Pounds	Value	Value	Value	Pounds	Value
Haul seines:								
Illinois River	58,900	$418					7,414,176	$397,428
Mississippi River	12,000	40					479,700	35,574
Total	70,900	458					7,893,876	433,002
Fykes:								
Big Muddy River							13,500	990
Embarras River							8,800	880
Illinois River	650	26					2,009,947	117,804
Kaskaskia River							27,500	3,445
Mississippi River							1,599,894	119,811
Ohio River							293,100	26,324
Wabash River							224,000	15,256
Total	650	26					4,176,741	284,510
Crowfoot bars:								
Embarras River			8,000	$160	$25	$16	8,000	201
Fox River			238,000	9,520	420	260	238,000	10,200
Illinois River			596,000	5,906	675	386	596,000	6,967
Mississippi River			342,000	8,180	755	615	342,000	9,550
Ohio River			1,806,000	32,045	1,050	3,100	1,806,000	36,195
Pecatonica River			210,000	5,150	100	177	210,000	5,427
Rock River			2,828,000	99,890	1,845	6,655	2,828,000	108,390
Wabash River			911,000	16,255	1,515	1,820	911,000	19,590
Total			6,939,000	177,106	6,385	13,029	6,939,000	196,520
Set lines:								
Big Muddy River							8,000	945
Embarras River							3,500	350
Illinois River							195,300	11,834
Mississippi River							404,900	36,971
Ohio River							141,400	12,606
Wabash River							144,500	9,970
Total							897,600	72,676
Gill nets:								
Illinois River							268,220	14,853
Mississippi River							30,000	4,020
Total							298,220	18,873
Trammel nets: Mississippi River							51,030	3,392
Dip nets: Illinois River							11,000	570
Hand lines: Kaskaskia River							1,800	275
Forks, dredges, etc.:								
Embarras River			88,000	2,560	65	116	88,000	2,741
Fox River			400,000	13,530	645	419	400,000	14,594
Illinois River			110,000	1,210		75	112,729	1,557
Iroquois River			150,000	4,500	150	152	150,000	4,802
Kankakee River			726,000	21,780	620	920	726,000	23,320
Kaskaskia River			104,000	1,560	1,285	35	104,000	2,880
Little Vermillion River			44,000	660	25	44	44,000	729
Little Wabash River			30,000	900	25	40	30,000	965
Mississippi River			126,000	3,256			126,000	3,256
Rock River			44,000	1,320	45	65	44,000	1,430
Wabash River			504,000	9,215	1,650	1,008	504,000	11,873
Total			2,326,000	60,491	4,510	2,874	2,328,729	68,147
Total by waters:								
Big Muddy River							21,500	1,935
Embarras River			96,000	2,720	90	132	108,300	4,172
Fox River			638,000	23,050	1,065	679	638,000	24,794
Illinois River	59,550	444	706,000	7,116	675	461	10,607,372	551,013
Iroquois River			150,000	4,500	150	152	150,000	4,802
Kankakee River			726,000	21,780	620	920	726,000	23,320
Kaskaskia River			104,000	1,560	1,285	35	133,300	6,600
Little Vermillion River			44,000	660	25	44	44,000	729
Little Wabash River			30,000	900	25	40	30,000	965
Mississippi River	12,000	40	468,000	11,436	755	615	3,033,524	212,574
Ohio River			1,806,000	32,045	1,050	3,100	2,240,500	75,125
Pecatonica River			210,000	5,150	100	177	210,000	5,427
Rock River			2,872,000	101,210	1,890	6,720	2,872,000	109,820
Wabash River			1,415,000	25,470	3,165	2,828	1,783,500	56,689
Total	71,550	484	9,265,000	237,597	10,895	15,903	22,597,996	1,077,965

INDIANA

In 1922 there were 1,821 fishermen and 568 shoresmen engaged in the fisheries of the Mississippi River and its tributaries in Indiana. Practically all of the shoresmen were connected with the pearl-button or allied industries. The total investment was $212,700. Some of the more important items of this investment were 675 gasoline boats, 1,375 rowboats, and 27 house boats, with a combined value of $73,540; 1,296 pairs of crowfoot bars, valued at $25,820, and 1,149 fyke nets, valued at $11,780; and shore property valued at $96,117. The total production of the State amounted to 12,577,050 pounds, valued at $437,411. Of this total, mussel shells contributed 11,144,-000 pounds, valued at $281,374, including pearls and slugs. This State ranked second, or next to Arkansas, in the value of its mussel fisheries. Among the more important species of fish taken were carp, with a production of 356,700 pounds, valued at $37,654; catfish, 284,700 pounds, valued at $30,519; drum or sheepshead, 233,700 pounds, valued at $26,204; quillback or American carp, 178,000 pounds, valued at $20,675; suckers, 156,100 pounds, valued at $18,050; and buffalofish, 174,650 pounds, valued at $17,841.

The more important rivers of the State, due to their mussel fisheries, are the Wabash, Ohio, East Fork of the White, and the Tippecanoe. Several rivers in the State produced shells only, no fish being taken commercially.

The following tables show in detail the statistics of the fisheries of this State in 1922:

Persons engaged and investment in the fisheries of Indiana, 1922

Waters	Persons engaged			Gasoline boats		Rowboats	
	Fishermen	Shoresmen	Total	No.	Value	No.	Value
	Number	Number	Number	No.	Value	No.	Value
Blackwater River	2		2			2	$20
Driftwood River	6		6			6	60
East Fork of White River	270	95	365	87	$8,700	245	2,450
Eel River	16		16			16	160
Mississinnewa River	5		5			5	50
Muscatook River	2		2			2	20
Ohio River	324	194	518	99	9,950	261	3,925
Tippecanoe River	303		303			303	3,030
Wabash River	798	53	851	461	34,275	440	4,525
West Fork of White River	31		31			31	310
White River	60	26	86	28	2,800	60	600
Yellow River	4		4			4	40
Total	1,821	368	2,189	675	55,725	1,375	15,190

Waters	House boats		Crowfoot bars, pairs		Fyke nets		Forks	
	No.	Value	No.	Value	No.	Value	No.	Value
East Fork of White River			194	$3,880			182	$910
Ohio River	17	$1,675	252	4,940	886	$9,150		
Wabash River	7	650	790	15,800	263	2,630	448	1,646
White River	3	300	60	1,200			60	300
Total	27	2,625	1,296	25,820	1,149	11,780	690	2,856

Persons engaged and investment in the fisheries of Indiana, 1922—Continued

Water	Set lines		Haul seines			Tongs		Shore property	Total investment
	No.	Value	No.	Yards	Value	No.	Value	Value	Value
Blackwater River								$40	$60
Driftwood River								120	180
East Fork of White River	262	$132				12	$60	20,246	36,378
Eel River								320	480
Mississinnewa River								100	150
Muscatook River								40	60
Ohio River	815	815	8	800	$775			32,736	63,966
Tippecanoe River								4,060	7,090
Wabash River	630	630				30	90	28,985	89,231
West Fork of White River								600	910
White River	115	85						8,790	14,075
Yellow River								80	120
Total	1,822	1,662	8	800	775	42	150	96,117	212,700

Yield, by apparatus, of the fisheries of Indiana, 1922

Apparatus	Buffalofish		Carp		Catfish		Drum, freshwater, or sheepshead	
	Pounds	Value	Pounds	Value	Pounds	Value	Pounds	Value
Fyke nets:								
Ohio River	75,700	$8,160	128,700	$14,794	78,300	$9,266	90,000	$10,848
Wabash River	19,600	1,408	27,800	2,052	22,100	1,608	16,900	1,236
Total	95,300	9,568	156,500	16,846	100,400	10,874	106,900	12,084
Set lines:								
East Fork of White River	10,600	1,220	21,600	2,380	21,400	2,500	12,800	1,440
Ohio River	25,550	2,797	63,600	7,062	81,700	9,372	44,800	5,504
Wabash River	32,200	2,936	99,000	9,436	69,700	6,478	45,200	4,146
White River	5,000	500	7,000	700	7,000	700	5,000	500
Total	73,350	7,453	191,200	19,578	179,800	19,050	107,800	11,590
Haul seines: Ohio River	6,000	820	9,000	1,230	4,500	595	19,000	2,530
Total by waters:								
East Fork of White River	10,600	1,220	21,600	2,380	21,400	2,500	12,800	1,440
Ohio River	107,250	11,777	201,300	23,086	164,500	19,233	153,800	18,882
Wabash River	51,800	4,344	126,800	11,488	91,800	8,086	62,100	5,382
White River	5,000	500	7,000	700	7,000	700	5,000	500
Total	174,650	17,841	356,700	37,654	284,700	30,519	233,700	26,204

Apparatus	Paddlefish or spoonbill cat		Quillback or American carp		Sturgeon, shovelnose		Sturgeon, shovelnose, caviar		Suckers	
	Lbs.	Value	Pounds	Value	Pounds	Value	Pounds	Value	Pounds	Value
Fyke nets:										
Ohio River			133,800	$16,105	8,950	$913			112,200	$12,916
Wabash River			21,200	1,520	4,800	384			12,900	884
Total			155,000	17,625	13,750	1,297			125,100	13,800
Set lines:										
East Fork of White River					3,300	394				
Ohio River					12,650	1,233			6,000	900
Wabash River					15,200	1,310				
White River					1,250	125				
Total					32,400	3,062			6,000	900
Haul seines: Ohio River	1,500	$195	23,000	3,050	1,100	149	250	$375	25,000	3,350
Total by waters:										
East Fork of White River					3,300	394				
Ohio River	1,500	195	156,800	19,155	22,700	2,295	250	375	143,200	17,166
Wabash River			21,200	1,520	20,000	1,694			12,900	884
White River					1,250	125				
Total	1,500	195	178,000	20,675	47,250	4,508	250	375	156,100	18,050

Yield, by apparatus, of the fisheries of Indiana, 1922—Continued

Apparatus	Sunfish		Mussel shells		Pearls	Slugs	Total	
	Pounds	Value	Pounds	Value	Value	Value	Pounds	Value
Crowfoot bars:								
East Fork of White River			910,000	$18,200	$1,940	$972	910,000	$21,112
Ohio River			1,499,000	26,361	650	2,168	1,499,000	29,179
Wabash River			2,441,000	56,710	1,882	2,948	2,441,000	61,540
White River			176,000	3,520	200	176	176,000	3,896
Total			5,026,000	104,791	4,672	6,264	5,026,000	115,727
Fyke nets:								
Ohio River							627,650	73,002
Wabash River	200	$16					125,500	9,108
Total	200	16					753,150	82,110
Forks:								
East Fork of White River			912,000	18,240	2,370	972	912,000	21,582
Wabash River			1,629,000	33,525	1,337	1,992	1,629,000	36,854
White River			178,000	3,560	300	176	178,000	4,036
Total			2,719,000	55,325	4,007	3,140	2,719,000	62,472
Set lines:								
East Fork of White River							69,700	7,934
Ohio River							234,300	26,868
Wabash River							261,300	24,306
White River							25,250	2,525
Total							590,550	61,633
Haul seines: Ohio River							89,350	12,294
Tongs: Wabash River			60,000	1,050	25	120	60,000	1,195
By hand:								
Blackwater River			4,000	120		4	4,000	124
Driftwood River			58,000	1,170	50	56	58,000	1,276
East Fork of White River			332,000	9,960	275	390	332,000	10,625
Eel River			134,000	4,020	125	132	134,000	4,277
Mississinewa River			62,000	1,560	50	50	62,000	1,660
Muscatook River			20,000	400		20	20,000	420
Tippecanoe River			1,490,000	44,700			1,490,000	44,700
Wabash River			1,078,000	32,340	535	1,042	1,078,000	33,917
West Fork of White River			131,000	3,930	110	151	131,000	4,191
Yellow River			30,000	750		40	30,000	790
Total			3,339,000	98,950	1,145	1,885	3,339,000	101,980
Total by waters:								
Blackwater River			4,000	120		4	4,000	124
Driftwood River			58,000	1,170	50	56	58,000	1,276
East Fork of White River			2,154,000	46,400	4,585	2,334	2,223,700	61,253
Eel River			134,000	4,020	125	132	134,000	4,277
Mississinewa River			62,000	1,560	50	50	62,000	1,660
Muscatook River			20,000	400		20	20,000	420
Ohio River			1,499,000	26,361	650	2,168	2,450,300	141,343
Tippecanoe River			1,490,000	44,700			1,490,000	44,700
Wabash River	200	16	5,208,000	123,625	3,779	6,102	5,594,800	166,920
West Fork of White River			131,000	3,930	110	151	131,000	4,191
White River			354,000	7,080	500	352	379,250	10,457
Yellow River			30,000	750		40	30,000	790
Total	200	16	11,144,000	260,116	9,849	11,409	12,577,050	437,411

IOWA

In 1922 there were 794 fishermen, 3,131 shoresmen, and 5 men on transporting vessels engaged in the fisheries and related industries of Iowa, and an investment in boats, apparatus, shore property, and cash capital of $1,981,570, giving the State first place among those in the Mississippi Valley both in number of persons engaged and investment. This is due to its pearl-button industry, centered at Muscatine, where it was first established in 1891. The total fishery production of the State amounted to 6,760,662 pounds, valued at $326,177, of which 2,453,000 pounds, valued at $56,793, belong to the mussel industry. The more important species of fish were carp, catfish, buffalofish, and drum or sheepshead.

The most important fisheries in this State are located on the Mississippi River, where the production in 1922 amounted to 77 per cent in amount and 82 per cent in value of the total output of fish and mussel shells in this State. Some fishing of lesser importance was done in various lakes and rivers under supervision of game wardens.

The following tables show in detail the statistics of the fisheries of this State in 1922:

Persons engaged and investment in the fisheries of Iowa, 1922

Waters	Persons engaged			Gasoline boats		Rowboats		House boats	
	Fishermen	Shoresmen	Total	Number	Value	Number	Value	Number	Value
	Number	Number	Number	Number	Value	Number	Value	Number	Value
Cedar River	2	2	4			1	$10		
Des Moines River	96	24	120	3	$450	60	600		
Iowa River	9	33	42			8	90		
Mississippi River	580	2,901	[1] 3,486	[2] 321	57,573	400	8,688	48	$9,085
Missouri River	36		36	2	350	31	849		
Skunk River	7	149	156			5	75		
Wapsipinicon River	24	11	35	1	150	21	215		
Miscellaneous lakes	40	11	51	1	700	3	125		
Total	794	3,131	3,930	328	59,223	529	10,652	48	9,085

Waters	Fyke nets		Haul seines			Set lines		Trammel nets		
	No.	Value	No.	Yards	Value	No.	Value	No.	Yards	Value
Des Moines River						35	$70			
Mississippi River	5,139	$65,720	65	13,485	$10,545	47	65	160	17,875	$12,905
Missouri River	203	1,196	5	580	458	3	4	21	1,478	958
Wapsipinicon River			1	400	1,000					
Miscellaneous lakes			5	4,416	4,750					
Total	5,342	66,916	76	18,881	16,753	85	139	181	19,353	13,863

Waters	Crowfoot bars, pairs		Forks		Hand lines	Dip nets		Shore property	Cash capital	Total investment
	No.	Value	No.	Value	Value	No.	Value	Value	Value	Value
Cedar River	1	$10						$10		$30
Des Moines River			38	$190	$64			2,240		3,614
Iowa River	9	90						12,303		12,483
Mississippi River	82	693	46	76		1	$12	1,606,965	$21,800	1,794,127
Missouri River								2,331		6,146
Skunk River								156,010		156,085
Wapsipinicon River	17	170						325		1,860
Miscellaneous lakes								1,650		7,225
Total	109	963	84	266	64	1	12	1,781,834	21,800	1,981,570

[1] Includes crew of one transporting vessel.
[2] Includes one transporting vessel of 14 net tonnage, valued at $4,000.

. : Yield, by apparatus and waters, of the fisheries of Iowa, 1922

Apparatus and waters	Black bass		Bowfin		Buffalofish		Carp	
	Pounds	*Value*	*Pounds*	*Value*	*Pounds*	*Value*	*Pounds*	*Value*
Fyke nets:								
Mississippi River	400	$52			355,016	$25,155	693,806	$28,369
Missouri River					2,475	223	16,900	1,475
Total	400	52			357,491	25,378	710,706	29,844
Haul seines:								
Mississippi River			4,000	$80	180,875	11,744	520,075	19,328
Missouri River					4,350	526	41,450	4,934
Wapsipinicon River					24,840	1,440	40,000	1,632
Miscellaneous lakes					60,165	5,081	164,450	12,971
Total			4,000	80	270,230	18,791	765,975	38,865
Trammel nets:								
Mississippi River					187,765	13,059	451,510	17,676
Missouri River					11,270	1,374	34,180	3,595
Total					199,035	14,433	485,690	21,271
Set lines:								
Des Moines River	200	24			4,900	560	23,800	1,600
Mississippi River					600	48	4,500	195
Total	200	24			5,500	608	28,300	1,795
Hand lines: Des Moines River	550	118			2,300	264	9,000	680
Dip nets: Mississippi River							1,500	75
Total by waters:								
Des Moines River	750	142			7,200	824	32,800	2,280
Mississippi River	400	52	4,000	80	724,256	50,006	1,671,391	65,643
Missouri River					18,095	2,123	92,560	10,004
Wapsipinicon River					24,840	1,440	40,000	1,632
Miscellaneous lakes					60,165	5,081	164,450	12,971
Total	1,150	194	4,000	80	834,556	59,474	2,001,171	92,530

Apparatus and waters	Catfish and bull heads		Crappie		Drum, fresh-water, or sheeps-head		Paddlefish, or spoonbill cat	
	Pounds	*Value*	*Pounds*	*Value*	*Pounds*	*Value*	*Pounds*	*Value*
Fyke nets:								
Mississippi River	389,239	$37,755	22,425	$1,454	169,888	$8,390	24,095	$1,550
Missouri River	13,083	2,255						
Total	402,322	40,010	22,425	1,454	169,888	8,390	24,095	1,550
Haul seines:								
Mississippi River	101,050	9,895	15,500	1,085	83,450	4,160	10,460	688
Missouri River	200	40						
Total	101,250	9,935	15,500	1,085	83,450	4,160	10,460	688
Trammel nets:								
Mississippi River	234,420	23,565	15,520	953	77,205	3,700	13,575	858
Missouri River	6,050	1,250						
Total	240,470	24,815	15,520	953	77,205	3,700	13,575	858
Set lines:								
Des Moines River	7,200	1,440	150	18				
Mississippi River	12,250	1,475			1,450	73	200	10
Missouri River	400	80						
Total	19,850	2,995	150	18	1,450	73	200	10
Hand lines: Des Moines River	4,000	900	1,400	159				
Dip nets: Mississippi River	250	30			150	8	600	30
Total by waters:								
Des Moines River	11,200	2,340	1,550	177				
Mississippi River	737,209	72,720	53,445	3,492	332,143	16,331	48,930	3,136
Missouri River	19,733	3,625						
Total	768,142	78,685	54,995	3,669	332,143	16,331	48,930	3,136

Yield, by apparatus and waters, of the fisheries of Iowa, 1922—Continued

Apparatus and waters	Pike perch, sauger		Pike perch, wall-eyed		Pike and pickerel		Quillback or American carp	
	Pounds	*Value*	*Pounds*	*Value*	*Pounds*	*Value*	*Pounds*	*Value*
Fyke nets: Mississippi River	400	$48					28,000	$810
Haul seines:								
Mississippi River	150	18	12,400	$1,800	15,000	$1,380	73,000	2,150
Wapsipinicon River							500	50
Total	150	18	12,400	1,800	15,000	1,380	73,500	2,200
Trammel nets: Mississippi River	1,700	204	3,000	450	5,100	470	26,200	673
Set lines:								
Des Moines River			350	35				
Mississippi River	30	4						
Total	30	4	350	35				
Hand lines: Des Moines River			400	46				
Total by waters:								
Des Moines River			750	81				
Mississippi River	2,280	274	15,400	2,250	20,100	1,850	127,200	3,633
Wapsipinicon River							500	50
Total	2,280	274	16,150	2,331	20,100	1,850	127,700	3,683

Apparatus and waters	Sturgeon, shovelnose		Sturgeon, shovelnose, caviar		Sunfish		White bass	
	Pounds	*Value*	*Pounds*	*Value*	*Pounds*	*Value*	*Pounds*	*Value*
Fyke nets: Mississippi River	100	$10			15,255	$772		
Haul seines: Missouri River	400	40			25,950	1,559	6,700	$665
Trammel nets: Mississippi River	30,500	2,280	795	$905	16,445	894		
Set lines:								
Des Moines River							100	12
Mississippi River	100	10						
Total	100	10					100	12
Total by waters:								
Des Moines River							100	12
Mississippi River	31,100	2,340	795	905	57,650	3,225	6,700	665
Total	31,100	2,340	795	905	57,650	3,225	6,800	677

Yield, by apparatus and waters, of the fisheries of Iowa, 1922—Continued

Apparatus and waters	Mussel shells		Pearls	Slugs	Total	
	Pounds	Value	Value	Value	Pounds	Value
Fyke nets:						
Mississippi River					1,698,624	$104,365
Missouri River					32,458	3,953
Total					1,731,082	108,318
Haul seines:						
Mississippi River					1,049,010	54,592
Missouri River					46,000	5,500
Wapsipinicon River					65,340	3,122
Miscellaneous lakes					224,615	18,052
Total					1,384,965	81,266
Trammel nets:						
Mississippi River					1,063,735	65,687
Missouri River					51,500	6,219
Total					1,115,235	71,906
Crowfoot bars:						
Cedar River	4,000	$80		$12	4,000	92
Iowa River	104,000	1,965	$90	215	104,000	2,270
Mississippi River	1,042,000	25,105	3,531	2,360	1,042,000	30,996
Wapsipinicon River	196,000	3,048	150	400	196,000	3,598
Total	1,346,000	30,198	3,771	2,987	1,346,000	36,956
Forks:						
Des Moines River	706,000	5,095		3,530	706,000	8,625
Mississippi River	212,000	6,245		1,240	212,000	7,485
Total	918,000	11,340		4,770	918,000	16,110
Set lines:						
Des Moines River					36,700	3,689
Mississippi River					19,130	1,815
Missouri River					400	80
Total					56,230	5,584
Hand lines: Des Moines River					17,650	2,167
Dip nets: Mississippi River					2,500	143
Hand:						
Mississippi River	154,000	2,620	150	150	154,000	2,920
Skunk River	35,000	737	10	60	35,000	807
Total	189,000	3,357	160	210	189,000	3,727
Total by waters:						
Cedar River	4,000	80		12	4,000	92
Des Moines River	706,000	5,095		3,530	760,350	14,481
Iowa River	104,000	1,965	90	215	104,000	2,270
Mississippi River	1,408,000	33,970	3,681	3,750	5,240,999	268,003
Missouri River					130,358	15,752
Skunk River	35,000	737	10	60	35,000	807
Wapsipinicon River	196,000	3,048	150	400	261,340	6,720
Miscellaneous lakes					224,615	18,052
Total	2,453,000	44,895	3,931	7,967	6,760,662	326,177

KANSAS

In the commercial fisheries of Kansas there were engaged 124 fishermen and 56 shoresmen, most of the latter being connected with the pearl-button industry. The investment of $25,793 was also mainly in the latter business. The total output of fishery products amounted to 615,236 pounds, valued at $26,062. The production of the more important species was as follows: 79,852 pounds of carp, valued at $7,754; 33,447 pounds of catfish, valued at $6,213; 48,967 pounds of buffalofish, valued at $4,831; and 437,100 pounds of mussel shells, valued, together with the slugs, at $5,255. Fyke nets, haul seines, set lines, and forks for mussels were the most important forms of apparatus used. The Kansas, Neosho, and Missouri Rivers were the main fishery streams.

The following tables show in detail the statistics of the fisheries of this State:

Persons engaged and investment in the fisheries of Kansas, 1922.

Waters	Persons engaged			Gasoline boats		Rowboats		House boats	
	Fishermen	Shoresmen	Total	No.	Value	No.	Value	No.	Value
	Number	*Number*	*Number*	*No.*	*Value*	*No.*	*Value*	*No.*	*Value*
Blue River	12		12			11	$155		
Cottonwood River	1		1			1	10		
Fall River	2		2			1	10		
Kansas River	40	1	41			31	595	3	$125
Missouri River	19		19	2	$135	15	205	1	50
Neosho River	49	55	104			41	438		
Osage River	1		1			1	12		
Total	124	56	180	2	135	101	1,425	4	175

Waters	Fyke nets		Haul seines			Set lines		Trammel nets		
	No.	Value	No.	Yards	Value	No.	Value	No.	Yards	Value
	No.	*Value*	*No.*	*Yards*	*Value*	*No.*	*Value*	*No.*	*Yards*	*Value*
Blue River	57	$456	6	425	$207	47	$75			
Kansas River	146	1,443	4	335	190	101	87	4	170	$90
Missouri River	55	470	3	430	430	2	4	8	410	288
Neosho River	30	254	5	275	165	59	81			
Total	288	2,623	18	1,465	992	209	247	12	580	378

Waters	Gill nets			Forks		Hand lines	Shore property	Total investment
	No.	Yards	Value	No.	Value	Value	Value	Value
	No.	*Yards*	*Value*	*No.*	*Value*	*Value*	*Value*	*Value*
Blue River							$1,455	$2,348
Cottonwood River				1	$3		50	63
Fall River				2	7		50	67
Kansas River							1,885	4,415
Missouri River	6	500	$230				775	2,587
Neosho River				21	67	$3	15,240	16,248
Osage River				1	3		50	65
Total	6	500	230	25	80	3	19,505	25,793

Yield, by apparatus and waters, of the fisheries of Kansas; 1922.

Apparatus and waters	Buffalofish		Carp		Catfish		Drum, fresh-water, or sheepshead	
	Pounds	Value	Pounds	Value	Pounds	Value	Pounds	Value
Fyke nets:								
Blue River	1,350	$196			2,450	$445		
Kansas River	3,905	577	22,210	$2,701	1,865	334	75	$10
Missouri River	1,430	143	7,620	762	600	120		
Neosho River	3,340	361	4,350	435	2,162	397	150	17
Total	10,025	1,277	34,180	3,898	7,077	1,296	225	27
Haul seines:								
Blue River	5,800	290			100	20		
Kansas River	5,300	625	3,000	300	2,600	520		
Missouri River	7,500	525	10,000	300	1,700	170		
Neosho River	13,400	1,360	9,400	940	1,200	240		
Total	32,000	2,800	22,400	1,540	5,600	950		
Set lines:								
Blue River	550	65			4,050	780		
Kansas River	125	17	1,730	209	9,200	1,750	80	8
Missouri River			100	10	200	40		
Neosho River	1,550	175	2,300	230	5,670	1,109	535	65
Total	2,225	257	4,130	449	19,120	3,679	615	73
Trammel nets:								
Kansas River	1,242	179	1,867	244	450	83	50	3
Missouri River	2,600	230	10,200	915	1,000	170		
Total	3,842	409	12,067	1,159	1,450	253	50	3
Gill nets: Missouri River	875	88	6,925	693	100	20		
Hand lines: Neosho River			150	15	100	15	100	15
Total by waters:								
Blue River	7,700	551			6,600	1,245		
Kansas River	10,572	1,398	28,807	3,454	14,115	2,687	205	21
Missouri River	12,405	986	34,845	2,680	3,600	520		
Neosho River	18,290	1,896	16,200	1,620	9,132	1,761	785	97
Total	48,967	4,831	79,852	7,754	33,447	6,213	990	118

24309—25†——7

Yield, by apparatus and waters, of the fisheries of Kansas, 1922—Continued

Apparatus and waters	Quillback, or American carp		Mussel shells		Slugs	Total	
	Pounds	Value	Pounds	Value	Value	Pounds	Value
Fyke nets:							
Blue River	3,050	$448				6,850	$1,089
Kansas River	2,855	425				30,910	4,047
Missouri River	1,375	138				11,025	1,163
Neosho River						10,002	1,210
Total	7,280	1,011				58,787	7,509
Haul seines:							
Blue River	2,100	135				7,600	445
Kansas River	3,300	555				14,600	2,000
Missouri River	400	8				19,600	1,003
Neosho River						24,000	2,540
Total	5,800	698				65,800	5,988
Set lines:							
Blue River						4,600	845
Kansas River						11,135	1,984
Missouri River						300	50
Neosho River						10,055	1,579
Total						26,090	4,458
Trammel nets:							
Kansas River	200	30				3,809	539
Missouri River	500	42				14,300	1,357
Total	700	72				18,109	1,896
Gill nets: Missouri River	1,100	110				9,000	911
Forks:							
Cottonwood River			95,945	$1,679	$50	95,945	1,729
Fall River			83,455	838	40	83,455	878
Neosho River			208,590	2,086	108	208,590	2,194
Osage River			49,110	430	24	49,110	454
Total			437,100	5,033	222	437,100	5,255
Hand lines: Neosho River						350	45
Total by waters:							
Blue River	5,150	583				19,050	2,379
Cottonwood River			95,945	1,679	50	95,945	1,729
Fall River			83,455	838	40	83,455	878
Kansas River	6,355	1,010				60,454	8,570
Missouri River	3,375	298				54,225	4,484
Neosho River			208,590	2,086	108	252,997	7,568
Osage River			49,110	430	24	49,110	454
Total	14,880	1,891	437,100	5,033	222	615,236	26,062

KENTUCKY

In 1922 there were 496 persons engaged in the fisheries and fishery industries of Kentucky, about one-third being shoresmen connected with the wholesale fish trade of Louisville and the pearl-button blank factories. Of the total investment of $250,446 a similar portion was employed in the above-mentioned industries. The total production amounted to 2,893,219 pounds, valued at $167,360, comprised mainly of catfish, buffalofish, carp, drum, suckers, and quillback, with mussels ranking between drum and suckers in value. Of the total output, 1,777,679 pounds, valued at $113,293, were taken in the Ohio River, and 490,500 pounds, valued at $32,850, in the comparatively small portion of the State bordering on the Mississippi River. The other rivers were of comparative unimportance.

The following tables show in detail the statistics of the fisheries of this State:

Persons engaged and investment in the fisheries of Kentucky, 1922

Waters	Persons engaged			Gasoline boats		Rowboats	
	Fisher-men	Shores-men	Total	Number	Value	Number	Value
	Number	Number	Number	Number	Value	Number	Value
Big Barren River	2		2			2	$25
Big Sandy River	2		2			2	70
Cumberland River	24		24	3	'$350	24	240
Green River	30		30			30	450
Mississippi River	41		41	12	2,250	23	240
Ohio River	259	128	387	85	12,800	216	3,365
Tennessee River	10		10	9	900	10	150
Total	368	128	496	109	16,300	307	4,540

Waters	House boats		Fyke nets		Set lines		Haul seines '		
	Number	Value	Number	Value	Number	Value	Number	Yards	Value
Big Sandy River			12	$300					
Cumberland River			106	1,060	30	$43			
Green River			180	1,800	180	180			
Mississippi River			310	3,400	140	140	2	200	$200
Ohio River	32	$3,350	843	8,855	808	808	10	1,000	1,000
Tennessee River	2	200	37	390	43	43			
Total	34	3,550	1,488	15,805	1,201	1,214	12	1,200	1,200

Waters	Crowfoot bars, pairs		Tongs		Shore property	Cash capital	Total in-vestment
	Number	Value	Number	Value	Value	Value	Value
Big Barren River					$25		$50
Big Sandy River					10		380
Cumberland River	9	$115	9	$90	150		2,048
Green River					360		2,790
Mississippi River					325		6,555
Ohio River	137	2,740			184,822	$19,000	236,740
Tennessee River	10	100			100		1,883
Total	156	2,955	9	90	185,792	19,000	250,446

Yield, by apparatus and waters, of the fisheries of Kentucky, 1922

Apparatus and waters	Black bass		Buffalofish		Carp		Catfish	
	Pounds	*Value*	*Pounds*	*Value*	*Pounds*	*Value*	*Pounds*	*Value*
Fyke nets:								
Big Sandy River			20	$4	367	$69	1,735	$325
Cumberland River			11,500	1,475	1,600	195	2,600	360
Green River			13,800	1,104	15,000	1,200	4,500	360
Mississippi River			110,000	8,300	102,500	4,625	50,000	5,000
Ohio River	60	$10	95,245	11,428	111,336	12,821	52,593	6,733
Tennessee River			2,400	258	2,300	248	2,700	405
Total	60	10	232,965	22,569	233,103	19,158	114,128	13,183
Set lines:								
Cumberland River			2,000	245	500	64	5,500	775
Green River			3,000	240	4,200	336	15,000	1,200
Mississippi River			12,000	860	12,000	500	68,000	6,800
Ohio River			17,700	1,982	37,900	4,121	78,200	9,801
Tennessee River			1,100	126	500	54	8,200	1,230
Total			35,800	3,453	55,100	5,075	174,900	19,806
Haul seines:								
Mississippi River			5,000	300	5,000	150	500	50
Ohio River			5,000	650	5,000	650	4,000	600
Total			10,000	950	10,000	800	4,500	650
Total by waters:								
Big Sandy River			20	4	367	69	1,735	325
Cumberland River			13,500	1,720	2,100	259	8,100	1,135
Green River			16,800	1,344	19,200	1,536	19,500	1,560
Mississippi River			127,000	9,460	119,500	5,275	118,500	11,850
Ohio River	60	10	117,945	14,060	154,236	17,592	134,793	17,134
Tennessee River			3,500	384	2,800	302	10,900	1,635
Grand total	60	10	278,765	26,972	298,203	25,033	293,528	33,639

Apparatus and waters	Crappie		Drum		Paddlefish or spoonbill cat		Paddlefish caviar	
	Pounds	*Value*	*Pounds*	*Value*	*Pounds*	*Value*	*Pounds*	*Value*
Fyke nets:								
Big Sandy River	33	$6	3,400	$637				
Cumberland River			1,900	235	450	$68		
Green River			4,800	384				
Mississippi River			79,500	3,905	10,000	600		
Ohio River	442	33	86,528	10,448	1,135	175		
Tennessee River			5,100	546	230	27		
Total	475	39	181,228	16,155	11,815	870		
Set lines:								
Cumberland River			700	85				
Green River			3,000	240				
Mississippi River			34,000	1,620				
Ohio River			36,300	4,757				
Tennessee River			2,300	248				
Total			76,300	6,950				
Haul seines:								
Mississippi River					2,000	140		
Ohio River			12,000	1,500	1,200	166	150	$225
Total			12,000	1,500	3,200	306	150	225
Total by waters:								
Big Sandy River	33	6	3,400	637				
Cumberland River			2,600	320	450	68		
Green River			7,800	624				
Mississippi River			113,500	5,525	12,000	740		
Ohio River	442	33	134,828	16,705	2,335	341	150	225
Tennessee River			7,400	794	230	27		
Grand total	475	39	269,528	24,605	15,015	1,176	150	225

Yield, by apparatus and waters, of the fisheries of Kentucky, 1922—Continued

Apparatus and waters	Pike perch, sauger		Pike perch, wall-eyed		Quillback, or American carp		Sturgeon, lake	
	Pounds	*Value*	*Pounds*	*Value*	*Pounds*	*Value*	*Pounds*	*Value*
Fyke nets:								
Big Sandy River			670	$125	600	$113		
Cumberland River			450	68				
Green River					3,000	240		
Ohio River	1,765	$329	4,275	769	107,450	11,556	580	$85
Tennessee River					2,400	258		
Total	1,765	329	5,395	962	113,450	12,167	580	85
Haul seines: Ohio River					10,000	1,300		
Total by waters:								
Big Sandy River			670	125	600	113		
Green River			450	68	3,000	240		
Ohio River	1,765	329	4,275	769	117,450	12,856	580	85
Tennessee River					2,400	258		
Grand total	1,765	329	5,395	962	123,450	13,467	580	85

Apparatus and waters	Sturgeon, shovelnose		Sturgeon, shovelnose, caviar		Suckers		Sunfish	
	Pounds	*Value*	*Pounds*	*Value*	*Pounds*	*Value*	*Pounds*	*Value*
Fyke nets:								
Big Sandy River					935	$175		
Cumberland River					750	95		
Green River	200	$16			28,200	2,256		
Ohio River	5,850	637	50	$75	97,762	12,172	25	$4
Tennessee River					1,200	128		
Total	6,050	653	50	75	128,847	14,826	25	4
Set lines:								
Green River	100	8						
Ohio River	7,600	732						
Total	7,700	740						
Haul seines: Ohio River	500	65			14,000	1,820		
Total by waters:								
Big Sandy River					935	175		
Cumberland River					750	95		
Green River	300	24			28,200	2,256		
Ohio River	13,950	1,434	50	75	111,762	13,992	25	4
Tennessee River					1,200	128		
Grand total	14,250	1,458	50	75	142,847	16,646	25	4

Yield, by apparatus and waters, of the fisheries of Kentucky, 1922—Continued

Apparatus and waters	White bass		Mussel shells		Pearls	Slugs	Total	
	Pounds	*Value*	*Pounds*	*Value*	*Value*	*Value*	*Pounds*	*Value*
Fyke nets:								
Big Sandy River	100	$19					7, 860	$1, 47
Cumberland River							19, 250	2, 49
Green River							69, 500	5, 56
Mississippi River							352, 000	22, 43
Ohio River	33	7					565, 129	67, 28
Tennessee River							16, 330	1, 87
Total	133	26					1, 030, 069	101, 11
Set lines:								
Cumberland River							8, 700	1, 16
Green River							25, 300	2, 02
Mississippi River							126, 000	9, 78
Ohio River							177, 700	21, 39
Tennessee River							12, 100	1, 658
Total							349, 800	36, 024
Haul seines:								
Mississippi River							12, 500	640
Ohio River							51, 850	6, 976
Total							64, 350	7, 616
Crowfoot bars:								
Cumberland River			170, 000	$1, 275		$28	170, 000	1, 303
Ohio River			939, 000	16, 077	$95	1, 140	939, 000	17, 312
Tennessee River			216, 000	2, 970		28	216, 000	2, 998
Total			1, 325, 000	20, 322	95	1, 196	1, 325, 000	21, 613
Tongs, etc.:								
Big Barren River			40, 000	360			40, 000	360
Cumberland River			40, 000	300		6	40, 000	306
Ohio River			44, 000	330			44, 000	330
Total			124, 000	990		6	124, 000	996
Total by waters:								
Big Barren River			40, 000	360			40, 000	360
Big Sandy River	100	19					7, 860	1, 473
Cumberland River			210, 000	1, 575		34	237, 500	5, 206
Green River							95, 250	7, 652
Mississippi River							490, 500	32, 850
Ohio River	33	7	983, 000	16, 407	95	1, 140	1, 777, 679	113, 293
Tennessee River			216, 000	2, 970		28	244, 430	6, 526
Grand total	133	26	1, 449, 000	21, 312	95	1, 202	2, 893, 219	167, 360

LOUISIANA

In 1922 there were 2,088 fishermen, 157 shoresmen, and 7 men engaged in transporting vessels in Louisiana. Out of a total investment of $715,071 there were 969 gasoline boats, valued at $149,765, 1,958 rowboats, with a value of $33,864; 816 houseboats, valued at $100,685; 11,946 fyke nets, valued at $151,970; 102 haul seines, valued at $19,008; lines of all kinds, valued at $12,116; and shore property and cash capital, valued at $193,445 and $47,500, respectively, the remainder of the investment being divided among apparatus of lesser importance. Nearly one-half of the persons engaged and more than one-half of the investment are credited to the Atchafalaya River. Of a total catch from the Mississippi and all of its tributaries in the State, of 10,485,588 pounds, valued at $572,863, 4,579,220 pounds, valued at $254,651, were taken from the Atchafalaya River. Among other important fishery streams, in the order of their importance, were the Mississippi River with a catch of 915,011 pounds, valued at $67,569; Ouachita River, 818,354 pounds, valued at $58,284; Black River, 977,493 pounds, valued at $39,329;

and Lake Larto, with a catch of 1,096,504 pounds, valued at $38,234. The more important species, with the amount of each taken, were as follows: Buffalofish, 4,938,777 pounds, valued at $222,944; catfish, 3,229,056 pounds, valued at $207,350; drum or sheepshead, 1,439,368 pounds, valued at $52,633; and paddlefish or spoonbill cat, 422,478 pounds, valued at $36,560. To the paddlefish may be added 5,908 pounds of caviar, having a value to the fishermen of $13,956. Most of the paddlefish meat and caviar was shipped to New York City.

The following tables show in detail the statistics of the fisheries of this State:

Persons engaged and investment in the fisheries of Louisiana, 1922

Waters	Persons engaged			Gasoline boats		Rowboats, etc.	
	Fishermen	Shoresmen	Total	Number	Value	Number	Value
	Number	*Number*	*Number*	*Number*	*Value*	*Number*	*Value*
Atchafalaya River	920	88	1,012	672	$85,300	1,046	$21,160
Black River	112	13	125	35	4,650	107	1,615
Little River and Catahoula Lake	162	4	166	29	4,445	125	1,036
Mississippi River	313	6	319	61	17,710	263	3,906
Ouachita River	156	6	162	65	11,805	133	1,865
Red River	214	25	242	58	14,575	186	2,437
Tensas River	13	3	16	2	175	3	60
Lake Allemands	98	12	110	23	6,500	55	1,210
Lake Larto	46	--------	46	18	3,455	22	270
Miscellaneous waters	54	--------	54	6	1,150	18	305
Total	2,088	157	[1] 2,252	[2] 969	149,765	1,958	33,864

Waters	House boats		Fyke nets		Haul seines			Lines	Spears and gigs	
	Number	Value	Number	Value	Number	Yards	Value	Value	Number	Value
	Number	*Value*	*Number*	*Value*	*Number*	*Yards*	*Value*	*Value*	*Number*	*Value*
Atchafalaya River	679	$64,600	8,150	$119,000	15	3,200	$4,075	$7,300	398	$373
Black River	13	4,400	684	5,610	6	1,800	1,650	487	--------	------
Little River and Catahoula Lake	17	2,615	408	3,396	22	4,475	3,375	346	2	1
Mississippi River	17	3,190	170	1,404	6	1,225	1,358	1,174	--------	------
Ouachita River	37	9,855	987	8,566	10	2,050	1,940	1,452	--------	------
Red River	53	16,025	1,410	12,656	9	1,232	810	849	--------	------
Tensas River	--------	--------	26	238	2	400	400	7	--------	------
Lake Allemands	--------	--------	--------	--------	12	1,900	1,500	110	--------	------
Lake Larto	--------	--------	45	450	14	3,225	3,025	104	2	1
Miscellaneous waters	--------	--------	66	650	6	815	875	287	--------	------
Total	816	100,685	11,946	151,970	102	20,322	19,008	12,116	402	375

Waters	Shrimp traps		Guns		Dip nets		Shore property	Cash capital	Total investment
	Number	Value	Number	Value	Number	Value	Value	Value	Value
	Number	*Value*	*Number*	*Value*	*Number*	*Value*	*Value*	*Value*	*Value*
Atchafalaya River	--------	--------	30	$900	50	$100	$147,820	$35,700	$486,328
Black River	--------	--------	--------	--------	--------	--------	10,385	4,000	32,797
Little River and Catahoula Lake	--------	--------	--------	--------	--------	--------	2,655	800	18,669
Mississippi River	4,060	$3,963	40	1,200	--------	--------	3,295	500	37,700
Ouachita River	--------	--------	--------	--------	--------	--------	3,025	--------	38,508
Red River	--------	--------	--------	--------	--------	--------	21,300	4,000	72,652
Tensas River	--------	--------	--------	--------	--------	--------	1,180	--------	2,060
Lake Allemands	--------	--------	6	180	--------	--------	1,775	2,500	13,775
Lake Larto	--------	--------	--------	--------	--------	--------	735	--------	8,040
Miscellaneous waters	--------	--------	--------	--------	--------	--------	1,275	--------	4,542
Total	4,060	3,963	76	2,280	50	100	193,445	47,500	715,071

[1] Includes 7 men on three transporting vessels.
[2] Includes three transporting vessels with a net tonnage of 32 and value of $7,400.

Yield, by apparatus and waters, of the fisheries of Louisiana, 1922

Apparatus and waters	Buffalofish		Carp, German		Catfish		Drum, fresh-water or sheepshead	
	Pounds	*Value*	*Pounds*	*Value*	*Pounds*	*Value*	*Pounds*	*Value*
Fyke nets:								
Atchafalaya River	783, 412	$38, 390					356, 727	$12, 902
Black River	283, 104	9, 117			4, 600	$256	94, 452	1, 902
Little River and Catahoula Lake	219, 934	7, 939			2, 333	140	38, 948	714
Mississippi River	115, 150	5, 286	200	$20	29, 500	2, 233	25, 250	1, 198
Ouachita River	374, 534	17, 706			3, 950	248	76, 905	2, 958
Red River	562, 325	30, 621	430	35	15, 400	1, 528	153, 541	9, 442
Tensas River	14, 026	700					1, 458	30
Lake Larto	34, 200	1, 200			500	22	4, 000	100
Miscellaneous waters	22, 950	1, 970			2, 600	260	4, 550	333
Total	2, 409, 635	112, 929	630	55	58, 883	4, 687	755, 831	29, 579
Haul seines:								
Atchafalaya River	995, 000	47, 520					365, 000	12, 950
Black River	120, 000	3, 600					20, 000	300
Little River and Catahoula Lake	159, 219	4, 816			1, 371	40	19, 171	226
Mississippi River	87, 725	5, 143	41, 000	2, 500	12, 950	877	8, 500	252
Ouachita River	86, 400	4, 643			8, 600	677	7, 150	266
Red River	32, 200	2, 596			1, 155	87	3, 850	355
Lake Allemands	29, 992	909			200, 153	10, 007	5, 136	108
Lake Larto	733, 905	24, 300			88, 359	4, 149	99, 055	1, 975
Miscellaneous waters	157, 456	8, 459			650	43	3, 630	641
Total	2, 401, 897	101, 986	41, 000	2, 500	313, 238	15, 880	531, 492	17, 073
Lines:								
Atchafalaya River					1, 829, 665	121, 161		
Black River	7, 700	260			177, 714	8, 930	51, 000	1, 109
Little River and Catahoula Lake	4, 000	120			66, 485	3, 960	8, 676	130
Mississippi River	43, 395	2, 011			365, 200	28, 553	11, 925	505
Ouachita River	3, 600	138			145, 011	9, 972	8, 500	178
Red River	1, 250	50			74, 179	4, 295	65, 944	3, 896
Tensas River	60, 100	4, 803			3, 323	236	500	18
Lake Allemands					95, 000	4, 750		
Lake Larto	1, 000	35			95, 358	4, 476	5, 000	120
Miscellaneous waters	200	12			5, 000	450	500	25
Total	121, 245	7, 429			2, 856, 935	186, 783	152, 045	5, 981
Dipnets, etc: Miscellaneous waters	6, 000	600						
Total by waters:								
Atchafalaya River	1, 778, 412	85, 910			1, 829, 665	121, 161	721, 727	25, 852
Black River	510, 804	12, 977			182, 314	9, 186	165, 452	3, 311
Little River and Catahoula Lake	383, 153	12, 875			70, 189	4, 140	66, 795	1, 070
Mississippi River	246, 270	12, 440	41, 200	2, 520	407, 650	31, 663	45, 675	1, 955
Ouachita River	464, 534	22, 487			157, 561	10, 897	92, 555	3, 402
Red River	595, 775	33, 267	430	35	90, 734	5, 910	223, 335	13, 693
Tensas River	74, 126	5, 503			3, 323	236	1, 958	48
Lake Allemands	29, 992	909			295, 153	14, 757	5, 136	108
Lake Larto	769, 105	25, 535			184, 217	8, 647	108, 055	2, 195
Miscellaneous waters	186, 606	11, 041			8, 250	753	8, 680	999
Grand total	4, 938, 777	222, 944	41, 630	2, 555	3, 229, 056	207, 350	1, 439, 368	52, 633

Yield, by apparatus and waters, of the fisheries of Louisiana, 1922—Continued

Apparatus and waters	Eels		Garfish		Paddlefish or spoonbill cat		Paddlefish caviar	
	Pounds	Value	Pounds	Value	Pounds	Value	Pounds	Value
Fyke nets:								
Black River					2,500	$100		
Mississippi River			2,500	$50				
Ouachita River					3,500	350		
Red River					450	59	50	$141
Total			2,500	50	6,450	509	50	141
Haul seines:								
Black River					202,554	10,664	769	2,136
Little River and Catahoula Lake					6,637	477	375	658
Mississippi River					5,420	688	595	1,780
Ouachita River					30,900	4,385	1,430	3,544
Red River					6,850	998	200	605
Lake Larto			845	9	33,700	1,485	183	334
Miscellaneous waters			25	1	14,176	1,301	168	348
Total			870	10	300,237	19,998	3,720	9,405
Lines:								
Black River					13,000	655	100	300
Little River and Catahoula Lake					5,000	255	50	135
Mississippi River	1,100	$100			18,800	1,618	50	135
Ouachita River					66,554	11,051	1,320	2,168
Red River					4,088	639	218	657
Tensas River					2,349	235		
Miscellaneous waters					6,000	1,600	400	1,000
Total	1,100	100			115,791	16,053	2,138	4,410
Total by waters:								
Black River					218,054	11,419	869	2,436
Little River and Catahoula Lake					11,637	732	425	793
Mississippi River	1,100	100	2,500	50	24,220	2,306	645	1,930
Ouachita River					100,954	15,786	2,750	5,712
Red River					11,388	1,696	468	1,403
Tensas River					2,349	235		
Lake Larto			845	9	33,700	1,485	183	334
Miscellaneous waters			25	1	20,176	2,901	568	1,348
Grand total	1,100	100	3,370	60	422,478	36,560	5,908	13,956

Apparatus and waters	Sturgeon, shovelnose		Suckers		Shrimp		Crawfish	
	Pounds	Value	Pounds	Value	Pounds	Value	Pounds	Value
Fyke nets: Mississippi River	100	$10						
Lines: Mississippi River	180	15						
Shrimp traps: Mississippi River					142,182	$13,870		
Dip nets, etc:								
Atchafalaya River							7,265	$509
Red River			400	$28				
Total			400	28			7,265	509
Total by waters:								
Atchafalaya River							7,265	509
Mississippi River	280	25			142,182	13,870		
Red River			400	28				
Grand total	280	25	400	28	142,182	13,870	7,265	509

Yield, by apparatus and waters, of the fisheries of Louisiana, 1922—Continued

Apparatus and waters	Frogs		Turtles		Alligator hides		Total	
	Pounds	Value	Pounds	Value	Pounds	Value	Pounds	Value
Fyke nets:								
Atchafalaya River							1,140,139	$51,292
Black River							384,656	11,375
Little River and Catahoula Lake							261,215	8,793
Mississippi River							172,700	8,797
Ouachita River							458,889	21,262
Red River							732,196	41,826
Tensas River							15,484	730
Lake Larto							38,700	1,322
Miscellaneous waters							30,100	2,563
Total							3,234,079	147,960
Haul seines:								
Atchafalaya River							1,360,000	60,470
Black River							343,323	16,700
Little River and Catahoula Lake			1,500	$30			188,273	6,247
Mississippi River							156,190	11,240
Ouachita River							134,480	13,515
Red River							44,255	4,641
Lake Allemands							235,281	11,024
Lake Larto			169	3			956,216	32,255
Miscellaneous waters							176,105	10,793
Total			1,669	33			3,594,123	166,885
Lines:								
Atchafalaya River			10,227	290			1,839,892	121,451
Black River							249,514	11,254
Little River and Catahoula Lake			5,950	200			90,161	4,800
Mississippi River			300	8	1,242	$291	442,192	33,251
Ouachita River							224,985	23,507
Red River							145,679	9,537
Tensas River							66,272	5,292
Lake Allemands							95,000	4,750
Lake Larto							101,358	4,631
Miscellaneous waters							12,100	3,087
Total			16,477	498	1,242	291	3,267,153	221,560
Spears and gigs:								
Atchafalaya River	216,912	$17,367					216,912	17,367
Little River and Catahoula Lake	230	26					230	26
Lake Larto	230	26					230	26
Total	217,372	17,419					217,372	17,419
Shrimp traps: Mississippi River							142,182	13,870
Guns:								
Atchafalaya River					12,372	1,912	12,372	1,912
Mississippi River					1,747	411	1,747	411
Lake Allemands					255	59	255	59
Total					14,374	2,382	14,374	2,382
Dip nets, etc.:								
Atchafalaya River			2,640	1,650			9,905	2,159
Red River							400	28
Miscellaneous waters							6,000	600
Total			2,640	1,650			16,305	2,787
Total by waters:								
Atchafalaya River	216,912	17,367	12,867	1,940	12,372	1,912	4,579,220	254,651
Black River							977,493	39,329
Little River and Catahoula Lake	230	26	7,450	230			539,879	19,866
Mississippi River			300	8	2,989	702	915,011	67,569
Ouachita River							818,354	58,284
Red River							922,530	56,032
Tensas River							81,756	6,022
Lake Allemands					255	59	330,536	15,833
Lake Larto	230	26	169	3			1,096,504	38,234
Miscellaneous waters							224,305	17,043
Grand total	217,372	17,419	20,786	2,181	15,616	2,673	10,485,588	572,863

MINNESOTA

In 1922 a total of 514 fishermen and 205 shoresmen were engaged in the fisheries of the Mississippi River and its tributaries in Minnesota. Most of the shoresmen were connected with the wholesale fish trade of Minneapolis and St. Paul and the pearl-button industry. The same may be said of the shore property and cash capital, amounting, respectively, to $363,136 and $68,000. The total output of the State amounted to 5,659,555 pounds, valued at $230,425. Among the more valuable species were the carp, with a catch of 2,948,230 pounds, valued at $122,881, and buffalofish, 761,370 pounds, valued at $46,748. The output of mussel shells amounted to 1,571,196 pounds, valued at $36,427, together with $2,451 worth of pearls and slugs. Mussel shells were taken in various streams throughout the State, but about one-third of them were from the Mississippi River.

Important fisheries are conducted in many of the lakes throughout the State, under the supervision of State game wardens. The total catch from these amounted to 2,076,682 pounds, valued at $93,346, or more than one-third, in pounds and value, of the State's entire output from the Mississippi and its tributaries.

The following tables show in detail the statistics of the fisheries of this State:

Persons engaged and investment in the fisheries of Minnesota, 1922

Waters	Persons engaged			Gasoline boats		Row boats and scows		House boats	
	Fishermen	Shoresmen	Total						
	Number	Number	Number	Number	Value	Number	Value	Number	Value
Blue Earth River	2		2			3	$50		
Cedar River	2		2						
Cottonwood River	1		1			1	10		
Crow Wing River	10		10			10	150		
Des Moines River	6		6			6	60		
Minnesota River	54	1	55	7	$1,275	37	641		
Mississippi River	208	209	417	104	22,750	144	3,475	1	$150
Shell River	10		10	2	550	8	135		
St. Croix River	38		38	10	2,200	26	533		
Vermillion River	4		4	1	200	2	75		
White Water River	1		1			1	10		
Miscellaneous lakes	178	12	190	8	1,700	20	590		
Total	514	222	1 736	132	28,675	258	5,729	1	150

Waters	Haul seines			Crowfoot bars (pairs)		Fyke nets		Set lines	
	Number	Yards	Value	Number	Value	Number	Value	Number	Value
Blue Earth River				2	$25				
Cottonwood River				1	10				
Crow Wing River				10	150				
Des Moines River				2	20				
Minnesota River	9	1,262	$1,970	16	165	1	$35	9	$29
Mississippi River	49	13,100	16,890	30	300	353	5,190	43	56
Shell River				3	40				
St. Croix River	10	3,916	4,500					12	65
Vermillion River	1	235	225						
White Water River								1	5
Miscellaneous lakes	30	16,592	19,995	3	35				
Total	99	35,105	43,580	67	745	354	5,225	65	155

1 Includes 17 men connected with the wholesale fishery trade of North Dakota.

Persons engaged and investment in the fisheries of Minnesota, 1922—Continued

Waters	Gill nets			Pound nets		Forks		Rakes		Shore property	Cash capital	Total investment
	No.	Yards	Value	No.	Value	No.	Value	No.	Value	Value	Value	Value
Blue Earth River										$150		$225
Cedar River								2	$3			3
Cottonwood River										25		45
Crow Wing River										200		500
Des Moines River								1	4	100		184
Minnesota River				3	$160	1	$3			4,435		8,713
Mississippi River	10	6,730	$1,630							343,316	$73,000	466,757
Shell River						5	11			345		1,081
St. Croix River	14	650	210							4,180		11,688
Vermillion River										300		800
White Water River										15		30
Miscellaneous lakes										33,370		55,690
Total	24	7,380	1,840	3	160	6	14	3	7	386,436	73,000	[2] 545,716

[2] Includes $5,000 cash capital and $23,300 worth of shore property connected with the wholesale fishery trade of North Dakota.

Yield, by apparatus and waters, of the fisheries of Minnesota, 1922

Apparatus and waters	Bowfin		Buffalofish		Carp	
	Pounds	Value	Pounds	Value	Pounds	Value
Haul seines:						
Minnesota River	200	$10	15,024	$1,364	377,738	$14,475
Mississippi River	5,309	137	162,017	10,350	644,037	29,698
St. Croix River	2,658	45	54,596	2,428	304,020	7,001
Vermillion River					67,018	4,315
Miscellaneous lakes	5,632	179	494,747	29,511	1,385,722	58,294
Total	13,799	371	726,384	43,653	2,778,535	113,783
Fykes:						
Minnesota River			1,000	30	19,000	570
Mississippi River	1,000	20	21,900	2,195	98,500	6,445
St. Croix River			4,274	243		
Total	1,000	20	27,174	[2] 468	117,500	7,015
Set lines:						
Minnesota River			550	42	3,350	153
Mississippi River	600	19	82	5	12,445	485
St. Croix River					1,175	83
White Water River					500	50
Total	600	19	632	47	17,470	771
Gill nets:						
Mississippi River			3,430	296	23,100	867
St. Croix River			500	50	1,000	60
Total			3,930	346	24,100	927
Pound nets:						
Minnesota River	400	12	1,050	110	6,375	185
Mississippi River			2,200	124	4,250	200
Total	400	12	3,250	234	10,625	385
Total by waters:						
Minnesota River	600	22	17,624	1,546	406,463	15,383
Mississippi River	6,909	176	189,629	12,970	782,332	37,695
St. Croix River	2,658	45	59,370	2,721	306,195	7,144
Vermillion River					67,018	4,315
White Water River					500	50
Miscellaneous lakes	5,632	179	494,747	29,511	1,385,722	58,294
Total	15,799	422	761,370	46,748	2,948,230	122,881

Yield, by apparatus and waters, of the fisheries of Minnesota, 1922—Continued

Apparatus and waters	Catfish and bullheads		Drum, freshwater, or sheepshead		Eels		Quillback or American carp	
	Pounds	*Value*	*Pounds*	*Value*	*Pounds*	*Value*	*Pounds*	*Value*
Haul seines:								
Minnesota River	1,000	$100	4,030	$292			335	$19
Mississippi River	23,920	2,961	121,205	4,411			12,265	514
St Croix River	5,918	669	36,154	1,119	20	$2	2,330	83
Miscellaneous lakes			22,067	1,044				
Total	30,838	3,730	183,456	6,866	20	2	14,930	616
Fykes:								
Minnesota River	100	5						
Mississippi River	39,227	4,643	7,952	493	86	17		
St. Croix River	860	86	9,282	252				
Total	40,187	4,734	17,234	745	86	17		
Set lines:								
Minnesota River	2,600	230	400	40			50	5
Mississippi River	7,620	1,148	2,295	189	400	23	1,400	40
St. Croix River	991	114	50	5	34	6		
White Water River	100	15	50	5			200	20
Total	11,311	1,507	2,795	239	434	29	1,650	65
Gill nets: Mississippi River	1,015	87	700	22			2,500	77
Pound nets: Minnesota River	1,000	100	50	5				
Total by waters:								
Minnesota River	4,700	435	4,480	337			385	24
Mississippi River	71,782	8,839	132,152	5,115	486	40	16,165	631
St. Croix River	7,769	869	45,486	1,376	54	8	2,330	83
White Water River	100	15	50	5			200	20
Miscellaneous lakes			22,067	1,044				
Total	84,351	10,158	204,235	7,877	540	48	19,080	758

Apparatus and waters	Sturgeon, lake		Sturgeon, shovelnose		Suckers		Turtles	
	Pounds	*Value*	*Pounds*	*Value*	*Pounds*	*Value*	*Pounds*	*Value*
Haul seines:								
Minnesota River					500	$25		
Mississippi River	608	$101	1,580	$219	26,670	879		
St. Croix River			1,120	171	1,859	37		
Miscellaneous lakes					714	32		
Total	608	101	2,700	390	29,743	973		
Fykes:								
Mississippi River	3,471	649			2,868	92		
St. Croix River					11,820	123		
Total	3,471	649			14,688	215		
Set lines:								
Mississippi River	1,294	121	500	50	230	13	65	$2
St. Croix River			20	3				
White Water River			35	5				
Total	1,294	121	555	58	230	13	65	2
Gill nets: Mississippi River	800	112			600	21		
Total by waters:								
Minnesota River					500	25		
Mississippi River	6,173	983	2,080	269	30,368	1,005	65	2
St. Croix River			1,140	174	13,679	160		
White Water River			35	5				
Miscellaneous lakes					714	32		
Total	6,173	983	3,255	448	45,261	1,222	65	2

Yield, by apparatus and waters, of the fisheries of Minnesota, 1922—Continued

Apparatus and waters	Mussel shells		Pearls	Slugs	Total	
	Pounds	Value	Value	Value	Pounds	Value
Haul seines:						
Minnesota River					398, 827	$16, 285
Mississippi River					997, 611	49, 270
St. Croix River					408, 675	11, 555
Vermillion River					67, 018	4, 315
Miscellaneous lakes					1, 908, 882	89, 060
Total					3, 781, 013	170, 485
Crowfoot bars:						
Blue Earth River	86, 000	$1, 320	$25	$15	86, 000	1, 360
Cottonwood River	36, 000	630		9	36, 000	639
Crow Wing River	252, 065	6, 699	150	84	252, 065	6, 933
Des Moines River	37, 000	689	45	13	37, 000	747
Minnesota River	196, 200	5, 145	408	187	196, 200	5, 740
Mississippi River	549, 961	12, 104	590	522	549, 961	13, 216
Shell River	149, 800	3, 479		51	149, 800	3, 530
Miscellaneous lakes	167, 800	4, 286			167, 800	4, 286
Total	1, 474, 826	34, 352	1, 218	881	1, 474, 826	36, 451
Fykes:						
Minnesota River					20, 100	605
Mississippi River					175, 004	14, 554
St. Croix River					26, 236	704
Total					221, 340	15, 863
Set lines:						
Minnesota River					6, 950	470
Mississippi River					26, 931	2, 095
St. Croix River					2, 270	211
White Water River					885	95
Total					37, 036	2, 871
Gill nets:						
Mississippi River					32, 145	1, 482
St. Croix River					1, 500	110
Total					33, 645	1, 592
Pound nets:						
Minnesota River					8, 875	412
Mississippi River					6, 450	324
Total					15, 325	736
Forks, rakes, etc.:						
Cedar River			100	50		150
Des Moines River	33, 100	646	31	21	33, 100	698
Minnesota River	30, 270	735	47	17	30, 270	799
Mississippi River	10, 000	175	35	9	10, 000	219
St. Croix River	10, 000	169	25		10, 000	194
Shell River	13, 000	350		17	13, 000	367
Total	96, 370	2, 075	238	114	96, 370	2, 427
Total by waters:						
Blue Earth River	86, 000	1, 320	25	15	86, 000	1, 360
Cedar River			100	50		150
Cottonwood River	36, 000	630		9	36, 000	639
Crow Wing River	252, 065	6, 699	150	84	252, 065	6, 933
Des Moines River	70, 100	1, 335	76	34	70, 100	1, 445
Minnesota River	226, 470	5, 880	455	204	661, 222	24, 311
Mississippi River	559, 961	12, 279	625	531	1, 798, 102	81, 160
Shell River	162, 800	3, 829		68	162, 800	3, 897
St. Croix River	10, 000	169	25		448, 681	12, 774
Vermillion River					67, 018	4, 315
White Water River					885	95
Miscellaneous lakes	167, 800	4, 286			2, 076, 682	93, 346
Total	1, 571, 196	36, 427	1, 456	995	5, 659, 555	230, 425

MISSISSIPPI

The fisheries of the Mississippi River and its tributaries, in Mississippi, gave employment in 1922 to 379 fishermen and 55 shoresmen, most of the latter being connected with the wholesale trades. The total investment in boats, apparatus, shore property, and cash capital amounted to $203,286. Based on the value of the catch, the more important forms of apparatus used were fyke nets, haul seines, and set lines. The total output of the State amounted to 3,327,501 pounds, valued at $191,449. The leading species taken were the buffalofish, with a catch of 2,096,288 pounds, valued at $105,188; paddlefish, 352,260 pounds, valued at $36,672, and paddlefish caviar, 1,563 pounds, valued at $3,037; catfish, 448,690 pounds, valued at $27,566; and drum or sheepshead, 329,109 pounds, valued at $11,636.

The Mississippi and Yazoo were the most productive of the rivers, the value of the catch of these two being about 70 per cent of that of the Mississippi River and all of its tributaries combined. Besides the Big Sunflower and Homochitto Rivers, several lakes tributary to the Mississippi were quite productive.

The following tables show in detail the statistics of the fisheries of this State.

Persons engaged and investment in the fisheries of Mississippi, 1922

Waters	Persons engaged			Gasoline boats		Rowboats		House boats	
	Fishermen	Shoresmen	Total						
	No.	No.	No.	No.	Value	No.	Value	No.	Value
Big Sunflower River	25		25	16	$1,625	18	$340	10	$1,700
Homochitto River	24		24	9	1,135	13	124	2	200
Mississippi River	178	34	212	94	25,395	107	1,842	53	4,823
Yazoo River	99	10	109	60	8,670	72	1,151	35	9,240
Beulah Lake	12	1	13	2	450	2	40		
Flower Lake	5		5			6	90		
Lake Lee	6	6	12	3	1,750	3	150	1	800
Moon Lake	15	2	17	1	100	6	100		
Washington Lake	15	2	17	1	600	5	750		
Total	379	55	434	186	39,725	232	4,587	101	16,763

Waters	Fyke nets		Haul seines			Set lines		Gill nets		
	No.	Value	No.	Yards	Value	No.	Value	No.	Yards	Value
Big Sunflower River	170	$1,700	5	1,055	$870	62	$90	8	640	$115
Homochitto River	34	328	1	450	450	820	115			
Mississippi River	1,235	12,466	8	1,940	1,525	697	1,248	7	1,150	308
Yazoo River	1,480	14,675	17	5,789	5,115	318	1,654	3	700	295
Beulah Lake			2	1,600	1,600					
Flower Lake	13	150	1	700	200	5	8	1	100	40
Lake Lee	30	300	1	735	500	10	20	7	700	300
Moon Lake			2	2,000	1,800	76	180			
Washington Lake			5	3,100	3,900					
Total	2,962	29,619	42	17,369	15,960	1,988	3,315	26	3,290	1,058

Waters	Trammel nets			Shrimp traps		Shore property	Cash capital	Total investment
	No.	Yards	Value	No.	Value	Value	Value	Value
Big Sunflower River						$425		$6,865
Homochitto River						150		2,502
Mississippi River	8	1,110	$483	300	$200	49,820	$11,000	109,110
Yazoo River						8,965	2,300	52,065
Beulah Lake						100		2,190
Flower Lake						80		568
Lake Lee						14,736	2,500	21,056
Moon Lake	2	240	100			1,000		3,280
Washington Lake						400		5,650
Total	10	1,350	583	300	200	75,676	15,800	203,286

Yield, by apparatus and waters, of the fisheries of Mississippi, 1922

Apparatus and waters	Black bass		Buffalofish		Carp	
	Pounds	*Value*	*Pounds*	*Value*	*Pounds*	*Value*
Fyke nets:						
Big Sunflower River			76,000	$5,410	2,000	$90
Homochitto River			49,500	1,570		
Mississippi River	100	$10	674,470	32,751	8,896	562
Yazoo River			490,808	21,206	1,785	59
Flower Lake			4,000	320	500	15
Lake Lee			30,000	1,200		
Total	100	10	1,324,778	62,457	13,181	726
Haul seines:						
Big Sunflower River			24,000	1,580		
Homochitto River			1,000	40		
Mississippi River	447	60	92,881	5,479	5,345	330
Yazoo River	120	12	141,659	6,248		
Beulah Lake			40,000	2,400	100	4
Flower Lake			8,000	480	1,000	30
Lake Lee			70,000	4,200		
Moon Lake			60,000	3,000		
Lake Washington			193,729	11,836	1,084	33
Total	567	72	631,269	35,263	7,529	397
Set lines:						
Big Sunflower River			500	25		
Mississippi River	100	10	16,500	705		
Yazoo River			11,353	507	400	12
Total	100	10	28,353	1,237	400	12
Gill nets:						
Big Sunflower River			2,000	100		
Mississippi River			13,688	877	1,000	80
Yazoo River			25,200	974		
Flower Lake			2,000	160		
Lake Lee			5,000	300		
Total			47,888	2,411	1,000	80
Trammel nets:						
Mississippi River			14,000	1,320	1,000	60
Moon Lake			50,000	2,500		
Total			64,000	3,820	1,000	60
Total by waters:						
Big Sunflower River			102,500	7,115	2,000	90
Homochitto River			50,500	1,610		
Mississippi River	647	80	811,539	41,132	16,241	1,032
Yazoo River	120	12	669,020	28,935	2,185	71
Beulah Lake			40,000	2,400	100	4
Flower Lake			14,000	960	1,500	45
Lake Lee			105,000	5,700		
Moon Lake			110,000	5,500		
Washington Lake			193,729	11,836	1,084	33
Total	767	92	2,096,288	105,188	23,110	1,275

Yield, by apparatus and waters, of the fisheries of Mississippi, 1922—Continued

Apparatus and waters	Catfish		Crappie		Drum, fresh-water or sheepshead	
	Pounds	Value	Pounds	Value	Pounds	Value
Fyke nets:						
Big Sunflower River	500	$30			21,010	$845
Homochitto River	1,000	50			5,760	140
Mississippi River	24,476	1,474	14,003	$1,230	116,625	3,843
Yazoo River	14,549	874	400	28	67,300	2,562
Flower Lake					1,000	30
Lake Lee			300	30	2,000	40
Total	40,525	2,428	14,703	1,288	213,695	7,460
Haul seines:						
Big Sunflower River					5,000	175
Homochitto River	3,000	150			2,000	60
Mississippi River	11,688	948	25,008	1,864	35,612	1,086
Yazoo River	17,322	1,051	7,679	537	16,803	589
Beulah Lake	4,000	320			500	20
Flower Lake	1,000	80			1,000	30
Lake Lee	1,000	80	1,200	144	12,000	480
Lake Washington	3,155	238			447	13
Total	41,165	2,867	33,887	2,545	73,362	2,453
Set lines:						
Big Sunflower River	20,000	1,490			2,500	93
Homochitto River	33,000	1,662				
Mississippi River	208,003	12,422	2,349	258	17,452	726
Yazoo River	84,106	4,908	200	14	9,450	310
Flower Lake	3,000	240			500	15
Lake Lee	9,000	720				
Moon Lake	2,000	160				
Total	359,109	21,602	2,549	272	29,902	1,144
Gill nets:						
Mississippi River	3,311	305			950	76
Yazoo River	1,580	84	300	21	4,200	133
Flower Lake					1,000	30
Lake Lee	2,000	160			3,000	120
Total	6,891	549	300	21	9,150	359
Trammel nets: Mississippi River	1,000	120	150	15	3,000	220
Total by waters:						
Big Sunflower River	20,500	1,520			28,510	1,113
Homochitto River	37,000	1,862			7,760	200
Mississippi River	248,478	15,269	41,510	3,367	173,639	5,951
Yazoo River	117,557	6,917	8,579	600	97,753	3,594
Beulah Lake	4,000	320			500	20
Flower Lake	4,000	320			3,500	105
Lake Lee	12,000	960	1,500	174	17,000	640
Moon Lake	2,000	160				
Washington Lake	3,155	238			447	13
Total	448,690	27,566	51,589	4,141	329,109	11,636

Yield, by apparatus and waters, of the fisheries of Mississippi, 1922—Continued

Apparatus and waters	Eels		Paddlefish, or spoonbill cat		Paddlefish caviar		Sturgeon, shovelnose	
	Pounds	*Value*	*Pounds*	*Value*	*Pounds*	*Value*	*Pounds*	*Value*
Fyke nets:								
Mississippi River			3, 129	$320			311	$9
Yazoo River			3, 300	361				
Total			6, 429	681			311	9
Haul seines:								
Big Sunflower River			27, 300	3, 863				
Homochitto River			20, 000	2, 000				
Mississippi River			21, 640	2, 528	15	$15		
Yazoo River			34, 122	3, 815	75	138	300	3
Beulah Lake			10, 000	600	50	150		
Lake Lee			10, 000	1, 500	50	150		
Moon Lake			5, 000	250	3	8		
Lake Washington			25, 022	1, 674	215	679		
Total			153, 084	16, 230	408	1, 140	300	3
Set lines:								
Big Sunflower River			10, 100	1, 240	30	90		
Homochitto River			3, 800	272				
Mississippi River	29	$2	62, 100	6, 415	60	130	800	80
Yazoo River			81, 747	9, 128	1, 030	1, 583		
Lake Lee			1, 000	80				
Moon Lake			10, 000	500	6	16		
Total	29	2	168, 747	17, 635	1, 126	1, 819	800	80
Gill nets:								
Big Sunflower River			5, 000	650				
Mississippi River			10, 600	758	26	70		
Yazoo River			1, 400	168				
Lake Lee			2, 000	300				
Total			19, 000	1, 876	26	70		
Trammel nets: Moon Lake			5, 000	250	3	8		
Total by waters:								
Big Sunflower River			42, 400	5, 753	30	90		
Homochitto River			23, 800	2, 272				
Mississippi River	29	2	97, 469	10, 021	101	215	1, 111	89
Yazoo River			120, 569	13, 472	1, 105	1, 721	300	3
Beulah Lake			10, 000	600	50	150		
Lake Lee			13, 000	1, 880	50	150		
Moon Lake			20, 000	1, 000	12	32		
Washington Lake			25, 022	1, 674	215	679		
Total	29	2	352, 260	36, 672	1, 563	3, 037	1, 411	92

Yield, by apparatus and waters, of the fisheries of Mississippi, 1922—Continued

Apparatus and waters	White bass		Shrimp		Turtles		Total	
	Pounds	*Value*	*Pounds*	*Value*	*Pounds*	*Value*	*Pounds*	*Value*
Fyke nets:								
Big Sunflower River							99,510	$6,375
Homochitto River							56,260	1,760
Mississippi River	2,433	$227			800	$24	845,243	40,450
Yazoo River	331	23					578,473	25,113
Flower Lake							5,500	365
Lake Lee	300	30					32,600	1,300
Total	3,064	280			800	24	1,617,586	75,363
Haul seines:								
Big Sunflower River							56,300	5,615
Homochitto River							26,060	2,250
Mississippi River	7,100	545					199,736	12,855
Yazoo River	4,000	280					222,080	12,673
Beulah Lake							54,650	3,494
Flower Lake							11,000	620
Lake Lee	1,000	120					95,250	6,674
Moon Lake							65,003	3,258
Lake Washington							223,652	14,473
Total	12,100	945					953,671	61,915
Set lines:								
Big Sunflower River							33,130	2,938
Homochitto River					300	8	37,100	1,942
Mississippi River	700	49			500	15	306,593	20,812
Yazoo River							188,286	16,462
Flower Lake							3,500	255
Lake Lee							10,000	800
Moon Lake							12,006	676
Total	700	49			800	23	592,615	43,885
Gill nets:								
Big Sunflower River							7,000	750
Mississippi River	221	27					29,796	2,193
Yazoo River							32,680	1,380
Flower Lake							3,000	190
Lake Lee							12,000	880
Total	221	27					84,476	5,393
Trammel nets:								
Mississippi River							19,150	1,735
Moon Lake							55,003	2,758
Total							74,153	4,493
Shrimp traps: Mississippi River			5,000	$400			5,000	400
Total by waters:								
Big Sunflower River							195,940	15,681
Homochitto River					300	8	119,360	5,952
Mississippi River	10,454	848	5,000	400	1,300	39	1,407,515	78,445
Yazoo River	4,331	303					1,021,519	55,628
Beulah Lake							54,650	3,494
Flower Lake							23,000	1,430
Lake Lee	1,300	150					149,850	9,654
Moon Lake							132,012	6,692
Washington Lake							223,652	14,473
Total	16,085	1,301	5,000	400	1,600	47	3,327,501	191,449

MISSOURI

The fisheries of Missouri are confined entirely to the Mississippi River and tributaries, including the Missouri River. In 1922 there were 1,023 persons engaged in the fisheries or fishery industries of this State, more than two-thirds of this number being connected with the wholesale fish trade of St. Louis and Kansas City and the pearl-button industry in factories located at various places in the State. The total investment amounted to $1,152,007, most of which is credited to the wholesale fish trade and the button industry already mentioned. Also contributing to the investment were 78 gas boats, valued at

Yield, by apparatus and waters, of the fisheries of Mississippi, 1922—Continued

Apparatus and waters	Eels		Paddlefish, or spoonbill cat		Paddlefish caviar		Sturgeon, shovelnose	
	Pounds	*Value*	*Pounds*	*Value*	*Pounds*	*Value*	*Pounds*	*Value*
Fyke nets:								
Mississippi River			3,129	$320			311	$9
Yazoo River			3,300	361				
Total			6,429	681			311	9
Haul seines:								
Big Sunflower River			27,300	3,863				
Homochitto River			20,000	2,000				
Mississippi River			21,640	2,528	15	$15		
Yazoo River			34,122	3,815	75	138	300	3
Beulah Lake			10,000	600	50	150		
Lake Lee			10,000	1,500	50	150		
Moon Lake			5,000	250	3	8		
Lake Washington			25,022	1,674	215	679		
Total			153,084	16,230	408	1,140	300	3
Set lines:								
Big Sunflower River			10,100	1,240	30	90		
Homochitto River			3,800	272				
Mississippi River	29	$2	62,100	6,415	60	130	800	80
Yazoo River			81,747	9,128	1,030	1,583		
Lake Lee			1,000	80				
Moon Lake			10,000	500	6	16		
Total	29	2	168,747	17,635	1,126	1,819	800	80
Gill nets:								
Big Sunflower River			5,000	650				
Mississippi River			10,600	758	26	70		
Yazoo River			1,400	168				
Lake Lee			2,000	300				
Total			19,000	1,876	26	70		
Trammel nets: Moon Lake			5,000	250	3	8		
Total by waters:								
Big Sunflower River			42,400	5,753	30	90		
Homochitto River			23,800	2,272				
Mississippi River	29	2	97,469	10,021	101	215	1,111	89
Yazoo River			120,569	13,472	1,105	1,721	300	3
Beulah Lake			10,000	600	50	150		
Lake Lee			13,000	1,880	50	150		
Moon Lake			20,000	1,000	12	32		
Washington Lake			25,022	1,674	215	679		
Total	29	2	352,260	36,672	1,563	3,037	1,411	92

Yield, by apparatus and waters, of the fisheries of Mississippi, 1922—Continued

Apparatus and waters	White bass		Shrimp		Turtles		Total	
	Pounds	*Value*	*Pounds*	*Value*	*Pounds*	*Value*	*Pounds*	*Value*
Fyke nets:								
Big Sunflower River							99,510	$6,375
Homochitto River							56,260	1,760
Mississippi River	2,433	$227			800	$24	845,243	40,450
Yazoo River	331	23					578,473	25,113
Flower Lake							5,500	365
Lake Lee	300	30					32,600	1,300
Total	3,064	280			800	24	1,617,586	75,363
Haul seines:								
Big Sunflower River							56,300	5,618
Homochitto River							26,000	2,250
Mississippi River	7,100	545					199,736	12,855
Yazoo River	4,000	280					222,080	12,673
Beulah Lake							54,650	3,494
Flower Lake							11,000	620
Lake Lee	1,000	120					95,250	6,674
Moon Lake							65,003	3,258
Lake Washington							223,652	14,473
Total	12,100	945					953,671	61,915
Set lines:								
Big Sunflower River							33,130	2,938
Homochitto River					300	8	37,100	1,942
Mississippi River	700	49			500	15	308,593	20,812
Yazoo River							188,286	16,462
Flower Lake							3,500	255
Lake Lee							10,000	800
Moon Lake							12,006	676
Total	700	49			800	23	592,615	43,885
Gill nets:								
Big Sunflower River							7,000	750
Mississippi River	221	27					29,796	2,193
Yazoo River							32,680	1,380
Flower Lake							3,000	190
Lake Lee							12,000	880
Total	221	27					84,476	5,393
Trammel nets:								
Mississippi River							19,150	1,735
Moon Lake							55,003	2,758
Total							74,153	4,493
Shrimp traps: Mississippi River			5,000	$400			5,000	400
Total by waters:								
Big Sunflower River							195,940	15,681
Homochitto River					300	8	119,360	5,952
Mississippi River	10,454	848	5,000	400	1,300	39	1,407,518	78,445
Yazoo River	4,331	303					1,021,519	55,628
Beulah Lake							54,650	3,494
Flower Lake							23,000	1,430
Lake Lee	1,300	150					149,850	9,654
Moon Lake							132,012	6,692
Washington Lake							223,652	14,473
Total	16,085	1,301	5,000	400	1,600	47	3,327,501	191,449

MISSOURI

The fisheries of Missouri are confined entirely to the Mississippi River and tributaries, including the Missouri River. In 1922 there were 1,023 persons engaged in the fisheries or fishery industries of this State, more than two-thirds of this number being connected with the wholesale fish trade of St. Louis and Kansas City and the pearl-button industry in factories located at various places in the State. The total investment amounted to $1,152,007, most of which is credited to the wholesale fish trade and the button industry already mentioned. Also contributing to the investment were 78 gas boats, valued at

$11,215; 235 rowboats, valued at $4,255; 23 houseboats, valued at $5,515; 1,422 fyke nets, valued at $12,248; 85 trammel nets, valued at $3,630; 434 set lines, valued at $1,186; 37 haul seines, valued at $3,238; and a few minor forms of apparatus. Based on the catch, the fyke net was the most important form of apparatus.

The total production of the State amounted to 1,566,162 pounds, valued at $103,755. Some of the more important species contributing to this output were 551,536 pounds of carp, valued at $35,160; 194,371 pounds of catfish and bullheads, valued at $24,745; and 287,474 pounds of buffalofish, valued at $21,536. The Mississippi and Missouri Rivers furnished the greater part of the State's output. The production of mussel shells amounted to 327,500 pounds, valued at $4,042, together with $1,178 worth of pearls and slugs. The shell catch was divided among the White, Maramec, Osage, and Mississippi Rivers.

The following tables show in detail the statistics of the fisheries of this State:

Persons engaged and investment in the fisheries of Missouri, 1922

Waters	Persons engaged			Gasoline boats		Rowboats		House boats	
	Fishermen	Shoresmen	Total	Number	Value	Number	Value	Number	Value
	Number	Number	Number	Number	Value	Number	Value	Number	Value
Black River	10		10			4	$40		
Gasconade River	6		6	3	$755	8	190	2	$1,000
Little River	15		15	1	300	15	150		
Maramec River	9		9			8	76	1	200
Mississippi River	113	551	664	55	8,015	87	1,645	10	2,225
Missouri River	108	130	238	15	1,445	73	1,394	9	2,010
Osage River	18	26	44	4	700	14	280		
Platte River	1		1			1	15	1	80
White River	10		10			10	100		
Miscellaneous lakes	26		26			15	365		
Total	316	707	1,023	78	11,215	235	4,255	23	5,515

Waters	Fyke nets		Set lines		Trammel nets			Haul seines		
	Number	Value	Number	Value	Number	Yards	Value	Number	Yards	Value
Black River			8	$4				2	10	$5
Gasconade River	15	$109	28	32	1	60	$80	1	67	30
Little River	204	770	45	45				4	600	500
Maramec River			6	6						
Mississippi River	864	8,314	240	364	12	1,620	525	16	4,429	608
Missouri River	223	2,057	63	111	52	2,468	1,450	11	1,814	1,665
Osage River	102	870	19	24	6	540	245			
Platte River	8	80			1	40	35	1	45	30
Miscellaneous lakes	6	48	25	600	13	1,960	1,295	2	500	400
Total	1,422	12,248	434	1,186	85	6,688	3,630	37	7,465	3,238

Waters	Crowfoot bars, pairs		Rakes		Forks		Shore property	Cash capital	Total investment
	Number	Value	Number	Value	Number	Value	Value	Value	Value
Black River							$15		$64
Gasconade River							100		2,296
Little River							150		1,915
Maramec River					9	$16	198		496
Mississippi River	1	$7	9	$68	9	45	658,571	$56,800	737,187
Missouri River							362,625	26,000	308,757
Osage River					3	10	4,955		7,084
Platte River							200		440
White River					10	20	40		160
Miscellaneous lakes							900		3,608
Total	1	7	9	68	31	91	1,027,754	82,800	1,152,007

Yield, by apparatus and waters, of the fisheries of Missouri, 1922

Apparatus and waters	Black bass		Buffalofish		Carp		Catfish and bullheads	
	Pounds	Value	Pounds	Value	Pounds	Value	Pounds	Value
Fyke nets:								
Gasconade River			650	$65	725	$73	1,600	$320
Little River	500	$75	5,000	250	7,000	140	3,000	240
Mississippi River			88,875	6,453	236,840	14,721	47,849	5,489
Missouri River			11,055	1,074	57,780	5,248	6,840	1,117
Osage River			15,400	1,554	2,400	199	600	120
Platte River			500		2,000	200	500	100
Total	500	75	121,480	9,446	306,745	20,581	60,389	7,386
Set lines:								
Black River			200	30			1,500	225
Gasconade River			100	10	100	10	3,600	660
Little River							7,500	585
Maramec River					1,280	204	414	83
Mississippi River			12,300	1,003	37,770	1,945	45,770	5,661
Missouri River			420	53	2,425	278	6,679	1,144
Osage River			200	30	350	36	3,100	620
Miscellaneous lakes			16,000	960	4,000	200		
Total			29,220	2,086	45,925	2,673	68,563	8,978
Trammel nets:								
Gasconade River			700	70	700	70		
Mississippi River	37	2	10,825	393	36,950	687	10,825	1,093
Missouri River			24,217	2,158	71,334	6,861	39,524	5,418
Osage River			11,950	1,346	1,200	90	1,145	220
Platte River			300	30	2,000	200	400	80
Miscellaneous lakes	125	25	56,900	3,688	14,100	765		
Total	162	27	104,892	7,686	126,284	8,673	51,894	6,811
Haul seines:								
Gasconade River			50	5	75			
Little River			2,000	100	15,000	300		
Mississippi River	140	21	21,180	1,654	40,620	1,643	13,025	1,470
Missouri River			8,652	559	15,387	1,133	500	100
Platte River					1,500	150		
Total	140	21	31,882	2,318	72,582	3,233	13,525	1,570
Total by waters:								
Black River			200	30			1,500	225
Gasconade River			1,500	150	1,600	160	5,200	980
Little River	500	75	7,000	350	22,000	440	10,500	825
Maramec River					1,280	204	414	83
Mississippi River	177	23	133,180	9,503	352,180	18,996	117,469	13,713
Missouri River			44,344	3,844	146,926	13,520	53,543	7,779
Osage River			27,550	2,930	3,950	325	4,845	960
Platte River			800	80	5,500	550	900	180
Miscellaneous lakes	125	25	72,900	4,649	18,100	965		
Grand total	802	123	287,474	21,536	551,536	35,160	194,371	24,745

Yield, by apparatus and waters, of the fisheries of Missouri, 1922—Continued

Apparatus and waters	Crappie		Drum		Eels		Minnows	
	Pounds	*Value*	*Pounds*	*Value*	*Pounds*	*Value*	*Pounds*	*Value*
Fyke nets:								
Gasconade River			625	$63				
Little River	1,500	$120	4,000	120	200	$10		
Mississippi River			41,797	3,008	2,000	249		
Missouri River	200	40	2,020	212				
Osage River	600	120	4,500	328				
Total	2,300	280	52,942	3,731	2,200	259		
Set lines:								
Gasconade River			200	20				
Little River			1,000	30	300	15		
Maramec River			256	41				
Mississippi River			7,765	744	500	51		
Missouri River			340	42				
Osage River			525	78				
Total			10,086	955	800	66		
Trammel nets:								
Gasconade River			700	70				
Mississippi River			4,570	140				
Missouri River			1,300	110				
Osage River			1,100	76				
Miscellaneous lakes	1,200	190	150	15				
Total	1,200	190	7,820	411				
Haul seines:								
Black River							165	$50
Gasconade River			50	5				
Mississippi River			11,130	765				
Missouri River	1,225	123	860	83			1,000	400
Total	1,225	123	12,040	853			1,165	450
Total by waters:								
Black River							165	50
Gasconade River			1,575	158				
Little River	1,500	120	5,000	150	500	25		
Maramec River			256	41				
Mississippi River			65,262	4,657	2,500	300		
Missouri River	1,425	163	4,520	447			1,000	400
Osage River	600	120	6,125	482				
Miscellaneous lakes	1,200	190	150	15				
Grand total	4,725	593	82,888	5,950	3,000	325	1,165	450

Apparatus and waters	Mooneye		Paddlefish or spoonbill cat		Pike perch, wall-eyed		Quillback or American carp	
	Pounds	*Value*	*Pounds*	*Value*	*Pounds*	*Value*	*Pounds*	*Value*
Fyke nets:								
Mississippi River			10,170	$567				
Missouri River	200	$16	600	44	150	$30	12,425	$1,245
Osage River			1,300	186	50	10	750	73
Platte River							500	50
Total	200	16	12,070	797	200	40	13,675	1,368
Set lines:								
Black River					500	125		
Missouri River							100	13
Total					500	125	100	13
Trammel nets:								
Mississippi River			1,600	160	75	5		
Missouri River	2,050	69	9,665	498			5,155	406
Osage River			100	19			50	3
Platte River			100	5			100	10
Total	2,050	69	11,465	682	75	5	5,305	419
Haul seines:								
Little River	1,000	50	500	35	500	40		
Mississippi River			3,880	170				
Missouri River	200	31	8,935	449			1,312	74
Platte River							100	10
Total	1,200	81	13,315	654	500	40	1,412	84
Total by waters:								
Black River					500	125		
Little River	1,000	50	500	35	500	40		
Mississippi River			15,650	897	75	5		
Missouri River	2,450	116	19,200	991	150	30	18,992	1,738
Osage River			1,400	205	50	10	800	76
Platte River			100	5			700	70
Grand total	3,450	166	36,850	2,133	1,275	210	20,492	1,884

Yield, by apparatus and waters, of the fisheries of Missouri, 1922—Continued

Apparatus and waters	Rock bass		Sturgeon, lake		Sturgeon, shovelnose		Sturgeon, shovelnose, caviar	
	Pounds	Value	Pounds	Value	Pounds	Value	Pounds	Value
Fyke nets:								
Mississippi River			600	$51	3,960	$238	200	$300
Missouri River			300	20				
Osage River			900	102				
Total			1,800	173	3,960	238	200	300
Set lines: Mississippi River					5,244	330		
Trammel nets:								
Mississippi River					19,300	1,771	400	640
Missouri River			2,200	118				
Osage River			100	5				
Total			2,300	123	19,300	1,771	400	640
Haul seines:								
Mississippi River	275	$33			2,000	180	90	135
Missouri River			100	5				
Total	275	33	100	5	2,000	180	90	135
Total by waters:								
Mississippi River	275	33	600	51	30,504	2,519	690	1,075
Missouri River			2,600	143				
Osage River			1,000	107				
Grand total	275	33	4,200	301	30,504	2,519	690	1,075

Apparatus and waters	Suckers		Sunfish		Crawfish		Turtles	
	Pounds	Value	Pounds	Value	Pounds	Value	Pounds	Value
Fyke nets:								
Little River			1,500	$45			2,000	$40
Mississippi River	4,500	$330						
Missouri River	1,100	96						
Osage River	2,400	243						
Total	8,000	669	1,500	45			2,000	40
Set lines:								
Black River	1,500	150						
Maramec River	700	112						
Total	2,200	262						
Trammel nets:								
Missouri River	315	33						
Osage River	250	23						
Miscellaneous lakes			50	8				
Total	565	56	50	8				
Haul seines:								
Gasconade River	25	2						
Miscellaneous lakes					625	$250		
Total	25	2			625	250		
Total by waters:								
Black River	1,500	150						
Gasconade River	25	2						
Little River			1,500	45			2,000	40
Maramec River	700	112						
Mississippi River	4,500	330						
Missouri River	1,415	129						
Osage River	2,650	266						
Miscellaneous lakes			50	8	625	250		
Grand total	10,790	989	1,550	53	625	250	2,000	40

Yield, by apparatus and waters, of the fisheries of Missouri, 1922—Continued

Apparatus and waters	Mussel shells		Pearls	Slugs	Total	
	Pounds	Value	Value	Value	Pounds	Value
Fyke nets:						
Gasconade River					3,600	$521
Little River					24,700	1,040
Mississippi River					436,791	31,406
Missouri River					92,670	9,142
Osage River					28,900	2,935
Platte River					3,500	400
Total					590,161	45,444
Set lines:						
Black River					3,700	530
Gasconade River					4,000	700
Little River					8,800	630
Maramec River					2,650	440
Mississippi River					109,349	9,734
Missouri River					9,964	1,530
Osage River					4,175	764
Miscellaneous lakes					20,000	1,160
Total					·162,638	15,488
Trammel nets:						
Gasconade River					·2,100	210
Mississippi River					84,582	4,891
Missouri River					155,760	15,671
Osage River					15,895	1,782
Platte River					2,900	325
Miscellaneous lakes					72,525	4,692
Total					333,762	27,571
Haul seines:						
Black River					165	50
Gasconade River					200	19
Little River					19,000	525
Mississippi River					92,340	6,071
Missouri River					38,171	2,957
Platte River					1,600	160
Miscellaneous lakes					625	250
Total					152,101	10,032
Crowfoot bars: Mississippi River	6,000	$157			6,000	157
Rakes and forks:						
Maramec River	124,000	1,000	$368	$760	124,000	2,128
Mississippi River	18,000	390			18,000	390
Osage River	79,500	995		50	79,500	1,045
White River	100,000	1,500			100,000	1,500
Total	321,500	3,885	368	810	321,500	5,063
Total by waters:						
Black River					3,865	580
Gasconade River					9,900	1,450
Little River					52,500	2,195
Maramec River	124,000	1,000	368	760	126,650	2,568
Mississippi River	24,000	547			747,062	52,649
Missouri River					296,565	29,300
Osage River	79,500	995		50	·128,470	6,526
Platte River					8,000	885
White River	100,000	1,500			100,000	1,500
Miscellaneous lakes					93,150	6,102
Grand total	327,500	4,042	368	810	1,566,162	103,755

NEBRASKA

The fisheries of Nebraska were conducted entirely in the Missouri River. In 1922 there were 89 fishermen engaged, a total investment (represented mainly in the wholesale trade of Omaha) of $184,664, and a total catch of 135,440 pounds, valued at $15;477, consisting mainly of carp, catfish, and buffalofish.

The following tables show in detail the statistics of the fisheries of this State:

Persons engaged and investment in the fisheries of Nebraska, 1922

Items	Number	Value	Items	Number	Value
Persons engaged:			Investment—continued:		
Fishermen	52		Trammel nets	1 35	$1,269
Shoresmen	37		Haul seines	2 3	314
			Fyke nets	44	369
Total	89		Set lines	2	3
			Shore property		171,115
Investment:			Cash capital		10,000
Gasoline boats	5	$510			
Rowboats	40	1,084	Total		184,664

1 1,900 yards in length.
2 650 yards in length.

Yield, by apparatus, of the fisheries of Nebraska, 1922

Species	Trammel nets		Haul seines		Fyke nets		Set lines		Total	
	Pounds	*Value*	*Pounds*	*Value*	*Pounds*	*Value*	*Pounds*	*Value*	*Pounds*	*Value*
Buffalofish	7,180	$716	8,165	$737	1,100	$98			16,445	$1,551
Carp	63,500	6,606	10,500	950	8,300	702			82,300	8,258
Catfish	17,460	3,222	2,085	350	4,850	956	1,000	$200	25,395	4,728
Drum, fresh-water, or sheepshead					100	10			100	10
Paddlefish, or spoonbill cat			10,000	850	800	40			10,800	890
Suckers					400	40			400	40
Total	88,140	10,544	30,750	2,887	15,550	1,846	1,000	200	135,440	15,477

OHIO

In 1922 there were engaged in the fisheries of Ohio 75 fishermen, 173 shoresmen, and 4 men on transporting vessels. Most of the shoresmen were connected with the wholesale fish trade of Cincinnati and button-blank factories at Manchester and Marietta. The total investment amounted to $173,646, mainly connected with the wholesale fish and button-blank industries mentioned above. The apparatus, in the order of their importance, consisted of fyke nets, crowfoot bars, set lines, and forks.

The total production was 702,323 pounds, valued at $30,120, consisting of 597,500 pounds of mussel shells, with a value of $11,940, including pearls and slugs; 26,345 pounds of suckers, valued at $4,114; 20,450 pounds of quillbacks, valued at $3,515; 18,320 pounds of drum or sheepshead, valued at $3,226; 17,420 pounds of catfish, valued at $3,154; 11,045 pounds of buffalofish, valued at $2,017, and several species of minor importance.

The following tables show in detail the statistics of the fisheries of this State:

Persons engaged and investment in the fisheries of Ohio, 1922

Waters	Persons engaged			Gasoline boats		Rowboats		House boats		Fyke nets	
	Fishermen	Shoresmen	Total	No.	Value	No.	Value	No.	Value	No.	Value
	No.	No.	No.	No.	Value	No.	Value	No.	Value	No.	Value
Muskingum River	6	------	6	2	$125	5	$90	----	------	----	------
Ohio River	51	173	1 228	2 15	4,820	49	753	12	$1,675	110	$1,228
Tuscarawas River	6	------	6	----	------	7	170	----	------	----	------
Killbuck Creek	4	------	4	----	------	4	60	----	------	----	------
Mohican Creek	6	------	6	----	------	6	90	----	------	----	------
Wills Creek	2	------	2	----	------	1	10	----	------	----	------
Total	75	173	252	17	4,945	72	1,173	12	1,675	110	1,228

Waters	Set lines		Crowfoot bars, pairs		Forks		Shore property	Cash capital	Total investment
	Number	Value	Number	Value	Number	Value	Value	Value	Value
Muskingum River	------	------	6	$120	5	$6	$35	------	$376
Ohio River	71	$105	25	490	------	------	148,455	$15,000	172,526
Tuscarawas River	------	------	6	120	3	4	25	------	319
Killbuck Creek	------	------	4	80	------	------	20	------	160
Mohican Creek	------	------	6	120	------	------	35	------	245
Wills Creek	------	------	------	------	------	------	10	------	20
Total	71	105	47	930	8	10	148,580	15,000	173,646

, 1 Includes 4 men on two transporting vessels.
2 Includes two transporting vessels with a net tonnage of 28 and value of $3,600.

Yield, by apparatus and waters, of the fisheries of Ohio, 1922

Apparatus and waters	Black bass		Buffalofish		Carp		Catfish		Crappie	
	Pounds	Value	Pounds	Value	Pounds	Value	Pounds	Value	Pounds	Value
Fyke nets: Ohio River	5	$1	8,150	$1,445	7,750	$1,480	3,720	$744	5	$1
Set lines: Ohio River	------	------	2,895	572	2,055	369	13,700	2,410	------	------
Total, by waters: Ohio River	5	1	11,045	2,017	9,805	1,849	17,420	3,154	5	1

Apparatus and waters	Drum, freshwater, or sheepshead		Pike perch, sauger		Pike perch, wall-eyed		Quillback, or American carp		Sturgeon, shovelnose	
	Pounds	Value	Pounds	Value	Pounds	Value	Pounds	Value	Pounds	Value
Fyke nets: Ohio River	10,550	$1,905	700	$165	170	$44	19,825	$3,390	130	$20
Set lines: Ohio River	7,770	1,321	------	------	60	13	625	125	330	50
Total, by waters: Ohio River	18,320	3,226	700	165	230	57	20,450	3,515	460	70

Yield, by apparatus and waters, of the fisheries of Ohio, 1922—Continued

Apparatus and waters	Suckers		White bass		Mussel shells		Pearls	Slugs	Total	
	Pounds	*Value*	*Pounds*	*Value*	*Pounds*	*Value*	*Value*	*Value*	*Pounds*	*Value*
Fyke nets: Ohio River	26,225	$4,107	38	$11					77,268	$13,313
Set lines: Ohio River	120	7							27,555	4,867
Crowfoot bars:										
Muskingum River					56,000	$1,440	$55	$115	56,000	1,610
Ohio River					261,500	3,465	35	214	261,500	3,714
Tuscarawas River					28,000	730	30	38	28,000	798
Killbuck Creek					80,000	1,800	100	180	80,000	2,080
Mohican Creek					20,000	400	150	200	20,000	750
Total					445,500	7,835	370	747	445,500	8,952
Forks, etc.:										
Muskingum River					16,000	420	10	28	16,000	458
Tuscarawas River					8,000	205			8,000	205
Killbuck Creek					30,000	675			30,000	675
Mohican Creek					60,000	1,200			60,000	1,200
Wills Creek					38,000	430		20	38,000	450
Total					152,000	2,930	10	48	152,000	2,988
Total, by waters:										
Muskingum River					72,000	1,860	65	143	72,000	2,068
Ohio River	26,345	4,114	38	11	261,500	3,465	35	214	366,323	21,894
Tuscarawas River					36,000	935	30	38	36,000	1,003
Killbuck Creek					110,000	2,475	100	180	110,000	2,755
Mohican Creek					80,000	1,600	150	200	80,000	1,950
Wills Creek					38,000	430		20	38,000	450
Total	26,345	4,114	38	11	597,500	10,765	380	795	702,323	30,120

OKLAHOMA

The fisheries of Oklahoma were confined mainly to the Arkansas, Poteau, and Grand, or Neosho, Rivers, though some mussel shells were taken from the Verdigris River, and a few catfish and drum or sheepshead from the Illinois River.

The total number of persons engaged on all of the rivers in 1922 was 109, the investment was $12,261, and the output 363,170 pounds, valued at $31,215 to the fishermen. Fyke nets, set lines, and forks were the only forms of apparatus used. The catch consisted of 110,725 pounds of drum or sheepshead, valued at $10,076; 86,550 pounds of buffalofish, valued at $7,723; 55,425 pounds of catfish, valued at $7,172; 61,050 pounds of carp, valued at $5,646; small quantities of a few other species; and 44,870 pounds of mussel shells, valued at $383, including slugs.

The following tables show in detail the statistics of the fisheries of this State:

Persons engaged and investment in the fisheries of Oklahoma, 1922

Waters	Persons engaged			Gasoline boats		Rowboats		House boats	
	Fisher-men	Shores-men	Total	Number	Value	Number	Value	Number	Value
	Number	*Number*	*Number*	*Number*	*Value*	*Number*	*Value*	*Number*	*Value*
Arkansas River	53		53	7	$700	51	$610	5	$900
Grand River	27		27	1	100	27	270	6	1,500
Illinois River	6		6			6	60		
Poteau River	21	1	22	2	250	21	220	4	1,000
Verdigris River	1		1			1	10		
Total	108	1	109	10	1,050	106	1,170	15	3,400

*Persons engaged and investment in the fisheries of Oklahoma, 1922—*Continued

Waters	Fyke nets		Set lines		Forks		Shore property	Total investment
	Number	Value	Number	Value	Number	Value	Value	Value
Arkansas River	238	$2,380	163	$172			$1,150	$5,912
Grand River	100	700	75	75			300	2,945
Illinois River			12	6			10	76
Poteau River	127	1,270	34	25			525	3,290
Verdigris River					1	$3	25	38
Total	465	4,350	284	278	1	3	2,010	12,261

Yield, by apparatus and waters, of the fisheries of Oklahoma, 1922

Apparatus and waters	Buffalofish		Carp		Catfish		Drum, fresh-water, or sheepshead	
	Pounds	Value	Pounds	Value	Pounds	Value	Pounds	Value
Fyke nets:								
Arkansas River	55,300	$4,800	56,500	$5,258	15,025	$2,123	20,500	$1,826
Grand River	5,100	408	2,600	208	4,200	504	625	50
Poteau River	25,000	2,400	1,450	140	1,200	180	9,100	898
Total	85,400	7,608	60,550	5,606	20,425	2,807	30,225	2,774
Set lines:								
Arkansas River					6,400	880	46,200	4,372
Grand River			500	40	26,000	3,120	20,000	1,600
Illinois River					500	50	2,500	150
Poteau River	1,150	115			2,100	315	11,800	1,180
Total	1,150	115	500	40	35,000	4,365	80,500	7,302
Total by waters:								
Arkansas River	55,300	4,800	56,500	5,258	21,425	3,003	66,700	6,198
Grand River (Neosho River)	5,100	408	3,100	248	30,200	3,624	20,625	1,650
Illinois River					500	50	2,500	150
Poteau River	26,150	2,515	1,450	140	3,300	495	20,900	2,078
Total	86,550	7,723	61,050	5,646	55,425	7,172	110,725	10,076

Apparatus and waters	Paddlefish or spoonbill cat		Quillback, or American carp		Mussel shells		Slugs	Total	
	Pounds	Value	Pounds	Value	Pounds	Value	Value	Pounds	Value
Fyke nets:									
Arkansas River	550	$55						147,875	$14,062
Grand River			4,000	$160				16,525	1,330
Poteau River								36,750	3,618
Total	550	55	4,000	160				201,150	19,010
Set lines:									
Arkansas River								52,600	5,252
Grand River								46,500	4,760
Illinois River								3,000	200
Poteau River								15,050	1,610
Total								117,150	11,822
Forks: Verdigris River					44,870	$359	$24	44,870	383
Total by waters:									
Arkansas River	550	55						200,475	19,314
Grand River (Neosho River)			4,000	160				63,025	6,090
Illinois River								3,000	200
Poteau River								51,800	5,228
Verdigris River					44,870	359	24	44,870	383
Total	550	55	4,000	160	44,870	359	24	363,170	31,215

PENNSYLVANIA

No fishing was prosecuted in tributaries of the Mississippi River in Pennsylvania during 1922, except that a few tons of mussel shells, together with a few dollars worth of pearls and slugs, were taken from the Shenango River. All of the persons shown as shoremen were connected with the wholesale fish trade of Pittsburgh. Comparatively few of the fish handled at the latter city were from the Mississippi River and its tributaries, but were mainly Great Lakes and salt-water species. The investment of $126,380 was practically all in the wholesale trade just mentioned.

The following tables show in detail the statistics of the fisheries of this State:

Persons engaged and investment in the fisheries of Pennsylvania, 1922

Items	Number	Value	Items	Number	Value
Persons engaged:			Investment:		
Fishermen	2		Rowboats	2	$25
Shoremen (wholesale trade)	38		Crowfoot bars (pairs)	2	40
			Shore property		109,315
			Cash capital (wholesale trade)		17,000
Total	40		Total		126,380

Yield, by apparatus, of the fisheries of Pennsylvania, 1922

Species	Crowfoot bars		By hand		Total	
	Pounds	*Value*	*Pounds*	*Value*	*Pounds*	*Value*
Mussel shells	25,000	$813	24,000	$780	49,000	$1,593
Pearls		5				5
Slugs		80		80		160
Total	25,000	898	24,000	860	49,000	1,758

SOUTH DAKOTA

The fisheries of South Dakota were confined to the James and Missouri Rivers. On the former river the output consisted of 80,000 pounds of mussel shells, valued at $1,136, including the value of a few pearls and slugs. On the Missouri River the catch consisted of 9,900 pounds of catfish, valued at $2,120; 5,875 pounds of carp, valued at $587; and 5,675 pounds of buffalofish, valued at $568. The apparatus used were fyke nets, trammel nets, and set lines for the fish, and forks and rakes for taking the mussels.

The following tables show in detail the statistics of the fisheries of this State:

Persons engaged and investment in the fisheries of South Dakota, 1922

Items	James River		Missouri River		Total	
	Number	*Value*	*Number*	*Value*	*Number*	*Value*
Persons engaged: Fishermen	6		11		17	
Investment:						
Gasoline boats	1	$50	1	$150	2	$200
Rowboats	6	50	7	215	13	265
House boats			1	600	1	600
Fyke nets			55	434	55	434
Trammel nets			[1] 3	95	3	95
Forks	6	8			6	8
Rakes	6	8			6	8
Set lines			22	46	22	46
Shore property		35		510		545
Total		151		2,050		2,201

[1] 150 yards.

Yield, by apparatus and waters, of the fisheries of South Dakota, 1922

Items	James River		Missouri River		Total	
	Pounds	*Value*	*Pounds*	*Value*	*Pounds*	*Value*
Fyke nets:						
Buffalofish			2, 875	$288	2, 875	$288
Carp			3, 175	317	3, 175	317
Catfish			7, 400	1, 580	7, 400	1, 580
Total			13, 450	2, 185	13, 450	2, 185
Trammel nets:						
Buffalofish			2, 800	280	2, 800	280
Carp			2, 700	270	2, 700	270
Total			5, 500	550	5, 500	550
Forks and rakes:						
Mussel shells	80, 000	$1, 080			80, 000	1, 080
Pearls		50				50
Slugs		6				6
Total	80, 000	1, 136			80, 000	1, 136
Set lines: Catfish			2, 500	540	2, 500	540
Total, by species:						
Buffalofish			5, 675	568	5, 675	568
Carp			5, 875	587	5, 875	587
Catfish			9, 900	2, 120	9, 900	2, 120
Mussel shells	80, 000	1, 080			80, 000	1; 080
Pearls		50				50
Slugs		6				6
Total	80,.000	1, 136	21, 450	3, 275	101, 450	4, 411

TENNESSEE

The total number of persons engaged in the fisheries of Tennessee in 1922 was 562, of which number 468 were fishermen and 94 shoresmen, most of the latter being connected with the wholesale trade. The total investment amounted to $268,712, made up of 113 gasoline boats, valued at $17,525; 437 rowboats, valued at $6,480; 48 houseboats, valued at $12,775; 3,182 fyke nets, valued at $30,075; 10 haul seines, valued at $3,556; 22 trammel nets, valued at $2,495; 117 pairs of crowfoot bars, valued at $1,325; and several other less important forms of apparatus, together with $174,407 worth of shore property and $18,600 cash capital. Based on the catch, the fyke net is the leading form of apparatus used, followed in importance by the crowfoot bars for mussels.

The total output of 5,493,793 pounds, valued at $187,561, included 3,766,000 pounds of mussel shells, valued (including pearls and slugs) at $48,500. The more important fish products were buffalofish, catfish, drum or sheepshead, crappie, paddlefish or spoonbill cat, and carp.

Owing to its important mussel fishery, the Tennessee River, with its total production of 3,143,500 pounds, valued at $59,195, ranked first among the waters of the State, followed in importance by Reelfoot Lake, with a production of 698,472 pounds of fish, valued to the fishermen at $55,646. The Mississippi River ranked third, with a catch of 533,121 pounds, valued at $34,791. The combined output of several lakes tributary to the Mississippi River amounted to 101,850 pounds, valued at $13,302. Mussels were taken in the Cumberland, Holston, and Clinch Rivers, as well as in the Tennessee River.

The following tables show in detail the statistics of the fisheries of this State:

Persons engaged and investment in the fisheries of Tennessee, 1922

Waters	Persons engaged			Gasoline boats		Rowboats		House boats	
	Fisher-men	Shores-men	Total	No.	Value	No.	Value	No.	Value
	No.	*No.*	*No.*	*No.*	*Value*	*No.*	*Value*	*No.*	*Value*
Clinch River	20		20			20	$120		
Cumberland River	70		70	9	$1,100	70	684		
Hatchee River	8		8	4	650	4	60		
Holston River	25		25			25	150		
Obion River	27	7	34	10	2,000	15	255	8	$2,500
Mississippi River	105	42	147	43	8,950	52	995	23	8,550
Tennessee River	76	21	97	40	4,000	90	1,261	17	1,725
Reelfoot Lake	125	21	146	6	625	156	2,865		
Miscellaneous lakes	12	3	15	1	200	5	90		
Total	468	94	562	113	17,525	437	6,480	48	12,775

Waters	Fyke nets		Crowfoot bars, pairs		Set lines		Haul seines			Hand lines
	No.	Value	No.	Value	No.	Value	No.	Yards	Value	Value
	No.	*Value*	*No.*	*Value*	*No.*	*Value*	*No.*	*Yards*	*Value*	*Value*
Cumberland River	86	$880	42	$575	47	$71				
Hatchee River	50	1,250			6	9				
Obion River	155	2,175			36	85	1	1,200	$1,000	
Mississippi River	446	7,900			110	224	7	2,400	2,056	
Tennessee River	216	2,160	75	750	94	84				
Reelfoot Lake	2,223	15,650			53	698				$140
Miscellaneous lakes	6	60					2	600	500	
Total	3,182	30,075	117	1,325	346	1,171	10	4,200	3,556	140

Waters	Trammel nets			Gigs		Tongs		Shore prop-erty	Cash capital	Total invest-ment
	No.	Yards	Value	No.	Value	No.	Value			
	No.	*Yards*	*Value*	*No.*	*Value*	*No.*	*Value*			
Clinch River								$30		$150
Cumberland River						13	$140	255		3,705
Hatchee River								50		2,019
Holston River								25		175
Obion River								3,900	$1,000	12,915
Mississippi River	1	100	$60					123,072	13,000	164,807
Tennessee River								27,805		37,785
Reelfoot Lake	20	2,964	2,360	30	$23			17,970	4,600	44,931
Miscellaneous lakes	1	150	75					1,300		2,225
Total	22	3,214	2,495	30	23	13	140	174,407	18,600	268,712

Yield, by apparatus and waters, of the fisheries of Tennessee, 1922

Apparatus and waters	Black bass		Bowfin		Buffalofish		Carp	
	Pounds	*Value*	*Pounds*	*Value*	*Pounds*	*Value*	*Pounds*	*Value*
Fyke nets:								
Cumberland River					6,800	$540	3,250	$293
Hatchee River					13,000	650	36,000	1,800
Obion River					21,000	1,280	10,000	490
Mississippi River					186,222	10,865	64,000	2,610
Tennessee River					2,200	220	9,600	960
Reelfoot Lake			3,000	$60	150,000	12,000	41,000	1,640
Miscellaneous lakes					2,000	160	500	35
Total			3,000	60	381,222	25,715	164,350	7,828
Set lines:								
Cumberland River					1,550	137	1,500	141
Obion River					1,000	60		
Mississippi River					2,600	156		
Tennessee River					550	55	1,500	150
Reelfoot Lake					3,353	284		
Total					9,253	692	3,000	291
Haul seines:								
Mississippi River					56,100	3,300	7,500	320
Obion River					25,000	1,500	5,000	250
Miscellaneous lakes			500	30	20,800	1,630	2,150	150
Total			500	30	101,900	6,430	14,650	720
Trammel nets:								
Mississippi River					3,500	175	2,000	100
Reelfoot Lake			1,873	37	52,813	4,225	14,111	564
Miscellaneous lakes					12,450	995	2,150	150
Total			1,873	37	68,763	5,395	18,261	814
Hand lines: Reelfoot Lake	33,962	$6,105						
Total by waters:								
Cumberland River					8,350	677	4,750	434
Hatchee River					13,000	650	36,000	1,800
Obion River					47,000	2,840	15,000	740
Mississippi River					248,422	14,496	73,500	3,030
Tennessee River					2,750	275	11,100	1,110
Reelfoot Lake	33,962	6,105	4,873	97	206,366	16,509	55,111	2,204
Miscellaneous lakes			500	30	35,250	2,785	4,800	335
Grand total	33,962	6,105	5,373	127	561,138	38,232	200,261	9,653

Yield, by apparatus and waters, of the fisheries of Tennessee, 1922—Continued

Apparatus and waters	Catfish		Crappie		Drum, fresh-water, or sheepshead	
	Pounds	Value	Pounds	Value	Pounds	Value
Fyke nets:						
Cumberland River	3,300	$459			6,150	$580
Hatchee River	1,700	119			1,500	75
Obion River	2,000	200	50	$5	6,800	392
Mississippi River	25,500	2,525	750	75	46,722	2,557
Tennessee River	49,700	6,220			50,700	5,070
Reelfoot Lake	3,000	240	16,231	2,435	60,000	1,200
Miscellaneous lakes	200	20			300	6
Total	85,400	9,783	17,031	2,515	172,172	9,880
Set lines:						
Cumberland River	11,800	1,625			1,500	141
Hatchee River	4,000	280				
Obion River	16,000	1,600			5,200	308
Mississippi River	57,200	5,595			36,100	1,951
Tennessee River	22,800	3,020			4,000	400
Reelfoot Lake	86,000	6,880	1,000	150	1,500	30
Total	197,800	19,000	1,000	150	48,300	2,830
Haul seines:						
Mississippi River	3,250	323	300	31	11,500	628
Obion River	1,500	150	200	20	10,000	600
Miscellaneous lakes	5,200	484	400	60	10,000	200
Total	9,950	957	900	111	31,500	1,428
Trammel nets:						
Mississippi River	300	20			300	15
Reelfoot Lake	7,360	589	6,000	900	9,794	196
Miscellaneous lakes	1,100	107	300	45	3,000	60
Total	8,760	716	6,300	945	13,094	271
Hand lines: Reelfoot Lake	1,000	80	60,787	9,118		
Total by waters:						
Cumberland River	15,100	2,084			7,650	721
Hatchee River	5,700	399			1,500	75
Obion River	19,500	1,950	250	25	22,000	1,300
Mississippi River	86,250	8,463	1,050	106	94,622	5,151
Tennessee River	72,500	9,240			54,700	5,470
Reelfoot Lake	97,360	7,789	84,018	12,603	71,294	1,426
Miscellaneous lakes	6,500	611	700	105	13,300	266
Grand total	302,910	30,536	86,018	12,839	265,066	14,409

Apparatus and waters	Eels		Minnows		Paddlefish or spoonbill cat		Paddlefish caviar	
	Pounds	Value	Pounds	Value	Pounds	Value	Pounds	Value
Fyke nets:								
Cumberland River					1,050	$95		
Obion River					100	20		
Mississippi River					1,750	222		
Total					2,900	337		
Set lines: Reelfoot Lake	200	$12			1,888	142		
Haul seines:								
Mississippi River			500	$500	8,227	1,800		
Obion River					400	80		
Miscellaneous lakes					40,600	8,570	200	$600
Total			500	500	49,227	10,450	200	600
Hand lines: Reelfoot Lake	378	23						
Total by waters:								
Cumberland River					1,050	95		
Obion River					500	100		
Mississippi River			500	500	9,977	2,022		
Reelfoot Lake	578	35			1,888	142		
Miscellaneous lakes					40,600	8,570	200	600
Grand total	578	35	500	500	54,015	10,929	200	600

Yield, by apparatus and waters, of the fisheries of Tennessee, 1922—Continued

Apparatus and waters	Quillback or American carp		Rock bass		Sturgeon, shovelnose		Suckers	
	Pounds	Value	Pounds	Value	Pounds	Value	Pounds	Value
Fyke nets:								
Cumberland River					1,400	$120	6,650	$645
Obion River	2,000	$120						
Mississippi River	14,300	508						
Tennessee River	1,200	120					41,250	4,125
Reelfoot Lake			463	$69				
Total	17,500	748	463	69	1,400	120	47,900	4,770
Haul seines:								
Mississippi River	3,000	75						
Obion River	3,000	180						
Total	6,000	255						
Hand lines: Reelfoot Lake			400	60				
Total by waters:								
Cumberland River					1,400	120	6,650	645
Obion River	5,000	300						
Mississippi River	17,300	583						
Tennessee River	1,200	120					41,250	4,125
Reelfoot Lake			863	129				
Grand total	23,500	1,003	863	129	1,400	120	47,900	4,770

Apparatus and waters	Sunfish		White bass		Shrimp		Frogs	
	Pounds	Value	Pounds	Value	Pounds	Value	Pounds	Value
Fyke nets:								
Obion River			200	$12				
Mississippi River			1,200	140				
Reelfoot Lake	85,008	$4,250	668	33				
Total	85,008	4,250	2,068	185				
Set lines: Reelfoot Lake	183	9						
Haul seines:								
Mississippi River					300	$300		
Obion River			250	15				
Total			250	15	300	300		
Trammel nets: Reelfoot Lake	4,000	200	300	15				
Gigs: Reelfoot Lake							6,000	$1,800
Hand lines: Reelfoot Lake	45,000	2,250	1,000	50				
Total by waters:								
Obion River			450	27				
Mississippi River			1,200	140	300	300		
Reelfoot Lake	134,191	6,709	1,968	98			6,000	1,800
Grand total	134,191	6,709	3,618	265	300	300	6,000	1,800

Yield, by apparatus and waters, of the fisheries of Tennessee, 1922—Continued

Apparatus and waters	Mussel shells		Pearls	Slugs	Total	
	Pounds	Value	Value	Value	Pounds	Value
Fyke nets:						
Cumberland River					28,600	$2,732
Hatchee River					52,200	2,644
Obion River					42,150	2,519
Mississippi River					340,444	19,502
Tennessee River					154,650	16,715
Reelfoot Lake					359,370	21,927
Miscellaneous lakes					3,000	221
Total					980,414	66,260
Crowfoot bars:						
Cumberland River	374,000	$3,825	$50	$249	374,000	4,124
Tennessee River	2,960,000	38,465		390	2,960,000	38,855
Total	3,334,000	42,290	50	639	3,334,000	42,979
Set lines:						
Cumberland River					16,350	2,044
Hatchee River					4,000	280
Obion River					22,200	1,968
Mississippi River					95,900	7,702
Tennessee River					28,850	3,625
Reelfoot Lake					94,324	7,507
Total					261,624	23,126
Haul seines:						
Mississippi River					90,677	7,277
Obion River					45,350	2,795
Miscellaneous lakes					79,850	11,724
Total					215,877	21,796
Trammel nets:						
Mississippi River					6,100	310
Reelfoot Lake					96,251	6,726
Miscellaneous lakes					19,000	1,357
Total					121,351	8,393
Gigs: Reelfoot Lake					6,000	1,800
Tongs, etc.:						
Clinch River	160,000	1,600	200	400	160,000	2,200
Cumberland River	72,000	565		6	72,000	571
Holston River	200,000	2,000	250	500	200,000	2,750
Total	432,000	4,165	450	906	432,000	5,521
Hand lines: Reelfoot Lake					142,527	17,686
Total by waters:						
Clinch River	160,000	1,600	200	400	160,000	2,200
Cumberland River	446,000	4,390	50	255	490,950	9,471
Hatchee River					56,200	2,924
Holston River	200,000	2,000	250	500	200,000	2,750
Obion River					109,700	7,282
Mississippi River					533,121	34,791
Tennessee River	2,960,000	38,465		390	3,143,500	59,195
Reelfoot Lake					698,472	55,646
Miscellaneous lakes					101,850	13,302
Grand total	3,766,000	46,455	500	1,545	5,493,793	187,561

TEXAS

The only waters in Texas tributary to the Mississippi River in which fisheries were prosecuted in 1922 were the Sulphur River and Caddo Lake, in which 50 fishermen and 7 shoresmen were engaged. The total investment amounted to $11,662, with a total production of 183,949 pounds, valued at $18,547. Based on the catch, the fyke net was the most important form of apparatus used, followed by hand lines, trammel nets, pound nets, gill nets, and set lines. The most important species taken were crappie, buffalofish, paddlefish cr spoonbill cat, catfish, and black bass.

The following tables show in detail the statistics of the fisheries of this State:

Persons engaged and investment in the fisheries of Texas, 1922

Items	Sulphur River			Caddo Lake			Total		
	Number	*Yards*	*Value*	*Number*	*Yards*	*Value*	*Number*	*Yards*	*Value*
Persons engaged:									
Fishermen	12			38			50		
Shoresmen				7			7		
Total	12			45			57		
Investment:									
Gasoline boats				10		$2,250	10		$2,250
Rowboats	7		$95	38		760	45		855
Fyke nets	15		150	260		2,600	275		2,750
Gill nets	1	100	40	15	1,275	700	16	1,375	740
Trammel nets	2	200	80	12	1,020	480	14	1,220	560
Pound nets	5		125				5		125
Hand lines						28			28
Set lines	2		4				2		4
Shore property			100			3,250			3,350
Cash capital						1,000			1,000
Total			594			11,068			11,662

Yield, by apparatus and waters, of the fisheries of Texas, 1922

Apparatus and Waters	Black bass		Buffalofish		Carp		Catfish		Crappie	
	Pounds	*Value*	*Pounds*	*Value*	*Pounds*	*Value*	*Pounds*	*Value*	*Pounds*	*Value*
Fyke nets:										
Sulphur River			6,000	$360	1,000	$60	300	$24		
Caddo Lake			5,715	667			2,000	220	31,882	$3,784
Total			11,715	1,027	1,000	60	2,300	244	31,882	3,784
Gill nets:										
Sulphur River			3,000	180	500	30				
Caddo Lake			5,715	667						
Total			8,715	847	500	30				
Trammel nets:										
Sulphur River			4,000	240	600	36				
Caddo Lake			5,715	667					2,000	235
Total			9,715	907	600	36			2,000	235
Pound nets: Sulphur River			25,000	1,500	6,000	360	1,000	80		
Set lines: Sulphur River							2,000	240		
Hand lines: Caddo Lake	11,028	$1,309	2,000	140			11,061	1,216	21,254	2,523
Total by waters:										
Sulphur River			38,000	2,280	8,100	486	3,300	344		
Caddo Lake	11,028	1,309	19,145	2,141			13,061	1,436	55,136	6,542
Total	11,028	1,309	57,145	4,421	8,100	486	16,361	1,780	55,136	6,542

Yield, by apparatus and waters, of the fisheries of Texas, 1922—Continued

Apparatus and waters	Drum, fresh-water, or sheepshead		Paddlefish or spoonbill cat		Paddlefish caviar		Total	
	Pounds	*Value*	*Pounds*	*Value*	*Pounds*	*Value*	*Pounds*	*Value*
Fyke nets:								
Sulphur River	1,500	$90					8,800	$534
Caddo Lake	1,669	166	8,436	$742	170	$375	49,872	5,954
Total	3,169	256	8,436	742	170	375	58,672	6,488
Gill nets:								
Sulphur River	600	36					4,100	246
Caddo Lake			8,436	742	165	375	14,316	1,784
Total	600	36	8,436	742	165	375	18,416	2,030
Trammel nets:								
Sulphur River	600	36					5,200	312
Caddo Lake			8,438	742	165	375	16,318	2,019
Total	600	36	8,438	742	165	375	21,518	2,331
Pound nets: Sulphur River	4,000	240	1,000	30			37,000	2,210
Set lines: Sulphur River	1,000	60					3,000	300
Hand lines: Caddo Lake							45,343	5,188
Total by waters:								
Sulphur River	7,700	462	1,000	30			58,100	3,602
Caddo Lake	1,669	166	25,310	2,226	500	1,125	125,849	14,945
Total	9,369	628	26,310	2,256	500	1,125	183,949	18,547

WEST VIRGINIA

In 1922 there were 129 persons engaged in the fishing and related industries of West Virginia. The total investment in boats, apparatus, and shore property amounted to $11,673. The fishery was confined to the Kanawa and Ohio rivers, the total output being 37,200 pounds, valued at $5,976, from the Kanawa River and 58,045 pounds, valued at $1,989, from the Ohio River. Of the latter 50,500 pounds were mussel shells, valued (including slugs) at $699.

The following tables show in detail the statistics of the fisheries of this State:

Persons engaged and investment in the fisheries of West Virginia, 1922

Items	Kanawa River		Ohio River		Total	
	Number	*Value*	*Number*	*Value*	*Number*	*Value*
Persons engaged:						
Fishermen	38		14		52	
Shoresmen			77		77	
Total	38		91		129	
Investment:						
Gasoline boats	2	$200	6	$650	8	$850
Rowboats	38	475	13	225	51	700
House boats			6	625	6	625
Set lines	46	132	9	13	55	145
Crowfoot bars, (pairs)			8	160	8	160
Shore property		128		9,065		9,193
Total		935		10,738		11,673

Yield, by apparatus and waters, of the fisheries of West Virginia, 1922

Apparatus and species	Kanawa River		Ohio River		Total	
	Pounds	Value	Pounds	Value	Pounds	Value
Set lines:						
Buffalofish	2,380	$450	990	$200	3,370	$650
Carp	2,250	426	540	100	2,790	526
Catfish	28,150	4,225	4,340	655	32,490	4,880
Drum, fresh-water, or sheepshead	4,420	875	1,610	325	6,030	1,200
Sturgeon, shovelnose			65	10	65	10
Total	37,200	5,976	7,545	1,290	44,745	7,266
Crowfoot bars:						
Mussel shells			50,500	631	50,500	631
Slugs				68		68
Total			50,500	699	50,500	699
Total, by species:						
Buffalofish	2,380	450	990	200	3,370	650
Carp	2,250	426	540	100	2,790	526
Catfish	28,150	4,225	4,340	655	32,490	4,880
Drum, fresh-water, or sheepshead	4,420	875	1,610	325	6,030	1,200
Sturgeon, shovelnose			65	10	65	10
Mussel shells			50,500	631	50,500	631
Slugs				68		68
Total	37,200	5,976	58,045	1,989	95,245	7,965

WISCONSIN

The fisheries of Wisconsin, prosecuted on the Mississippi River and tributaries in 1922, gave employment to 587 fishermen and 302 shoresmen, most of the latter being connected with the pearl-button industry. The total investment amounted to $442,950, most of which was also represented in the pearl-button industry. Other important items were 343 gasoline boats, valued at $76,255; 87 haul seines, valued at $28,875; 1,100 fyke nets, valued at $23,700; and 518 gill nets, valued at $6,930.

The products of the State amounted to 8,089,494 pounds, valued at $285,624. Of this total mussel shells contributed 3,105,140 pounds, valued at $68,064, including pearls and slugs. The carp fishery in Wisconsin has increased in importance within recent years; and in 1922 the value of the catch was nearly one-half that of all the products of the State taken from the Mississippi River and tributaries. Other important species worthy of mention were buffalofish, catfish, and drum or sheepshead. Based on the catch, the most important form of apparatus was the haul seine, followed by the crowfoot bar for taking mussels, the fyke net, gill net, set line, and spear. Large quantities of mussels were taken by hand while wading. Mussels were taken from several of the rivers, including the Mississippi and St. Croix, but the latter two were the only ones from which fish were taken commercially.

The following tables show in detail the statistics of the fisheries, of this State:

Persons engaged and investment in the fisheries of Wisconsin, 1922

Waters	Persons engaged			Gasoline boats		Rowboats		House boats	
	Fisher-men	Shores-men	Total	Number	Value	Number	Value	Number	Value
	Number	Number	Number	Number	Value	Number	Value	Number	Value
Baraboo River	7		7	2	$300	5	$75		
Fox River	50	5	55	26	2,445	19	365		
Mississippi River	490	277	767	306	71,310	231	5,175	2	$735
Rock River	7		7	4	600	2	40		
St. Croix River	26		26	3	1,100	9	365		
Wisconsin River	7	20	27	2	500	6	115		
Total	587	302	889	343	76,255	272	6,135	2	735

Waters	Haul seines			Crowfoot bars, pairs		Fyke nets		Gill nets		
	Number	Yards	Value	Number	Value	Number	Value	Number	Yards	Value
Baraboo River				4	$40					
Fox River				48	805					
Mississippi River	84	27,025	$25,675	187	2,040	1,100	$23,700	434	12,700	$5,670
Rock River				7	70					
St. Croix River	3	1,935	3,200	1	15			84	4,025	1,260
Wisconsin River				2	20					
Total	87	28,960	28,875	249	2,990	1,100	23,700	518	16,725	6,930

Waters	Set lines		Spears		Shore property	Cash capital	Total invest-ment
	Number	Value	Number	Value	Value	Value	Value
Baraboo River					$75		$490
Fox River					3,270		6,885
Mississippi River	159	$289	7	$17	272,709	$10,100	417,420
Rock River					15		725
St. Croix River					4,000		9,940
Wisconsin River					6,855		7,490
Total	159	289	7	17	286,924	10,100	442,950

Yield, by apparatus and waters, of the fisheries of Wisconsin, 1922.

Apparatus and waters	Bowfin		Buffalofish		Carp		Catfish and bullheads	
	Pounds	Value	Pounds	Value	Pounds	Value	Pounds	Value
Haul seines:								
Mississippi River	16,250	$231	299,953	$18,804	2,254,278	$80,019	155,572	$16,066
St. Croix River			19,000	1,225	164,500	7,006	200	30
Total	16,250	.231	318,953	20,029	2,418,778	87,025	155,772	16,096
Fyke nets: Mississippi River	736	11	168,059	10,800	430,414	17,357	40,900	4,275
Gill nets:								
Mississippi River	750	10	96,191	5,228	469,855	17,067	20,050	1,271
St. Croix River			2,700	166	36,400	1,662		
Total	750	10	98,891	5,394	506,255	18,729	20,050	1,271
Set lines: Mississippi River			2,079	93	5,659	159	63,015	7,068
Spears: Mississippi River			1,399	46	25,092	802	347	22
Total by waters:								
Mississippi River	17,736	252	567,681	34,971	3,185,298	115,404	279,884	28,702
St. Croix River			21,700	1,391	200,900	8,668	200	30
Grand total	17,736	252	589,381	36,362	3,386,198	124,072	280,084	28,732

Yield, by apparatus and waters, of the fisheries of Wisconsin, 1922—Continued

Apparatus and waters	Drum, fresh-water, or sheepshead		Eels		Paddlefish or spoonbill cat		Quillback, or American carp		Suckers	
	Pounds	Value	Pounds	Value	Pounds	Value	Pounds	Value	Pounds	Value
Haul seines:										
Mississippi River	197,086	$8,815	263	$6	27,085	$1,517	87,417	$3,470	24,431	$1,241
St. Croix River							3,000	150	700	40
Total	197,086	8,815	263	6	27,085	1,517	90,417	3,620	25,131	1,281
Fyke nets: Mississippi River	138,118	5,765	50	1	2,100	163	24,000	615	8,050	169
Gill nets: Mississippi River	141,643	4,376			250	7	26,000	585	13,035	313
Set lines: Mississippi River	16,584	920					120	4		
Spears: Mississippi River	495	18			36	2			50	3
Total by waters:										
Mississippi River	493,926	19,894	313	7	29,471	1,689	137,537	4,624	45,566	1,726
St. Croix River							3,000	150	700	40
Grand total	493,926	19,894	313	7	29,471	1,689	140,537	4,774	46,266	1,766

Apparatus and waters	Turtles		Mussel Shells		Pearls	Slugs	Total	
	Pounds	Value	Pounds	Value	Value	Value	Pounds	Value
Haul seines:								
Mississippi River	367	$10					3,062,702	$130,179
St. Croix River							187,400	8,451
Total	367	10					3,250,102	138,630
Crowfoot bars:								
Baraboo River			44,000	$660	$20	$75	44,000	755
Fox River			481,140	10,545	195	890	481,140	11,630
Mississippi River			2,000,000	34,840	3,900	5,405	2,000,000	44,145
Rock River			102,000	2,550		100	102,000	2,650
St. Croix River			6,000	75		7	6,000	82
Wisconsin River			16,000	240	25	50	16,000	315
Total			2,649,140	48,910	4,140	6,527	2,649,140	59,577
Fyke nets: Mississippi River							812,427	39,156
Gill nets:								
Mississippi River	75	2					767,849	28,809
St. Croix River							39,100	1,828
Total	75	2					806,949	30,637
Set lines: Mississippi River							87,457	8,244
Spears: Mississippi River							27,419	893
By hand:								
Baraboo River			60,000	900	30	75	60,000	1,005
Fox River			28,000	800	85	20	28,000	905
Mississippi River			336,000	5,685	250	125	336,000	6,060
St. Croix River			8,000	120		12	8,000	132
Wisconsin River			24,000	360		25	24,000	385
Total			456,000	7,865	365	257	456,000	8,487
Total by waters:								
Baraboo River			104,000	1,560	50	150	104,000	· 1,760
Fox River			509,140	11,345	280	910	509,140	12,535
Mississippi River	442	12	2,336,000	40,525	4,150	5,530	7,093,854	257,486
Rock River			102,000	2,550		100	102,000	2,650
St. Croix River			14,000	195		19	240,500	10,493
Wisconsin River			40,000	600	25	75	40,000	700
Grand total	442	12	3,105,140	56,775	4,505	6,784	8,089,494	285,624

FISHERIES OF THE GREAT LAKES, LAKE OF THE WOODS, AND RAINY LAKE, 1922

The statistics of the fisheries of the Great Lakes, Lake of the Woods, and Rainy Lake, presented herewith, are the result of a statistical canvass covering the calender year 1922. The canvass was so planned and conducted as to make its results comparable with the statistics for the year 1917, with the exception that the mussel fisheries of certain rivers tributary to Lake Michigan and Lake Erie were included, although they had not heretofore been covered by statistical canvasses of the Great Lakes. The statistics obtained have already been published in condensed form in Statistical Bulletin No. 618. The detailed statistics are published for the first time in the present report.

EARLIER PUBLICATIONS

Earlier publications relating to the fisheries of the Great Lakes, published in Washington, D. C., follow:

1887. The fisheries of the Great Lakes. By Frederick W. True. Elaborated from notes gathered by Mr. Ludwig Kumlien. *In* The Fisheries and Fishery Industries of the United States, by George Brown Goode and associates, 1880 (1887), Section II, Part XVII, pp. 631–673.

1887. The fisheries of the Great Lakes. By Ludwig Kumlien. *In* The Fisheries and Fishery Industries of the United States, by George Brown Goode and associates, 1880 (1887), Section V, Vol. I, Part XIV, pp. 757–769.

1891. Review of the fisheries of the Great Lakes in 1885, compiled by Hugh M. Smith and Merwin-Marie Snell, with introduction and description of fishing vessels and boats by J. W. Collins. Appendix, Report of the Commissioner, United States Commission of Fish and Fisheries, 1887 (1891), pp. 1–133.

1892. Report on an investigation of the fisheries of Lake Ontario. By Hugh M. Smith. Bulletin, United States Fish Commission, Vol. X. 1890 (1892), pp. 177–215.

1894. The fisheries of the Great Lakes. By Hugh M. Smith. Report of the Commissioner, United States Commission of Fish and Fisheries, 1892 (1894), pp. 363–462.

1896. Report of the Division of Statistics and Methods of the Fisheries. By Hugh M. Smith. Report of the Commissioner, United States Commission of Fish and Fisheries, 1895 (1896), pp. 93–103.

1898. Report of the Joint Commission relative to the preservation of the fisheries in waters contiguous to Canada and the United States. By Richard Rathbun and William Wakeham. House Executive Document No. 315, Fifty-fourth Congress, second session, 1897, pp. 1–178.

1899. Fisheries of Lake Ontario. Report of the Commissioner, United States Commission of Fish and Fisheries, 1898 (1899), pp. clii–clvi.

1899. Statistics of certain fisheries of the New England and Middle Atlantic States and the Great Lakes. Report of the Commissioner, United States Commission of Fish and Fisheries, 1898 (1899), pp. clxvi–clxxv. [In this report the figures presented relate to the fiscal year 1897.]

1902. Statistics of the fisheries of the Great Lakes. By C. H. Townsend. Report of the Commissioner, United States Commission of Fish and Fisheries, 1901 (1902), pp. 575–657.

1905. Statistics of the fisheries of the Great Lakes in 1903. By A. B. Alexander. Report of the Bureau of Fisheries, 1904 (1905), pp. 643–731.

1911. Fisheries of the United States, 1908. Special Report, Bureau of the Census, 1911.

1917. Fresh-water mussel fishery. *In* Report, United States Commission of Fisheries, 1915 (1917), Document No. 827, pp. 63–69.

1920. Fisheries of the Great Lakes, Lake of the Woods, and Rainy Lake in 1917. *In* Fishery Industries of the United States. Report of the Division of Statistics and Methods of the Fisheries for 1919, by Lewis Radcliffe. Appendix X, Report, United States Commissioner of Fisheries, 1919 (1921), pp. 52–128. Bureau of Fisheries Document No. 892.

COMMON AND SCIENTIFIC NAMES OF THE FISHES OF THE GREAT LAKES

For the sake of clarity as to the species referred to in the tables and discussions of the fisheries of the Great Lakes, the following list of common and scientific names of fishes is appended:

Black bass	*Micropterus salmoides.*
Bowfin	*Amiatus calvus.*
Buffalofish	*Ictiobus cyprinella.*
Burbot	*Lota maculosa.*
Carp, German	*Cyprinus carpio.*
Catfish and bullheads	{*Ameiurus* (species). {*Ictalurus punctatus.*
Ciscoes [6]	*Leucichthys* (species).
Eel	*Anguilla chrysypa.*
Goldeye	*Hiodon alosoides.*
Mooneye	*Hiodon tergisus.*
Muskellunge	*Esox masquinongy.*
Pike	{*Esox lucius.* {*Esox vermiculatus.*
Pike perch (blue perch)	*Stizostedion vitreum.*
Pike perch (sauger)	*Stizostedion vitreum.*
Pike perch (wall-eyed)	*Stizostedion canadense griseum.*
Rock bass	*Ambloplites rupestris.*
Sheepshead or drum	*Aplodinotus grunniens.*
Sturgeon	*Acipenser rubicundus.*
Suckers	Catostomidæ (species).
Sunfishes	Centrarchidæ (species).
Trout, lake	*Cristivomer namaycush.*
Trout, steelhead	*Salmo gairdneri.*
White bass	*Roccus chrysops.*
Whitefish, common	{*Coregonus clupeiformis.* {*Coregonus albus.*
Whitefish, Menominee	*Coregonus quadrilateralis.*
Yellow perch	*Perca flavescens.*

GENERAL STATISTICS

The number of persons engaged in the fisheries of the entire region covered by this canvass in 1922 was 8,162, the investment amounted to $12,186,413, and the products, 110,410,442 pounds, were valued at $6,799,633.

In the fisheries of the Great Lakes, not including the Lake of the Woods and Rainy Lake Region, the number of persons engaged was 8,039, of whom 1,777 were on vessels fishing, 4,357 in the shore or boat fisheries, and 1,905 employed on boats transporting and as shoresmen in the fisheries and wholesale fishery trade. In the fisheries of the various lakes, the number of persons engaged was as follows: Superior, 773; Michigan, 3,107; Huron, 1,001; St. Clair and the St. Clair River, 90; Erie, 2,628; and Ontario, including the St. Lawrence and Niagara Rivers, 440. Compared with the statistics for 1917, there were decreases in the number of persons employed in all but the St. Clair and the Lake Ontario regions. The total decrease amounted to 1,182 persons.

The investment in the fisheries and related industries amounted to $12,046,458, apportioned among the lakes as follows: Superior, $697,572; Michigan, $4,333,451; Huron, $1,648,767; St. Clair and St. Clair River, $17,857; Erie, $5,166,531; and Ontario, $182,280. The investment, as compared with 1917, has increased in all the fisheries excepting those of Lake Superior.

---

[6] Includes lake herring, chub, longjaw, bluefin and blackfin, and tullibee.

The products of the fisheries amounted to 108,732,443 pounds, having a value to the fishermen of $6,689,611. The yields of the various lakes were as follows: Superior, 10,988,020 pounds, valued at $484,273; Michigan, 26,128,199 pounds, valued at $2,133,849; Huron, 13,942,115 pounds, valued at $945,259; St. Clair and St. Clair River, 310,012 pounds, valued at $17,365; Erie, 56,338,298 pounds, valued at $2,977,064; and Ontario, 1,025,799 pounds, valued at $131,801.

The principal species taken, in order of value, including fresh, salted, and smoked fish, were lake trout, 13,726,039 pounds, valued at $1,647,638; pike perch, all species, 23,967,086 pounds, valued at $1,516,332; ciscoes, all species, 36,009,659 pounds, valued at $1,377,-055; whitefish, all species, 4,378,128 pounds, valued at $710,280; carp 8,119,441 pounds, valued at $330,874; yellow perch, 4,902,250 pounds, valued at $314,928; suckers, 5,395,213 pounds, valued at $263,575; catfish and bullheads, 1,662,298 pounds, valued at $117,417; and other fishes, 4,242,182 pounds, valued at $174,639. The production of shellfish totaled 6,330,147 pounds, valued at $236,873, of which mussel shells from rivers tributary to lakes Michigan and Erie constituted the largest item, 6,245,975 pounds, valued (together with the pearls and slugs) at $233,873.

The following table presents, by lakes, the number of persons engaged, the amount of capital invested, and the quantity and value of the products of the fisheries of the Great Lakes in 1922.

Persons engaged, investment, and products of the fisheries of the Great Lakes in 1922

Items	Lake Superior		Lake Michigan [1]		Lake Huron		Lake St. Clair [2]	
PERSONS ENGAGED	*Number*	*Value*	*Number*	*Value*	*Number*	*Value*	*Number*	*Value*
On vessels fishing	53		1,011		131			
On vessels transporting	10		115		9			
In shore or boat fisheries	640		1,146		705		90	
Shoresmen	70		835		156			
Total	773		3,107		1,001		90	
INVESTMENT								
Vessels, fishing, steam	6	$19,150	87	$341,100	18	$84,500		
Tonnage	115		1,709		443			
Outfit		12,545		65,282		25,190		
Vessels, fishing, gasoline	7	8,800	269	348,850	11	9,400		
Tonnage	64		2,442		89			
Outfit		5,030		60,346		2,385		
Vessels, transporting, steam					1	1,000		
Tonnage					8			
Outfit						65		
Vessles, transporting, gasoline	4	12,500	62	56,100	13	25,950		
Tonnage	35		528		110			
Outfit		2,700		6,410		2,000		
Sail and row boats	319	9,475	807	18,155	224	11,825	52	$2,770
Power boats	267	78,310	312	70,221	248	118,225	30	6,900
Apparatus, vessel fisheries:								
Gill nets	1,510	25,225	35,930	357,653	4,043	78,885		
Lines		2,830		23,525		7,275		
Apparatus, shore fisheries:								
Pound nets and trap nets	303	43,475	704	174,815	1,474	366,390		
Gill nets	8,087	94,257	10,453	51,102	2,960	36,139		
Fyke nets	28	1,200	1,196	27,655	425	26,290		
Seines, haul	7	420	40	7,945	75	18,290	3	2,700
Lines		6,070		430		1,070		87
Crawfish pots			5,255	1,409				
Other apparatus				4,968				
Shore and accessory property		291,557		1,889,033		644,388		5,400
Cash capital		84,028		828,452		189,500		
Total		697,572		4,333,451		1,648,767		17,857

[1] Includes mussel fisheries of the St. Joseph, Grand, Kalamazoo, Maple, Muskegon, Pigeon, Thornapple, and Wolf Rivers.
[2] Includes St. Clair River.

Persons engaged, investment, and products of the fisheries of the Great Lakes in 1922—Continued

Items	Lake Superior		Lake Michigan		Lake Huron		Lake St. Clair	
PRODUCTS	Pounds	Value	Pounds	Value	Pounds	Value	Pounds	Value
Black bass							2,000	$200
Buffalofish			892	$50	63	$3		
Burbot	829	$16	14,241	519	3,075	62		
Carp, German			754,027	25,222	1,065,116	41,256	260,000	10,400
Catfish and bullheads			148,629	7,520	64,826	4,518	1,005	148
Ciscoes:								
Fresh	5,158,254	99,259	5,435,013	202,461	2,775,403	90,176		
Frozen	936,151	18,981						
Salted	1,292,200	39,839	1,290,105	35,933	2,721,060	63,437		
Smoked	7,500	375	38,415	5,998				
Pike	16,201	2,063	46,388	5,421	39,473	2,985	4,040	404
Pike perch:								
Wall-eyed or yellow pike	23,298	3,268	132,948	21,185	1,260,374	171,102	38,620	5,741
Sheepshead or drum			4,472	107	46,760	1,400	16	1
Sturgeon	343	123	9,203	3,581	2,374	928	231	61
Sturgeon caviar			670	314	126	269		
Suckers, fresh	284,330	11,721	1,513,907	88,972	1,889,129	104,204		
Suckers, salted	11,800	413	5,760	147				
Trout, lake, fresh	2,807,490	252,685	8,735,585	1,171,801	2,108,249	215,501		
Trout, lake, salted	26,000	1,652	120	5				
Trout, steelhead			11,165	2,233				
White bass	6,900	207	1,005	38				
Whitefish, common, fresh	380,400	51,488	1,547,049	263,935	1,300,621	199,503		
Whitefish, common, salted	50	35						
Whitefish, common, caviar					1,289	1,009		
Whitefish, Menominee, fresh	10,827	478	107,163	7,977	30,029	1,708		
Whitefish, Menominee, salted	8,100	405	14,480	677	960	60		
Yellow perch	17,347	1,265	1,244,768	85,748	633,188	47,138	4,100	410
Crawfish			82,764	2,887				
Mussel shells			4,986,805	187,568				
Pearls				7,996				
Slugs				5,449				
Oil			2,625	105				
Total	10,988,020	484,273	26,128,199	2,133,849	13,942,115	945,259	310,012	17,365

Items	Lake Erie [3]		Lake Ontario [4]		Total	
PERSONS ENGAGED	Number	Value	Number	Value	Number	Value
On vessels fishing	582				1,777	
On vessels transporting	26				160	
In shore or boat fisheries	1,350		426		4,357	
Shoresmen	670		14		1,745	
Total	2,628		440		8,039	
INVESTMENT						
Vessels, fishing, steam	69	$438,100			180	$882,850
Tonnage	1,601				3,868	
Outfit		102,506				205,523
Vessels, fishing, gasoline	37	113,900			324	480,950
Tonnage	473				3,068	
Outfit		30,397				98,158
Vessels, transporting, steam	5	21,500			6	22,500
Tonnage	118				126	
Outfit		5,198				5,263
Vessels, transporting, gasoline	17	44,750			96	139,300
Tonnage	147				820	
Outfit		5,583				16,693
Sail and row boats	679	22,060	232	$7,498	2,313	71,783
Power boats	380	167,540	111	35,745	1,348	476,941
Apparatus, vessel fisheries:						
Gill nets	36,555	260,999			78,038	722,762
Lines						33,630
Apparatus, shore fisheries:						
Pound nets and trap nets	3,931	554,510	419	33,589	6,831	1,172,779
Gill nets	5,849	36,995	2,319	24,215	29,668	242,708
Fyke nets	752	35,190	204	3,362	2,605	93,697
Seines, haul	213	29,685	25	1,479	363	60,519
Lines		87		2,045		9,789
Crawfish pots					5,255	1,409
Fishing machines		44	9	1,175	9	1,175
Other apparatus				272		5,284
Shore and accessory property		2,148,230		47,900		5,026,508
Cash capital		1,149,257		25,000		2,276,237
Total		5,166,531		182,280		12,046,458

[3] Includes mussel fisheries of the Anglaize, Moumee, Sandusky, Tiffin, St. Marys, St. Joseph of the Moumee, Huron, and Raisin Rivers, and also men and investment in the wholesale fish trade of Detroit.
[4] Includes St. Lawrence and Niagara Rivers.

Persons engaged, investment, and products of the fisheries of the Great Lakes in 1922—Continued

Items	Lake Erie		Lake Ontario		Total	
PRODUCTS	*Pounds*	*Value*	*Pounds*	*Value*	*Pounds*	*Value*
Black bass					2,000	$200
Bowfin			1,558	$86	1,558	86
Buffalofish					955	53
Burbot	354,004	$6,089	15,641	1,587	387,790	8,273
Carp, German	5,899,181	242,937	141,117	11,059	8,119,441	330,874
Catfish and bullheads	1,337,519	96,883	110,319	8,348	1,662,298	117,417
Ciscoes:						
Fresh	16,158,239	804,601	194,319	15,545	29,721,228	1,212,042
Frozen					936,151	18,981
Salted			3,000	450	5,306,365	139,659
Smoked					45,915	6,373
Eels			55,323	4,931	55,323	4,931
Goldeye and mooneye	13,438	140			13,438	140
Muskellunge	85	9			85	9
Pike	65,095	3,878	19,448	2,304	190,645	17,055
Pike perch:						
Blue pike	14,542,195	720,970	47,540	4,247	14,589,735	725,217
Sauger	6,002,378	295,337			6,002,378	295,337
Wall-eyed or yellow pike	1,813,423	269,092	106,310	25,390	3,374,973	495,778
Rock bass			5,974	308	5,974	308
Sheephead or drum	2,362,343	56,952			2,413,591	58,460
Shiner			13,450	10,088	13,450	10,088
Sturgeon	15,475	4,293	68,698	17,130	96,324	26,116
Sturgeon caviar	127	256	935	2,796	1,858	3,635
Suckers, fresh	1,598,171	49,586	92,116	8,532	5,377,653	263,015
Suckers, salted					17,560	560
Sunfishes			13,687	636	13,687	636
Trout, lake, fresh	1,897	168	46,698	5,826	13,699,919	1,645,981
Trout, lake, salted					26,120	1,657
Trout, steelhead					11,165	2,233
White bass	1,022,609	42,006			1,030,514	42,251
Whitefish, common, fresh	922,209	173,402	54,951	9,603	4,205,230	697,931
Whitefish, common, salted					50	35
Whitefish, common, caviar					1,289	1,009
Whitefish, Menominee, fresh					148,019	10,163
Whitefish, Menominee, salted					23,540	1,142
Yellow perch	2,969,332	177,492	33,515	2,875	4,902,250	314,928
Other fish			1,200	60	1,200	60
Crawfish					82,764	2,887
Turtles	1,408	113			1,408	113
Mussel shells	1,259,170	30,580			6,245,975	218,148
Pearls		816				8,812
Slugs		1,464				6,913
Oil					2,625	105
Total	56,338,298	2,977,064	1,025,799	131,801	108,732,443	6,689,611

NOTE.—Ciscoes include lake herring, chub, longjaw, bluefin or blackfin, and tullibee. The mussel fisheries of the rivers tributary to Lake Michigan and Lake Erie have not previously been included in the statistics of the fisheries of the Great Lakes.

COMPARISON WITH PREVIOUS STATISTICS

An examination of the available statistics for previous years shows that there was a marked increase in all phases of the Great Lakes fisheries during the years 1880 to 1885; the number of persons employed doubled, the number of vessels and boats more than doubled, the number of pound nets, gill nets, and seines doubled, the investment more than tripled, and the catch of fish increased 45 per cent.

Subsequent to 1885 we find a general decline in most aspects of the fishery. The number of persons employed has never exceeded the 10,355 reported in 1885, and the number in 1922 (8,039) is the lowest reported in any canvass since 1880. Similarly, the number of vessels and boats reported in 1885 exceeds that of any later canvass, although not much in excess of the number reported in 1922. The number of pound nets reported has increased with each canvass until in 1917, when the maximum number, 8,433, was reported, but in 1922 the number dropped to 6,809. Gill nets also increased in number, until in 1917 there were 153,277. In 1922 the number dropped to 107,706. The history of the seines is somewhat different. After 1885 there was a distinct decline in the numbers reported, until in 1893 a minimum was reached, which was even below the number reported in 1880. Since then the number again increased, reaching 446 in 1917, but it declined to 363 in 1922. The investment in the fishery has constantly increased, the amount reported in 1922 being $11,720,821, which is greater than that of any previous report, and is almost nine times as great as that of 1880.

The total yield of the fisheries of the Great Lakes since 1885 has fluctuated between 86,000,000 and 114,000,000 pounds, the catch in 1922, amounting to 108,732,443 pounds, not being conspicuously greater or smaller than those of previous reports. The same is not true of the catches of individual species. The lake sturgeon has suffered the most serious decline, the catch in 1922 being less than 1.3 per cent that of 1880. The yield of whitefish was also considerably reduced in 1922, being less than 20 per cent that of 1880, though above that of 1903. The confusion existing in the early nomenclature of the fishes of the Great Lakes, and the various conditions in which they were reported (fresh, salted, smoked, etc.), prevent one from venturing too far in definite comparisons; but it is safe to say that the production of some of the most highly prized species has seriously declined, their places being taken by hitherto undesired species and the total yield thus sustained.

The following tables present summary statistics of the Great Lakes for various years, 1880 to 1922. The figures in the table on products include the fresh, frozen, salted, and smoked fish, none of which have been converted to a fresh basis and for that reason do not represent accurately comparable amounts. They may be useful, however, in indicating the general trend of the yield.

Comparative statistics of the fisheries of the Great Lakes for various years, from 1880 to 1922

PERSONS ENGAGED

Lakes	1880	1885	1890	1893	1899	1903	1908	1917	1922
Superior	414	914	653	916	613	918	792	1,348	773
Michigan	1,578	3,379	2,877	3,928	3,255	3,241	2,706	3,313	[4] 3,107
Huron	470	892	726	944	1,241	1,704	1,382	1,348	1,001
St. Clair [1]	356	272	611	529	442	355	221	64	90
Erie [2]	1,620	4,298	4,482	3,622	3,728	2,727	3,142	2,770	[4] 2,628
Ontario [3]	612	600	389	241	391	388	296	378	440
Total	5,050	10,355	9,738	10,180	9,670	9,333	8,539	9,221	8,039

[1] Includes St. Clair and Detroit Rivers. There was no fishing in Detroit River in 1917 and 1922.
[2] Includes persons in wholesale trade of Detroit, Mich.
[3] Includes St. Lawrence and Niagara Rivers.
[4] Includes persons engaged in the mussel fisheries of tributary rivers not shown in previous canvasses.

Comparative statistics of the fisheries of the Great Lakes for various years, from 1880 to 1922—Continued

APPARATUS AND CAPITAL EMPLOYED

Lakes and years	Vessels and boats [1]		Pound nets and trap nets		Gill nets		Seines		Other apparatus [2]	Shore property and cash capital	Total
	No.	Value	No.	Value	No.	Value	No.	Value	Value	Value	Value
Superior:											
1880	161	$26,240	43	$14,950	4,630	$25,280	32	$2,010	$200	$12,700	$81,380
1885	519	100,735	230	67,520	7,557	78,082	43	2,920	1,155	177,521	427,933
1890	328	85,275	140	34,435	5,974	63,476	19	955	2,763	179,778	366,682
1893	447	139,035	276	63,415	8,899	87,680	14	500	1,565	209,512	529,024
1899	315	69,045	162	25,820	7,229	99,283	1	50	1,058	167,023	372,083
1903	378	141,109	218	27,793	10,169	127,238	8	335	815	299,032	596,322
1908		149,000							159,000	83,000	391,000
1917	724	241,425	204	26,262	11,117	144,986	5	325	5,773	383,810	802,581
1922	603	128,235	303	43,475	9,597	119,482	7	420	10,100	375,585	677,297
Michigan: [3]											
1880	836	133,375	476	185,425	24,599	124,740	19	2,040	1,455	104,100	551,135
1885	1,402	368,326	715	253,840	58,516	326,902	87	6,950	13,457	788,356	1,757,831
1890	1,102	266,331	844	244,880	40,896	215,914	30	3,480	13,460	693,159	1,437,224
1893	1,549	357,987	785	181,385	54,237	352,084	28	2,520	27,863	1,092,219	2,063,497
1899	1,178	281,968	805	186,349	49,857	288,395	11	510	29,285	2,087,829	2,915,241
1903	1,363	386,396	980	198,960	48,645	269,754	44	2,384	37,743	2,593,950	3,489,187
1908		692,000							753,000	519,000	1,964,000
1917	1,131	771,723	1,134	242,570	83,807	645,074	61	18,120	69,263	2,108,141	3,854,891
1922	1,536	834,426	704	174,815	46,383	408,755	40	7,945	57,987	2,717,485	4,201,413
Huron:											
1880	111	20,905	189	49,425	3,360	20,600	28	5,600	3,500	3,700	103,730
1885	561	72,946	586	113,350	3,444	35,333			23,100	140,620	385,349
1890	417	36,898	551	88,515	2,206	21,665	6	600	7,155	254,025	408,858
1893	520	87,645	731	108,508	4,923	53,071	1	75	3,807	236,285	503,700
1899	539	87,585	996	111,839	5,676	54,384	9	673	8,188	203,989	474,953
1903	643	126,418	1,685	176,495	6,129	51,526	18	608	13,977	482,615	851,639
1908		185,000							281,000	267,000	733,000
1917	617	228,980	1,731	207,904	10,610	102,835	77	7,960	19,594	588,192	1,155,465
1922	515	250,900	1,474	366,390	7,003	115,024	75	18,290	34,635	833,888	1,619,127
St. Clair: [4]											
1880	52	8,000			180	1,080	42	6,000	1,500	24,000	40,580
1885	215	7,457	57	12,550	23	160	34	8,825	3,819	218,270	251,081
1890	166	28,775	34	9,450	814	9,418	28	6,240	5,580	150,682	210,145
1893	211	13,728	91	7,400	380	4,260	20	3,025	2,346	206,672	240,076
1899	188	3,770	5	1,050	60	600	13	1,255	915	46,945	54,535
1903	150	3,150					6	890	961	234,884	239,885
1908		10,000							8,000	28,000	46,000
1917	64	2,540					6	1,365	50	12,000	15,955
1922	82	9,670					3	2,700	87	5,400	17,857
Erie: [3]											
1880	602	83,880	758	233,600	5,775	22,500	18	2,800	8,645	163,675	515,100
1885	1,536	298,757	1,028	259,785	22,644	75,507	71	8,320	72,205	847,564	1,562,138
1890	1,449	520,033	1,893	548,100	49,320	169,513	44	5,305	70,601	1,502,750	2,816,302
1893	1,146	424,227	1,783	439,060	35,369	164,683	47	4,440	23,339	1,423,017	2,506,842
1899	980	435,566	1,724	329,500	41,678	229,182	104	8,390	19,362	1,614,677	2,720,554
1903	608	490,236	1,469	172,805	35,150	180,581	110	8,040	18,350	1,326,385	2,196,397
1908		603,000							615,000	426,000	1,644,000
1917	1,133	780,683	5,011	681,060	47,578	329,632	285	38,867	45,154	2,341,051	4,216,447
1922	1,187	807,850	3,909	554,510	42,404	297,994	213	29,685	35,321	3,297,487	5,022,847
Ontario: [5]											
1880	167	13,100	34	14,000	6,000	20,000	9	1,950		5,000	54,050
1885	467	20,448	350	19,445	4,722	23,952	69	3,177	12,627	56,100	135,749
1890	376	31,162	288	24,577	2,345	18,110	27	656	10,361	38,667	123,533
1893	177	9,619	77	2,310	1,185	8,794	7	175	2,240	32,250	-56,131
1899	289	9,482	145	5,850	1,187	18,674	24	420	7,194	38,640	80,350
1903	234	15,457	176	9,945	1,796	13,862	8	205	9,303	52,220	100,992
1908		11,000							16,000	7,900	34,900
1917	270	24,395	353	21,460	165	15,175	12	610	6,349	70,235	138,224
1922	343	43,243	419	33,589	2,319	24,215	25	1,479	6,854	72,900	182,280
All lakes:											
1880	1,929	285,500	1,500	497,400	44,544	214,200	148	20,400	15,300	313,175	1,345,975
1885	4,700	868,669	2,966	726,490	96,906	539,936	304	30,192	126,363	2,228,431	4,520,081
1890	3,838	968,474	3,750	949,957	101,555	498,096	154	17,236	109,920	2,819,061	5,362,774
1893	4,050	1,032,241	3,743	802,078	104,988	670,572	117	10,735	61,160	3,199,955	5,899,270
1899	3,489	887,416	3,837	660,408	105,687	690,518	162	11,298	66,002	4,159,103	6,617,716
1903	3,376	1,162,766	4,528	585,998	101,889	642,961	194	12,462	81,149	4,989,006	7,474,422
1908		1,651,000							1,831,000	1,332,000	4,814,000
1917	3,939	2,049,746	8,433	1,179,256	153,277	1,237,702	446	67,247	115,586	5,503,429	10,183,563
1922	4,266	2,074,324	6,809	1,172,779	107,706	965,470	363	60,519	144,984	7,302,745	11,720,821

[1] In 1908 the outfit of the vessels is included in the value.
[2] Includes all forms of apparatus in 1908.
[3] Includes investment in the vessel fisheries of tributary rivers not shown in previous canvasses.
[4] Includes St. Clair and Detroit Rivers. There was no fishing in Detroit River in 1917 and 1922.
[5] Includes St. Lawrence and Niagara Rivers.

PRODUCTS [1]

Lakes and years	Whitefish	Trout	Ciscoes	Sturgeon	All other fish	Total	
	Pounds	*Pounds*	*Pounds*	*Pounds*	*Pounds*	*Pounds*	*Value*
Superior:							
1880	2,257,000	1,464,750	34,000		60,875	3,816,625	$118,370
1885	4,571,947	3,488,177	324,680	182,760	258,416	8,825,980	291,523
1890	3,213,176	2,613,378	199,121	47,482	42,835	6,115,992	220,968
1893	2,732,270	4,342,122	660,272	62,052	300,211	8,096,927	252,107
1899	693,191	3,118,169	1,125,478	4,415	488,401	5,429,654	150,862
1903	794,022	4,954,830	4,742,805	13,137	2,700,219	13,205,013	343,671
1908	910,100	2,752,200	5,587,600	67,600	878,000	10,195,500	342,000
1917	302,210	2,588,353	12,258,482		398,387	15,547,432	726,674
1922	380,450	2,3,490	7,394,105	343	379,632	10,988,020	484,273
Michigan:							
1880	12,030,400	2,639,450	3,050,400	3,839,600	1,562,025	23,141,875	668,400
1885	8,682,986	6,1,298	3,312,493	1,406,678	3,684,693	23,518,148	878,788
1890	5,455,079	8,464,167	6,082,082	946,897	5,586,041	26,434,266	830,465
1893	2,330,060	8,3,920	11,580,895	311,780	8,308,100	30,747,755	828,611
1899	1,510,364	5,4,947	21,573,716	108,279	5,818,690	34,499,996	876,743
1903	1,972,594	9,,299	13,863,617	56,420	8,637,568	33,579,498	1,090,550
1908	2,490,900	7,8,000	21,842,000	70,500	7,521,900	39,817,300	1,554,000
1917	3,047,393	8,616,715	18,259,354	10,805	5,492,361	35,460,628	2,270,859
1922 [2]	1,547,049	8,060,705	6,763,533	9,203	9,072,709	26,128,199	2,133,849
Huron:							
1880	2,700,778	2,084,500	246,800	204,000	1,969,195	7,205,273	195,277
1885	1,425,380	2,539,780	1,265,650	215,500	6,010,860	11,457,170	276,397
1890	1,004,094	1,505,61	2,514,551	365,718	4,666,399	10,056,381	221,067
1893	1,178,271	3,439,57	2,758,628	79,553	4,608,311	12,064,338	306,381
1899	592,308	1,887,105	3,699,807	30,497	6,208,614	12,418,327	308,078
1903	692,863	2,1,632	4,640,967	34,343	6,978,404	14,455,209	450,318
1908	719,000	1,3,800	4,791,000	9,900	6,053,300	12,932,000	486,000
1917	996,851	2,008,455	5,381,365	4,886	4,900,650	13,363,207	857,478
1922	1,300,621	2,160,249	5,496,463	2,374	5,034,408	13,942,115	945,259
St. Clair: [3]							
1880	77,922		250,700	998,500	523,805	1,850,927	36,273
1885	41,125		1,208,150	227,780	708,740	2,185,795	40,193
1890	238,764	244,847	490,334	309,003	1,711,623	2,994,571	73,577
1893	50,950	72,000	140,112	54,106	1,497,143	1,814,311	46,030
1899	69,902	69,915		7,600	431,650	579,067	23,864
1903	25,591			8,800	487,550	521,941	21,594
1908				13,000	724,700	737,700	32,000
1917					133,330	133,330	11,852
1922				231	309,781	310,012	17,365
Erie:							
1880	3,333,800	26,200	11,774,400	1,970,000	11,982,900	29,087,300	474,880
1885	3,531,855	106,900	19,354,900	4,727,950	23,734,912	51,456,517	1,109,096
1890	2,341,451	121,420	38,868,283	2,078,907	21,440,812	64,850,873	1,000,905
1893	1,292,410	203,132	20,931,076	793,800	19,747,907	42,968,325	805,979
1899	2,066,314	32,024	33,427,797	789,402	22,078,327	58,393,864	1,150,895
1903	302,805	15,127	8,788,625	300,103	13,781,896	23,188,556	780,015
1908	1,503,000	6,900	10,599,100	63,900	29,733,600	41,906,500	1,280,000
1917	1,755,947	1,922	17,160,852	28,384	19,763,133	38,710,238	2,327,299
1922 [2]	922,209	1,897	16,158,239	15,475	39,240,478	56,338,298	2,977,064
Ontario: [4]							
1880	1,064,000	569,700	611,217	545,283	849,800	3,640,000	159,700
1885	90,711	20,510	403,585	386,974	1,496,686	2,398,466	95,869
1890	148,771	41,010	598,978	541,752	2,115,937	3,446,448	124,786
1893	45,380	6,204	164,998	125,293	586,140	928,015	31,510
1899	161,935	15,432	86,778	189,155	1,953,032	2,406,332	100,997
1903	25,384	4,050	121,315	226,095	867,756	1,244,600	59,353
1908	56,000	14,000	35,000	37,000	679,800	821,800	74,000
1917	88,347	23,694	469,272	51,141	421,934	1,054,388	100,857
1922	54,951	46,698	197,319	68,698	658,133	1,025,799	131,801
All lakes:							
1880	21,463,900	6,804,600	15,967,517	7,557,383	16,948,600	68,742,000	1,652,900
1885	18,344,004	12,586,665	25,869,458	7,147,642	35,894,307	99,842,076	2,691,866
1890	12,401,335	12,890,441	48,753,349	4,289,759	35,563,647	113,898,531	2,471,768
1893	7,629,341	16,279,953	36,235,981	1,426,584	35,047,812	96,619,671	270,618
1899	5,094,014	10,611,588	59,913,576	1,129,348	36,978,714	113,727,240	611,439
1903	3,813,259	16,131,938	32,157,319	638,898	33,453,393	86,194,817	745,501
1908	5,679,000	12,023,900	42,854,700	261,900	45,591,300	106,410,800	2,768,000
1917	6,190,748	13,344,139	53,529,325	95,216	31,109,795	104,269,223	6,295,019
1922	4,205,280	13,726,039	36,009,659	96,324	54,695,141	108,732,443	6,689,611

NOTE.—The statistics for 1908 in these tables are from data published by the Bureau of the Census.

[1] In this table caviar and other secondary products are omitted in 1880, 1885, and 1890. In 1880, 1885, and 1890 bluefin, longjaw, and Menominee in Lake Michigan, and Menominee in Lake Huron are included with whitefish. In 1893 and 1899 bluefin in Lake Superior, bluefin and Menominee in Lake Michigan, and Menominee in Lake Huron are included with "all other fish" and longjaw in Lake Michigan with ciscoes. In 1903, bluefin, Menominee, longjaw, and steelhead trout are included with "all other fish." In 1908, 1917, and 1922 ciscoes (herring) include longjaw, bluefin or blackfin, and tullibee.
[2] Includes the mussel fisheries of tributary rivers not shown in previous canvasses.
[3] Includes St. Clair and Detroit Rivers. There was no fishing in Detroit River in 1917 and 1922.
[4] Includes St. Lawrence and Niagara Rivers.

FISHERIES OF LAKE SUPERIOR

The number of persons engaged in the fisheries of Lake Superior in 1922 was 773, of whom 53 were on fishing vessels, 640 in the shore and boat fisheries, and 80 on transporting vessels, in the wholesale trade and related industries.

The investment amounted to $697,572. This included 13 steam and gasoline vessels, with a total net tonnage of 179, valued, together with their outfits, at $45,525; 4 gasoline transporting vessels, with a total net tonnage of 35, valued, together with their outfits, at $15,200; 586 power and row boats, valued at $87,785; fishing apparatus employed on vessels to a value of $28,055; fishing apparatus employed in the shore and boat fisheries to the value of $145,422; shore and accessory property valued at $291,557; and cash capital amounting to $84,028.

The products of the fisheries of Lake Superior amounted to 10,988,020 pounds, valued at $484,273. Among the species of importance were the following: Ciscoes, 7,394,105 pounds, valued at $158,454; lake trout, 2,833,490 pounds, valued at $254,337; common whitefish, 380,450 pounds, valued at $51,523; and suckers, 296,130 pounds, valued at $12,134.

Compared with the other lakes, Lake Superior ranked fourth in persons engaged, investment, and quantity and value of products. Compared with 1917, there was a decrease in the number of persons employed, investment, and quantity and value of products. The number of persons employed and the investment approximate that of 1903, and the quantity and value of products somewhat exceed those of 1903.

FISHERIES BY STATES AND COUNTIES

The following tables show, by States and counties, the number of persons employed, investment, and quantity and value of the products of the fisheries of Lake Superior in 1922:

Statistics of the fisheries of Lake Superior in 1922, by States and counties

PERSONS ENGAGED

State and county	On vessels fishing	On vessels transporting	In shore or boat fisheries	Shoresmen	Total
Michigan:					
Alger	8		48	4	60
Baraga			40		40
Chippewa			40	4	44
Gogebic			9		9
Houghton		3	75		78
Keweenaw			34		34
Marquette	18		35	7	60
Ontonagon	8		7		15
Total	34	3	288	15	340
Wisconsin:					
Ashland			8	4	12
Bayfield	13		100	14	127
Douglas	2		2	12	16
Iron			1		1
Total	15		111	30	156
Minnesota:					
Cook			63		63
Lake		2	131		133
St. Louis	4	5	47	25	81
Total	4	7	241	25	277
Grand total	53	10	640	70	773

Statistics of the fisheries of Lake Superior in 1922, by States and counties—Continued

INVESTMENT

State and county	Vessels fishing							
	Steam				Gasoline			
	Number	Tonnage	Value	Outfit	Number	Tonnage	Value	Outfit
Michigan:								
Alger	1	6	$1,000	$350	1	12	$700	$1,500
Marquette	2	76	11,500	8,250	1	7	1,000	500
Ontonagon	2	18	1,650	370	1	5	800	700
Total	5	100	14,150	8,970	3	24	2,500	2,700
Wisconsin:								
Bayfield	1	15	5,000	3,575	1	14	1,500	1,700
Douglas					1	5	800	130
Total	1	15	5,000	3,575	2	19	2,300	1,830
Minnesota: St. Louis					2	21	4,000	500
Grand total	6	115	19,150	12,545	7	64	8,800	5,030

State and county	Vessels transporting (gasoline)				Rowboats		Power boats	
	Number	Tonnage	Value	Outfit	Number	Value	Number	Value
Michigan:								
Alger					11	$280	21	$6,560
Baraga					21	605	10	2,700
Chippewa					17	545	14	5,150
Gogebic					1	30	7	2,450
Houghton	1	10	$1,500	$300	15	370	39	10,575
Keweenaw					7	190	17	4,400
Marquette					2	55	[1] 8	2,750
Ontonagon					4	170	2	1,800
Total	1	10	1,500	300	78	2,245	118	36,385
Wisconsin:								
Ashland					4	115	5	775
Bayfield					20	605	46	13,900
Douglas							2	150
Iron							1	300
Total					24	720	54	15,125
Minnesota:								
Cook					64	1,890	26	6,350
Lake	1	7	1,500	300	111	3,345	42	10,950
St. Louis	2	18	9,500	2,100	42	1,275	27	9,500
Total	3	25	11,000	2,400	217	6,510	95	26,800
Grand total	4	35	12,500	2,700	319	9,475	267	78,310

[1] Includes one small steamer. valued at $500.

Statistics of the fisheries of Lake Superior in 1922, by States and counties—Continued

INVESTMENT—Continued

State and county	Apparatus of capture, vessel fisheries			Apparatus of capture, shore fisheries			
	Gill nets		Lines	Pound nets and trap nets		Gill nets	
	Number	Value	Value	Number	Value	Number	Value
Michigan:							
Alger	230	$3,000	$300	34	$6,675	424	$6,102
Baraga				39	3,575	121	1,182
Chippewa				178	21,550	501	6,250
Gogebic						57	570
Houghton				6	2,400	1,400	14,798
Keweenaw				7	525	546	5,566
Marquette	760	15,100	2,200	4	1,000	90	1,620
Ontonagon	165	2,025	330	3	750	110	1,100
Total	1,155	20,125	2,830	271	36,475	3,249	37,188
Wisconsin:							
Ashland				1	250	75	750
Bayfield	195	3,300		27	5,950	1,256	14,574
Douglas	40	400				8	80
Iron						6	60
Total	235	3,700		28	6,200	1,345	15,464
Minnesota:							
Cook						1,024	11,740
Lake						1,592	18,400
St. Louis	120	1,400		4	800	877	11,465
Total	120	1,400		4	800	3,493	41,605
Grand total	1,510	25,225	2,830	303	43,475	8,087	94,257

State and county	Apparatus of capture, shore fisheries—Con.				Shore and accessory property	Cash capital	Total investment
	Fyke nets		Seines (hand)		Lines			
	Number	Value	Number	Value	Value	Value	Value	Value
Michigan:								
Alger					$1,750	$8,690		$36,907
Baraga	8	$200			300	1,790		10,352
Chippewa					375	12,540	$5,000	51,410
Gogebic					50	1,700		4,800
Houghton			7	$420	575	6,450		37,388
Keweenaw					1,125	250		12,056
Marquette					600	7,650		52,225
Ontonagon					160	800		10,655
Total	8	200	7	420	4,935	39,870	5,000	215,793
Wisconsin:								
Ashland	6	300				11,975	25,000	39,165
Bayfield	14	700			15	42,400	18,528	111,747
Douglas						27,500	11,500	40,560
Iron								360
Total	20	1,000			15	81,875	55,028	191,832
Minnesota:								
Cook					500	8,450		28,930
Lake					420	7,600		42,515
St. Louis					200	153,762	24,000	218,502
Total					1,120	169,812	24,000	289,947
Grand total	28	1,200	7	420	6,070	291,557	84,028	697,572

Statistics of the fisheries of Lake Superior in 1922, by States and counties—Continued

YIELD, BY SPECIES

State and county	Burbot		Ciscoes					
			Fresh		Frozen		Salted	
	Pounds	Value	Pounds	Value	Pounds	Value	Pounds	Value
Michigan:								
Alger			8,457	$340				
Baraga			44,092	1,327				
Chippewa	575	$10	77,776	3,373				
Gogebic			33,993	839				
Houghton	115	1	83,736	1,999				
Keweenaw	139	5	26,814	894				
Marquette			21,278	634				
Ontonagon			36,267	833				
Total	829	16	332,413	10,239				
Wisconsin:								
Ashland			2,985	79				
Bayfield			1,103,609	16,955	110,400	$2,302	3,000	$97
Douglas			63,705	994				
Iron			805	14				
Total			1,171,104	18,042	110,400	2,302	3,000	97
Minnesota:								
Cook			1,273,972	25,478	37,000	740	479,400	15,565
Lake			1,635,497	31,698	511,203	10,168	521,200	14,797
St. Louis			745,268	13,802	277,548	5,771	288,600	9,380
Total			3,654,737	70,978	825,751	16,679	1,289,200	39,742
Grand total	829	16	5,158,254	99,259	936,151	18,981	1,292,200	39,839

State and county	Ciscoes, smoked		Pike		Pike perch (wall-eyed) or yellow pike		Sturgeon	
	Pounds	Value	Pounds	Value	Pounds	Value	Pounds	Value
Michigan:								
Alger			25	$3	2,297	$251		
Baraga			1,098	134	675	36		
Chippewa			8,489	1,132	6,124	805	318	$115
Houghton			100	18			25	8
Keweenaw			345	27	2,215	250		
Ontonagon			115	15				
Total			10,172	1,329	11,311	1,342	343	123
Wisconsin:								
Ashland			2,120	297	1,875	339		
Bayfield			2,462	250	10,112	1,587		
Douglas			875	86				
Total			5,457	633	11,987	1,926		
Minnesota:								
Lake	4,500	$225	155	80				
St. Louis	3,000	150	417	21				
Total	7,500	375	572	101				
Grand total	7,500	375	16,201	2,063	23,298	3,268	343	123

Statistics of the fisheries of Lake Superior in 1922, by States and counties—Continued

YIELD, BY SPECIES—Continued

State and county	Suckers				Trout			
	Fresh		Salted		Fresh		Salted	
	Pounds	Value	Pounds	Value	Pounds	Value	Pounds	Value
Michigan:								
Alger	17,422	$576			216,088	$17,178		
Baraga	34,972	1,372			14,919	1,577		
Chippewa	121,881	5,563			42,931	4,020		
Gogebic	2,070	72			36,045	3,329		
Houghton	6,154	165			224,038	20,988		
Keweenaw	4,629	220			132,406	9,352		
Marquette	7,041	107			586,778	60,593		
Ontonagon	4,782	250			103,026	11,738		
Total	198,951	8,325			1,356,231	128,775		
Wisconsin:								
Ashland	6,354	251			8,070	894		
Bayfield	46,050	2,425	11,800	$413	700,738	70,656	8,900	$496
Douglas	31,000	600			3,900	360		
Total	83,404	3,276	11,800	413	712,708	71,910	8,900	496
Minnesota:								
Cook					175,033	17,372	3,400	204
Lake					271,973	25,160	6,800	408
St. Louis	1,975	120			291,545	9,468	6,900	544
Total	1,975	120			738,551	52,000	17,100	1,156
Grand total	284,330	11,721	11,800	413	2,807,490	252,685	26,000	1,652

State and county	White bass		Whitefish, common			
			Fresh		Salted	
	Pounds	Value	Pounds	Value	Pounds	Value
Michigan:						
Alger			102,797	$10,504		
Baraga			29,615	4,233		
Chippewa			92,918	18,030		
Gogebic			2,100	182		
Houghton			17,453	2,184		
Keweenaw			6,780	680		
Marquette			24,767	3,978		
Ontonagon			13,224	774		
Total			289,654	40,565		
Wisconsin:						
Ashland			886	125		
Bayfield			54,935	6,693		
Douglas	6,900	$207				
Total	6,900	207	55,821	6,818		
Minnesota:						
Cook			8,777	887		
Lake			4,613	532	50	$35
St. Louis			21,535	2,686		
Total			34,925	4,105	50	35
Grand total	6,900	207	380,400	51,488	50	35

Statistics of the fisheries of Lake Superior in 1922, by States and counties—Continued

YIELD, BY SPECIES—Continued

State and county	Whitefish, Menominee				Yellow perch		Total	
	Fresh		Salted					
	Pounds	Value	Pounds	Value	Pounds	Value	Pounds	Value
Michigan								
Alger	60	$5					347,146	$28,857
Baraga					2,942	$275	128,313	8,954
Chippewa					13,844	949	364,856	33,997
Gogebic	400	14					74,608	4,436
Houghton							331,621	25,363
Keweenaw							173,328	11,428
Marquette							639,864	65,312
Ontonagon							157,414	13,610
Total	460	19			16,786	1,224	2,217,150	191,957
Wisconsin:								
Ashland					61	6	22,351	1,991
Bayfield	1,599	89			500	35	2,054,105	101,998
Douglas							106,380	2,247
Iron							805	14
Total	1,599	89			561	41	2,183,641	106,250
Minnesota:								
Cook	1,000	50					1,978,582	60,296
Lake	300	30	2,300	$115			2,958,591	83,248
St. Louis	7,468	290	5,800	290			1,650,056	42,522
Total	8,768	370	8,100	405			6,587,229	186,066
Grand total	10,827	478	8,100	405	17,347	1,265	10,988,020	484,273

FISHERIES BY APPARATUS

The catch of the vessel fisheries amounted to 1,454,461 pounds, valued at $83,893, and of the shore and boat fisheries to 9,533,559 pounds, valued at $400,380. In the vessel fisheries the catch of ciscoes, suckers, lake trout, and whitefish, with gill nets, amounted to 1,359,981 pounds, valued at $72,159; the balance of the catch, consisting of lake trout, was taken on lines. In the shore and boat fisheries 8,610,155 pounds, consisting of burbot, ciscoes, pike, pike perch, suckers, lake trout, white bass, whitefish, and yellow perch, valued at $310,532, were taken with gill nets; the pound-net fishery yielded 633,999 pounds of ciscoes, pike, pike perch, sturgeon, suckers, lake trout, whitefish, and yellow perch, valued at $65,287; fyke nets took 42,966 pounds of pike, pike perch, suckers and yellow perch, valued at $2,485; 26,587 pounds of burbot, ciscoes and suckers, valued at $427, were taken with seines; and 219,852 pounds of lake trout, valued at $21,649, were taken on lines.

The following tables give the statistics of the yield of the vessel, and the shore and boat fisheries of Lake Superior in 1922:

Yield of the vessel fisheries of Lake Superior in 1922, by States, counties, apparatus, and species

Apparatus and species	Michigan							
	Alger		Marquette		Ontonagon		Total	
	Pounds	Value	Pounds	Value	Pounds	Value	Pounds	Value
Gill nets:								
Ciscoes, fresh			12,963	$335	30,000	$600	42,963	$935
Suckers			6,981	104	2,300	100	9,281	204
Trout	108,391	$6,775	462,743	45,842	23,000	2,500	594,134	55,117
Whitefish	349	45	2,754	478	4,600	400	7,703	923
Total	108,740	6,820	485,441	46,759	59,900	3,600	654,081	57,179
Lines: Trout	14,915	1,297	50,995	6,812	28,570	3,625	94,480	11,734
Grand total	123,655	8,117	536,436	53,571	88,470	7,225	748,561	68,913

Yield of the vessel fisheries of Lake Superior in 1922, by States, counties, apparatus, and species—Continued

| Apparatus and species | Wisconsin | | | | | | Minnesota | | Grand total | |
	Bayfield		Douglas		Total		St. Louis			
	Pounds	*Value*	*Pounds*	*Value*	*Pounds*	*Value*	*Pounds*	*Value*	*Pounds*	*Value*
Gill nets:										
Ciscoes, fresh	525,000	$10,500	56,000	$800	581,000	$11,300			623,963	$12,235
Ciscoes, frozen							80,000	$1,820	80,000	1,820
Suckers			31,000	600	31,000	600			40,281	804
Trout			3,900	360	3,900	360	10,000	900	608,034	56,377
Whitefish									7,703	923
Total	525,000	10,500	90,900	1,760	615,900	12,260	90,000	2,720	1,359,981	72,159
Lines: Trout									94,480	11,734
Grand total	525,000	10,500	90,900	1,760	615,900	12,260	90,000	2,720	1,454,461	83,893

Yield of the shore fisheries of Lake Superior in 1922, by States, counties, apparatus, and species

| Apparatus and species | Michigan | | | | | |
	Alger		Baraga		Chippewa	
	Pounds	*Value*	*Pounds*	*Value*	*Pounds*	*Value*
Pound nets and trap nets:						
Ciscoe			560	$22	4,025	$115
Pike	25	$3	230	20	8,489	1,132
Pike perch (wall-eyed) or yellow pike	2,297	251	215	28	6,124	805
Sturgeon					318	115
Suckers	15,363	504	30,662	1,128	101,348	4,683
Trout, lake, fresh	14,684	1,520	4,600	510	23,466	2,199
Whitefish, common	57,791	5,957	25,324	3,693	85,951	17,121
Yellow perch			742	48	12,600	853
Total	90,160	8,235	62,333	5,449	242,321	27,023
Gill nets:						
Burbot					575	10
Ciscoe, fresh	8,457	340	43,532	1,305	73,751	3,258
Pike			868	114		
Suckers, fresh	2,059	72	4,310	244	20,533	880
Trout, fresh	51,194	4,989	5,719	667	9,920	867
Whitefish, common, fresh	44,657	4,502	4,291	540	6,967	909
Whitefish, Menominee, fresh	60	5				
Yellow perch			2,200	227	1,244	96
Total	106,427	9,908	60,920	3,097	112,990	6,020
Fyke nets: Pike perch (wall-eyed) or yellow pike			460	8		
Lines: Trout, lake	26,904	2,597	4,600	400	9,545	954
Grand total	223,491	20,740	128,313	8,954	364,856	33,997

Yield of shore fisheries of Lake Superior in 1922, by States, counties, apparatus, and species—Continued

Apparatus and species	Michigan—Continued					
	Gogebic		Houghton		Keweenaw	
	Pounds	Value	Pounds	Value	Pounds	Value
Pound nets and trap nets:						
Pike			100	$18	345	$27
Pike perch (wall-eyed) or yellow pike					2,215	250
Sturgeon			25	8		
Suckers	2,070	$72	950	25	4,200	207
Trout, lake, fresh			34,183	3,023		
Whitefish, common	2,100	182	1,429	296		
Total	4,170	254	36,687	3,370	6,760	484
Gill nets:						
Burbot					139	5
Ciscoes, fresh	33,993	839	59,736	1,599	26,814	894
Suckers, fresh			2,732	114	429	13
Trout, fresh	36,045	3,329	157,742	15,213	101,592	6,673
Whitefish, common, fresh			16,024	1,888	6,780	680
Whitefish, Menominee, fresh	400	14				
Total	70,438	4,182	236,234	18,814	135,754	8,265
Seines:						
Burbot			115	1		
Ciscoe			24,000	400		
Suckers			2,472	26		
Total			26,587	427		
Lines: Trout, lake			32,113	2,752	30,814	2,679
Grand total	74,608	4,436	331,621	25,363	173,328	11,428

Apparatus and species	Michigan—Continued					
	Marquette		Ontonagon		Total	
	Pounds	Value	Pounds	Value	Pounds	Value
Pound nets and trap nets:						
Ciscoe	7,740	$249			12,325	$386
Pike					9,189	1,200
Pike perch (wall-eyed) or yellow pike					10,851	1,334
Sturgeon					343	123
Suckers			1,241	$75	155,834	6,694
Trout, lake, fresh	16,435	1,786	17,152	1,871	110,520	10,909
Whitefish, common	12,726	2,215	8,624	374	193,945	29,838
Yellow perch					13,342	901
Total	36,901	4,250	27,017	2,320	506,349	51,385
Gill nets:						
Burbot					714	15
Ciscoes, fresh	575	50	6,267	233	253,125	8,518
Pike			115	15	983	129
Suckers, fresh	60	3	1,241	75	31,364	1,401
Trout, fresh	46,715	5,078	17,152	1,871	426,079	38,687
Whitefish, common, fresh	9,287	1,285			88,006	9,804
Whitefish, Menominee, fresh					460	19
Yellow perch					3,444	323
Total	56,637	6,416	24,775	2,194	804,175	58,896
Fyke nets: Pike perch (wall-eyed) or yellow pike					460	8
Seines:						
Burbot					115	1
Ciscoe					24,000	400
Suckers					2,472	26
Total					26,587	427
Lines: Trout, lake	9,890	1,075	17,152	1,871	131,018	12,328
Grand total	103,428	11,741	68,944	6,385	1,468,589	123,044

Yield of shore fisheries of Lake Superior in 1922, by States, counties, apparatus, and species—Continued

| Apparatus and species | Wisconsin | | | | | |
	Ashland		Bayfield		Douglas	
	Pounds	Value	Pounds	Value	Pounds	Value
Pound nets and trap nets:						
Ciscoe			85	$7		
Pike			1,373	131		
Pike perch (wall-eyed) or yellow pike			6,020	892		
Suckers			7,196	94		
Trout, lake, fresh	1,344	$116	68,212	7,540		
Trout, lake, salted			1,500	90		
Whitefish, common			14,593	1,997		
Whitefish, Menominee			535	32		
Total	1,344	116	99,514	10,783		
Gill nets:						
Ciscoes, fresh	2,985	79	578,524	6,448	7,705	$194
Ciscoes, frozen			110,400	2,302		
Ciscoes, salted			3,000	97		
Pike	1,500	210	1,089	119	875	86
Pike perch (wall-eyed) or yellow pike	1,875	339	4,092	695		
Suckers, fresh			3,883	233		
Suckers, salted			11,800	413		
Trout, fresh	6,726	778	601,064	59,341		
Trout, salted			7,400	406		
White bass					6,900	207
Whitefish, common, fresh	886	125	40,342	4,696		
Whitefish, Menominee, fresh			1,064	57		
Total	13,972	1,531	1,362,658	74,807	15,480	487
Fyke nets:						
Pike	620	87				
Suckers	6,354	251	34,971	2,098		
Yellow perch	61	6	500	35		
Total	7,035	344	35,471	2,133		
Lines: Trout, lake			31,462	3,775		
Grand total	22,351	1,991	1,529,105	91,498	15,480	487

| Apparatus and species | Wisconsin—Continued | | | | Minnesota | | | |
	Iron		Total		Cook		Lake	
	Pounds	Value	Pounds	Value	Pounds	Value	Pounds	Value
Pound nets and trap nets:								
Ciscoe			85	$7				
Pike			1,373	131				
Pike perch (wall-eyed) or yellow pike			6,020	892				
Suckers			7,196	94				
Trout, lake, fresh			69,556	7,656				
Trout, lake, salted			1,500	90				
Whitefish, common			14,593	1,997				
Whitefish, Menominee			535	32				
Total			100,858	10,899				
Gill nets:								
Ciscoes, fresh	805	$14	590,019	6,735	1,273,972	$25,478	1,635,497	$31,698
Ciscoes, frozen			110,400	2,302	37,000	740	511,203	10,168
Ciscoes, salted			3,000	97	479,400	15,565	521,200	14,797
Ciscoes, smoked							4,500	225
Pike			3,464	415			155	80
Pike perch (wall-eyed) or yellow pike			5,967	1,034				
Suckers, fresh			3,883	233				
Suckers, salted			11,800	413				
Trout, fresh			607,790	60,119	147,506	14,752	253,128	23,334
Trout, salted			7,400	406	3,400	204	6,800	408
White bass			6,900	207				
Whitefish, common, fresh			41,228	4,821	8,777	887	4,613	532
Whitefish, common, salted							50	35
Whitefish, Menominee, fresh			1,064	57	1,000	50	300	30
Whitefish, Menominee, salted							2,300	115
Total	805	14	1,392,915	76,839	1,951,055	57,676	2,939,746	81,422
Fyke nets:								
Pike			620	87				
Suckers			41,325	2,349				
Yellow perch			561	41				
Total			42,506	2,477				
Lines: Trout, lake			31,462	3,775	27,527	2,620	18,845	1,826
Grand total	805	14	1,567,741	93,990	1,978,582	60,296	2,958,591	83,248

Yield of shore fisheries of Lake Superior in 1922, by States, counties, apparatus, and species—Continued

Apparatus and species	Minnesota—Continued				Grand total	
	St. Louis		Total			
	Pounds	Value	Pounds	Value	Pounds	Value
Pound nets and trap nets:						
Ciscoe					12,410	$393
Pike	392	$19	392	$19	10,954	1,350
Pike perch (wall-eyed) or yellow pike					16,871	2,226
Sturgeon					343	123
Suckers					163,030	6,788
Trout, lake, fresh	8,000	800	8,000	800	188,076	19,365
Trout, lake, salted	400	24	400	24	1,900	114
Whitefish, common	18,000	2,160	18,000	2,160	226,538	33,995
Whitefish, Menominee					535	32
Yellow perch					13,342	901
Total	26,792	3,003	26,792	3,003	633,999	65,287
Gill nets:						
Burbot					714	15
Ciscoes, fresh	745,268	13,802	3,654,737	70,978	4,497,881	86,231
Ciscoes, frozen	197,548	3,951	745,751	14,859	856,151	17,161
Ciscoes, salted	288,600	9,380	1,289,200	39,742	1,292,200	39,839
Ciscoes, smoked	3,000	150	7,500	375	7,500	375
Pike	25	2	180	82	4,627	626
Pike perch (wall-eyed) or yellow pike					5,967	1,034
Suckers, fresh	1,975	120	1,975	120	37,222	1,754
Suckers, salted					11,800	413
Trout, fresh	262,545	6,668	663,179	44,754	1,697,048	143,560
Trout, salted	6,500	520	16,700	1,132	24,100	1,538
White bass					6,900	207
Whitefish, common, fresh	3,535	526	16,925	1,945	146,159	16,570
Whitefish, common, salted				50	35	50	35
Whitefish, Menominee, fresh	7,468	290	8,768	370	10,292	446
Whitefish, Menominee, salted	5,800	290	8,100	405	8,100	405
Yellow perch					3,444	323
Total	1,522,264	35,699	6,413,065	174,797	8,610,155	310,532
Fyke nets:						
Pike					620	87
Pike perch (wall-eyed) or yellow pike					460	8
Suckers					41,325	2,349
Yellow perch					561	41
Total					42,966	2,485
Seines:						
Burbot					115	1
Ciscoe					24,000	400
Suckers					2,472	26
Total					26,587	427
Lines: Trout, lake	11,000	1,100	57,372	5,546	219,852	21,649
Grand total	1,560,056	39,802	6,497,229	183,346	9,533,559	400,380

WHOLESALE FISHERY TRADE

The wholesale fishery trade of Lake Superior in 1922 was conducted by 11 establishments, of which 6 were in Duluth, Minn., and 5 in Ashland, Bayfield, and Superior, Wis. The total number of persons employed in these establishments was 55; wages paid, $51,568; investment in shore and accessory property, $212,912; and cash capital, $79,028.

Compared with 1917, there was a decrease of 4 in the number of establishments, a decrease of 194 in the number of persons employed, and an increase of $25,255 in the total investment.

The following table shows the statistics of the wholesale trade of Lake Superior in 1922:

Wholesale fishery trade of Lake Superior in 1922

Localities	State	Number of firms	Persons engaged	Wages paid	Shore and accessory property	Cash capital
Duluth	Minnesota	6	25	$24,968	$142,812	$24,000
Ashland, Bayfield, and Superior	Wisconsin	5	30	26,600	70,100	55,028
Total		11	55	51,568	212,912	79,028

FISHERIES OF LAKE MICHIGAN

In 1922 Lake Michigan ranked first among the Great Lakes in the number of persons employed and second only to Lake Erie in the amount of invested capital and quantity and value of products.

The total number of persons employed was 2,617, of whom 1,011 were on vessels fishing, 707 in the shore and boat fisheries, and 899 employed as shoresmen and on vessels transporting. Comparing the total number with previous statistics, it is seen that there were fewer men reported in this canvass than in any previous one except that of 1880.

The total investment in the fisheries of the lake amounted to $4,247,964, of which $947,838 was invested in vessels and boats, $644,599 in gear, and $2,655,527 in shore and accessory property and cash capital. There were 356 vessels above 5 tons net engaged in the fishery, 87 of them being operated by steam and 269 by gasoline. The gear employed by these vessels consisted of 35,930 gill nets, valued at $357,653, and lines to the value of $23,525. The principal gear in the shore and boat fisheries consisted of pound nets and gill nets, 704 of the former valued at $174,815, and 10,453 of the latter, valued at $51,102. There was a very distinct decrease in the number of all types of gear as compared to 1917.

The fishery products of Lake Michigan amounted to 21,141,394 pounds, valued at $1,932,836. The more important species taken in this lake were ciscoes, 6,763,533 pounds, valued at $244,392; lake trout, 8,735,705 pounds, valued at $1,171,806; common whitefish, 1,547,049 pounds, valued at $263,935; yellow perch, 1,244,768 pounds, valued at $85,748; and suckers, 1,519,667 pounds, valued at $89,119.

Compared with previous years, this is a distinct decrease in the yield of ciscoes and whitefish and an ordinary production of lake trout. The 1922 catch of sturgeon, amounting to 9,203 pounds, was the lowest on record. In 1880 the yield of this species from Lake Michigan amounted to 3,839,600 pounds.

The following tables present in detail the statistics of the fisheries of Lake Michigan in 1922:

Statistics of the fisheries of Lake Michigan in 1922, by States and counties

PERSONS ENGAGED

State and county	On vessels fishing	On vessels transporting	In shore or boat fisheries	Shoresmen	Total
Michigan:					
Allegan	2		6		8
Antrim			9		9
Benzie	31		4	6	41
Berrien	24		23	11	58
Charlevoix	99	2	15	21	137
Delta	53	10	69	7	139
Emmet		3	23		26
Grand Traverse	6	8	17		31
Leelanau	36		24	6	66
Mackinac	16	16	46		78
Manistee	17		7		24
Mason	30	2	5	4	41
Menominee	13		39	15	67
Muskegon	13		16	2	31
Oceana	4		1		5
Ottawa	20	2	13	22	57
Schoolcraft	33	2	10	7	52
Van Buren	20		2	6	28
Total	417	45	329	107	898
Indiana:					
Lake			5		5
Laporte	22		11	11	44
Porter			6		6
Total	22		22	11	55
Illinois:					
Cook	14		9	413	436
Lake	24		3	13	40
Total	38		12	426	476
Wisconsin:					
Brown	44	30	81	69	224
Door	142	24	113	24	303
Kenosha	24		2	7	33
Kewaunee	31	2	19		52
Manitowoc	42		26	19	87
Marinette	46	1	38	14	99
Milwaukee	61		1	35	97
Oconto	55	13	28	11	107
Ozaukee	25		4	23	52
Racine	31		4	8	43
Sheboygan	33		28	30	91
Total	534	70	344	240	1,188
Grand total	1,011	115	707	784	2,617

Statistics of the fisheries of Lake Michigan in 1922, by States and counties—Con.

INVESTMENT

State and county	Vessels fishing							
	Steam				Gasoline			
	Number	*Tonnage*	*Value*	*Outfit*	*Number*	*Tonnage*	*Value*	*Outfit*
Michigan:								
Allegan	1	7	$2,000	$100				
Benzie	4	79	17,000	3,500	4	38	$4,900	$780
Berrien	3	111	16,500	3,500	3	21	1,700	360
Charlevoix	5	55	13,000	5,700	28	226	32,800	8,375
Delta	3	55	7,500	1,525	20	123	8,800	1,155
Grand Traverse	1	6	600	125	2	18	3,000	90
Leelanau	5	52	7,400	3,900	9	67	7,600	1,840
Mackinac	1	30	2,000	2,250	7	48	3,150	720
Manistee					7	48	5,250	1,253
Mason	2	40	5,000	400	11	99	10,150	1,600
Menominee	1	15	2,500	1,820	3	30	2,700	698
Muskegon	2	23	2,500	200	4	22	2,600	220
Oceana					2	17	1,400	140
Ottawa	5	78	14,500	2,870				
Schoolcraft	1	7	800	120	9	135	17,950	7,580
Van Buren	6	98	12,800	2,650				
Total	40	656	104,100	28,660	109	892	102,000	24,811
Indiana: Laporte	4	92	14,000	3,700	1	8	500	20
Illinois:								
Cook	1	24	7,000	25	3	16	6,000	2,100
Lake	1	19	5,000	900	5	67	14,000	3,445
Total	2	43	12,000	925	8	83	20,000	5,545
Wisconsin:								
Brown	1	8	1,500	300	19	159	14,050	1,665
Door	2	19	6,500	750	56	538	98,250	11,805
Kenosha	1	32	5,000	150	6	79	23,000	1,000
Kewaunee	1	19	9,000	1,400	11	105	15,300	4,250
Manitowoc	3	54	10,500	2,700	10	146	32,700	4,065
Marinette	1	13	4,000	627	18	144	14,250	3,215
Milwaukee	12	240	52,500	8,870	4	33	4,800	340
Oconto					26	206	17,000	2,380
Ozaukee	6	138	29,500	4,550				
Racine	8	195	55,500	5,450				
Sheboygan	6	200	37,000	7,200	1	49	7,000	1,250
Total	41	918	211,000	31,997	151	1,459	226,350	29,970
Grand total	87	1,709	341,100	65,282	269	2,442	348,850	60,346

Statistics of the fisheries of Lake Michigan in 1922, by States and counties—Con.

INVESTMENT—Continued

State and county	Vessels transporting (gasoline)				Sail and row boats		Power boats	
	Number	*Tonnage*	*Value*	*Outfit*	*Number*	*Value*	*Number*	*Value*
Michigan:								
Allegan					3	$110	3	$550
Antrim					7	175	2	200
Benzie					2	50	1	500
Berrien					11	290	10	2,950
Charlevoix	1	11	$2,500	$300	9	265	7	2,350
Delta	5	34	1,650	385	58	1,910	27	4,750
Emmet	1	7	400	100	9	350	8	1,975
Grand Traverse	7	52	5,450	610	16	610	6	1,100
Leelanau					18	525	7	1,100
Mackinac	8	52	5,550	580	23	675	21	5,150
Manistee					7	240	1	300
Mason	1	5	300	40	4	115	1	150
Menominee					34	925	3	700
Muskegon					12	455	5	1,700
Oceana					1	80		
Ottawa	1	8	800	145	13	455	2	400
Schoolcraft	1	5	500	80	9	435	2	650
Van Buren					2	50		
Total	25	174	17,150	2,240	238	7,715	106	24,525
Indiana:								
Lake					1	40	2	1,800
Laporte					5	150	4	1,150
Porter					1	25	2	950
Total					7	215	8	3,900
Illinois:								
Cook					4	110	3	2,600
Lake					1	25	1	200
Total					5	135	4	2,800
Wisconsin:								
Brown	16	100	8,700	565	85	2,400	22	4,250
Door	12	191	24,150	3,210	27	1,105	38	7,160
Kenosha					2	50		
Kewaunee	1	9	300	45	1	30	2	575
Manitowoc					17	775	9	5,250
Marinette	1	10	1,000	50	7	200	5	850
Milwaukee					1	25		
Oconto	7	44	4,800	300	30	925	10	2,200
Ozaukee							1	300
Racine					4	100		
Sheboygan					21	1,065	8	3,200
Total	37	354	38,950	4,170	195	6,675	95	23,785
Grand total	62	528	56,100	6,410	445	14,740	213	55,010

Statistics of the fisheries of Lake Michigan in 1922, by States and counties—Con.

INVESTMENT—Continued

State and county	Apparatus of capture, vessel fisheries			Apparatus of capture, shore fisheries				
	Gill nets		Lines	Pound nets and trap nets		Gill nets		Fyke nets
	Number	Value	Value	Number	Value	Number	Value	Number	Value
Michigan:	Number	Value	Value	Number	Value	Number	Value	Number	Value
Allegan	40	$320		3	$800	125	$980		
Antrim				5	1,100	39	260		
Benzie	1,246	10,884	$300			109	930		
Berrien	1,150	16,150	3,000	8	3,300	338	2,025		
Charlevoix	3,294	29,720	2,100	20	5,800	177	1,250		
Delta	1,273	9,428	1,150	87	15,950	1,354	5,665	63	$4,675
Emmet				8	5,500	383	1,871		
Grand Traverse	100	800	150	94	13,390	45	280		
Leelanau	1,999	15,400	300	26	3,700	260	2,025		
Mackinac	490	5,255		93	13,700	139	795		
Manistee	886	8,185	925	3	750	35	345		
Mason	1,482	15,560	350	28	1,540	10	120		
Menominee	414	6,760		37	4,450	106	1,060	2	40
Muskegon	345	3,840	200	18	4,400	261	2,770		
Oceana	164	1,600				30	240		
Ottawa	987	4,650	2,000	19	5,110	156	760		
Schoolcraft	1,105	16,600	1,200	40	5,200	26	262		
Van Buren	615	4,360	1,500			6	30		
Total	15,590	149,512	13,175	489	84,690	3,599	21,668	65	4,715
Indiana:									
Lake				3	1,500	106	530		
Laporte	1,206	22,120	800	5	3,000	27	115		
Porter				5	3,100	16	80		
Total	1,206	22,120	800	13	7,600	149	725		
Illinois:									
Cook	342	1,658				155	477		
Lake	1,368	13,560				35	165		
Total	1,710	15,218				190	642		
Wisconsin:									
Brown	988	4,880		21	2,300	907	4,185	896	17,255
Door	7,738	54,940	3,720	61	20,400	1,649	8,220		
Kenosha	351	2,270	350			930	4,640		
Kewaunee	545	3,745	2,200			930	4,640		
Manitowoc	1,546	36,150		36	16,250	10	110	27	500
Marinette	1,820	21,631		10	1,950	2,252	6,756	11	370
Milwaukee	826	7,914	560	1	100				
Oconto	1,882	12,943		38	9,225	706	3,896	197	4,815
Ozaukee	821	7,970	480	4	2,000				
Racine	472	4,060	1,120			50	150		
Sheboygan	435	14,300	1,120	31	30,300	11	110		
Total	17,424	170,803	9,550	202	82,525	6,515	28,067	1,131	22,940
Grand total	35,930	357,653	23,525	704	174,815	10,453	51,102	1,196	27,655

Statistics of the fisheries of Lake Michigan in 1922, by State and counties—Con.

INVESTMENT—Continued

State and county	Apparatus of capture, shore fisheries—Continued							Shore and accessory property	Cash capital	Total investment
	Seines (haul)		Trammel nets		Lines	Crawfish pots				
	Number	Value	Number	Value	Value	Number	Value	Value	Value	Value
Michigan:										
Allegan										$4,860
Antrim								$500		2,235
Benzie								8,900		47,744
Berrien								4,825	$3,000	57,600
Charlevoix								58,800	23,000	185,960
Delta								17,855	2,300	84,698
Emmet								2,175		12,371
Grand Traverse					$75			400		26,680
Leelanau					150			4,325		48,265
Mackinac								4,650		44,475
Manistee								1,245		18,493
Mason								5,800	1,500	42,625
Menominee								39,580	70,000	131,233
Muskegon								5,225		24,110
Oceana								250		3,710
Ottawa								37,175	36,257	105,122
Schoolcraft								2,350		53,727
Van Buren								1,000		22,390
Total					225			195,055	136,057	916,298
Indiana:										
Lake								1,000		4,870
Laporte								7,010	1,000	53,565
Porter								1,400		5,555
Total								9,410	1,000	63,990
Illinois:										
Cook								992,487	518,000	1,530,457
Lake								12,500		49,795
Total								1,004,987	518,000	1,580,252
Wisconsin:										
Brown	31	$7,300				4,450	$1,187	149,832	90,000	310,369
Door					195			68,160	6,000	314,565
Kenosha					10			4,500	1,000	37,330
Kewaunee								6,205		47,690
Manitowoc	4	105	3	$65				37,980	11,000	158,150
Marinette								18,956	7,000	80,855
Milwaukee								258,450	32,000	365,559
Oconto	2	450				805	222	20,170	7,895	87,221
Ozaukee								21,760	12,000	78,560
Racine								12,100		78,480
Sheboygan	3	90						19,510	6,500	128,645
Total	40	7,945	3	65	205	5,255	1,409	617,623	173,395	1,687,424
Grand total	40	7,945	3	65	430	5,255	1,409	1,827,075	828,452	4,247,964

Statistics of the fisheries of Lake Michigan in 1922, by States and counties—Con.

YIELD, BY SPECIES

State and county	Buffalofish		Burbot		Carp, German		Catfish and bullheads	
	Pounds	Value	Pounds	Value	Pounds	Value	Pounds	Value
Michigan:								
Allegan	60	$4	1,720	$50	1,000	$30	160	$16
Berrien	62	4	200	10	502	20		
Delta			1,400	28	2,245	63	3,260	195
Emmet			400	20				
Grand Traverse					750	28		
Mason			100	2				
Menominee			400	4	100	4		
Muskegon			720	36	100	2		
Ottawa			140	5	400	8	245	16
Total	122	8	5,080	155	5,097	155	3,665	227
Indiana:								
Lake	100	5	300	6	100	5		
Laporte	620	34	120	12	5,100	203		
Porter	50	3			150	12		
Total	770	42	420	18	5,350	220		
Wisconsin:								
Brown			1,141	16	481,388	10,591	129,269	5,869
Door					65,000	5,200		
Kenosha			2,000	100				
Kewaunee					116,544	5,827		
Manitowoc			600	30	2,518	140		
Marinette					3,500	95	2,500	250
Oconto					73,930	2,944	13,195	1,174
Ozaukee			5,000	200	200	10		
Sheboygan					500	40		
Total			8,741	346	743,580	24,847	144,964	7,293
Grand total	892	50	14,241	519	754,027	25,222	148,629	7,520

24309—25†——11

*Statistics of the fisheries of Lake Michigan in 1922, by States and counties—*Con.

YIELD, BY SPECIES—Continued

State and county	Ciscoes						Pike	
	Fresh		Salted		Smoked			
	Pounds	Value	Pounds	Value	Pounds	Value	Pounds	Value
Michigan:								
Allegan	9,060	$451						
Antrim	7,725	299						
Benzie	17,853	1,093						
Berrien	130,742	5,319						
Charlevoix	37,237	2,582						
Delta	95,189	3,013					17,003	$2,455
Emmet	1,563	129						
Grand Traverse	25,605	1,255					400	60
Leelanau	40,646	2,356					70	10
Mackinac	550	27					300	44
Manistee	6,449	257						
Mason	62,105	3,292						
Menominee	238,037	5,852	13,680	$399				
Muskegon	100,910	4,296					1,991	299
Oceana	6,000	420						
Ottawa	38,130	1,500					475	71
Schoolcraft	30,781	1,229					88	12
Van Buren	6,135	384						
Total	854,717	33,754	13,680	399			20,327	2,951
Indiana:								
Lake	58,000	2,500						
Laporte	176,800	10,884					25	3
Porter	61,800	3,090						
Total	296,600	16,474					25	3
Illinois:								
Cook	154,000	15,340						
Lake	98,000	4,230			29,165	$4,893		
Total	252,000	19,570			29,165	4,893		
Wisconsin:								
Brown	564,635	11,549					15,404	1,440
Door	753,998	22,611	974,280	26,158			1,236	119
Kenosha	23,200	1,028						
Kewaunee	87,363	2,479						
Manitowoc	481,274	23,389					174	28
Marinette	657,500	19,520	29,325	895			1,510	155
Milwaukee	274,649	16,321						
Oconto	807,700	18,786	272,820	8,481	250	25	7,712	725
Ozaukee	116,340	5,221			9,000	1,080		
Racine	500	40						
Sheboygan	264,537	11,719						
Total	4,031,696	132,663	1,276,425	35,534	9,250	1,105	26,036	2,467
Grand total	5,435,013	202,461	1,290,105	35,933	38,415	5,998	46,388	5,421

State and county	Pike perch (wall-eyed) or yellow pike		Sheepshead or drum		Steelhead trout		Sturgeon		Sturgeon caviar	
	Pounds	Value	Pounds	Value	Pounds	Value	Pounds	Value	Pounds	Value
Michigan:										
Allegan	2,700	$405								
Berrien	308	46					2,089	$1,046	25	$75
Delta	53,846	7,933					1,001	402	8	12
Mackinac	250	25					2,387	1,020	467	142
Manistee	520	93					325	162	170	85
Mason	6,584	987								
Menominee	915	125					81	23		
Muskegon	3,015	509	60	$2			650	325		
Ottawa	2,435	365	500	25			300	125		
Schoolcraft	469	75					210	74		
Total	71,042	10,563	560	27			7,043	3,177	670	314
Indiana:										
Lake					8,000	$1,600	500	250		
Laporte	150	37			115	23	820	121		
Porter					3,050	610	840	33		
Total	150	37			11,165	2,233	2,160	404		
Wisconsin:										
Brown	43,704	7,461	3,912	80						
Door	550	128								
Kewaunee	140	32								
Marinette	860	129								
Oconto	16,502	2,835								
Total	61,756	10,585	3,912	80						
Grand total	132,948	21,185	4,472	107	11,165	2,233	9,203	3,581	670	314

Statistics of the fisheries of Lake Michigan·in⸱ 1922, by States and. counties—Con.

YIELD, BY SPECIES—Continued·

State and county	Suckers				Trout, lake			
	Fresh		Salted		Fresh		Salted	
	Pounds	Value	Pounds	Value	Pounds	Value	Pounds	Value
Michigan:								
Allegan	6, 500	$264			750	$112		
Antrim					3, 340	410		
Benzie	18, 784	802			290, 255	39, 018		
Berrien	4, 070	270			168, 486	24, 885		
Charlevoix					1, 125, 847	130, 540		
Delta	448, 601	19, 264			203, 160	26, 851		
Emmet	130	5			99, 050	12, 469		
Grand Traverse	38, 506	3, 080			42, 102	4, 971		
Leelanau	11, 384	907			336, 670	38, 729		
Mackinac	15, 343	909			112, 283	14, 564		
Manistee	21, 155	1, 144			135, 725	20, 304		
Mason	17, 060	1, 023			147, 454	18, 158		
Menominee	10, 638	635			48, 290	4, 900		
Muskegon	2, 685	126			27, 516	4, 531		
Oceana					14, 800	1, 856		
Ottawa	4, 070	194			140, 650	19, 526		
Schoolcraft	10, 366	329			461, 341	63, 164		
Van Buren	600	30			96, 706	13, 397		
Total	609, 892	28, 982			3, 454, 425	438, 385		
Indiana:								
Lake	100	5			3, 000	310		
Laporte	750	54			265, 270	37, 145		
Porter	125	6			3, 300	330		
Total	975	65			271, 570	37, 785		
Illinois:								
Cook					35, 300	4, 210		
Lake					167, 775	25, 894		
Total					203, 075	30, 104		
Wisconsin:								
Brown	286, 380	15, 505			2, 000	249		
Door	26, 853	1, 650	5, 760	$147	1, 289, 407	156, 383	120	$5
Kenosha					122, 860	19, 596		
Kewaunee	13, 949	1, 216			515, 200	77, 280		
Manitowoc	54, 527	2, 765			546, 277	76, 973		
Marinette	214, 800	16, 439			128, 200	13, 320		
Milwaukee	50	3			620, 140	93, 495		
Oconto	294, 065	21, 723			12, 950	1, 475		
Ozaukee	1, 850	111			396, 555	57, 751		
Racine					400, 703	55, 687		
Sheboygan	10, 566	513			772, 223	113, 318		
Total	903, 040	59, 925	5, 760	147	4, 806, 515	665, 527	120	5
Grand total	1, 513, 907	88, 972	5, 760	147	8, 735, 585	1, 171, 801	120	5

Statistics of the fisheries of Lake Michigan in 1922, by States and counties—Con.

YIELD, BY SPECIES—Continued

State and county	White bass		Whitefish, common		Whitefish, Menominee			
					Fresh		Salted	
	Pounds	Value	Pounds	Value	Pounds	Value	Pounds	Value
Michigan:								
Allegan			8, 815	$1, 763				
Antrim			5, 425	795	30	$4		
Benzie			76, 469	12, 211				
Berrien			39, 610	7, 777				
Charlevoix			242, 295	36, 388	10, 053	663		
Delta			113, 947	21, 570	17, 037	1, 081		
Emmet			20, 562	3, 260	800	56		
Grand Traverse			52, 564	7, 824	1, 424	142		
Leelanau			84, 076	14, 983	1, 658	150		
Mackinac			276, 327	49, 781	39, 043	3, 018		
Manistee			8, 881	1, 466	50	5		
Mason			20, 803	3, 795	300	24		
Menominee			62, 992	9, 434	225	20		
Muskegon			53, 998	9, 811	100	8		
Oceana			2, 600	470				
Ottawa			28, 955	5, 744	200	16		
Schoolcraft			95, 167	17, 930	4, 805	480		
Van Buren			47, 195	9, 233				
Total			1, 240, 681	214, 235	75, 725	5, 667		
Indiana:								
Lake			1, 100	178				
Laporte			16, 000	2, 690				
Porter			3, 700	592				
Total			20, 800	3, 460				
Wisconsin:								
Brown	1, 005	$38	313	75				
Door			170, 845	28, 651	9, 038	430	14, 480	$677
Kewaunee					20, 000	1, 600		
Manitowoc			11, 753	1, 509	1, 400	210		
Marinette			90, 667	13, 601				
Oconto			2, 300	384	800	40		
Ozaukee			5, 055	1, 110	200	30		
Sheboygan			4, 635	910				
Total	1, 005	38	285, 568	46, 240	31, 438	2, 310	14, 480	677
Grand total	1, 005	38	1, 547, 049	263, 935	107, 163	7, 977	14, 480	677

Statistics of the fisheries of Lake Michigan in 1922, by State and counties—Con.

YIELD, BY SPECIES—Continued

State and county	Yellow perch		Crawfish		Oil		Total	
	Pounds	Value	Pounds	Value	Pounds	Value	Pounds	Value
Michigan:								
Allegan	1,610	$96					32,375	$3,191
Antrim							16,520	1,508
Benzie	1,250	100					404,611	53,224
Berrien	7,288	438					353,382	39,890
Charlevoix	33,255	1,995					1,448,687	172,168
Delta	161,744	9,768					1,118,441	92,635
Emmet	1,990	254					124,495	16,193
Grand Traverse	2,450	178					163,801	17,538
Leelanau	5,178	362					479,682	57,497
Mackinac	1,590	96					448,540	69,626
Manistee	1,370	92					174,645	23,608
Mason	100	6					254,506	27,287
Menominee	17,525	598					392,883	21,994
Muskegon	7,380	483					199,125	20,428
Oceana							23,400	2,746
Ottawa	3,450	220					219,950	27,815
Schoolcraft	25	1					603,252	83,294
Van Buren	3,745	307					154,381	23,351
Total	249,950	14,994					6,612,676	753,993
Indiana:								
Lake	2,500	200					73,700	5,059
Laporte	8,800	1,181					474,570	52,387
Porter	2,200	110					75,215	4,786
Total	13,500	1,491					623,485	62,232
Illinois:								
Cook	26,300	3,642					215,600	23,192
Lake	3,100	310					298,040	35,327
Total	29,400	3,952					513,640	58,519
Wisconsin:								
Brown	299,358	17,764	68,764	$2,446			1,897,273	73,083
Door	250,250	22,584					3,561,817	264,743
Kenosha	1,250	225					149,310	20,949
Kewaunee	21,934	2,296					775,130	90,730
Manitowoc	11,294	1,122					1,109,817	106,166
Marinette	53,850	3,532					1,182,712	67,936
Milwaukee	27,590	2,345					922,429	112,164
Oconto	279,700	14,632	14,000	441			1,795,924	73,665
Ozaukee	260	16					534,460	65,529
Racine	3,270	450					404,473	56,177
Sheboygan	3,162	345			2,625	$105	1,058,248	126,950
Total	951,918	65,311	82,764	2,887	2,625	105	13,391,593	1,058,092
Grand total	1,244,768	85,748	82,764	2,887	2,625	105	21,141,394	1,932,836

FISHERIES BY APPARATUS

Of the total yield of Lake Michigan in 1922, the vessel fishery produced 13,294,749 pounds, valued at $1,395,396, and the shore and boat fisheries produced 7,846,645 pounds, valued at $537,440. Gill nets and lines were employed, the former catching 11,152,890 pounds of fish, mainly ciscoes, lake trout, whitefish, yellow perch, and pike perch, and the latter catching 2,141,859 pounds of lake trout and 260 pounds of pike. In the shore and boat fisheries the pound nets were most important, yielding 3,771,600 pounds, followed by gill nets with a yield of 2,397,435 pounds.

The following tables show in detail the products of the fisheries of Lake Michigan by gear.

Yield of vessel fisheries of Lake Michigan in 1922, by States, counties, apparatus, and species

Apparatus and species	Michigan							
	Allegan		Benzie		Berrien		Charlevoix	
	Pounds	Value	Pounds	Value	Pounds	Value	Pounds	Value
Gill nets:								
Burbot	120	$2						
Ciscoes, fresh	1,480	148	17,853	$1,093	3,000	$210	33,262	$2,304
Suckers	100	8	16,484	664	1,100	98		
Trout, lake	125	22	265,914	35,527	92,664	13,945	950,589	109,533
Whitefish—								
Common	695	139	74,289	11,819	16,906	3,238	223,005	33,621
Menominee, fresh							8,953	558
Yellow perch	150	9	650	52			11,655	699
Total	2,670	328	375,190	49,155	113,670	17,491	1,227,464	146,715
Lines: Trout, lake			8,256	1,239	63,900	9,148	110,900	13,367
Grand total	2,670	328	383,446	50,394	177,570	26,639	1,338,364	160,082

Apparatus and species	Michigan—Continued							
	Delta		Grand Traverse		Leelanau		Mackinac	
	Pounds	Value	Pounds	Value	Pounds	Value	Pounds	Value
Gill nets:								
Ciscoes, fresh	54,806	$1,809	10,995	$609	33,491	$2,037	150	$15
Pike	150	22					200	29
Pike perch (wall-eyed)	210	31					250	25
Suckers	56,840	2,728			100	4	7,000	408
Trout, lake	136,112	18,282	3,686	452	302,644	34,696	84,733	11,259
Whitefish—								
Common	37,600	6,614	200	31	70,716	12,470	41,350	6,442
Menominee, fresh	5,647	512					19,709	1,679
Yellow perch	76,230	4,584					1,265	76
Total	367,595	34,582	14,881	1,092	406,951	49,207	154,657	19,933
Lines: Trout, lake	62,450	7,920	4,468	536	7,000	790		
Grand total	430,045	42,502	19,349	1,628	413,951	49,997	154,657	19,933

Apparatus and species	Michigan—Continued							
	Manistee		Mason		Menominee		Muskegon	
	Pounds	Value	Pounds	Value	Pounds	Value	Pounds	Value
Gill nets:								
Ciscoes, fresh			45,105	$2,782	105,200	$3,150	73,634	$3,191
Pike perch (wall-eyed)	300	$60			565	85	1,000	200
Sturgeon	325	162						
Sturgeon caviar	170	85						
Suckers	9,038	417			2,875	100		
Trout, lake	114,375	17,111	137,564	17,010	41,265	4,126	20,885	3,406
Whitefish, common	7,420	1,174	20,703	3,780	62,530	9,379	6,000	1,080
Yellow perch	810	60			15,725	493	2,000	160
Total	132,438	19,069	203,372	23,572	228,160	17,333	103,519	8,037
Lines: Trout, lake	21,000	3,150	9,490	1,088			2,600	520
Grand total	153,438	22,219	212,862	24,660	228,160	17,333	106,119	8,557

Yield of vessel fisheries of Lake Michigan in 1922, by States, counties, apparatus, and species—Continued

Apparatus and species	Michigan—Continued									
	Oceana		Ottawa		Schoolcraft		Van Buren		Total	
	Pounds	Value	Pounds	Value	Pounds	Value	Pounds	Value	Pounds	Value
Gill nets:										
Burbot									120	$2
Ciscoes, fresh	6,000	$420	10,170	$632	30,756	$1,228	6,135	$384	432,037	20,012
Pike									350	.51
Pike perch (walleyed)									2,325	401
Sturgeon									325	162
Sturgeon caviar									170	85
Suckers					1,967	71	600	30	96,104	4,528
Trout, lake	14,700	1,844	41,785	5,501	379,387	51,828	35,076	5,401	2,621,504	329,943
Whitefish—										
Common	1,000	150	3,395	632	30,748	5,046	47,195	9,233	643,752	104,848
Menominee, fresh					1,500	150			35,809	2,899
Yellow perch							2,045	137	110,530	6,270
Total	21,700	2,414	55,350	6,765	444,358	58,323	91,051	15,185	3,943,026	469,201
Lines: Trout, lake			95,100	13,564	38,608	5,268	61,630	7,996	485,402	64,586
Grand total	21,700	2,414	150,450	20,329	482,966	63,591	152,681	23,181	4,428,428	533,787

Apparatus and species	Illinois						Indiana	
	Cook		Lake		Total		Laporte	
	Pounds	Value	Pounds	Value	Pounds	Value	Pounds	Value
Gill nets:								
Ciscoes—	105,000	$10,500	95,000	$4,050	200,000	$14,550	150,000	$9,000
Fresh			28,165	4,733	28,165	4,733		
Smoked	25,000	2,980	167,275	25,814	192,275	28,794	215,200	30,128
Trout, lake								
Whitefish, common							10,000	1,400
Yellow perch	16,000	2,340	100	10	16,100	2,350	1,000	100
Total	146,000	15,820	290,540	34,607	436,540	50,427	376,200	40,628
Lines: Trout, lake							50,000	7,000
Grand total	146,000	15,820	290,540	34,607	436,540	50,427	426,200	47,628

Apparatus and species	Wisconsin							
	Brown		Door		Kenosha		Kewaunee	
	Pounds	Value	Pounds	Value	Pounds	Value	Pounds	Value
Gill nets:								
Burbot					2,000	$100		
Ciscoes, fresh	394,755	$7,490	582,580	$17,128	23,200	1,028	10,000	$200
Pike	156	14	720	72				
Pike perch (wall-eyed)	5,968	1,158	150	23				
Suckers	12,260	823	5,406	129			1,000	80
Trout, lake	2,000	249	810,703	95,550	48,600	6,804	212,000	31,800
Whitefish—								
Common	163	30	102,080	15,834			20,000	1,600
Menominee, fresh			1,945	38				
Menominee, salted			5,640	235				
Yellow perch	73,542	4,782	27,039	1,465	250	25	19,000	2,030
Total	488,844	14,546	1,536,263	130,474	74,050	7,957	262,000	35,710
Lines:								
Pike			260	21				
Trout, lake			381,653	46,545	74,260	12,792	302,200	45,330
Total			381,913	46,566	74,260	12,792	302,200	45,330
Grand total	488,844	14,546	1,918,176	177,040	148,310	20,749	564,200	81,040

Yield of vessel fisheries of Lake Michigan in 1922, by States, counties, apparatus, and species—Continued

Apparatus and species	Wisconsin—Continued									
	Manitowoc		Marinette		Milwaukee		Oconto		Ozaukee	
	Pounds	Value	Pounds	Value	Pounds	Value	Pounds	Value	Pounds	Value
Gill nets:										
Burbot	600	$30							5,000	$200
Carp, German							1,200	$60		
Ciscoes—										
Fresh	407,494	20,762	441,000	$13,130	274,320	$16,307	453,500	9,120	106,340	4,921
Salted			24,265	741			146,100	4,784		
Smoked							250	.25		
Pike			60	10						
Pike perch (wall-eyed)							7,372	1,229		
Suckers	250	13	13,250	576			44,065	2,753		
Trout, lake	405,327	55,913	115,900	12,090	540,140	81,295	12,500	1,430	197,335	28,926
Whitefish—										
Common	50	13	81,367	12,205			2,100	348		
Menominee, fresh	600	90								
Yellow perch	4,500	450	15,500	475	27,000	2,310	123,260	6,222		
Total	818,821	77,271	691,342	39,227	841,460	99,912	790,287	25,971	308,675	34,047
Lines:Trout,lake					80,000	12,200			195,220	28,105
Grand total	818,821	77,271	691,342	39,227	921,460	112,112	790,287	25,971	503,895	62,152

Apparatus and species	Wisconsin—Continued						Grand total	
	Racine		Sheboygan		Total			
	Pounds	Value	Pounds	Value	Pounds	Value	Pounds	Value
Gill nets:								
Burbot					7,600	$330	7,720	$332
Carp, German					1,200	60	1,200	60
Ciscoes—								
Fresh			122,830	$8,831	2,816,019	98,917	3,598,056	142,479
Salted					170,365	5,525	170,365	5,525
Smoked					250	25	28,415	4,758
Pike					936	96	1,286	147
Pike perch (wall-eyed)					13,490	2,410	15,815	2,811
Sturgeon							325	162
Sturgeon caviar							170	85
Suckers					76,231	4,374	172,335	8,902
Trout, lake	114,642	$15,198	345,285	51,649	2,804,432	380,904	5,833,411	769,769
Whitefish—								
Common					185,760	28,430	839,512	134,678
Menominee, fresh					22,545	1,728	58,354	4,627
Menominee, salted					5,640	235	5,640	235
Yellow perch					290,031	17,759	417,661	26,479
Oil			2,625	105	2,625	105	2,625	105
Total	114,642	15,198	470,740	60,585	6,397,124	540,898	11,152,890	1,101,154
Lines:								
Pike					260	21	260	21
Trout, lake	286,061	40,489	286,803	37,174	1,606,197	222,635	2,141,599	294,221
Total	286,061	40,489	286,803	37,174	1,606,457	222,656	2,141,859	294,242
Grand total	400,703	55,687	757,543	97,759	8,003,581	763,554	13,294,749	1,395,396

Yield of the shore fisheries of Lake Michigan in 1922, by States, counties, apparatus, and species

Apparatus and species	Michigan							
	Allegan		Antrim		Benzie		Berrien	
	Pounds	Value	Pounds	Value	Pounds	Value	Pounds	Value
Pound nets and trap nets:								
Buffalofish	60	$4					62	$4
Carp, German							502	20
Catfish and bullheads	160	16						
Ciscoes, fresh			4,100	$164			121,692	4,867
Pike perch (wall-eyed) or yellow pike	1,400	210					308	46
Sturgeon							454	226
Sturgeon caviar							25	75
Suckers, fresh	1,350	54					640	32
Trout, lake			800	105				
Whitefish, common	320	64	3,665	531			3,810	760
Yellow perch	190	11					1,570	94
Total	3,480	359	8,565	800			129,063	6,124
Gill nets:								
Burbot	1,600	48					200	10
Carp, German	1,000	30						
Ciscoes, fresh	7,580	303	3,625	135			6,050	242
Pike perch (wall-eyed) or yellow pike	1,300	195					1,635	820
Sturgeon								
Suckers	5,050	202			2,300	$138	2,330	140
Trout, lake	625	90	2,540	305	16,085	2,252	11,922	1,792
Whitefish, common	7,800	1,560	1,760	264	2,180	392	18,894	3,779
Whitefish, Menominee			30	4				
Yellow perch	1,270	76			600	48	5,718	344
Total	26,225	2,504	7,955	708	21,165	2,830	46,749	7,127
Grand total	29,705	2,863	16,520	1,508	21,165	2,830	175,812	13,251

24309—25†——12

Yield of the shore fisheries of Lake Michigan in 1922, by States, counties, apparatus and species—Continued

Apparatus and species	Michigan—Continued							
	Charlevoix		Delta		Emmet		Grand Traverse	
	Pounds	*Value*	*Pounds*	*Value*	*Pounds*	*Value*	*Pounds*	*Value*
Pound nets and trap nets:								
Carp, German			235	$5			750	$28
Catfish and bullheads			971	41				
Ciscoes, fresh			11,103	324				
Pike			9,323	1,305			400	60
Pike perch (wall-eyed) or yellow pike			15,143	2,127				
Sturgeon			890	347				
Sturgeon caviar			8	12				
Suckers, fresh			175,911	7,283			37,606	3,008
Trout, lake	37,541	$4,505	288	32	34,000	$4,080	29,989	3,517
Whitefish, common	13,590	1,912	30,797	5,866	18,000	2,700	51,464	7,637
Whitefish, Menominee, fresh			2,230	111			1,424	142
Yellow perch			24,089	1,499			2,000	135
Total	51,131	6,417	270,988	18,952	52,000	6,780	136,993	15,061
Gill nets:								
Burbot					400	20		
Carp, German			60	2				
Catfish and bullheads			1,589	112				
Ciscoes, fresh	3,975	278	22,555	678	1,563	129	1,250	112
Pike			2,760	413				
Pike perch (wall-eyed) or yellow pike			1,168	176				
Suckers			97,050	4,704	130	5	900	72
Trout, lake	26,817	3,135	4,210	605	65,050	8,389	2,090	242
Whitefish, common	5,700	855	44,500	8,880	2,562	560	900	156
Whitefish, Menominee	1,100	105	8,960	448	800	56		
Yellow perch	21,600	1,296	51,850	3,111	1,990	254	450	43
Total	59,192	5,669	234,702	19,129	72,495	9,413	5,590	625
Fyke nets:								
Burbot			1,400	28				
Carp, German			1,950	56				
Catfish and bullheads			700	42				
Ciscoes			6,725	202				
Pike			4,770	715				
Pike perch (wall-eyed) or yellow pike			37,325	5,599				
Sturgeon			111	55				
Suckers			118,800	4,549				
Trout, lake			100	12				
Whitefish, common			1,050	210				
Whitefish, Menominee			200	10				
Yellow perch			9,575	574				
Total			182,706	12,052				
Lines: Trout							1,869	224
Grand total	110,323	12,086	688,396	50,133	124,495	16,193	144,452	15,910

Yield of the shore fisheries of Lake Michigan in 1922, by States, counties, apparatus, and species—Continued

Apparatus and species	Michigan—Continued							
	Leelanau		Mackinac		Manistee		Mason	
	Pounds	Value	Pounds	Value	Pounds	Value	Pounds	Value
Pound nets and trap nets:								
Burbot							100	$2
Ciscoes, fresh	100	$3			6,299	$252	17,000	510
Pike	70	10	100	$15				
Pike perch (wall-eyed) or yellow pike							6,084	912
Sturgeon			1,787	705				
Sturgeon caviar			395	106				
Suckers, fresh	11,284	903	1,800	108	9,057	543	16,060	963
Trout, lake	5,677	681	23,786	2,853			400	60
Whitefish, common	10,940	2,078	233,202	42,985	1,461	292	100	15
Whitefish, Menominee, fresh	208	20	2,381	208	50	5	300	24
Yellow perch	1,152	91	300	18	330	19	100	6
Total	29,431	3,786	263,751	46,998	17,197	1,111	40,144	2,492
Gill nets:								
Ciscoes, fresh	7,055	316	400	12	150	5		
Pike perch (wall-eyed) or yellow pike					220	33	500	75
Sturgeon			600	315				
Sturgeon caviar			72	36				
Suckers			6,543	393	3,060	184	1,000	60
Trout, lake	17,775	2,133	3,764	452	350	43		
Whitefish, common	2,420	435	1,775	354				
Whitefish, Menominee	1,450	130	16,953	1,131				
Yellow perch	4,026	271	25	2	230	13		
Total	32,726	3,285	30,132	2,695	4,010	278	1,500	135
Lines: Trout	3,574	429						
Grand total	65,731	7,500	293,883	49,693	21,207	1,389	41,644	2,627

Apparatus and species	Michigan—Continued							
	Menominee		Muskegon		Oceana		Ottawa	
	Pounds	Value	Pounds	Value	Pounds	Value	Pounds	Value
Pound nets and trap nets:								
Burbot	400	$4	720	$36			140	$5
Carp, German	100	4	100	2			400	8
Catfish and bullheads							245	16
Ciscoes, fresh	111,137	2,146					960	38
Ciscoes, salted	13,680	399						
Pike			1,391	209			475	71
Pike perch (wall-eyed) or yellow pike	350	40	690	103			2,435	365
Sheepshead or drum							500	25
Sturgeon	81	23					300	125
Suckers, fresh	650	14	1,155	46			2,770	139
Trout, lake	3,925	459	500	75			3,465	416
Whitefish, common	462	55	21,174	4,234			22,610	4,522
Whitefish, Menominee, fresh	25	2						
Yellow perch	800	34	1,300	78			1,800	108
Total	131,610	3,180	27,030	4,783			36,100	5,838
Gill nets:								
Ciscoes, fresh	21,700	556	27,276	1,105			27,000	830
Pike			600	90				
Pike perch (wall-eyed) or yellow pike			1,325	206				
Sheepshead or drum			60	2				
Sturgeon			650	325				
Suckers	7,013	517	1,530	80			1,300	55
Trout, lake	3,100	315	3,531	530	100	$12	300	45
Whitefish, common			26,824	4,497	1,600	320	2,950	590
Whitefish, Menominee	200	18	100	8			200	16
Yellow perch	900	65	4,080	245			1,650	112
Total	32,913	1,471	65,976	7,088	1,700	332	33,400	1,648
Fyke nets:								
Suckers	100	4						
Yellow perch	100	6						
Total	200	10						
Grand total	164,723	4,661	93,006	11,871	1,700	332	69,500	7,486

Yield of the shore fisheries of Lake Michigan in 1922, by States, counties, apparatus, and species—Continued

Apparatus and species	Michigan—Continued					
	Schoolcraft		Van Buren		Total	
	Pounds	*Value*	*Pounds*	*Value*	*Pounds*	*Value*
Pound nets and trap nets:						
Buffalofish					122	$8
Burbot					1,360	47
Carp, German					2,087	67
Catfish and bullheads					1,376	73
Ciscoes, fresh					285,751	8,838
Ciscoes, salted					13,680	399
Pike	88	$12			11,847	1,682
Pike perch (wall-eyed) or yellow pike	469	75			26,879	3,878
Sheepshead or drum					500	25
Sturgeon	210	74			3,722	1,500
Sturgeon caviar					428	193
Suckers, fresh	7,813	225			266,096	13,318
Trout, lake	43,346	6,068			183,717	22,851
Whitefish, common	62,951	12,590			474,546	86,241
Whitefish, Menominee, fresh					6,618	512
Yellow perch					33,631	2,093
Total	114,877	19,044			1,312,360	141,725
Gill nets:						
Burbot					2,200	78
Carp, German					1,060	32
Catfish and bullheads					1,589	112
Ciscoes, fresh	25	1			130,204	4,702
Pike					3,360	503
Pike perch (wall-eyed) or yellow pike					4,513	685
Sheepshead or drum					60	2
Sturgeon					2,885	1,460
Sturgeon caviar					72	36
Suckers	586	33			128,792	6,583
Trout, lake					158,259	20,340
Whitefish, common	1,468	294			121,333	22,936
Whitefish, Menominee	3,305	330			33,098	2,246
Yellow perch	25	1	1,700	$170	96,114	6,051
Total	5,409	659	1,700	170	683,539	65,766
Fyke nets:						
Burbot					1,400	28
Carp, German					1,950	56
Catfish and bullheads					700	42
Ciscoes					6,725	202
Pike					4,770	715
Pike perch (wall-eyed) or yellow pike					37,325	5,599
Sturgeon					111	55
Suckers					118,900	4,553
Trout, lake					100	12
Whitefish, common					1,050	210
Whitefish, Menominee					200	10
Yellow perch					9,675	580
Total					182,906	12,062
Lines: Trout					5,443	653
Grand total	120,286	19,703	1,700	170	2,184,248	220,206

Yield of the shore fisheries of Lake Michigan in 1922, by States, counties, apparatus, and species—Continued

Apparatus and species	Indiana							
	Lake		Laporte		Porter		Total	
	Pounds	Value	Pounds	Value	Pounds	Value	Pounds	Value
Pound nets and trap nets:								
Buffalofish	100	$5	620	$34	50	$3	770	$42
Burbot	300	6	120	12			420	18
Carp, German	100	5	5,100	203	150	12	5,350	220
Ciscoes, fresh	40,000	1,600	22,000	1,500	59,000	2,950	121,000	6,050
Pike			25	3			25	3
Pike perch (wall-eyed) or yellow pike			150	37			150	37
Steelhead	500	100	115	23	3,050	610	3,665	733
Sturgeon	500	250	620	61	840	33	1,960	344
Suckers, fresh	100	5	550	34	125	6	775	45
Trout, lake	2,500	250	70	17	3,300	330	5,870	597
Whitefish, common	1,000	160	6,000	1,290	3,700	592	10,700	2,042
Yellow perch	1,000	50	5,000	800	1,100	55	7,100	905
Total	46,100	2,431	40,370	4,014	71,315	4,591	157,785	11,036
Gill nets:								
Ciscoes, fresh	18,000	900	4,800	384	2,800	140	25,600	1,424
Steelhead	7,500	1,500					7,500	1,500
Sturgeon			200	60			200	60
Suckers			200	20			200	20
Trout, lake	500	60					500	60
Whitefish, common	100	18					100	18
Yellow perch	1,500	150	2,800	281	1,100	55	5,400	486
Total	27,600	2,628	8,000	745	3,900	195	39,500	3,568
Grand total	73,700	5,059	48,370	4,759	75,215	4,786	197,285	14,604

Apparatus and species	Illinois					
	Cook		Lake		Total	
	Pounds	Value	Pounds	Value	Pounds	Value
Gill nets:						
Ciscoes, fresh	49,000	$4,840	3,000	$180	52,000	$5,020
Ciscoes, smoked			1,000	160	1,000	160
Trout, lake	10,300	1,230	500	80	10,800	1,310
Yellow perch	10,300	1,302	3,000	300	13,300	1,602
Grand total	69,600	7,372	7,500	720	77,100	8,092

Yield of the shore fisheries of Lake Michigan in 1922, by States, counties, apparatus, and species—Continued

Apparatus and species	Wisconsin							
	Brown		Door		Kenosha		Kewaunee	
	Pounds	Value	Pounds	Value	Pounds	Value	Pounds	Value
Pound nets and trap nets:								
Ciscoes, fresh	42,000	$840	118,800	$3,562				
Ciscoes, salted			974,280	26,158				
Pike			200	20				
Pike perch (wall-eyed) or yellow pike	2,200	330	100	15				
Suckers, fresh			4,247	147				
Suckers, salted			5,760	147				
Trout, lake			37,167	4,475				
Trout, lake, salted			120	5				
Whitefish, common			18,818	2,627				
Whitefish, Menominee, fresh			5,093	252				
Whitefish, Menominee, salted			8,840	442				
Yellow perch	14,000	980	3,728	305				
Total	58,200	2,150	1,177,153	38,155				
Gill nets:								
Carp, German			65,000	5,200			116,544	$5,827
Catfish and bullheads	5,000	500						
Ciscoes, fresh	127,280	3,202	52,618	1,921			77,363	2,279
Pike	740	87	56	6				
Pike perch (wall-eyed) or yellow pike	7,516	1,547	300	90			140	32
Suckers	90,676	7,003	17,200	1,374			12,949	1,136
Trout, lake			50,570	8,600			1,000	150
Whitefish, common	150	45	49,947	10,190				
Whitefish, Menominee			2,000	140				
Yellow perch	17,690	1,152	219,483	20,814			2,934	266
Total	249,052	13,536	457,174	48,335			210,930	9,690
Fyke nets:								
Burbot	1,141	16						
Carp, German	31,736	846						
Catfish and bullheads	119,669	5,099						
Ciscoes	600	17						
Pike	14,458	1,335						
Pike perch (wall-eyed) or yellow pike	23,000	3,523						
Sheepshead or drum	2,262	47						
Suckers	170,204	6,674						
White bass	1,005	38						
Yellow perch	194,126	10,850						
Total	558,201	28,445						
Seines (haul):								
Carp, German	449,652	9,745						
Catfish and bullheads	4,600	270						
Pike	50	4						
Pike perch (wall-eyed) or yellow pike	5,020	903						
Sheepshead or drum	1,650	33						
Suckers	13,240	1,005						
Total	474,212	11,960						
Lines:								
Trout			9,314	1,213				
Yellow perch					1,000	$200		
Total			9,314	1,213	1,000	200		
Crawfish pots: Crawfish	68,764	2,446						
Grand total	1,408,429	58,537	1,643,641	87,703	1,000	200	210,930	9,690

Yield of the shore fisheries of Lake Michigan in 1922, by States, counties, apparatus, and species—Continued

Apparatus and species	Manitowoc		Marinette		Milwaukee		Oconto		Ozaukee	
	Pounds	*Value*	*Pounds*	*Value*	*Pounds*	*Value*	*Pounds*	*Value*	*Pounds*	*Value*
Pound nets and trap nets:										
Carp, German	550	$34					100	$4	200	$10
Ciscoes, fresh	72,000	2,520	21,000	$600	329	$14	311,000	8,480	10,000	300
Ciscoes, salted			5,060	154			120,720	3,522		
Ciscoes, smoked									9,000	1,080
Pike							1,500	150		
Pike perch (wall-eyed) or yellow pike			500	75			1,200	190		
Suckers, fresh	16,000	470	450	18	50	3	11,200	812	1,850	111
Trout, lake	139,950	21,000	3,800	380			450	45	4,000	720
Whitefish, common	11,583	1,474	6,800	1,021			200	36	5,055	1,110
Whitefish, Menominee, fresh									200	30
Yellow perch	100	10	1,200	52	590	35	20,000	1,190	260	16
Total	240,183	25,508	38,810	2,300	969	52	466,370	14,429	30,565	3,377
Gill nets:										
Ciscoes, fresh	1,500	90	195,500	5,790			43,200	1,186		
Ciscoes, salted							6,000	175		
Pike							200	30		
Pike perch (wall-eyed) or yellow pike							150	22		
Suckers			196,200	15,696			171,500	13,760		
Trout, lake	1,000	60	8,500	850						
Whitefish, common	120	22	2,500	375						
Whitefish, Menominee	800	120					800	40		
Yellow perch	3,400	350	27,000	2,700			13,000	910		
Total	6,820	642	429,700	25,411			234,850	16,123		
Fyke nets:										
Carp, German	1,968	106	3,500	95			2,630	80		
Catfish and bullheads			2,500	250			11,195	1,054		
Ciscoes	280	17								
Pike	174	28	1,450	145			6,012	545		
Pike perch (wall-eyed) or yellow pike			360	54			5,780	1,094		
Suckers	36,777	2,207	4,900	149			37,300	1,998		
Yellow perch	2,794	287	10,150	305			123,500	6,310		
Total	41,993	2,645	22,860	998			186,417	11,081		
Seines (haul):										
Carp, German							70,000	2,800		
Catfish and bullheads							2,000	120		
Pike perch (wall-eyed) or yellow pike							2,000	300		
Suckers	1,500	75					30,000	2,400		
Yellow perch	500	25								
Total	2,000	100					104,000	5,620		
Crawfish pots: Crawfish							14,000	441		
Grand total	290,996	28,895	491,370	28,709	969	52	1,005,637	47,694	30,565	3,377

Yield of the shore fisheries of Lake Michigan in 1922, by States, counties, apparatus, and species—Continued

Apparatus and species	Wisconsin—Continued						Grand total	
	Racine		Sheboygan		Total			
	Pounds	Value	Pounds	Value	Pounds	Value	Pounds	Value
Pound nets and trap nets:								
Buffalofish							892	$50
Burbot							1,780	65
Carp, German					850	$48	8,287	335
Catfish and bullheads							1,376	73
Ciscoes, fresh			141,707	$2,888	716,836	19,204	1,123,587	34,092
Ciscoes, salted					1,100,060	29,834	1,113,740	30,233
Ciscoes, smoked					9,000	1,080	9,000	1,080
Pike					1,700	170	13,572	1,855
Pike perch (wall-eyed) or yellow pike					4,000	610	31,029	4,525
Sheepshead or drum							500	25
Steelhead							3,665	733
Sturgeon							5,682	1,844
Sturgeon caviar							428	193
Suckers, fresh			1,566	63	35,363	1,624	302,234	14,987
Suckers, salted					5,760	147	5,760	147
Trout, lake			140,135	24,495	325,502	51,115	515,089	74,563
Trout, lake, salted					120	5	120	5
Whitefish, common			4,635	910	47,091	7,178	532,337	95,461
Whitefish, Menominee, fresh					5,293	282	11,911	794
Whitefish, Menominee, salted					8,840	442	8,840	442
Yellow perch			1,162	105	41,040	2,693	81,771	5,691
Total			289,205	28,461	2,301,455	114,432	3,771,600	267,193
Gill nets:								
Burbot							2,200	78
Carp, German					181,544	11,027	182,604	11,059
Catfish and bullheads					5,000	500	6,589	612
Ciscoes, fresh	500	$40			497,961	14,508	705,765	25,654
Ciscoes, salted					6,000	175	6,000	175
Ciscoes, smoked							1,000	160
Pike					996	123	4,356	626
Pike perch (wall-eyed) or yellow pike					8,106	1,691	12,619	2,376
Sheepshead or drum							60	2
Steelhead							7,500	1,500
Sturgeon							3,085	1,520
Sturgeon caviar							72	36
Suckers			3,000	150	491,525	39,119	620,517	45,722
Trout, lake					61,070	9,660	230,629	31,370
Whitefish, common					52,717	10,632	174,150	33,586
Whitefish, Menominee					3,600	300	36,698	2,546
Yellow perch	3,270	450	2,000	240	288,777	26,882	403,591	35,021
Total	3,770	490	5,000	390	1,597,296	114,617	2,397,435	192,043
Fyke nets:								
Burbot					1,141	16	2,541	44
Carp, German					39,834	1,127	41,784	1,183
Catfish and bullheads					133,364	6,403	134,064	6,445
Ciscoes					880	34	7,605	236
Pike					22,094	2,053	26,864	2,768
Pike perch (wall-eyed) or yellow pike					29,140	4,671	66,465	10,270
Sheepshead or drum					2,262	47	2,262	47
Sturgeon							111	55
Suckers					249,181	11,028	368,081	15,581
Trout, lake							100	12
White bass					1,005	38	1,005	38
Whitefish, common							1,050	210
Whitefish, Menominee							200	10
Yellow perch					330,570	17,752	340,245	18,332
Total					809,471	43,169	992,377	55,231
Seines (haul):								
Carp, German			500	40	520,152	12,585	520,152	12,585
Catfish and bullheads					6,600	390	6,600	390
Pike					50	4	50	4
Pike perch (wall-eyed) or yellow pike					7,020	1,203	7,020	1,203
Sheepshead or drum					1,650	33	1,650	33
Suckers			6,000	300	50,740	3,780	50,740	3,780
Yellow perch					500	25	500	25
Total			6,500	340	586,712	18,020	586,712	18,020
Lines:								
Trout					9,314	1,213	14,757	1,866
Yellow perch					1,000	200	1,000	200
Total					10,314	1,413	15,757	2,066
Crawfish pots: Crawfish					82,764	2,887	82,764	2,887
Grand total	3,770	490	300,705	29,191	5,388,012	294,538	7,846,645	537,440

MUSSEL FISHERIES OF RIVERS TRIBUTARY TO LAKE MICHIGAN

In 1922 the mussel fisheries of rivers tributary to Lake Michigan were found to be of sufficient importance to be canvassed in connection with the Great Lakes canvass. Though not formerly canvassed with the Great Lakes, earlier statistics on certain of the rivers are available as the result of a special mussel canvass for the year 1913. In order to avoid confusion in comparisons, the statistics of the mussel fishery have been omitted from the foregoing treatment of the fisheries of Lake Michigan and are shown in the following table:

Persons engaged, investment, and products in the mussel fisheries of rivers tributary to Lake Michigan in 1922, by apparatus, States, and counties

	St. Joseph River					
	Michigan					
Items	Berrien		St. Joseph		Total	
PERSONS ENGAGED	Number	Value	Number	Value	Number	Value
Fishermen	44		56		100	
Shoresmen	26		12		38	
Total	70		68		138	
INVESTMENT						
Rowboats	22	$230	56	$340	78	$570
Bower boats	23	3,450	20	3,000	43	6,450
Crowfoot bars (pairs)	44	660	7	105	51	765
Picks			54	54	54	54
Shore and accessory property		12,726		2,450		15,176
Total		17,066		5,949		23,015
PRODUCTS						
By crowfoot bars:	Pounds		Pounds		Pounds	
Mussel shells	536,000	12,255	90,000	3,270	626,000	15,525
Pearls		1,310		460		1,770
Slugs		1,070		50		1,120
By picks:						
Mussel shells			740,000	25,600	740,000	25,600
Pearls				3,200		3,200
Slugs				560		560
Total, all apparatus:						
Mussel shells	536,000	12,255	830,000	28,870	1,366,000	41,125
Pearls		1,310		3,660		4,970
Slugs		1,070		610		1,680

NOTE.—The mussel fisheries on the above rivers have not previously been shown with Great Lakes statistics, but those of some of them were shown in an independent mussel canvass for the year 1913.

Persons engaged, investment, and products in the mussel fisheries of rivers tributary to Lake Michigan in 1922, by apparatus, States, and counties—Continued

	St. Joseph River—Continued							
Items	Indiana						Total	
	Elkhart		St. Joseph		Total			
PERSONS ENGAGED	Number	Value	Number	Value	Number	Value	Number	Value
Fishermen	8		6		14		114	
Shoresmen							38	
Total	8		6		14		152	
INVESTMENT								
Rowboats	3	$35	2	$30	5	$65	83	$635
Power boats	5	750	4	600	9	1,350	52	7,800
Crowfoot bars (pairs)	8	120	6	90	14	210	65	975
Picks							54	54
Shore and accessory property		500		450		950		16,126
Total		1,405		1,170		2,575		25,590
PRODUCTS								
By crowfoot bars:	Pounds		Pounds		Pounds		Pounds	
Mussel shells	108,000	3,330	117,000	3,465	225,000	6,795	851,000	22,320
Pearls		190		180		370		2,140
Slugs		350		400		750		1,870
By picks:								
Mussel shells							740,000	25,600
Pearls								3,200
Slugs								560
Total, all apparatus:								
Mussel shells	108,000	3,330	117,000	3,465	225,000	6,795	1,591,000	47,920
Pearls		190		180		370		5,340
Slugs		350		400		750		2,430

	Grand River						Kalamazoo River: Michigan, Allegan	
Items	Michigan				Total			
	Ionia		Kent					
PERSONS ENGAGED	Number	Value	Number	Value	Number	Value	Number	Value
Fishermen	150		150		300		4	
Shoresmen			13		13			
Total	150		163		313		4	
INVESTMENT								
Rowboats	129	$1,290	129	$1,290	258	$2,580	2	$20
Power boats	21	3,318	21	3,318	42	6,636	2	300
Crowfoot bars (pairs)	120	1,800	120	1,800	240	3,600	4	60
Picks	75	75	75	75	150	150		
Shore and accessory property		15,375		27,775		43,150		1,150
Total		21,858		34,258		56,116		1,530
PRODUCTS								
By crowfoot bars:	Pounds		Pounds		Pounds		Pounds	
Mussel shells	1,200,000	49,800	1,200,000	49,800	2,400,000	99,600	80,000	3,600
Pearls		600		600		1,200		25
Slugs		900		900		1,800		75
By picks:								
Mussel shells	300,000	12,450	300,000	12,450	600,000	24,900		
Pearls		375		75		450		
Slugs				300		300		
Total, all apparatus:								
Mussel shells	1,500,000	62,250	1,500,000	62,250	3,000,000	124,500	80,000	3,600
Pearls		975		675		1,650		25
Slugs		900		1,200		2,100		75

NOTE.—The mussel fisheries on the above rivers have not previously been shown with Great Lakes statistics, but those of some of them were shown in an independent mussel canvass for the year 1913.

Persons engaged, investment, and products in the mussel fisheries of rivers tributary to Lake Michigan in 1922, by apparatus, States, and counties—Continued

Items	Maple River: Michigan, Ionia		Muskegon River: Michigan, Newaygo		Pigeon River					
					Michigan, St. Joseph		Indiana, La Grange		Total	
PERSONS ENGAGED	Number	Value	Number	Value	Number	Value	Number	Value	Number	Value
Fishermen	4	-----	7	-----	2	-----	3	-----	5	-----
INVESTMENT										
Rowboats	4	$40	5	$50	2	$10	3	$30	5	$40
Power boats			2	300						
Forks	4	12								
Picks	4	4	7	7	2	2			2	2
Shore and accessory property		400		700		100		60		160
Total		456		1,057		112		90		202
PRODUCTS	Pounds		Pounds		Pounds		Pounds		Pounds	
By forks:										
Mussel shells	35,000	1,200								
Pearls		100								
Slugs		200								
By picks:										
Mussel shells	35,000	1,200	150,000	6,500	20,000	140			20,000	140
Pearls		100		75		60				60
Slugs		200		300		40				40
By hand:										
Mussel shells							10,000	300	10,000	300
Slugs								12		12
Total, all apparatus:										
Mussel shells	70,000	2,400	150,000	6,500	20,000	140	10,000	300	30,000	440
Pearls		200		75		60				60
Slugs		400		300		40		12		52

Items	Thornapple River: Michigan, Kent		Wolf River: Wisconsin, Waupaca		Grand total	
PERSONS ENGAGED	Number	Value	Number	Value	Number	Value
Fishermen	3	-----	2	-----	439	-----
Shoresmen					51	-----
Total	3	-----	2	-----	490	-----
INVESTMENT						
Rowboats	3	$30	2	$20	362	$3,415
Power boats			1	175	99	15,211
Crowfoot bars (pairs)			2	30	311	4,665
Forks			2	6	6	18
Picks	3	3			220	220
Shore and accessory property		75		197		61,958
Total		108		428		85,487
PRODUCTS	Pounds		Pounds		Pounds	
By crowfoot bars:						
Mussel shells			20,000	336	3,351,000	125,856
Pearls				20		3,385
Slugs				12		3,757
By forks:						
Mussel shells			5,805	72	40,805	1,272
Pearls				6		106
Slugs						200
By picks:						
Mussel shells	40,000	1,800			1,585,000	60,140
Pearls		20				3,905
Slugs		80				1,480
By hand:						
Mussel shells					10,000	300
Slugs						12
Total, all apparatus:						
Mussel shells	40,000	1,800	25,805	408	4,986,805	187,568
Pearls		20		26		7,396
Slugs		80		12		5,449

NOTE.—The mussel fisheries on the above rivers have not previously been shown with Great Lakes statistics, but those of some of them were shown in an independent mussel canvass for the year 1913.

In 1922 the wholesale fishery trade of Lake Michigan was carried on by 59 establishments, which employed 615 persons; paid $1,023,224 in wages; had $1,547,805 invested in property; and used $827,952 of cash capital to carry on the business. Compared with 1917 there was a material decrease in the number of establishments and number of persons employed and an increase in all phases of the investment. The detailed statistics are shown in the following table:

Wholesale fishery trade of Lake Michigan

Cities and towns	State	Number of firms	Persons engaged	Wages paid	Shore and accessory property	Cash capital
Chicago [1]	Illinois	22	416	$837,104	$990,397	$519,000
Milwaukee and Kenosha	Wisconsin	4	19	25,200	241,900	33,000
Sheboygan, Cedar Grove, and Port Washington.	do	5	21	11,900	17,140	18,000
Two Rivers, Manitowoc, and Sturgeon Bay.	do	5	14	9,397	38,250	17,000
Green Bay and Big Suamico	do	7	69	74,077	133,832	90,000
Marinette and Oconto	do	5	25	7,250	20,476	14,895
Menominee, Escanaba, and Fairport	Michigan	4	20	25,196	41,410	72,300
Charlevoix and Ludington	do	4	15	20,400	38,300	24,500
St. Joseph and Grand Haven	do	3	16	12,700	26,100	39,257
Total		59	615	1,023,224	1,547,805	827,952

[1] Includes two firms at Michigan City, Ind.

FISHERIES OF LAKE HURON

Lake Huron ranks third in importance among the Great Lakes. Reference to previous statistics indicates that her fisheries have suffered a lesser diminution than those of the other lakes, with the possible exception of Lake Erie.

In 1922 there were 1,001 persons engaged in the fisheries of Lake Huron, 131 of them on vessels fishing, 705 in the shore and boat fisheries, and 165 employed as shoresmen and on transporting vessels.

The total investment in the fisheries amounted to $1,648,767, of which $280,540 was invested in vessels and boats, $534,339 in gear, and $833,888 in shore and accessory property and cash capital. There were 29 fishing vessels over 5 tons net, 18 of them operated by steam and 11 by gasoline. Their fishing gear consisted of 4,043 gill nets, valued at $78,885, and lines valued at $7,275. There were 472 sail, power, and row boats engaged in the shore fishery. These operated 1,474 pound nets, 2,960 gill nets, 425 fyke nets, 75 haul seines, and a small number of lines.

The products of Lake Huron in 1922 aggregated 13,942,115 pounds, valued at $945,259. The more important species were ciscoes, 5,496,463 pounds, valued at $153,613; lake trout, 2,108,249 pounds, valued at $215,501; common whitefish, 1,300,621 pounds, valued at $199,503; pike perch, 1,260,374 pounds, valued at $171,102; suckers, 1,889,129 pounds, valued at $104,204; and yellow perch, 633,188 pounds, valued at $47,138.

FISHERIES BY COUNTIES

The number of persons engaged, investment, and quantity and value of products of the fisheries of Lake Huron in 1922 are shown by counties in the following tables:

Statistics of the fisheries of Lake Huron in 1922, by counties

PERSONS ENGAGED

Counties	On vessels fishing	On vessels transporting	In shore or boat fisheries	Shoresmen	Total
Alcona			15		15
Alpena	60		39	23	122
Arenac			39		39
Bay			149	57	206
Cheboygan	17	9	50	4	80
Chippewa	6		26	3	35
Huron	17		232	29	278
Iosco	14		36	17	67
Mackinac			46	8	54
Presque Isle	13		13	8	34
St. Clair	4		21	7	32
Sanilac			25		25
Tuscola			14		14
Total	131	9	705	156	1,001

INVESTMENT

Items	Alcona		Alpena		Arenac		Bay		Cheboygan	
	Number	Value	Number	Value	Number	Value	Number	Value	Number	Value
Vessels fishing:										
Steam			10	$55,000						
Tonnage			294							
Outfit				15,350						
Gasoline									7	$5,900
Tonnage									57	
Outfit										835
Vessels transporting:										
Gasoline [1]			2	2,000					12	24,950
Tonnage			15						103	
Outfit				200						1,865
Sail and row boats	4	$145	13	475	16	$1,625	36	$2,755	21	880
Power boats	5	1,450	14	8,950	14	3,950	44	16,275	19	6,950
Apparatus, vessel fisheries:										
Gill nets			2,123	53,405					324	4,340
Lines				4,800						50
Apparatus, shore fisheries:										
Pound nets and trap nets	8	1,500	178	52,740	38	5,200	114	29,480	409	36,600
Gill nets	130	1,295	71	1,345			61	610	406	6,816
Fyke nets					33	1,600	94	5,340	32	950
Seines (haul)					14	4,000	25	7,450		
Shore and accessory property		625		67,525		3,900		107,050		88,324
Cash capital				15,000				71,000		20,000
Total		5,015		276,790		20,275		239,960		198,460

Items	Chippewa		Huron		Iosco		Mackinac		Presque Isle	
	Number	Value	Number	Value	Number	Value	Number	Value	Number	Value
Vessels fishing:										
Steam	2	$2,000	3	$21,500	2	$3,000				
Tonnage	20		77		45					
Outfit		110		4,730		4,000				
Gasoline					1	500			3	$3,000
Tonnage					7				25	
Outfit						250				1,300
Sail and row boats	11	415	59	2,695	12	790	34	$1,105	2	45
Power boats	13	5,150	76	45,475	15	10,450	15	3,775	5	4,200
Apparatus, vessel fisheries:										
Gill nets	130	1,300	200	3,000	436	6,540			680	8,800
Lines				1,975						450
Apparatus, shore fisheries:										
Pound nets and trap nets	45	6,620	311	175,050	84	25,825	198	18,700	30	1,500
Gill nets	404	4,040	519	6,068	459	6,885	228	1,345	283	3,295
Fyke nets			254	17,300	2	100				
Seines (haul)			31	5,590						
Lines		10		495				90		
Shore and accessory property		11,240		250,814		46,775		13,740		7,900
Cash capital		5,000		33,000		23,000		7,500		
Total		35,885		567,692		128,115		46,255		30,490

[1] Includes 1 steamer in Cheboygan County.

Statistics of the fisheries of Lake Huron in 1922, by counties—Continued

INVESTMENT—Continued

Items	St. Clair		Sanilac		Tuscola		Total	
	Number	Value	Number	Value	Number	Value	Number	Value
Vessels fishing:								
Steam	1	$3,000					18	$84,500
Tonnage	7						443	
Outfit		1,000						25,190
Gasoline							11	9,400
Tonnage							89	
Outfit								2,385
Vessels transporting:								
Gasoline							14	26,950
Tonnage							118	
Outfit								2,065
Sail and row boats	7	300	6	$295	3	$300	224	11,825
Power boats	14	5,700	9	4,300	5	1,600	248	118,225
Apparatus, vessel fisheries:								
Gill nets	150	1,500					4,043	78,885
Lines								7,275
Apparatus, shore fisheries:								
Pound nets and trap nets	19	1,775	29	10,250	11	1,150	1,474	366,390
Gill nets	192	1,920	180	2,250	27	270	2,960	36,139
Fyke nets	10	1,000					425	26,290
Seines (haul)					5	1,250	75	18,290
Lines		475						1,070
Shore and accessory property		18,700		23,445		4,350		644,388
Cash capital		15,000						189,500
Total		50,370		40,540		8,920		1,648,767

YIELD, BY SPECIES

Species	Alcona		Alpena		Arenac		Bay	
	Pounds	Value	Pounds	Value	Pounds	Value	Pounds	Value
Burbot	3,000	$60					30	$1
Carp, German	40	1	1,915	$127	89,465	$2,850	218,162	7,254
Catfish and bullheads					7,996	276	19,737	1,150
Ciscoes, fresh	207,762	5,462	597,821	29,197	39,858	708	359,422	5,431
Pike	300	15	175	18	3,591	231	9,709	897
Pike perch (wall-eyed, or yellow pike)	7,440	953	23,153	5,358	46,887	6,546	218,218	27,265
Sheepshead or drum					150	5	2,326	67
Sturgeon	60	17	255	114				
Suckers	15,576	563	87,429	4,212	142,239	4,106	747,209	23,387
Trout, lake	17,618	1,756	671,681	75,183			402	60
Whitefish:								
Common	14,944	1,937	376,503	67,525	13,362	1,763	7,296	1,209
Menominee, fresh	200	10	9,142	476				
Caviar			889	889				
Yellow perch	2,020	197	14,962	1,652	68,223	4,636	212,920	16,437
Total	268,960	10,971	1,783,925	184,751	411,771	21,121	1,795,431	83,158

Species	Cheboygan		Chippewa		Huron		Iosco	
	Pounds	Value	Pounds	Value	Pounds	Value	Pounds	Value
Carp, German	126	$5	710	$42	700,867	$29,371	965	$31
Catfish and bullheads	16,529	1,146	200	12	18,671	1,814	20	1
Ciscoes:								
Fresh	58	2	5,128	233	408,217	13,242	581,766	6,258
Salted					2,641,500	60,790		
Pike	827	69	17,627	1,091	1,371	128	3,394	173
Pike perch (wall-eyed, or yellow pike)	8,660	1,623	9,606	1,899	605,281	76,105	256,157	39,267
Sheepshead or drum					14,744	539	115	5
Sturgeon			38	13	250	25	171	76
Sturgeon caviar							3	6
Suckers	299,623	48,730	93,005	4,024	244,466	6,447	115,095	5,438
Trout, lake	80,460	7,164	121,323	12,170	332,254	41,698	691,650	56,085
Whitefish:								
Common	138,762	19,260	20,479	3,117	202,862	31,328	268,182	30,027
Menominee, fresh	3,600	186	705	41			11,257	489
Caviar					400	120		
Yellow perch	8,897	836	16,921	1,072	177,219	13,089	29,190	1,811
Total	557,542	79,021	285,742	23,714	5,348,102	274,696	1,957,965	139,667

[1] Includes 1 steamer in Cheboygan County.

Statistics of the fisheries of Lake Huron in 1922, by counties—Continued

YIELD, BY SPECIES—Continued

Species	Mackinac		Presque Isle		St. Clair	
	Pounds	Value	Pounds	Value	Pounds	Value
Burbot			45	$1		
Carp, German					301	$7
Catfish and bullheads					506	34
Ciscoes:						
Fresh	1,745	$52	251,758	17,504	5,902	191
Salted	840	23				
Pike	2,022	303	310	46		
Pike perch (wall-eyed, or yellow pike)	1,331	200	25	3	12,656	970
Sheepshead or drum					1,213	33
Sturgeon	376	177			466	173
Sturgeon caviar					16	20
Suckers	94,102	5,646	5,000	150	19,117	544
Trout, lake	45,924	5,670	61,948	6,219	60,630	6,198
Whitefish:						
Common	103,562	20,712	17,751	2,928	103,524	14,268
Menominee, fresh	4,516	452	609	54		
Menominee, salted	960	60				
Yellow perch	23,222	1,394	690	66	46,535	3,081
Total	278,600	34,689	338,136	26,971	250,866	25,519

Species	Sanilac		Tuscola		Total	
	Pounds	Value	Pounds	Value	Pounds	Value
Buffalofish	63	$3			63	$3
Burbot					3,075	62
Carp, German	847	23	51,718	$1,545	1,065,116	41,256
Catfish and bullheads	294	26	873	59	64,826	4,518
Ciscoes:						
Fresh	308,001	11,714	7,965	182	2,775,403	90,176
Salted	78,720	2,624			2,721,060	63,437
Pike	12	1	135	13	39,473	2,985
Pike perch (wall-eyed, or yellow pike)	53,736	8,385	17,224	2,528	1,260,374	171,102
Sheepshead or drum	27,275	722	937	29	46,760	1,400
Sturgeon	758	333			2,374	928
Sturgeon caviar	107	243			126	269
Suckers	7,126	231	19,142	726	1,889,129	104,204
Trout, lake	24,359	3,298			2,108,249	215,501
Whitefish:						
Common	33,386	5,428	8	1	1,300,621	199,503
Menominee, fresh					30,029	1,708
Menominee, salted					960	60
Caviar					1,289	1,009
Yellow perch	26,818	2,433	5,571	434	633,188	47,138
Total	561,502	35,464	103,573	5,517	13,942,115	945,259

FISHERIES BY APPARATUS

The vessel fisheries of Lake Huron in 1922 produced 2,617,201 pounds, valued at $250,588, and the shore and boat fisheries, 11,324,-914 pounds, valued at $694,671. In the vessel fisheries most of the catch was made by gill nets and consisted chiefly of lake trout, ciscoes, and whitefish; the catch by lines consisted entirely of lake trout. In the shore fisheries the pound net was the chief form of apparatus, taking 8,724,330 pounds of fish, principally ciscoes, suckers, pike perch, and whitefish. The remainder of the catch was distributed among gill nets, seines, fyke nets, and lines, the first two named being the most important.

The following tables present in detail the products of the vessel and shore fisheries of Lake Huron by gear in 1922:

Yield of vessel fisheries of Lake Huron in 1922, by counties and apparatus

Apparatus and species	Alpena		Cheboygan		Chippewa		Huron	
	Pounds	*Value*	*Pounds*	*Value*	*Pounds*	*Value*	*Pounds*	*Value*
Gill nets:								
Ciscoes	473,916	$23,112						
Pike perch (wall-eyed or yellow pike)			4,487	$736				
Suckers			2,000	100				
Trout, lake	437,095	49,171	23,244	2,103	19,560	$2,174	60,000	$8,500
Whitefish—								
Common	162,030	26,920	25,377	3,740	1,075	131	14,015	1,962
Menominee	3,440	179						
Yellow perch			1,728	116				
Total	1,076,481	99,382	56,836	6,795	20,635	2,305	74,015	10,462
Lines: Trout, lake	229,611	25,488	2,400	240			241,044	29,406
Grand total	1,306,092	124,870	59,236	7,035	20,635	2,305	315,059	39,868

Apparatus and species	Iosco		Presque Isle		St. Clair		Total	
	Pounds	*Value*	*Pounds*	*Value*	*Pounds*	*Value*	*Pounds*	*Value*
Gill nets:								
Ciscoes			173,098	$12,040	150	$4	647,164	$35,156
Pike perch (wall-eyed or yellow pike)	8,075	$734			643	67	13,205	1,537
Suckers	7,050	141					9,050	241
Trout, lake	518,175	39,888	30,833	3,103	27,341	2,494	1,116,248	107,433
Whitefish—								
Common	61,693	5,532	10,447	1,635	54,956	8,601	329,593	48,521
Menominee							3,440	179
Yellow perch					3,318	231	5,046	347
Total	594,993	46,295	214,378	16,778	86,408	11,397	2,123,746	193,414
Lines: Trout, lake			20,400	2,040			493,455	57,174
Grand total	594,993	46,295	234,778	18,818	86,408	11,397	2,617,201	250,588

Yield of the shore fisheries of Lake Huron in 1922, by counties and apparatus

Apparatus and species	Alcona		Alpena		Arenac		Bay	
	Pounds	Value	Pounds	Value	Pounds	Value	Pounds	Value
Pound nets and trap nets:								
Burbot	3,000	$60					30	$1
Carp, German	40	1	1,915	$127	15,425	$469	76,810	2,373
Catfish and bullheads					1,274	52	7,607	430
Ciscoes, fresh	207,762	5,462	114,633	5,760	38,093	690	340,231	5,142
Pike	300	15	125	13	621	60	2,996	290
Pike perch (wall-eyed) or yellow pike	7,091	901	22,778	5,328	12,412	1,713	158,177	19,223
Sheepshead or drum					150	5	2,296	66
Sturgeon	60	17	255	114				
Suckers	14,815	536	87,229	4,205	43,368	1,231	560,173	17,282
Trout, lake			1,466	174			402	60
Whitefish—								
Common	9,231	1,082	212,535	40,332	13,362	1,763	7,161	1,189
Menominee	200	10						
Whitefish caviar			889					
Yellow perch	2,020	197	13,901	1,546	34,911	2,398	123,701	9,931
Total	244,519	8,281	455,726	58,488	159,616	8,381	1,279,584	55,987
Gill nets:								
Carp, German							400	12
Ciscoes, fresh			9,272	325				
Pike			50	5			128	13
Pike perch (wall-eyed) or yellow pike	349	52	375	30				
Suckers	761	27	200	7			3,908	117
Trout, lake	17,618	1,756	3,509	350				
Whitefish—								
Common	5,713	855	1,938	273				
Menominee, fresh			5,702	297				
Yellow perch			1,061	106			9,620	818
Total	24,441	2,690	22,107	1,393			14,056	960
Fyke nets:								
Carp, German					6,000	240	2,097	88
Catfish and bullheads					2,300	60	590	44
Ciscoes							100	2
Pike					600	48	676	63
Pike perch (wall-eyed) or yellow pike					633	113		
Suckers					7,757	164	47,413	2,222
Yellow perch					9,020	541	25,708	1,641
Total					26,310	1,166	76,584	4,060
Seines:								
Carp, German					68,040	2,141	138,855	4,781
Catfish and bullheads					4,422	164	11,540	676
Ciscoes					1,765	18	19,091	287
Pike					2,370	123	5,909	531
Pike perch (wall-eyed) or yellow pike					33,842	4,720	60,041	8,042
Sheepshead or drum							30	1
Suckers					91,114	2,711	135,715	3,766
Whitefish							135	20
Yellow perch					24,292	1,697	53,891	4,047
Total					225,845	11,574	425,207	22,151
Grand total	268,960	10,971	477,833	59,881	411,771	21,121	1,795,431	83,158

Yield of the shore fisheries of Lake Huron in 1922, by counties and apparatus—Con.

Apparatus and species	Cheboygan		Chippewa		Huron		Iosco	
	Pounds	*Value*	*Pounds*	*Value*	*Pounds*	*Value*	*Pounds*	*Value*
Pound nets and trap nets:								
Carp, German	126	$5	710	$42	68,327	$2,944	965	$31
Catfish and bullheads	16,529	1,146	200	12	13,407	1,335	20	1
Ciscoes—								
Fresh			1,978	103	405,306	13,106	581,296	6,241
Salted					2,641,500	60,790		
Pike	763	64	17,127	1,056	35	3	426	25
Pike perch (wall-eyed) or yellow pike	2,812	675	9,606	1,899	556,990	67,540	245,827	38,076
Sheepshead or drum					14,088	514	115	5
Sturgeon			38	13	250	25	171	76
Sturgeon caviar							3	6
Suckers	272,585	47,639	90,347	3,917	175,098	3,501	107,341	5,263
Trout, lake	14,355	1,291	18,246	1,663	7,704	855	21,206	1,653
Whitefish—								
Common	98,860	13,838	17,635	2,721	175,752	26,998	171,342	20,462
Menominee	2,900	146	170	8			2,691	117
Whitefish caviar					400	120		
Yellow perch	3,568	420	16,768	1,060	131,307	9,344	29,029	1,800
Total	412,498	65,224	172,825	12,494	4,190,164	187,075	1,160,432	73,756
Gill nets:								
Carp, German					32	1		
Ciscoes, fresh	58	2	3,150	130	1,338	105	470	17
Pike					82	11	2,968	148
Pike perch (wall-eyed) or yellow pike	1,100	173			33,606	6,302	2,255	457
Suckers			2,658	107	2,443	88	616	31
Trout, lake	40,461	3,530	83,517	8,333	17,604	2,135	152,269	14,544
Whitefish—								
Common	14,525	1,682	1,769	265	11,060	2,062	35,147	4,033
Menominee, fresh	700	40	535	33			8,566	372
Yellow perch	2,100	202	153	12	20,299	1,590		
Total	58,944	5,629	91,782	8,880	86,464	12,294	202,291	19,602
Fyke nets:								
Carp, German					9,300	392		
Catfish and bullheads					5,264	479		
Ciscoes					1,573	31		
Pike	64	5			1,254	114		
Pike perch (wall-eyed) or yellow pike	261	39			14,685	2,263		
Suckers	25,038	991			46,842	2,201	88	3
Trout, lake					500	60		
Whitefish					2,035	306		
Yellow perch	1,501	98			25,363	2,130	161	11
Total	26,864	1,133			106,816	7,976	249	14
Seines:								
Carp, German					623,208	26,034		
Sheepshead or drum					656	25		
Suckers					20,083	657		
Total					643,947	26,716		
Lines:								
Pike			500	35				
Trout, lake					5,402	742		
Yellow perch					250	25		
Total			500	35	5,652	767		
Grand total	498,306	71,986	265,107	21,409	5,033,043	234,828	1,362,972	93,372

Yield of the shore fisheries of Lake Huron in 1922, by counties and apparatus—Con.

Apparatus and species	Mackinac		Presque Isle		St. Clair	
	Pounds	Value	Pounds	Value	Pounds	Value
Pound nets and trap nets:						
Carp, German					132	$3
Catfish and bullheads					460	31
Ciscoes, fresh	1,745	$52			3,237	70
Pike	2,022	303	300	$45		
Pike perch (wall-eyed) or yellow pike	1,331	200			460	60
Sheepshead or drum					1,087	30
Sturgeon	376	177			196	68
Sturgeon caviar					16	20
Suckers	94,102	5,646	5,000	150	18,158	527
Trout, lake	25,077	3,133	1,150	120	980	98
Whitefish—						
Common	98,279	19,655	805	149	442	66
Menominee	300	30				
Yellow perch	17,956	1,078	600	60	2,765	144
Total	241,188	30,274	7,855	524	27,933	1,117
Gill nets:						
Burbot			45	1		
Ciscoes—						
Fresh			78,660	5,464	1,840	99
Salted	840	23				
Pike			10	1		
Pike perch (wall-eyed) or yellow pike			25	3	8,904	613
Trout, lake	18,480	2,253	9,565	956	19,717	2,178
Whitefish—						
Common	5,283	1,057	6,499	1,144	48,079	5,595
Menominee, fresh	4,216	422	609	54		
Menominee, salted	960	60				
Yellow perch	5,266	316	90	6	38,879	2,578
Total	35,045	4,131	95,503	7,629	117,419	11,063
Fyke nets:						
Carp, German					169	4
Catfish and bullheads					46	3
Ciscoes					675	18
Pike perch (wall-eyed) or yellow pike					2,649	230
Sheepshead or drum					126	3
Sturgeon					270	105
Suckers					959	17
Whitefish					47	6
Yellow perch					423	28
Total					5,364	414
Lines:						
Trout, lake	2,367	284			12,592	1,428
Yellow perch					1,150	100
Total	2,367	284			13,742	1,528
Grand total	278,600	34,689	103,358	8,153	164,458	14,122

Yield of the shore fisheries of Lake Huron in 1922, by counties and apparatus—Con.

Apparatus and species	Sanilac		Tuscola		Total	
	Pounds	Value	Pounds	Value	Pounds	Value
Pound nets and trap nets:						
Buffalofish	63	$3			63	$3
Burbot					3,030	61
Carp, German	847	23	37,659	$1,000	202,956	7,018
Catfish and bullheads	294	26	873	59	40,664	3,092
Ciscoes:—						
Fresh	204,541	8,103			1,898,822	44,729
Salted					2,641,500	60,790
Pike	12	1	110	10	24,837	1,885
Pike perch (wall-eyed) or yellow pike	31,475	4,955	10,333	1,450	1,059,292	142,020
Sheepshead or drum	17,828	470			35,564	1,090
Sturgeon	758	333			2,104	823
Sturgeon caviar	107	243			126	269
Suckers	7,126	231	11,179	407	1,486,521	90,535
Trout, lake	15,568	2,071			106,154	11,118
Whitefish:—						
Common	27,777	4,684			833,181	132,939
Menominee					6,261	311
Whitefish caviar					1,289	1,009
Yellow perch	2,300	200	3,140	188	381,966	28,366
Total	308,696	21,343	63,294	3,114	8,724,330	526,058
Gill nets:						
Burbot					45	1
Carp, German					432	13
Ciscoes:—						
Fresh	103,460	3,611			198,248	9,753
Salted	78,720	2,624			79,560	2,647
Pike					3,238	178
Pike perch (wall-eyed) or yellow pike	22,261	3,430	1,891	378	70,766	11,438
Sheepshead or drum	9,447	252			9,447	252
Suckers			963	39	11,549	416
Trout, lake	660	82			363,400	36,117
Whitefish:—						
Common	5,609	744	8	1	135,630	17,711
Menominee, fresh					20,328	1,218
Menominee, salted					960	60
Yellow perch	24,518	2,233	1,344	114	103,330	7,975
Total	244,675	12,976	4,206	532	996,933	87,779
Fyke nets:						
Carp, German					17,566	724
Catfish and bullheads					8,200	586
Ciscoes					2,348	51
Pike					2,594	230
Pike perch (wall-eyed) or yellow pike					18,228	2,645
Sheepshead or drum					126	3
Sturgeon					270	105
Suckers					128,097	5,598
Trout, lake					500	60
Whitefish					2,082	312
Yellow perch					62,176	4,449
Total					242,187	14,763
Seines:						
Carp, German			14,059	545	844,162	33,501
Catfish and bullheads					15,962	840
Ciscoes			7,965	182	28,821	487
Pike			25	3	8,304	657
Pike perch (wall-eyed) or yellow pike			5,000	700	98,883	13,462
Sheepshead or drum			937	29	1,623	55
Suckers			7,000	280	253,912	7,414
Whitefish					135	20
Yellow perch			1,087	132	79,270	5,876
Total			36,073	1,871	1,331,072	62,312
Lines:						
Pike					500	35
Trout, lake	8,131	1,145			28,492	3,599
Yellow perch					1,400	125
Total	8,131	1,145			30,392	3,759
Grand total	561,502	35,464	103,573	5,517	11,324,914	694,671

WHOLESALE FISHERY TRADE,

In 1922 there were 20 establishments engaged in the wholesale fishery trade of Lake Huron. These employed 115 persons, paid out $107,118 in wages, had $357,688 invested in property, and used $189,500 cash capital to carry on their business. Compared with 1917 this is a decrease in the number of firms and the number of persons engaged and an increase in the investment. The following table shows the detailed statistics of this business.

Wholesale fishery trade of Lake Huron in 1922

Cities and towns	State	Number of firms	Persons engaged	Wages paid	Shore and accessory property	Cash capital
Bay City	Michigan	5	57	$58,765	$78,525	$71,000
Alpena, Oscoda, and East Tawas	do	3	19	15,000	23,675	38,000
Cheboygan, St. Ignace, and Detour	do	4	12	10,832	22,574	32,500
Bayport, Sebewaing, and Caseville	do	5	16	13,300	208,054	27,000
Port Huron and Port Austin	do	3	11	9,221	24,860	21,000
Total		20	115	107,118	357,688	189,500

FISHERIES OF LAKE ST. CLAIR AND ST. CLAIR RIVER

The fisheries of Lake St. Clair and St. Clair River in 1922 show increases as compared to 1917, although not approaching their former importance. There were 90 persons, 82 power and row boats, and $17,857 in investment utilized in the fisheries, which in 1922 produced 310,012 pounds of fish, valued at $17,365. Carp and pike perch were the most important species.

The following table shows, by counties, the number of persons engaged, investment, and quantity and value of the products of these fisheries in 1922:

Persons engaged, investment, and products (by apparatus) in the fisheries of Lake St. Clair and St. Clair River in 1922, by counties

Items	Macomb		St. Clair		Total	
PERSONS ENGAGED	Number	Value	Number	Value	Number	Value
Fishermen	13		77		90	
INVESTMENT						
Rowboats	4	$170	48	$2,600	52	$2,770
Power boats	7	2,100	23	4,800	30	6,900
Seines (haul)	1	2,000	2	700	3	2,700
Hand lines			6		81		87
Shore and accessory property		1,500		3,900		5,400
Total		5,776		12,081		17,857
PRODUCTS	Pounds	Value	Pounds	Value	Pounds	Value
Seines: Carp	200,000	$8,000	60,000	$2,400	260,000	$10,400
Hand lines:						
Black bass			2,000	200	2,000	200
Catfish	1,005	148			1,005	148
Pike	40	4	4,000	400	4,040	404
Pike perch (wall-eyed or yellow pike)	185	30	38,435	5,711	38,620	5,741
Sheepshead or drum	16	1			16	1
Sturgeon	166	42	65	19	231	61
Yellow perch	100	10	4,000	400	4,100	410
Total	1,512	235	48,500	6,730	50,012	6,965
Grand total	201,512	8,235	108,500	9,130	310,012	17,365

FISHERIES OF LAKE ERIE

In 1922 Lake Erie ranked first among the Great Lakes except in the number of persons engaged, in which respect Lake Michigan ranked first. Lake Erie is one of the lakes whose production has been fairly well maintained throughout the period covered by the available statistics. Certain of the important species show material decreases, principal among these being sturgeon, lake trout, and whitefish. It is evident that the total production has been maintained through the greater catch of formerly unimportant species.

In 1922 the fisheries of Lake Erie gave employment to 2,504 persons. Of these, 582 were on fishing vessels, 1,226 in the shore and boat fisheries, and 696 employed as shoresmen and on transporting vessels.

The total investment in the fisheries and related industries amounted to $5,161,482, of which $950,359 was invested in vessels and boats, $917,466 in gear, and $3,293,657 in shore property and cash capital. There were 106 fishing vessels over 5 tons net, 69 of them operated by steam and 37 by gasoline; altogether carrying 36,555 gill nets valued at $260,999. In the shore fisheries there were 380 power boats and 555 rowboats operating 5,849 gill nets, valued at $36,995; 3,931 pound nets and trap nets, valued at $554,510; 752 fyke nets, valued at $35,190; 213 haul seines, valued at $29,685, and lines to the value of $87.

The products aggregated 55,079,128 pounds, valued at $2,944,204. Of this quantity, Ohio is credited with the greatest amount (37,342,813 pounds), followed, in order, by Pennsylvania, New York, and Michigan. The principal species were pike perch, all species, 22,357,996 pounds, valued at $1,285,399; ciscoes, 16,158,239 pounds, valued at $804,601; carp, 5,899,181 pounds, valued at $242,937; yellow perch, 2,969,332 pounds, valued at $177,492; and whitefish, 922,209 pounds, valued at $173,402.

FISHERIES BY STATES AND COUNTIES

The following tables show, by States and counties, the extent of the fisheries of Lake Erie in 1922:

Statistics of the fisheries of Lake Erie in 1922, by States and counties

PERSONS ENGAGED

State and county	On vessels fishing	On vessels transporting	In shore or boat fisheries	Shoresmen	Total
New York:					
Chatauqua	84		57	27	168
Erie	12		38	73	123
Total	96		95	100	291
Pennsylvania: Erie	249	2	33	195	479
Ohio:					
Ashtabula	46		57	25	128
Cuyahoga	55	2	45	69	171
Erie	112	10	269	140	531
Lake	18		71	12	101
Lorain	6		21	5	32
Lucas		1	119	21	141
Ottawa		11	337	25	373
Sandusky			26		26
Total	237	24	945	297	1,503
Michigan:					
Monroe			124	2	126
Wayne			29	76	[1] 105
Total			153	78	231
Grand total	582	26	1,226	670	2,504

[1] Includes persons engaged in the wholesale fish trade of Detroit.

Statistics of the fisheries of Lake Erie in 1922, by States and counties—Continued

INVESTMENT

State and county	Vessels fishing							
	Steam				Gasoline			
	Number	Tonnage	Value	Outfit	Number	Tonnage	Value	Outfit
New York								
Chautauqua	8	193	$57,500	$11,600	8	68	$21,500	$5,575
Erie	1	15	7,500	1,400	1	20	3,000	1,000
Total	9	208	65,000	13,000	9	88	24,500	6,575
Pennsylvania: Erie	34	850	229,000	57,874	10	120	28,000	7,607
Ohio:								
Ashtabula	6	109	41,500	4,775	2	15	3,000	650
Cuyahoga	7	167	40,100	14,042	3	20	4,400	1,250
Erie	11	224	49,500	10,415	10	211	48,000	10,115
Lake	1	9	3,000	900	3	19	6,000	4,200
Lorain	1	34	10,000	1,500				
Total	26	543	144,100	31,632	18	265	61,400	16,215
Grand total	69	1,601	438,100	102,506	37	473	113,900	30,397

State and county	Vessels transporting								Rowboats	
	Steam				Gasoline					
	Number	Tonnage	Value	Outfit	Number	Tonnage	Value	Outfit	Number	Value
New York:										
Chautauqua									15	$470
Erie									16	550
Total									31	1,020
Pennsylvania: Erie	2	66	$12,000	$4,148					15	520
Ohio:										
Ashtabula									15	360
Cuyahoga	1	24	1,500	250					19	580
Erie					6	53	$27,500	$2,898	97	3,055
Lake									21	650
Lorain									2	75
Lucas					6	40	8,250	1,435	76	2,420
Ottawa	2	28	8,000	800	5	54	9,000	1,250	207	7,775
Sandusky									10	405
Total	3	52	9,500	1,050	17	147	44,750	5,583	447	15,300
Michigan:										
Monroe									46	1,925
Wayne									16	2,120
Total									62	4,045
Grand total	5	118	21,500	5,198	17	147	44,750	5,583	555	20,885

Statistics of the fisheries of Lake Erie in 1922, by States and counties—Continued

INVESTMENT—Continued

State and county	Power boats		Apparatus, vessel fisheries		Apparatus of capture, shore fisheries			
			Gill nets		Gill nets		Pound nets and trap nets	
	Number	Value	Number	Value	Number	Value	Number	Value
New York:								
Chautauqua	11	$9,350	4,583	$55,795	2,245	$20,500		
Erie	13	3,050	234	3,520	250	3,000	22	$1,460
Total	24	12,400	4,819	59,315	2,495	23,500	22	1,460
Pennsylvania: Erie	12	8,800	15,212	113,108	370	1,450	65	19,950
Ohio:								
Ashtabula	12	8,500	4,848	36,924	76	765	232	37,685
Cuyahoga	16	9,300	3,540	15,080			269	39,500
Erie	118	46,180	7,068	30,672	1,000	4,000	1,607	251,000
Lake	24	13,600	768	4,700	624	2,300	380	42,750
Lorain	5	3,150	300	1,200			47	10,200
Lucas	37	11,800			25	125	395	37,675
Ottawa	96	38,710			1,231	4,743	864	110,350
Sandusky	4	750						
Total	312	131,990	16,524	88,576	2,956	11,933	3,794	529,160
Michigan:								
Monroe	27	11,650			28	112	50	3,940
Wayne	5	2,700						
Total	32	14,350			28	112	50	3,940
Grand total	380	167,540	36,555	260,999	5,849	36,995	3,931	554,510

State and county	Apparatus of capture, shore fisheries—Continued					Shore and accessory property	Cash capital	Total investment
	Fyke nets		Seines (haul)		Lines			
	Number	Value	Number	Value	Value	Value	Value	Value
New York:								
Chautauqua			12	$1,285	46	$77,875	$30,000	$291,496
Erie					41	244,639	376,157	645,317
Total			12	1,285	87	322,514	406,157	936,813
Pennsylvania: Erie						439,699	287,000	1,209,156
Ohio:								
Ashtabula			2	55		60,000	35,000	229,214
Cuyahoga						194,970	70,800	391,772
Erie	88	$3,840	16	2,010		421,832	180,200	1,091,217
Lake			3	75		45,729	10,000	133,884
Lorain						17,146	3,000	46,271
Lucas	278	17,140	15	1,525		222,200	28,000	330,570
Ottawa	66	5,640	107	17,545		152,600	65,000	421,413
Sandusky			8	1,100		500		2,755
Total	432	26,620	151	22,310		1,114,977	392,000	2,647,096
Michigan:								
Monroe	254	6,760	33	3,790		30,050	1,000	59,227
Wayne	66	1,810	17	2,300		237,160	63,100	[1] 309,190
Total	320	8,570	50	6,090		267,210	64,100	368,417
Grand total	752	35,190	213	29,685	87	2,144,400	1,149,257	5,161,482

[1] Includes investment in the wholesale fish trade of Detroit.

Statistics of the fisheries of Lake Erie in 1922, by States and counties—Continued

YIELD, BY SPECIES

State and county	Burbot		Carp, German		Catfish and bullheads		Ciscoes	
	Pounds	Value	Pounds	Value	Pounds	Value	Pounds	Value
New York:								
Chautauqua	350	$7	57,985	$2,924	1,190	$74	2,905,105	$141,771
Erie			1,075	30	20	2	210,949	10,562
Total	350	7	59,060	2,954	1,210	76	3,116,054	152,333
Pennsylvania: Erie	6,438	65	41,472	1,379	1,531	149	6,963,128	347,499
Ohio:								
Ashtabula	38,278	1,015	4,371	214	4,292	328	694,450	36,982
Cuyahoga	55,925	803	47,021	1,732	20,670	1,544	1,460,630	73,286
Erie	116,047	2,756	760,671	30,267	707,466	52,234	2,524,096	123,797
Lake	118,967	1,190	13,478	539	553	45	1,192,329	59,619
Lorain	3,060	63	13,250	478	4,800	374	207,342	11,071
Lucas			457,058	18,293	96,796	6,820		
Ottawa	14,939	190	2,117,839	84,971	438,523	29,789		
Sandusky			220,235	8,810	5,735	375		
Total	347,216	6,017	3,633,923	145,304	1,278,835	91,509	6,078,847	304,755
Michigan:								
Monroe			1,622,913	55,691	54,693	5,031		
Wayne			541,813	37,609	1,250	118	210	14
Total			2,164,726	93,300	55,943	5,149	210	14
Grand total	354,004	6,089	5,899,181	242,937	1,337,519	96,883	16,158,239	804,601

State and county	Goldeye or mooneye		Muskellunge		Pike		Pike perch — Blue pike	
	Pounds	Value	Pounds	Value	Pounds	Value	Pounds	Value
New York:								
Chautauqua							532,691	$17,251
Erie							31,838	1,624
Total							564,529	18,875
Pennsylvania: Erie							3,208,861	149,438
Ohio:								
Ashtabula			85	$9	2,362	$237	2,248,928	112,403
Cuyahoga					54,425	2,721	2,497,363	140,625
Erie	6,818	$73			16	1	1,577,379	76,480
Lake							4,111,574	206,470
Lorain							292,151	14,610
Lucas	1,285	13						
Ottawa	1,443	15			960	9	41,410	2,069
Total	9,546	101	85	9	57,763	2,968	10,768,805	552,657
Michigan:								
Monroe	3,892	39			4,732	530		
Wayne					2,600	380		
Total	3,892	39			7,332	910		
Grand total	13,438	140	85	9	65,095	3,878	14,542,195	720,970

Statistics of the fisheries of Lake Erie in 1922, by States and counties—Continued
YIELD, BY SPECIES—Continued

State and county	Pike perch—Continued				Sheepshead or drum		Sturgeon	
	Sauger		Wall-eyed or yellow pike					
	Pounds	Value	Pounds	Value	Pounds	Value	Pounds	Value
New York:								
Chautauqua	94,277	$4,711	5,367	$1,180	25	$1	6,127	$1,759
Erie			5,540	1,139			7,772	1,937
Total	94,277	4,711	10,907	2,319	25	1	13,899	3,696
Pennsylvania: Erie	139,480	6,973	25,962	4,348	58,509	1,449	1,341	503
Ohio:								
Ashtabula	325	10	2,030	605	8,784	268		
Cuyahoga	400,698	16,115	56,562	8,494	95,019	2,111		
Erie	4,350,275	217,595	837,990	122,676	1,319,151	32,100		
Lake	94,917	4,746	11,080	1,660	44,633	1,116		
Lorain	137,508	5,952	28,035	4,214	14,717	366		
Lucas	149,929	7,496	333,490	50,022	192,931	4,857		
Ottawa	634,969	31,739	475,715	71,256	603,374	14,173	235	94
Sandusky			65	9	12,815	256		
Total	5,768,621	283,653	1,744,967	258,936	2,291,424	55,237	235	94
Michigan:								
Monroe			30,827	3,337	12,385	265		
Wayne			760	152				
Total			31,587	3,489	12,385	265		
Grand total	6,002,378	295,337	1,813,423	269,092	2,362,343	56,952	15,475	4,293

State and county	Sturgeon caviar		Suckers		Trout, lake		White bass	
	Pounds	Value	Pounds	Value	Pounds	Value	Pounds	Value
New York:								
Chautauqua	14	$36	42,481	$3,018	1,079	$96	1,598	$113
Erie			27,254	1,167	202	20		
Total	14	36	69,735	4,185	1,281	116	1,598	113
Pennsylvania: Erie	105	200	45,664	1,488	585	49	14,257	566
Ohio:								
Ashtabula			48,161	1,925	31	3	16,346	966
Cuyahoga			83,408	1,975			37,286	1,719
Erie			533,978	16,091			381,479	15,257
Lake			43,926	1,318			7,719	308
Lorain			16,885	307			52,440	2,507
Lucas			303,921	9,173			243,324	9,732
Ottawa	8	20	307,771	9,222			263,439	10,555
Sandusky			600	24			2,740	85
Total	8	20	1,338,650	40,035	31	3	1,004,773	41,129
Michigan:								
Monroe			135,392	3,449			1,981	198
Wayne			8,730	429				
Total			144,122	3,878			1,981	198
Grand total	127	256	1,598,171	49,586	1,897	168	1,022,609	42,006

State and county	Whitefish		Yellow perch		Turtles		Total	
	Pounds	Value	Pounds	Value	Pounds	Value	Pounds	Value
New York:								
Chautauqua	199,411	$39,090	41,758	$2,820			3,889,458	$214,851
Erie	5,297	1,075	5,005	427			294,952	17,983
Total	204,708	40,165	46,763	3,247			4,184,410	232,834
Pennsylvania: Erie	375,972	75,093	160,354	8,398			11,043,659	597,597
Ohio:								
Ashtabula	33,726	6,100	123,394	11,078			3,225,563	172,143
Cuyahoga	4,702	846	262,882	14,480			5,076,591	266,441
Erie	146,391	23,862	1,576,058	94,261			14,837,815	807,450
Lake	23,058	4,579	307,360	15,401			5,969,594	296,991
Lorain	12,963	2,462	74,773	4,349			857,924	46,753
Lucas	14,335	2,294	71,716	5,562			1,864,785	114,262
Ottawa	103,290	17,470	263,028	15,779	85	$7	5,267,028	287,358
Sandusky					1,323	106	243,513	9,665
Total	338,465	57,613	2,679,211	160,910	1,408	113	37,342,813	2,001,063
Michigan:								
Monroe	3,064	531	81,724	4,719			1,951,603	73,790
Wayne			1,280	218			556,643	38,920
Total	3,064	531	83,004	4,937			2,508,246	112,710
Grand total	922,209	173,402	2,969,332	177,492	1,408	113	55,079,128	2,944,204

The catch of the vessel fisheries amounted to 24,297,307 pounds, valued at $1,280,146, and of the shore and boat fisheries to 30,781,821 pounds, valued at $1,664,058. The entire catch of the vessel fisheries was taken by gill nets, and consisted principally of ciscoes, pike perch, and yellow perch. In the shore fisheries the catch by pound nets was most important, amounting to 22,118,403 pounds, followed in order by haul seines with 5,618,210 pounds, gill nets with 1,636,282 pounds, fyke nets with 1,349,905 pounds, and other apparatus with 68,021 pounds.

The following tables give the products of the vessel and the shore fisheries of Lake Erie by States, counties, and species in 1922:

Yield of the gill-net vessel fisheries of Lake Erie in 1922, by States, counties, and species

Species	New York						Pennsylvania	
	Chautauqua		Erie		Total		Erie	
	Pounds	*Value*	*Pounds*	*Value*	*Pounds*	*Value*	*Pounds*	*Value*
Burbot							1,877	$19
Carp							37	1
Catfish							20	2
Ciscoes	2,427,019	$119,862	203,099	$10,154	2,630,118	$130,016	6,823,907	340,580
Pike perch:								
Blue pike	356,569	13,190	21,788	871	378,357	14,061	3,032,784	141,412
Sauger	94,277	4,711			94,277	4,711	139,480	6,973
Wall-eyed	867	130			867	130	1,022	156
Sheepshead or drum	25	1			25	1	5,295	117
Suckers	1,254	28	1,054	32	2,308	60	8,264	257
Trout, lake	1,066	95	202	20	1,268	115	585	49
White bass	378	15			378	15	4,143	165
Whitefish	123,816	24,571	2,560	512	126,376	25,083	328,256	65,559
Yellow perch	27,510	1,650			27,510	1,650	148,388	7,763
Total	3,032,781	164,253	228,703	11,589	3,261,484	175,842	10,494,058	563,053

Species	Ohio							
	Ashtabula		Cuyahoga		Erie		Lake	
	Pounds	*Value*	*Pounds*	*Value*	*Pounds*	*Value*	*Pounds*	*Value*
Burbot	12,225	$235	17,063	$213	210	$3		
Carp			27	1	4,466	156		
Catfish	40	4			700	55		
Ciscoes	617,329	31,584	1,452,434	72,796	2,485,268	121,477	807,856	$40,396
Pike perch:								
Blue pike	632,738	31,636	1,126,158	55,245	839,245	42,753	50,816	3,431
Sauger			1,746	88	1,097,646	54,977	32,505	1,625
Wall-eyed	30	5	110	17	10,768	1,595	610	90
Sheepshead or drum	705	17	2,380	50	3,682	148		
Suckers	690	25	1,307	66	6,926	280		
Trout, lake	31	3						
White bass	435	17	225	9	1,193	47		
Whitefish	32,272	5,809	49	9	12,711	2,250	6,437	1,255
Yellow perch	29,687	1,708	109,342	6,168	729,358	43,460	3,255	195
Total	1,326,182	71,043	2,710,841	134,662	5,192,173	267,201	901,479	46,992

Yield of the gill-net vessel fisheries of Lake Erie in 1922, by States, counties, and species—Continued

Species	Ohio—Continued				Grand total	
	Lorain		Total			
	Pounds	Value	Pounds	Value	Pounds	Value
Burbot			29,498	$451	31,375	$470
Carp			4,493	157	4,530	158
Catfish			740	59	760	61
Ciscoes	199,730	$10,463	5,562,617	276,716	15,016,642	747,312
Pike perch:						
Blue pike	148,540	7,427	2,797,497	140,492	6,208,638	295,965
Sauger	30,350	1,517	1,162,247	58,207	1,396,004	69,891
Wall-eyed			11,518	1,707	13,407	1,993
Sheepshead or drum			6,767	215	12,087	333
Suckers			8,923	371	19,495	688
Trout, lake			31	3	1,884	167
White bass	90	3	1,943	76	6,464	256
Whitefish			51,469	9,323	506,101	99,965
Yellow perch	32,380	1,943	904,022	53,474	1,079,920	62,887
Total	411,090	21,353	10,541,765	541,251	24,297,307	1,280,146

Yield of the shore fisheries of Lake Erie in 1922, by States, counties, apparatus, and species

Apparatus and species	New York					
	Chautauqua		Erie		Total	
	Pounds	Value	Pounds	Value	Pounds	Value
Pound nets and trap nets:						
Burbot	350	$7			350	$7
Carp			1,075	$30	1,075	30
Catfish and bullheads	50	5	20	2	70	7
Ciscoe			700	49	700	49
Pike perch—						
Blue pike	1,500	150	4,170	358	5,670	508
Wall-eyed or yellow pike	4,500	1,050	4,940	1,019	9,440	2,069
Sturgeon	665	416			665	416
Sturgeon caviar	14	36			14	36
Suckers	5,000	200	7,900	354	12,900	554
White bass	600	48			600	48
Yellow perch	600	48	2,580	205	3,180	253
Total	13,279	1,960	21,385	2,017	34,664	3,977
Gill nets:						
Ciscoes	473,415	21,042	7,150	359	480,565	21,401
Pike perch—						
Blue pike	174,622	3,911	5,880	395	180,502	4,306
Wall-eyed or yellow pike			600	120	600	120
Suckers	6,818	236	18,300	781	25,118	1,017
Trout, lake	13	1			13	1
White bass	620	50			620	50
Whitefish	75,595	14,519	2,737	563	78,332	15,082
Yellow perch	3,821	285	2,425	222	6,246	507
Total	734,904	40,044	37,092	2,440	771,996	42,484
Seines:						
Carp	57,985	2,924			57,985	2,924
Catfish and bullheads	1,140	69			1,140	69
Ciscoes	4,671	867			4,671	867
Suckers	29,409	2,554			29,409	2,554
Yellow perch	9,827	837			9,827	837
Total	103,032	7,251			103,032	7,251
Set lines: Sturgeon	5,462	1,343	7,772	1,937	13,234	3,280
Grand total	856,677	50,598	66,249	6,394	922,926	56,992

Yield of the shore fisheries of Lake Erie in 1922, by States, counties, apparatus, and species—Continued

Apparatus and species	Pennsylvania: Erie		Ohio			
			Ashtabula		Cuyahoga	
	Pounds	*Value*	*Pounds*	*Value*	*Pounds*	*Value*
Pound nets and trap nets:						
Burbot	4,171	$42	25,523	$764	38,312	$578
Carp	21,994	594	2,153	108	39,443	1,429
Catfish and bullheads	604	55	1,717	137	19,936	1,479
Ciscoe	88,713	4,394	32,443	2,271	1,014	60
Muskellunge			85	9		
Pike			2,287	229	54,425	2,721
Pike perch—						
Blue pike	157,709	7,357	1,586,847	79,293	1,368,571	85,248
Sauger			100	3	398,909	16,006
Wall-eyed or yellow pike	23,491	3,975	2,000	600	56,431	8,474
Sheepshead or drum	53,035	1,324	6,705	203	92,000	2,032
Sturgeon	1,341	503				
Sturgeon caviar	105	200				
Suckers	36,729	1,209	46,296	1,851	81,679	1,896
White bass	9,368	371	14,938	896	36,990	1,707
Whitefish	45,665	9,124	1,079	216	4,615	837
Yellow perch	5,321	302	92,024	9,202	153,055	8,282
Total	448,246	29,450	1,814,197	95,782	2,345,418	130,749
Gill nets:						
Burbot	390	4	440	13		
Carp	19,441	784	428	21		
Catfish and bullheads	907	92				
Ciscoes	50,508	2,525	44,678	3,127		
Pike			75	8		
Pike perch—						
Blue pike	18,368	669	28,993	1,455		
Sauger			225	7		
Wall-eyed or yellow pike	1,449	217				
Sheepshead or drum	179	8	490	15		
Suckers	671	22	825	33		
White bass	746	30	788	44		
Whitefish	2,051	410	110	22		
Yellow perch	6,645	333	1,633	163		
Total	101,355	5,094	78,685	4,908		
Seines:						
Carp			1,680	80		
Catfish and bullheads			195	19		
Pike perch, blue pike			325	18		
Sheepshead or drum			50	2		
Suckers			325	15		
White bass			175	8		
Whitefish			265	53		
Total			3,015	195		
Minor apparatus:						
Burbot			90	3	550	12
Carp			110	5	7,551	302
Catfish and bullheads			2,340	168	734	65
Ciscoes					7,182	430
Pike perch—						
Blue pike			25	1	2,634	132
Sauger					43	21
Wall-eyed or yellow pike					21	3
Sheepshead or drum			834	31	639	19
Suckers			25	1	422	13
White bass			10	1	71	3
Yellow perch			50	5	485	30
Total			3,484	215	20,332	1,030
Grand total	549,601	34,544	1,899,381	101,100	2,365,750	131,779

Yield of the shore fisheries of Lake Erie in 1922, by States, counties, apparatus, and species—Continued

Apparatus and species	Ohio—Continued					
	Erie		Lake		Lorain	
	Pounds	Value	Pounds	Value	Pounds	Value
Pound nets and trap nets:						
Burbot	115,738	$2,751	118,967	$1,190	2,930	$60
Carp	152,285	6,068	8,960	358	12,092	428
Catfish and bullheads	510,977	39,280	500	40	2,398	205
Ciscoe	38,183	2,289	125,680	6,284	7,612	608
Goldeye or mooneye	3,150	36				
Pike perch—						
Blue pike	737,848	33,713	4,057,538	202,877	143,318	7,166
Sauger	3,212,173	160,599	12,412	621	107,123	4,433
Wall-eyed or yellow pike	822,972	120,445	10,470	1,570	28,035	214
Sheepshead or drum	1,187,844	28,695	44,553	1,114	13,660	331
Suckers	508,682	15,260	43,806	1,314	16,835	305
White bass	317,748	12,710	7,444	298	52,340	2,503
Whitefish	120,721	19,385	8,191	1,638	12,963	2,462
Yellow perch	838,903	50,334	304,000	15,200	42,353	2,402
Total	8,567,224	491,565	4,742,521	232,504	441,659	25,117
Fyke nets:						
Burbot	50	1				
Carp	14,472	578				
Catfish and bullheads	49,803	3,238				
Goldeye or mooneye	193	2				
Pike perch—						
Sauger	11,167	558				
Wall-eyed or yellow pike	2,570	385				
Sheepshead or drum	52,666	1,316				
Suckers	15,730	472				
White bass	43,921	1,756				
Yellow perch	1,209	72				
Total	191,781	8,378				
Gill nets:						
Burbot	49	1				
Carp	209,072	8,251				
Catfish and bullheads	8,865	699				
Ciscoes	645	31	258,793	12,939		
Pike perch—						
Blue pike	286	14	2,035	102		
Sauger	22,076	1,100	50,000	2,500		
Wall-eyed or yellow pike	403	59				
Sheepshead or drum	20,279	574				
Suckers	1,433	43				
White bass	175	7				
Whitefish	12,959	2,227	8,430	1,686		
Yellow perch	6,538	392				
Total	282,780	13,398	319,258	17,227		
Seines:						
Carp	379,552	15,181	4,518	181		
Catfish and bullheads	131,912	8,549	53	5		
Goldeye or mooneye	3,475	35				
Pike	16	1				
Pike perch—						
Blue pike			1,185	60		
Sauger	7,213	361				
Wall-eyed or yellow pike	1,277	192				
Sheepshead or drum	54,680	1,367	80	2		
Suckers	1,207	36	120	4		
White bass	18,442	737	275	10		
Yellow perch	50	3	105	6		
Total	597,824	26,462	6,336	268		
Minor apparatus:						
Burbot					130	3
Carp	824	33			1,158	50
Catfish and bullheads	5,209	413			2,402	169
Pike perch—						
Blue pike					293	17
Sauger					35	2
Sheepshead or drum					1,057	35
Suckers					50	2
White bass					10	1
Yellow perch					40	4
Total	6,033	446			5,175	283
Grand total	9,645,642	540,249	5,068,115	249,999	446,834	25,400

Yield of the shore fisheries of Lake Erie in 1922, by States, counties, apparatus, and species—Continued

Apparatus and species	Ohio—Continued							
	Lucas		Ottawa		Sandusky		Total	
	Pounds	Value	Pounds	Value	Pounds	Value	Pounds	Value
Pound nets and trap nets:								
Burbot			14,887	$189			316,357	$5,532
Carp	126,734	$5,068	73,208	3,178			414,875	16,637
Catfish and bullheads	44,568	2,902	188,058	11,391			768,154	55,434
Ciscoe							204,932	11,512
Goldeye or mooneye	1,200	12	1,443	15			5,793	63
Muskellunge							85	9
Pike			960	9			57,672	2,959
Pike perch—								
Blue pike			41,410	2,069			7,935,532	410,366
Sauger	114,117	5,706	606,440	30,323			4,451,274	217,691
Wall-eyed or yellow pike	241,659	36,248	465,412	69,811			1,626,979	241,362
Sheepshead or drum	132,125	3,325	427,710	10,150			1,904,597	45,850
Sturgeon			235	94			235	94
Sturgeon caviar			8	20			8	20
Suckers	201,992	6,059	299,488	8,984			1,198,778	35,669
White bass	156,344	6,253	136,409	5,452			722,213	29,819
Whitefish	14,335	2,294	71,981	12,301			233,923	39,133
Yellow perch	44,626	3,395	256,235	15,372			1,731,196	104,187
Turtles			85	7			85	7
Total	1,077,700	71,262	2,583,969	169,365			21,572,688	1,216,344
Fyke nets:								
Burbot							50	1
Carp	56,860	2,276	38,650	1,556			109,982	4,410
Catfish and bullheads	31,709	2,027	90,931	6,823			172,443	12,088
Goldeye or mooneye	85	1					278	3
Pike perch—								
Sauger	34,548	1,727	5,570	278			51,285	2,563
Wall-eyed or yellow pike	88,635	13,295	3,460	419			94,665	14,099
Sheepshead or drum	55,986	1,399	28,740	574			137,392	3,289
Suckers	97,868	2,936	3,060	91			116,658	3,499
White bass	82,900	3,316	55,563	2,222			182,384	7,294
Yellow perch	26,419	2,113	430	25			28,058	2,210
Total	475,010	29,090	226,404	11,988			893,195	49,456
Gill nets:								
Burbot			52	1			541	15
Carp	320	13	24,168	966			233,988	9,251
Catfish and bullheads	996	77	181	14			10,042	790
Ciscoes							304,116	16,097
Pike							75	8
Pike perch—								
Blue pike							31,314	1,571
Sauger	264	13	10,905	546			83,470	4,166
Wall-eyed or yellow pike	85	13	846	127			1,334	199
Sheepshead or drum	625	16	1,179	56			22,573	661
Suckers	212	63	833	26			3,303	165
White bass			516	43			1,479	94
Whitefish			31,309	5,169			52,808	9,104
Yellow perch	140	11	4,577	274			12,888	840
Total	2,642	206	74,566	7,222			757,931	42,961
Seines:								
Carp	272,174	10,887	1,981,813	79,271	220,235	$8,810	2,859,972	114,410
Catfish and bullheads	4,438	322	156,568	11,339	5,735	375	298,901	20,609
Goldeye or mooneye							3,475	35
Pike							16	1
Pike perch—								
Blue pike							1,510	78
Sauger	1,000	50	12,054	592			20,267	1,003
Wall-eyed or yellow pike	3,040	456	5,987	897	65	9	10,369	1,554
Sheepshead or drum	3,394	85	145,745	3,393	12,815	256	216,764	5,105
Suckers	3,849	115	4,390	121	600	24	10,491	315
White bass	4,080	163	70,951	2,838	2,740	85	96,663	3,841
Whitefish							265	53
Yellow perch	500	40	1,776	107			2,431	156
Turtles					1,323	106	1,323	106
Total	292,475	12,118	2,379,284	98,558	243,513	9,665	3,522,447	147,266

Yield of the shore fisheries of Lake Erie in 1922, by States, counties, apparatus, and species—Continued

Apparatus and species	Ohio—Continued							
	Lucas		Ottawa		Sandusky		Total	
	Pounds	Value	Pounds	Value	Pounds	Value	Pounds	Value
Minor apparatus:								
Burbot							770	$18
Carp	970	$49					10,613	439
Catfish and bullheads	15,085	1,492	2,785	$222			28,555	2,529
Ciscoe							7,182	430
Pike perch—								
Blue pike							2,952	150
Sauger							78	23
Wall-eyed or yellow pike	71	10	10	2			102	15
Sheepshead or drum	801	32					3,331	117
Suckers							497	16
White bass							91	5
Yellow perch	31	3	10	1			616	43
Total	16,958	1,586	2,805	225			54,787	3,785
Grand total	1,864,785	114,262	5,267,028	287,358	243,513	$9,665	26,801,048	1,459,812

Apparatus and species	Michigan						Grand total	
	Monroe		Wayne		Total			
	Pounds	Value	Pounds	Value	Pounds	Value	Pounds	Value
Pound nets and trap nets:								
Burbot							320,878	$5,581
Carp	5,831	$173			5,831	$173	443,775	17,434
Catfish and bullheads	1,935	136			1,935	136	770,763	55,632
Ciscoe							294,345	15,955
Goldeye or mooneye	3,892	39			3,892	39	9,685	102
Muskellunge							85	9
Pike	40	4			40	4	57,712	2,963
Pike perch—								
Blue pike							8,098,911	418,231
Sauger							4,451,274	217,691
Wall-eyed or yellow pike	7,637	940			7,637	940	1,667,547	248,346
Sheepshead or drum	3,642	26			3,642	26	1,961,274	47,200
Sturgeon							2,241	1,013
Sturgeon caviar							127	256
Suckers	18,236	614			18,236	614	1,266,643	38,046
White bass	198	20			198	20	732,379	30,258
Whitefish	3,064	531			3,064	531	282,652	48,788
Yellow perch	18,330	1,400			18,330	1,400	1,758,027	106,142
Turtles							85	7
Total	62,805	3,883			62,805	3,883	22,118,403	1,253,654
Fyke nets:								
Burbot							50	1
Carp	50,761	2,006	123,323	$8,750	174,084	10,756	284,066	15,166
Catfish and bullheads	46,708	4,470	290	22	46,998	4,492	219,441	16,580
Goldeye or mooneye							278	3
Pike	2,842	320	2,600	380	5,442	700	5,442	700
Pike perch—								
Sauger							51,285	2,563
Wall-eyed or yellow pike	22,890	2,367	260	52	23,150	2,419	117,815	16,518
Sheepshead or drum	8,743	239			8,743	239	146,135	3,528
Suckers	115,756	2,721	8,580	422	124,336	3,143	240,994	6,642
White bass	1,783	178			1,783	178	184,167	7,472
Yellow perch	62,194	3,229	980	172	63,174	3,401	91,232	5,611
Total	311,677	15,530	136,033	9,798	447,710	25,328	1,340,905	74,784

Yield of the shore fisheries of Lake Erie in 1922, by States, counties, apparatus, and species—Continued

| Apparatus and species | Michigan | | | | | | Grand total | |
| | Monroe | | Wayne | | Total | | | |
	Pounds	Value	Pounds	Value	Pounds	Value	Pounds	Value
Gill nets:								
Burbot							931	$19
Carp	3,000	$240			3,000	$240	256,429	10,275
Catfish and bullheads							10,949	882
Ciscoes							835,189	40,023
Pike	1,000	120			1,000	120	1,075	128
Pike perch—								
Blue pike							230,184	6,546
Sauger							83,470	4,166
Wall-eyed or yellow pike							3,383	536
Sheepshead or drum							22,752	669
Suckers							29,092	1,204
Trout, lake							13	1
White bass							2,845	174
Whitefish							133,191	24,596
Yellow perch	1,000	70			1,000	70	26,779	1,750
Total	5,000	430			5,000	430	1,636,282	90,969
Seines:								
Carp	1,563,321	53,272	418,490	$28,859	1,981,811	82,131	4,899,768	199,465
Catfish and bullheads	6,050	425	960	96	7,010	521	307,051	21,199
Ciscoes			210	14	210	14	4,881	881
Goldeye or mooneye							3,475	35
Pike	850	86			850	86	866	87
Pike perch—								
Blue pike							1,510	78
Sauger							20,267	1,003
Wall-eyed or yellow pike	300	30	500	100	800	130	11,169	1,684
Sheepshead or drum							216,764	5,105
Suckers	1,400	114	150	7	1,550	121	41,450	2,990
White bass							96,663	3,841
Whitefish							265	53
Yellow perch	200	20	300	46	500	66	12,758	1,059
Turtles							1,323	106
Total	1,572,121	53,947	420,610	29,122	1,992,731	83,069	5,618,210	237,586
Set lines: Sturgeon							13,234	3,280
Minor apparatus:								
Burbot							770	18
Carp							10,613	439
Catfish and bullheads							28,555	2,529
Ciscoes							7,182	430
Pike perch—								
Blue pike							2,952	150
Sauger							78	23
Wall-eyed or yellow pike							102	15
Sheepshead or drum							3,331	117
Suckers							497	16
White bass							91	5
Yellow perch							616	43
Total							54,787	3,785
Grand total	1,951,603	73,790	556,643	38,920	2,508,246	112,710	30,781,821	1,664,058

MUSSEL FISHERIES OF RIVERS TRIBUTARY TO LAKE ERIE

The statistics of the mussel fisheries of rivers tributary to Lake Erie, not previously canvassed in connection with the Great Lakes, have been omitted from the foregoing treatment of the statistics of Lake Erie and are shown in the following table:

Persons engaged, investment, and products (by apparatus) in the mussel fisheries of rivers tributary to Lake Erie, in 1922, by States and counties

River, State, and county	Fisher-men	Rowboats		Apparatus				Shore and acces-sory prop-erty
				Forks		Picks		
	Number	Number	Value	Number	Value	Number	Value	Value
Auglaize River:								
Ohio: Defiance	2	2	$20					$40
Maumee River:								
Ohio—								
Defiance	22	22	220					440
Henry	28	28	280					560
Paulding	20	20	200					400
Wood	3	3	30					60
Total	73	73	730					1,460
Indiana: Allen	6	6	60					120
Total, Maumee River	79	79	790					1,580
Sandusky River:								
Ohio: Seneca	8	8	80					160
Tiffin River:								
Ohio: Defiance	2	2	20					40
St. Marys River:								
Indiana: DeKalb	3	3	30					60
St. Joseph of the Maumee River:								
Indiana—								
Allen	5	5	50					100
DeKalb	10	10	100					200
Total	15	15	150					300
Huron River:								
Michigan: Wayne	5	5	35	3	$9	5	$5	150
Raisin River:								
Michigan: Monroe	10	10	50	10	30			1,500
Grand total	124	124	1,175	13	39	5	5	3,830

River, State, and county	Products					
	By forks			By picks		
	Mussel shells	Pearls	Slugs	Mussel shells	Pearls	Slugs
	Pounds	Value	Value	Value	Pounds	Value	Value	Value
Huron River:								
Michigan: Wayne	14,000	$595	$75	$100	9,170	$390	$98	$20
Raisin River:								
Michigan—								
Lenawee	40,000	1,100	100	20				
Monroe	36,000	1,080	58	50				
Total	76,000	2,180	158	70				
Grand total	90,000	2,775	233	170	9,170	390	98	20

Persons engaged, investment, and products (by apparatus) in the mussel fisheries of rivers tributary to Lake Erie, in 1922, by States and counties—Continued

River, State, and county	Products—Continued							
	By hand				Total			
	Mussel shells	Pearls	Slugs		Mussel shells	Pearls	Slugs	
	Pounds	*Value*	*Value*	*Value*	*Pounds*	*Value*	*Value*	*Value*
Auglaize River: Ohio: Defiance	14,000	$210	--------	$12	14,000	$210	--------	$12
Maumee River: Ohio—								
Defiance	354,000	8,250	$150	392	354,000	8,250	$150	392
Henry	246,000	6,150	85	300	246,000	6,150	85	300
Paulding	270,000	6,750	150	272	270,000	6,750	150	272
Wood	28,000	700	5	35	28,000	700	5	35
Total	898,000	21,850	385	999	898,000	21,850	385	999
Indiana: Allen	80,000	2,000	40	80	80,000	2,000	40	80
Total, Maumee River	978,000	23,850	425	1,079	978,000	23,850	425	1,079
Sandusky River: Ohio: Seneca	42,000	1,050	50	55	42,000	1,050	50	55
Tiffin River: Ohio: Defiance	20,000	300	--------	20	20,000	300	--------	20
St. Marys River: Indiana: DeKalb	46,000	805	10	48	46,000	805	10	48
St. Joseph of the Maumee River: Indiana—								
Allen	20,000	400	--------	20	20,000	400	--------	20
DeKalb	40,000	800	--------	40	40,000	800	--------	40
Total	60,000	1,200	--------	60	60,000	1,200	--------	60
Huron River: Michigan: Wayne	--------	--------	--------	--------	23,170	985	173	120
Raisin River: Michigan—								
Lenawee	--------	--------	--------	--------	40,000	1,100	100	20
Monroe	--------	--------	--------	--------	36,000	1,080	58	50
Total	--------	--------	--------	--------	76,000	2,180	158	70
Grand total	1,160,000	27,415	485	1,274	1,259,170	30,580	816	1,464

WHOLESALE FISHERY TRADE

There were 69 establishments engaged in the wholesale fishery trade of Lake Erie in 1922. These employed 670 persons, to whom $775,716 were paid in wages, representing a total investment of $1,911,689. Cash capital to the amount of $1,149,257 was used. Compared with 1917, this shows a slight decrease in number of establishments and persons employed, although the investment has increased in all phases.

The following table shows the statistics of the wholesale fishery trade of Lake Erie in 1922:

Wholesale fishery trade of Lake Erie in 1922

Cities	State	Number of firms	Persons engaged	Wages paid	Shore and accessory property	Cash capital
Buffalo	New York	8	73	$141,568	$244,439	$376,157
Dunkirk and Westfield	do	3	27	30,750	74,100	30,000
Erie	Pennsylvania	9	195	150,149	437,959	287,000
Cleveland	Ohio	10	69	93,756	190,770	70,800
Toledo	do	4	21	13,456	207,000	28,000
Port Clinton	do	3	25	24,000	76,500	65,000
Sandusky	do	5	93	131,820	269,556	138,500
Ashtabula and Grand River	do	4	37	65,915	75,629	45,000
Vermilion and Lorain	do	4	29	23,506	40,577	28,000
Huron	do	3	23	31,810	59,199	16,700
Detroit [1]	Michigan	16	78	68,986	235,960	64,100
Total		69	670	775,716	1,911,689	1,149,257

[1] Includes one firm at Monroe, Mich.

FISHERIES OF LAKE ONTARIO

The fisheries of Lake Ontario in 1922 gave employment to 366 persons, of whom 352 were in the shore or boat fisheries and 14 were employed as shoresmen.

The investment amounted to $173,287, which included 192 rowboats, valued at $6,341; 100 power boats, valued at $31,920; fishing apparatus used on boats, valued at $62,511; shore and accessory property, valued at $47,515; and cash capital amounting to $25,000. The fishing apparatus included 419 trap nets, valued at $33,589; 2,319 gill nets, valued at $24,215; 204 fyke nets, valued at $3,362; and seines, lines, etc., to the value of $1,345.

The products of the fisheries amounted to 929,186 pounds, valued at $109,094, all of which were taken in the shore or boat fisheries, as no vessels were engaged in the fisheries of this lake in 1922. The principal species taken included ciscoes, 187,484 pounds, valued at $15,191; German carp, 138,711 pounds, valued at $10,927; bullheads, 107,481 pounds, valued at $8,209; pike perch, 141,210 pounds, valued at $28,490; suckers, 77,925 pounds, valued at $4,664; common whitefish, 54,951 pounds, valued at $9,603; and lake trout, 46,698 pounds, valued at $5,826.

Compared with 1917, the latest previous year for which statistics are available, there was an increase of 77 in the number of persons employed, of $40,634 in the investment, and of 13,570 pounds in the quantity and $24,981 in the value of the products.

FISHERIES BY COUNTIES

The following table shows, by counties, the number of persons employed, investment, and quantity and value of products of the fisheries in 1922:

Persons engaged, investment, and products (by species) in the fisheries of Lake Ontario in 1922, by counties

Item	Cayuga		Jefferson		Monroe		Niagara	
PERSONS ENGAGED	*No*	*Value*	*No.*	*Value*	*No.*	*Value*	*No.*	*Value*
In shore or boat fisheries	44		135		41		16	
Shoresmen			14					
Total	44		149		41		16	
INVESTMENT								
Rowboats	37	$1,050	62	$2,375	15	$380	4	$130
Power boats	4	1,400	54	18,720	5	1,075	12	2,425
Trap nets	46	3,830	289	22,344	1	75	5	2,000
Gill nets	30	395	998	6,888	86	866	66	3,054
Fyke nets			199	3,310	1	15		
Seines (haul)			10	465	2	45	2	155
Lines		8		215		40		70
Scap nets			3	11	17	51		
Spears			10	50				
Eel pots					3	10		
Shore and accessory property		280		35,610				500
Cash capital				25,000				
Total		6,963		114,988		2,557		8,334
PRODUCTS	*Pounds*	*Value*	*Pounds*	*Value*	*Pounds*	*Value*	*Pounds*	*Value*
Bowfin			530	$29	20	$2		
Bullheads	1,904	$43	89,465	7,038	1,070	60		
Burbot					6,815	655	496	$130
Carp, German	635	69	28,168	1,644	1,619	130	92,708	7,408
Ciscoes:								
Fresh	34,545	3,228	32,105	1,910	4,972	473	12,450	837
Salted			3,000	450				
Eels	856	89	43,832	3,463	297	43	160	16
Pike	124	13	19,258	2,284	46	5		
Pike perch:								
Blue pike	856	106	6,903	614	1,704	241	22,553	1,742
Wall-eyed or yellow pike	421	56	105,103	25,160	21	6		
Rock bass			5,496	260	78	8		
Shiner			6,600	4,950				
Sturgeon	576	187	13,322	3,717	1,094	181	8,730	2,217
Sturgeon caviar			62	222			125	345
Suckers	1,312	115	55,484	3,332	4,666	334	7,816	313
Sunfish	400	32	12,287	540	400	28		
Trout, lake			31,720	3,043	72	21	3,369	443
Whitefish			22,796	2,800	125	22	2,574	463
Yellow perch	1,430	146	25,708	2,035	1,237	163	310	55
Other fish							1,200	60
Total	43,059	4,084	501,839	63,491	24,236	2,372	152,491	14,029

Persons engaged, investment, and products (by species) in the fisheries of Lake Ontario, in 1922, by counties—Continued

Item	Orleans		Oswego		Wayne		Total	
PERSONS ENGAGED.	*No.*	*Value*	*No.*	*Value*	*No.*	*Value*	*No.*	*Value*
In shore or boat fisheries	7		26		83		352	
Shoresmen							14	
Total	7		26		83		366	
INVESTMENT								
Rowboats	4	$170	7	$880	63	$1,356	192	$6,341
Power boats	2	650	14	5,425	9	2,225	100	31,920
Trap nets					78	5,340	419	33,589
Gill nets	13	550	792	8,442	334	4,020	2,319	24,215
Fyke nets			2	30	2	7	204	3,362
Seines (haul)					1	150	15	815
Lines		10		65				408
Scap nets							20	62
Spears							10	50
Eel pots							3	10
Shore and accessory property				10,750		375		47,515
Cash capital								25,000
Total		1,380		25,592		13,473		173,287
PRODUCTS	*Pounds*	*Value*	*Pounds*	*Value*	*Pounds*	*Value*	*Pounds*	*Value*
Bowfin					1,008	$55	1,558	$86
Bullheads			236	$23	14,806	1,045	107,481	8,209
Burbot	3,810	$465			4,520	337	15,641	1,587
Carp, German			50	4	15,531	1,672	138,711	10,927
Ciscoes:								
Fresh	612	36	58,783	4,660	41,017	3,597	184,484	14,741
Salted							3,000	450
Eels			90	9	404	48	45,639	3,668
Pike					20	2	19,448	2,304
Pike perch:								
Blue pike	550	125	880	123	1,454	149	34,900	3,100
Wall-eyed or yellow pike			500	125	265	43	106,310	25,390
Rock bass					400	40	5,974	308
Shiner							6,600	4,950
Sturgeon	1,052	324	6,994	1,623	2,428	712	34,196	8,961
Sturgeon, caviar			150	450	8	26	345	1,043
Suckers	2,470	247	4,500	233	1,677	90	77,925	4,664
Sunfish			600	36			13,687	636
Trout, lake	417	100	10,822	2,148	298	71	46,698	5,826
Whitefish	2,365	663	25,767	5,350	1,324	305	54,951	9,603
Yellow perch			400	40	1,353	142	30,438	2,581
Other fish							1,200	60
Total	11,276	1,960	109,772	14,824	86,513	8,334	929,186	109,094

FISHERIES BY APPARATUS

The catch, as previously noted, was all taken in the shore or boat fisheries. Trap nets took 494,871 pounds of fish, valued at $57,168; gill nets, 263,337 pounds, valued at $33,232; fyke nets, 82,966 pounds, valued at $6,107; seines, 37,351 pounds, valued at $7,441; lines, 30,381 pounds, valued at $3,798; scap nets, 2,026 pounds, valued at $170; spears, 18,000 pounds, valued at $1,140; and eel pots, 254 pounds, valued at $38. The principal species taken with trap nets were bullheads, German carp, ciscoes, pike perch, and suckers; with gill nets, ciscoes, pike perch, sturgeon, lake trout, and whitefish; with fyke nets, bullheads, eels, pike, and suckers; with seines, German carp; and with lines, sturgeon, lake trout, and yellow perch. Scap nets took small quantities of bowfin, bullheads, German carp, eels, and suckers; and spears took German carp, eels, and suckers. Eel pots took a small catch of eels.

The following table gives the products of the fisheries of Lake Ontario by counties, apparatus, and species in 1922:

Yield of the fisheries of Lake Ontario in 1922, by counties, apparatus, and species

Apparatus and species	Cayuga		Jefferson		Monroe		Niagara	
	Pounds	Value	Pounds	Value	Pounds	Value	Pounds	Value
Trap nets:								
Bullheads	1,904	$43	39,724	$3,423	400	$20		
Carp, German	635	69	18,346	1,059			92,000	$7,360
Ciscoes—								
Fresh	31,206	2,918	9,573	556			6,310	378
Salted			2,800	420				
Eels	788	82	26,535	2,102				
Pike	18	3	10,290	1,209				
Pike perch—								
Blue pike	356	36	4,695	417			3,541	212
Wall-eyed or yellow pike	110	11	104,145	24,994				
Rock-bass			5,215	243				
Sturgeon			3,394	856				
Sturgeon caviar			42	137				
Suckers	252	54	37,648	2,282	200	20	3,600	108
Sunfish	400	32	8,276	380				
Trout, lake			5,248	555				
Whitefish			12,134	1,569				
Yellow perch	920	97	13,244	1,109	150	18		
Total	36,589	3,345	301,309	41,311	750	58	105,451	8,058
Gill nets:								
Bullheads					112	9		
Burbot					6,467	622	496	130
Ciscoes—								
Fresh	3,339	310	22,532	1,354	4,952	471	4,525	362
Salted			200	30				
Pike	106	10	1,788	219	46	5		
Pike perch—								
Blue pike	500	70	1,941	169	1,696	240	16,300	1,416
Wall-eyed or yellow pike	311	45	120	19	21	6		
Rock bass					78	8		
Sturgeon	576	187	8,872	2,584	542	104	5,560	1,449
Sturgeon caviar			20	85				
Suckers	1,060	61	343	16	3,779	253	1,910	100
Trout, lake			12,972	1,408	72	21	3,369	443
Whitefish			10,662	1,231	110	20	2,574	463
Yellow perch	510	49	1,644	142	1,077	144	310	55
Other fish							1,200	60
Total	6,402	732	61,094	7,257	18,952	1,903	36,244	4,478
Fyke nets:								
Bowfin			530	29				
Bullheads			48,814	3,544				
Burbot					300	30		
Carp, German			2,547	188				
Ciscoes					20	2		
Eels			6,222	483				
Pike			4,709	596				
Pike perch—								
Blue pike			267	28	8	1		
Wall-eyed or yellow pike			368	68				
Rock bass			281	17				
Suckers			12,447	805	15	1		
Sunfish			3,411	142				
Whitefish					15	2		
Yellow perch			2,470	116	10	1		
Total			82,066	6,016	368	37		
Seines:								
Bullheads			927	71	100	8		
Carp, German			2,275	147	1,000	80	708	48
Ciscoes							1,615	97
Eels			75	8			160	16
Pike			2,471	260				
Pike perch—								
Blue pike							2,712	114
Wall-eyed or yellow pike			470	79				
Shiner			6,600	4,950				
Suckers			1,582	89	250	20	2,306	105
Sunfish			600	18	400	28		
Yellow perch			350	28				
Total			15,350	5,650	1,750	136	7,501	380

Yield of the fisheries of Lake Ontario in 1922, by counties, apparatus, and species—Continued

Apparatus and species	Cayuga		Jefferson		Monroe		Niagara	
	Pounds	Value	Pounds	Value	Pounds	Value	Pounds	Value
Lines:								
Burbot					48	$3		
Eels	68	$7	1,000	$70				
Sturgeon			1,056	277	552	77	3,170	$768
Sturgeon caviar							125	345
Trout, lake			13,500	1,080				
Yellow perch			8,000	640				
Total	68	7	23,556	2,067	600	80	3,295	1,113
Scap nets:								
Bowfin					20	2		
Bullheads					458	23		
Carp, German					619	50		
Eels					43	5		
Suckers			464	50	422	40		
Total			464	50	1,562	120		
Spears:								
Carp, German			5,000	250				
Eels			10,000	800				
Suckers			3,000	90				
Total			18,000	1,140				
Eel pots: Eels					254	38		
Grand total	43,059	4,084	501,839	63,491	24,236	2,372	152,491	14,029

Apparatus and species	Orleans		Oswego		Wayne		Total	
	Pounds	Value	Pounds	Value	Pounds	Value	Pounds	Value
Trap nets:								
Bowfin					993	$54	993	$54
Bullheads					14,736	1,038	56,764	4,524
Carp, German					2,731	394	113,712	8,882
Ciscoes—								
Fresh					30,684	2,721	77,773	6,573
Salted							2,800	420
Eels					379	45	27,702	2,229
Pike							10,308	1,212
Pike perch—								
Blue pike					125	16	8,717	681
Wall-eyed or yellow pike							104,255	25,005
Rock bass					400	40	5,615	283
Sturgeon					112	36	3,506	892
Sturgeon caviar							42	137
Suckers					512	37	42,212	2,501
Sunfish							8,676	412
Trout, lake							5,248	555
Whitefish							12,134	1,569
Yellow perch					100	15	14,414	1,239
Total					50,772	4,396	494,871	57,168
Gill nets:								
Bullheads							112	9
Burbot	3,810	$465			4,520	337	15,293	1,554
Ciscoes—								
Fresh	612	36	58,783	$4,660	10,303	873	105,046	8,066
Salted							200	30
Pike					20	2	1,960	236
Pike perch—								
Blue pike	550	125	880	123	1,329	133	23,196	2,276
Wall-eyed or yellow pike			500	125	265	43	1,217	238
Rock bass							78	8
Sturgeon	740	231	4,544	1,190	2,316	676	23,150	6,421
Sturgeon caviar			150	450	8	26	178	561
Suckers	2,470	247	4,500	233	1,099	47	15,161	957
Sunfish			600	36			600	36
Trout, lake	417	100	10,822	2,148	298	71	27,950	4,191
Whitefish	2,365	663	25,767	5,350	1,324	305	42,802	8,032
Yellow perch			400	40	1,253	127	5,194	557
Other fish							1,200	60
Total	10,964	1,867	106,946	14,355	22,735	2,640	263,337	33,232

Yield of the fisheries of Lake Ontario, in 1922, by counties, apparatus, and species—Continued

Apparatus and species	Orleans		Oswego		Wayne		Total	
	Pounds	Value	Pounds	Value	Pounds	Value	Pounds	Value
Fyke nets:								
Bowfin					15	$1	545	$30
Bullheads			136	$18	70	7	49,020	3,569
Burbot							300	30
Carp, German			50	4	50	3	2,647	195
Ciscoes					30	3	50	5
Eels			90	9	25	3	6,337	495
Pike							4,709	596
Pike perch—								
Blue pike							275	29
Wall-eyed or yellow pike							368	68
Rock bass							281	17
Suckers					66	6	12,528	812
Sunfish							3,411	142
White fish							15	2
Yellow perch							2,480	117
Total			276	31	256	23	82,966	6,107
Seines:								
Bullheads							1,027	79
Carp, German					12,750	1,275	16,733	1,550
Ciscoes							1,615	97
Eels							235	24
Pike							2,471	260
Pike perch—								
Blue pike							2,712	114
Wall-eyed or yellow pike							470	79
Shiner							6,600	4,950
Suckers							4,138	214
Sunfish							1,000	46
Yellow perch							350	28
Total					12,750	1,275	37,351	7,441
Lines:								
Bullheads			100	5			100	5
Burbot							48	3
Eels							1,068	77
Sturgeon	312	$93	2,450	433			7,540	1,648
Sturgeon caviar							125	345
Trout, lake							13,500	1,080
Yellow perch							8,000	640
Total	312	93	2,550	438			30,381	3,798
Scap nets:								
Bowfin							20	2
Bullheads							458	23
Carp, German							619	50
Eels							43	5
Suckers							886	90
Total							2,026	170
Spears:								
Carp, German							5,000	250
Eels							10,000	800
Suckers							3,000	90
Total							18,000	1,140
Eel pots: Eels							254	38
Grand total	11,276	1,960	109,772	14,824	86,513	8,334	929,186	109,094

FISHERIES OF THE ST. LAWRENCE RIVER

The fisheries of the St. Lawrence River in 1922 gave employment to 47 persons. The investment amounted to $6,894, including 30 rowboats, valued at $903; 11 power boats, valued at $3,825; fishing apparatus valued at $2,141; and shore property valued at $25. The fishing apparatus included 5 seines, valued at $403; 2 weirs, valued at $150; and lines to the value of $1,588. The products of the fisheries amounted to 58,192 pounds, with a value of $19,641. The catch taken with seines amounted to 14,250 pounds, valued at $8,538; with lines, 37,442 pounds, valued at $10,128; and with weirs 6,500 pounds, valued at $975. The products included sturgeon, 34,502 pounds, valued at $8,169; sturgeon caviar, 590 pounds, valued $1,753; eels, 8,850 pounds, valued at $1,181; shiner, 6,850 pounds, valued at $5,138; and suckers, 7,400 pounds, valued at $3,400.

The following table gives, by counties, the persons, investment, and the quantity and value of the products of the fisheries of the St. Lawrence River in 1922:

Persons engaged, investment, and products (by apparatus) in the fisheries of the St. Lawrence River in 1922, by counties

Items	Jefferson		St. Lawrence		Total	
PERSONS ENGAGED	*Number*	*Value*	*Number*	*Value*	*Number*	*Value*
Fishermen	17		30		47	
INVESTMENT						
Rowboats	3	$175	27	$728	30	$903
Power boats	8	2,925	3	900	11	3,825
Seines (haul)	5	403			5	403
Lines (set)		120		1,468		1,588
Weirs			2	150	2	150
Shore and accessory property				25		25
Total		3,623		3,271		6,894
PRODUCTS	*Pounds*	*Value*	*Pounds*	*Value*	*Pounds*	*Value*
Seines:						
Shiner	6,850	$5,138			6,850	5,138
Suckers	7,400	3,400			7,400	3,400
Total	14,250	8,538			14,250	8,538
Lines:						
Eels			2,350	$206	2,350	206
Sturgeon	7,858	1,756	26,644	6,413	34,502	8,169
Sturgeon caviar	53	173	537	1,580	590	1,753
Total	7,911	1,929	29,531	8,199	37,442	10,128
Weirs: Eels			6,500	975	6,500	975
Grand total	22,161	10,467	36,031	9,174	58,192	19,641

FISHERIES OF THE NIAGARA RIVER

The fisheries of the Niagara River in 1922 were conducted in Niagara County, N. Y., and gave employment to 27 persons. The investment amounted to $2,099, including 10 power boats, valued at $254; 5 seines, valued at $261; 9 fishing machines, valued at $1,175; lines valued at $49; and shore and accessory property valued at $360. The products of the fisheries amounted to 38,421 pounds, with a value of $3,066. The catch taken with seines was 9,111 pounds, valued at $580; with fishing machines, 27,914 pounds, valued at $2,308; and with lines, 1,396 pounds, valued at $178. The species taken included bullheads, 2,838 pounds, valued at $139; German carp, 2,406 pounds, valued at $132; ciscoes, 9,835 pounds, valued at $804; eels, 834 pounds, valued at $82; pike perch, 12,640 pounds, valued at $1,147; suckers, 6,791 pounds, valued at $468; and yellow perch, 3,077 pounds, valued at $294.

The following table gives the number of persons employed, investment, and the quantity and value of the products of the fisheries of Niagara River in 1922:

Persons engaged, investment, and products (by apparatus) in the fisheries of the Niagara River in 1922

Items	Niagara County		Items	Niagara County	
PERSONS ENGAGED	Number	Value	PRODUCTS—continued		
Fisherman	27		Seines—Continued.	Pounds	Value
			Suckers	2,205	$118
INVESTMENT			Total	9,111	580
Rowboats	10	$254			
Seines (haul)	5	261	Fishing machines:		
Fishing machines	9	1,175	Bullheads	1,358	64
Lines (set)	6	49	Carp, German	803	45
Shore and accessory property		360	Ciscoes	9,535	789
			Eels	761	73
Total		2,099	Pike perch (blue pike)	9,190	871
			Suckers	3,190	172
PRODUCTS			Yellow perch	3,077	294
Seines:	Pounds	Value			
Bullheads	1,480	$75	Total	27,914	2,308
Carp, German	1,603	87			
Ciscoes	300	15	Lines: Suckers	1,396	178
Eels	73	9			
Pike perch (blue pike)	3,450	276	Grand total	38,421	3,066

FISHERIES CONSIDERED BY STATES

The fisheries of the Great Lakes are prosecuted in the following States: New York, Pennsylvania, Ohio, Indiana, Michigan, Illinois, Wisconsin and Minnesota. Michigan borders on Lakes Superior, Michigan, Huron, St. Clair, and Erie; Wisconsin on Lakes Superior and Michigan; and New York on Lakes Erie and Ontario. It is therefore of importance to consider these statistics by States as well as by lakes.

In 1922 there were 8,039 persons engaged in the fisheries of the Great Lakes, of whom 731 are credited to New York, 479 to Pennsylvania, 1,588 to Ohio, 96 to Indiana, 3,046 to Michigan, 476 to Illinois, 1,346 to Wisconsin, and 277 to Minnesota.

The investment, amounting to $12,046,458, was divided among the States as follows: New York, $1,119,093; Pennsylvania, $1,209,-156; Ohio, $2,649,646; Indiana, $67,375; Michigan $3,251,305; Illinois, $1,580,252; Wisconsin, $1,879,684; and Minnesota, $289,947.

The products, aggregating 108,732,443 pounds, valued at $6,689,-611, were distributed among the States as follows: New York, 5,210,209 pounds, valued at $364,635; Pennsylvania, 11,043,659 pounds, valued at $567,597; Ohio, 38,316,813 pounds, valued at $2,025,994; Indiana, 1,044,485 pounds, valued at $74,702; Michigan, 30,415,369 pounds, valued at $2,217,310; Illinois, 513,640 pounds, valued at $58,519; Wisconsin, 15,601,039 pounds, valued at $1,164,-788; and Minnesota, 6,587,229 pounds, valued at $186,066. Separate statistics, by lakes, are given for States whose fisheries are conducted in more than one lake.

The following table gives, by States, the number of persons engaged, apparatus and capital employed, and products of the fisheries of the Great Lakes in 1922:

Persons engaged, investment, and products in the fisheries of the Great Lakes in 1922, by States

Items	New York [1]		Pennsylvania		Ohio [2]	
PERSONS ENGAGED	Number	Value	Number	Value	Number	Value
On vessels fishing	96		249		237	
On vessels transporting			2		24	
In shore or boat fisheries	521		33		1,030	
Shoresmen	114		195		297	
Total	731		479		1,588	
INVESTMENT						
Vessels fishing:						
Steam	9	$65,000	34	$229,000	26	$144,100
Tonnage	208		850		543	
Outfit		13,000		57,874		31,632
Gasoline	9	24,500	10	28,000	18	61,400
Tonnage	88		120		265	
Outfit		6,575		7,607		16,215
Vessels transporting:						
Steam			2	12,000	3	9,500
Tonnage			66		52	
Outfit				4,148		1,050
Gasoline					17	44,750
Tonnage					147	
Outfit						5,583
Sail and row boats	263	8,518	15	520	532	16,150
Power boats	135	48,145	12	8,800	312	131,990
Apparatus, vessel fisheries:						
Gill nets	4,819	59,315	15,212	113,108	16,524	88,576
Apparatus, shore fisheries:						
Pound nets and trap nets	441	35,049	65	19,950	3,794	529,160
Gill nets	4,814	47,715	370	1,450	2,956	11,933
Fyke nets	204	3,362			432	26,620
Seines (haul)	37	2,764			151	22,310
Lines		2,132				
Fishing machines	9	1,175				
Other apparatus		272				
Shore and accessory property		370,414		439,699		1,116,677
Cash capital		431,157		287,000		392,000
Total		1,119,093		1,209,156		2,649,646
PRODUCTS	Pounds	Value	Pounds	Value	Pounds	Value
Bowfin	1,558	$86				
Burbot	15,991	1,594	6,438	$65	347,216	$6,017
Carp, German	200,177	14,013	41,472	1,379	3,633,923	145,304
Catfish and bullheads	111,529	8,424	1,531	149	1,278,835	91,509
Ciscoes:						
Fresh	3,310,373	167,878	6,963,128	347,499	6,078,847	304,755
Salted	3,000	450				
Eels	55,323	4,931				
Goldeye and mooneye					9,546	101
Muskellunge					85	9
Pike	19,448	2,304			57,763	2,968
Pike perch:						
Blue pike	612,069	23,122	3,208,861	149,438	10,768,805	552,657
Saugers	94,277	4,711	139,480	6,973	5,768,621	283,653
Wall-eyed or yellow pike	117,217	27,709	25,962	4,348	1,744,967	258,936
Rock bass	5,974	308				
Sheepshead or drum	25	1	58,509	1,449	2,291,424	55,237
Shiner	13,450	10,088				
Sturgeon	82,597	20,826	1,341	503	235	94
Sturgeon caviar	949	2,832	105	200	8	20
Suckers, fresh	161,851	12,717	45,664	1,488	1,338,650	40,035
Sunfishes	13,687	636				
Trout, lake, fresh	47,979	5,942	585	49	31	3
White bass	1,598	113	14,257	566	1,004,773	41,129
Whitefish, common, fresh	259,659	49,768	375,972	75,093	338,465	57,613
Yellow perch	80,278	6,122	160,354	8,398	2,679,211	160,910
Other fish	1,200	60				
Turtles					1,408	113
Mussel shells					974,000	23,410
Pearls						435
Slugs						1,086
Total	5,210,209	364,635	11,043,659	597,597	38,316,813	2,025,994

[1] Includes St. Lawrence and Niagara Rivers.
[2] Includes mussel fisheries of the Auglaize, Maumee, Sandusky, and Tiffin Rivers.

Persons engaged, investment, and products in the fisheries of the Great Lakes in 1922, by States—Continued

Items	Indiana [3]		Michigan [4]		Illinois	
PERSONS ENGAGED	*Number*	*Value*	*Number*	*Value*	*Number*	*Value*
On vessels fishing	22		582		38	
On vessels transporting			57			
In shore or boat fisheries	63		2,000		12	
Shoresmen	11		407		426	
Total	96		3,046		476	
INVESTMENT						
Vessels fishing:						
Steam	4	$14,000	63	$202,750	2	$12,000
Tonnage	92		1,199		43	
Outfit		3,700		62,820		925
Gasoline	1	500	123	113,900	8	20,000
Tonnage	8		1,005		83	
Outfit		20		29,896		5,545
Vessels transporting:						
Steam			1	1,000		
Tonnage			8			
Outfit				65		
Gasoline			39	44,600		
Tonnage			294			
Outfit				4,540		
Sail and row boats	39	550	1,021	31,985	5	135
Power boats	17	5,250	623	214,071	4	2,800
Apparatus, vessel fisheries:						
Gill nets	1,206	22,120	20,788	248,522	1,710	15,218
Lines		800		23,280		
Apparatus, shore fisheries:						
Pound nets and trap nets	13	7,600	2,284	491,495		
Gill nets	149	725	9,836	95,107	190	642
Fyke nets			818	39,775		
Seines (haul)			135	27,500		
Lines				6,317		
Other apparatus		210		4,701		
Shore and accessory property		10,900		1,214,324		1,004,987
Cash capital		1,000		394,657		518,000
Total		67,375		3,251,305		1,580,252
PRODUCTS	*Pounds*	*Value*	*Pounds*	*Value*	*Pounds*	*Value*
Black bass			2,000	$200		
Buffalofish	772	$42	185	11		
Burbot	420	18	8,984	233		
Carp, German	5,350	220	3,494,939	145,111		
Catfish and bullheads			125,439	10,042		
Ciscoes:						
Fresh	296,600	16,474	3,962,743	134,183	252,000	$19,570
Salted			2,734,740	63,836		
Smoked					29,165	4,893
Goldeye and mooneye			3,892	39		
Pike	25	3	81,344	8,579		
Pike perch: Wall-eyed or yellow pike	150	37	1,412,934	192,237		
Sheepshead or drum			59,721	1,693		
Sturgeon	2,160	404	9,991	4,289		
Sturgeon caviar			796	583		
Suckers, fresh	975	65	2,842,094	145,389		
Trout, lake, fresh	271,570	37,785	6,918,905	782,661	203,075	30,104
Trout, steelhead	11,165	2,233				
White bass			1,981	198		
Whitefish, common:						
Fresh	20,800	3,460	2,834,020	454,834		
Caviar			1,289	1,009		
Whitefish, Menominee:						
Fresh			106,214	7,394		
Salted			960	60		
Yellow perch	13,500	1,491	987,028	68,703	29,400	3,952
Mussel shells	421,000	11,100	4,825,170	183,230		
Pearls		420		7,931		
Slugs		950		4,865		
Total	1,044,485	74,702	30,415,369	2,217,310	513,640	58,519

NOTE.—The mussel fisheries in the rivers tributary to the Great Lakes have been prosecuted only a few years and have never previously been shown with statistics of the Great Lakes.

[3] Includes mussel fisheries of the Maumee, St. Marys, St. Joseph of the Maumee, St. Joseph, and Pigeon Rivers.

[4] Includes mussel fisheries of the St. Joseph, Grand, Kalamazoo, Maple, Muskegon, Pigeon, and Thornapple Rivers.

Persons engaged, investment, and products in the fisheries of the Great Lakes in 1922, by States—Continued

Items	Wisconsin [1]		Minnesota		Total	
PERSONS ENGAGED	*Number*	*Value*	*Number*	*Value*	*Number*	*Value*
On vessels, fishing	549		4		1,777	
On vessels, transporting	70		7		160	
In shore or boat fisheries	457		241		4,357	
Shoresmen	270		25		1,745	
Total	1,346		277		8,039	
INVESTMENT						
Vessels, fishing:						
Steam	42	$216,000			180	$882,850
Tonnage	933				3,868	
Outfit		35,572				205,523
Gasoline	153	228,650	2	$4,000	324	480,950
Tonnage	1,478		21		3,068	
Outfit		31,800		500		98,158
Vessels, transporting:						
Steam					6	22,500
Tonnage					126	
Outfit						5,263
Gasoline	37	38,950	3	11,000	96	139,300
Tonnage	354		25		820	
Outfit		4,170		2,400		16,693
Sail and row boats	221	7,415	217	6,510	2,313	71,783
P e boats	150	39,085	95	26,800	1,348	476,941
Apparatus, vessel fisheries:						
Gill nets	17,659	174,503	120	1,400	78,038	722,762
Lines		9,550				33,630
Apparatus, shore fisheries:						
Pound nets and trap nets	230	88,725	4	800	6,831	1,172,779
Gill nets	7,860	43,531	3,493	41,605	29,668	242,708
Fyke nets	1,151	23,940			2,605	93,697
Seines (haul)	40	7,945			363	60,519
Lines		220		1,120		9,789
Crawfish pots	5,255	1,409			5,255	1,409
Fishing machines					9	1,175
Other apparatus		101				5,284
Shore and accessory property		699,695		169,812		5,026,508
Cash capital		228,423		24,000		2,276,237
Total		1,879,684		289,947		12,046,458
PRODUCTS	*Pounds*	*Value*	*Pounds*	*Value*	*Pounds*	*Value*
Black bass					2,000	$200
Bowfin					1,558	86
Buffalofish					955	53
Burbot	8,741	$346			387,790	8,273
Carp, German	743,580	24,847			8,119,441	330,874
Catfish and bullheads	144,964	7,293			1,662,298	117,417
Ciscoes:						
Fresh	5,202,800	150,705	3,654,737	$70,978	29,721,228	1,212,042
Frozen	110,400	2,302	825,751	16,679	936,151	18,981
Salted	1,279,425	35,631	1,289,200	39,742	5,306,365	139,659
Smoked	9,250	1,105	7,500	375	45,915	6,373
Eels					55,323	4,931
Goldeye and mooneye					13,438	140
Muskellunge					85	9
Pike	31,493	3,100	572	101	190,645	17,055
Pike perch:						
Blue pike					14,589,735	725,217
Saugers					6,002,378	295,337
Wall-eyed or yellow pike	73,743	12,511			3,374,973	495,778
Rock bass					5,974	308
Sheepshead or drum	3,912	80			2,413,591	58,460
Shiner					13,450	10,088
Sturgeon					96,324	26,116
Sturgeon caviar					1,858	3,635
Suckers:						
Fresh	986,444	63,201	1,975	120	5,377,653	263,015
Salted	17,560	560			17,560	560
Sunfishes					13,687	636
Trout, lake:						
Fresh	5,519,223	737,437	738,551	52,000	13,699,919	1,645,981
Salted	9,020	501	17,100	1,156	26,120	1,657
Trout, steelhead					11,165	2,233
White bass	7,905	245			1,030,514	42,251

[1] Includes mussel fisheries of the Wolf River.

Persons engaged, investment, and products in the fisheries of the Great Lakes in 1922, by States—Continued

Items	Wisconsin		Minnesota		Total	
PRODUCTS—continued						
Whitefish, common:	*Pounds*	*Value*	*Pounds*	*Value*	*Pounds*	*Value*
Fresh	341,389	$53,058	34,925	$4,105	4,205,230	$697,931
Salted			50	35	50	35
Caviar					1,289	1,009
Whitefish, Menominee:						
Fresh	33,037	2,399	8,768	370	148,019	10,163
Salted	14,480	677	8,100	405	23,540	1,142
Yellow perch	952,479	65,352			4,902,250	314,928
Other fish					1,200	60
Crawfish	82,764	2,887			82,764	2,887
Turtles					1,408	113
Mussel shells	25,805	408			6,245,975	218,148
Pearls		26				8,812
Slugs		12				6,913
Oil	2,625	105			2,625	105
Total	15,601,039	1,164,788	6,587,229	186,066	108,732,443	6,689,611

NOTE.—The mussel fisheries in the rivers tributary to the Great Lakes have been prosecuted only a few years and have never previously been shown with statistics of the Great Lakes.

MICHIGAN

The fisheries of Michigan were prosecuted in Lakes Superior, Michigan, Huron, St. Clair and tributaries, and Erie, but were most extensive in Lake Huron and Lake Michigan. They are given in detail in the following table:

Persons engaged, investment, and products of the fisheries of Michigan in 1922, by lakes

Items	Lake Erie [1]		Lake St. Clair [2]		Lake Huron	
PERSONS ENGAGED	*Number*	*Value*	*Number*	*Value*	*Number*	*Value*
On vessels fishing					131	
On vessels transporting					9	
In shore or boat fisheries	168		90		705	
Shoresmen	78				156	
Total	246		90		1,001	
INVESTMENT						
Vessels fishing:						
Steam					18	$84,500
Tonnage					443	
Outfit						25,190
Gasoline					11	9,400
Tonnage					89	
Outfit						2,385
Vessels transporting:						
Steam					1	1,000
Tonnage					8	
Outfit						65
Gasoline					13	25,950
Tonnage					110	
Outfit						2,000
Sail and rowboats	77	$4,130	52	$2,770	224	11,825
Power boats	32	14,350	30	6,900	248	118,225
Apparatus, vessel fisheries:						
Gill nets					4,043	78,885
Lines						7,275
Apparatus, shore fisheries:						
Pound nets and trap nets	50	3,940			1,474	366,390
Gill nets	28	112			2,960	36,139
Fyke nets	320	8,570			425	26,290
Seines (haul)	50	6,090	3	2,700	75	18,290
Lines				87		1,070
Other apparatus		44				
Shore and accessory property		268,860		5,400		644,388
Cash capital		64,100				189,500
Total		370,196		17,857		1,648,767

[1] Includes the mussel fisheries of the Huron and Raisin Rivers.
[2] Includes St. Clair River.

Persons engaged, investment, and products of the fisheries of Michigan in 1922, by lakes—Continued

Items	Lake Erie		Lake St. Clair		Lake Huron	
PRODUCTS	*Pounds*	*Value*	*Pounds*	*Value*	*Pounds*	*Value*
Black bass			2,000	$200		
Buffalofish					63	$3
Burbot					3,075	62
Carp, German	2,164,726	$93,300	260,000	10,400	1,065,116	41,256
Catfish and bullheads	55,943	5,149	5,005	148	64,826	4,518
Ciscoes:						
Fresh	210	14			2,775,403	90,176
Salted					2,721,060	63,437
Goldeye and mooneye	3,892	39				
Pike	7,332	910	4,040	404	39,473	2,985
Pike perch: Wall-eyed or yellow pike	31,587	3,489	38,620	5,741	1,260,374	171,102
Sheepshead or drum	12,385	265	16	1	46,760	1,400
Sturgeon			231	61	2,374	928
Sturgeon caviar					126	269
Suckers	144,122	3,878			1,889,129	104,204
Trout, lake					2,108,249	215,501
White bass	1,981	198				
Whitefish:						
Common	3,064	531			1,300,621	199,503
Caviar					1,289	1,009
Menominee—						
Fresh					30,029	1,708
Salted					960	60
Yellow perch	83,004	4,937	4,100	410	633,188	47,138
Mussel shells	99,170	3,165				
Pearls		331				
Slugs		190				
Total	2,607,416	116,396	310,012	17,365	13,942,115	945,259

Items	Lake Michigan [3]		Lake Superior		Total	
PERSONS ENGAGED	*Number*	*Value*	*Number*	*Value*	*Number*	*Value*
On vessels fishing	417		34		582	
On vessels transporting	45		3		57	
In shore or boat fisheries	749		288		2,000	
Shoresmen	158		15		407	
Total	1,369		340		3,046	
INVESTMENT						
Vessels fishing:						
Steam	40	$104,100	5	$14,150	63	$202,750
Tonnage	656		100		1,199	
Outfit		28,660		8,970		62,820
Gasoline	109	102,000	3	2,500	123	113,900
Tonnage	892		24		1,005	
Outfit		24,811		2,700		29,896
Vessels transporting:						
Steam					1	1,000
Tonnage					8	
Outfit						65
Gasoline	25	17,150	1	1,500	39	44,600
Tonnage	174		10		294	
Outfit		2,240		300		4,540
Sail and row boats	590	11,015	78	2,245	1,021	31,985
Power boats	195	38,211	118	36,385	623	214,071
Apparatus, vessel fisheries:						
Gill nets	15,590	149,512	1,155	20,125	20,788	248,522
Lines		13,175		2,830		23,280
Apparatus, shore fisheries:						
Pound nets and trap nets	489	84,690	271	36,475	2,284	491,495
Gill nets	3,599	21,668	3,249	37,188	9,836	95,107
Fyke nets	65	4,715	8	200	818	39,775
Seines (haul)			7	420	135	27,500
Lines		225		4,935		6,317
Other apparatus		4,657				4,701
Shore and accessory property		255,806		39,870		1,214,324
Cash capital		136,057		5,000		394,657
Total		998,692		215,793		3,251,305

[3] Includes the mussel fisheries of the St. Joseph, Grand, Kalamazoo, Maple, Muskegon, Pigeon, and Thornapple Rivers.
[4] Includes one small steamer valued at $500.

NOTE:—The mussel fisheries in the rivers tributary to the Great Lakes have been prosecuted only a few years and have never previously been shown in the statistics of the fisheries of Great Lakes.

Persons engaged, investment, and products of the fisheries of Michigan in 1922, by lakes—Continued

Items	Lake Michigan		Lake Superior		Total	
PRODUCTS	Pounds	Value	Pounds	Value	Pounds	Value
Black bass					2,000	$200
Buffalo fish	122	$8			185	11
Burbot	5,080	155	829	$16	8,984	233
Carp, German	5,097	155			3,494,939	145,111
Catfish and bullheads	3,665	227			125,439	10,042
Ciscoes:						
Fresh	854,717	33,754	332,413	10,239	3,962,743	134,183
Salted	13,680	399			2,734,740	63,836
Goldeye and mooneye					3,892	39
Pike	20,327	2,951	10,172	1,329	81,344	8,579
Pike perch: Wall-eyed or yellow pike	71,042	10,563	11,311	1,342	1,412,934	192,237
Sheepshead or drum	560	27			59,721	1,693
Sturgeon	7,043	3,177	343	123	9,991	4,289
Sturgeon caviar	670	314			796	583
Suckers	609,892	28,982	198,951	8,325	2,842,094	145,389
Trout, lake	3,454,425	438,385	1,356,231	128,775	6,918,905	782,661
White bass					1,981	198
Whitefish:						
Common	1,240,681	214,235	289,654	40,565	2,834,020	454,834
Caviar					1,289	1,009
Menominee—						
Fresh	75,725	5,667	460	19	106,214	7,394
Salted					960	60
Yellow perch	249,950	14,994	16,786	1,224	987,028	68,703
Mussel shells	4,726,000	180,065			4,825,170	183,230
Pearls		7,600				7,931
Slugs		4,675				4,865
Total	11,338,676	946,333	2,217,150	191,957	30,415,369	2,217,310

WISCONSIN

The fisheries of Wisconsin, which were prosecuted in Lake Superior and Lake Michigan, are shown in detail in the following table:

Persons engaged, investment, and products of the fisheries of Wisconsin in 1922, by lakes

Items	Lake Michigan		Lake Superior		Total	
PERSONS ENGAGED	Number	Value	Number	Value	Number	Value
On vessels fishing	534		15		549	
On vessels transporting	70				70	
In shore or boat fisheries	346		111		457	
Shoresmen	240		30		270	
Total	1,190		156		1,346	
INVESTMENT						
Vessels fishing:						
Steam	41	$211,000	1	$5,000	42	$216,000
Tonnage	918		15		933	
Outfit		31,997		3,575		35,572
Gasoline	151	226,350	2	2,300	153	228,650
Tonnage	1,459		19		1,478	
Outfit		29,970		1,830		31,800
Vessels transporting:						
Gasoline	37	38,950			37	38,950
Tonnage	354				354	
Outfit		4,170				4,170
Rowboats	197	6,695	24	720	221	7,415
Power boats	96	23,960	54	15,125	150	39,085
Apparatus, vessel fisheries:						
Gill nets	17,424	170,803	235	3,700	17,659	174,503
Lines		9,550				9,550

Persons engaged, investment, and products of the fisheries of Wisconsin in 1922, by lakes—Continued

Items	Lake Michigan [1]		Lake Superior		Total	
	Pounds	*Value*	*Pounds*	*Value*	*Pounds*	*Value*
INVESTMENT—continued						
Apparatus, shore fisheries:						
Pound nets and trap nets	202	$82,525	28	$6,200	230	$88,725
Gill nets	6,515	28,067	1,345	15,464	7,860	43,531
Fyke nets	1,131	22,940	20	1,000	1,151	23,940
Trammel nets	3	65			3	65
Seines (haul)	40	7,945			40	7,945
Lines		205		15		220
Crowfoot bars	2	30			2	30
Forks	2	6			2	6
Crawfish pots	5,255	1,409			5,255	1,409
Shore and accessory property		617,820		81,875		699,695
Cash capital		173,395		55,028		228,423
Total		1,687,852		191,832		1,879,684
PRODUCTS						
Burbot	8,741	346			8,741	346
Carp, German	743,580	24,847			743,580	24,847
Catfish and bullheads	144,964	7,293			144,964	7,293
Ciscoes:						
Fresh	4,031,696	132,663	1,171,104	18,042	5,202,800	150,705
Frozen			110,400	2,302	110,400	2,302
Salted	1,276,425	35,534	3,000	97	1,279,425	35,631
Smoked	9,250	1,105			9,250	1,105
Pike	26,036	2,467	5,457	633	31,493	3,100
Pike perch: Wall-eyed, or yellow pike	61,756	10,585	11,987	1,926	73,743	12,511
Sheepshead, or drum	3,912	80			3,912	80
Suckers:						
Fresh	903,040	59,925	83,404	3,276	986,444	63,201
Salted	5,760	147	11,800	413	17,560	560
Trout:						
Fresh	4,806,515	665,527	712,708	71,910	5,519,223	737,437
Salted	120	5	8,900	496	9,020	501
White bass	1,005	38	6,900	207	7,905	245
Whitefish:						
Common	285,568	46,240	55,821	6,818	341,389	53,058
Menominee—						
Fresh	31,438	2,310	1,599	89	33,037	2,399
Salted	14,480	677			14,480	677
Yellow perch	951,918	65,311	561	41	952,479	65,352
Crawfish	82,764	2,887			82,764	2,887
Mussel shells	25,805	408			25,805	408
Pearls		26				26
Slugs		12				12
Oil	2,625	105			2,625	105
Total	13,417,398	1,058,538	2,183,641	106,250	15,601,039	1,164,788

[1] Includes mussel fishery of the Wolf River in Wisconsin, which has never previously been shown.

NEW YORK

The fisheries of New York in the Great Lakes were prosecuted in Lake Ontario and the St. Lawrence and Niagara Rivers and in two counties (Erie and Chautauqua) on Lake Erie. The number of persons engaged, investment, and products of these fisheries are given in detail in the following table:

Persons engaged, investment, and products of the fisheries of New York in 1922, by lakes

Items	Lake Ontario [1]		Lake Erie		Total	
PERSONS ENGAGED	*Number*	*Value*	*Number*	*Value*	*Number*	*Value*
On vessels fishing			96		96	
In shore or boat fisheries	426		95		521	
Shoresmen	14		100		114	
Total	440		291		731	
INVESTMENT						
Vessels fishing:						
Steam			9	$65,000	9	$65,000
Tonnage			208		208	
Outfit				13,000		13,000
Gasoline			9	24,500	9	24,500
Tonnage			88		88	
Outfit				6,575		6,575
Rowboats	232	$7,498	31	1,020	263	8,518
Power boats	111	35,745	24	12,400	135	48,145
Apparatus, vessel fisheries:						
Gill nets			4,819	59,315	4,819	59,315
Apparatus, shore fisheries:						
Trap nets and weirs	421	33,739	22	1,460	443	35,199
Gill nets	2,319	24,215	2,495	23,500	4,814	47,715
Fyke nets	204	3,362			204	3,362
Seines (haul)	25	1,479	12	1,285	37	2,764
Lines		2,045		87		2,132
Scap nets	20	62			20	62
Fishing machines	9	1,175			9	1,175
Other apparatus	13	60			13	60
Shore and accessory property		47,900		322,514		370,414
Cash capital		25,000		406,157		431,157
Total		182,280		936,813		1,119,093
PRODUCTS	*Pounds*	*Value*	*Pounds*	*Value*	*Pounds*	*Value*
Bowfin	1,558	$86			1,558	$86
Burbot	15,641	1,587	350	$7	15,991	1,594
Carp, German	141,117	11,059	59,060	2,954	200,177	14,013
Catfish and bullheads	110,319	8,348	1,210	76	111,529	8,424
Ciscoes:						
Fresh	194,319	15,545	3,116,054	152,333	3,310,373	167,878
Salted	3,000	450			3,000	450
Eels	55,323	4,931			55,323	4,931
Pike	19,448	2,304			19,448	2,304
Pike perch:						
Blue pike	47,540	4,247	564,529	18,875	612,069	23,122
Sauger			94,277	4,711	94,277	4,711
Wall-eyed or yellow pike	106,310	25,390	10,907	2,319	117,217	27,709
Rock bass	5,974	308			5,974	308
Sheepshead or drum			25	1	25	1
Shiner	13,450	10,088			13,450	10,088
Sturgeon	68,698	17,130	13,899	3,696	82,597	20,826
Sturgeon caviar	935	2,796	14	36	949	2,832
Suckers	92,116	8,532	69,735	4,185	161,851	12,717
Sunfish	13,687	636			13,687	636
Trout, lake	46,698	5,826	1,281	116	47,979	5,942
White, bass			1,598	113	1,598	113
Whitefish	54,951	9,603	204,708	40,165	259,659	49,768
Yellow perch	33,515	2,875	46,763	3,247	80,278	6,122
Other fish	1,200	60			1,200	60
Total	1,025,799	131,801	4,184,410	232,834	5,210,209	364,635

[1] Includes St. Lawrence and Niagara Rivers.

FISHERIES OF LAKE OF THE WOODS, RAINY LAKE, AND LAKES KABETO-GAMA, NAMAKAN, AND SAND POINT

The number of persons engaged in the fisheries of Lake of the Woods, Rainy Lake, and Lakes Kabetogama, Namakan, and Sand Point, in 1922, was 123, of whom 2 were on transporting vessels, 99 in the shore or boat fisheries, and 22 were shoresmen.

The investment amounted to $139,955, and included 1 transporting vessel, valued at $1,700, and outfit valued at $150; 95 row and gasoline boats valued at $29,680; fishing apparatus valued at $29,225; shore and accessory property valued at $51,150; and cash capital amounting to $28,050. The fishing apparatus included 94 pound nets and trap nets, valued at $22,375; 461 gill nets, valued at $4,525; and 80 fyke nets, valued at $2,325.

The products of the fisheries amounted to 1,677,999 pounds, valued at $110,022, which were divided among the different forms of fishing apparatus as follows: Pound nets and trap nets, 677,877 pounds, valued at $46,627; gill nets, 819,979 pounds, valued at $54,986; and fyke nets, 180,143 pounds, valued at $8,409. The principal species taken were pike perch, 831,558 pounds, valued at $71,761; pike, 305,888 pounds, valued at $15,474; ciscoes, 151,983 pounds, valued at $3,272; whitefish, 141,544 pounds, valued at $8,368; catfish and bullheads, 97,409 pounds, valued at $5,509; suckers, 96,703 pounds, valued at $1,500; yellow perch, 13,204 pounds, valued at $991; burbot, 11,750 pounds, valued at $204; German carp, 9,896 pounds, valued at $270; and sturgeon, 5,059 pounds, valued at $1,974.

The following table shows the extent of the fisheries of Lake of the Woods, Rainy Lake, and Lakes Kabetogama, Namakan, and Sand Point, Minn., in 1922:

Fisheries of Lake of the Woods, Rainy Lake, and Lakes Kabetogama, Namakan, and Sand Point, Minn., 1922

Items	Lake of the Woods		Rainy Lake, and Lakes Kabeto-gama, Namakan, and Sand Point		Total	
PERSONS ENGAGED	*Number*	*Value*	*Number*	*Value*	*Number*	*Value*
On vessels transporting			2		2	
In shore or boat fisheries	70		29		99	
Shoresmen	18		4		22	
Total	88		35		123	
INVESTMENT						
Transporting vessels:						
Gasoline			1	$1,700	1	$1,700
Tonnage			11		11	
Outfit				150		150
Rowboats	18	$745	6	360	24	1,105
Gasoline boats	45	21,925	26	6,650	71	28,575
Pound nets and trap nets	78	18,375	16	4,000	94	22,375
Gill nets	291	2,825	170	1,700	461	4,525
Fyke nets	80	2,325			80	2,325
Shore and accessory property		45,050		6,100		51,150
Cash capital		21,500		6,550		28,050
Total		112,745		27,210		139,955

Fisheries of Lake of the Woods, Rainy Lake, and Lakes Kabetogama, Namakan, and Sand Point, Minn., 1922—Continued

Items	Lake of the Woods		Rainy Lake, and Lakes Kabetogama, Namakan, and Sand Point		Total	
PRODUCTS						
Pound nets and trap nets:	*Pounds*	*Value*	*Pounds*	*Value*	*Pounds*	*Value*
Bullheads	6,300	$369			6,300	$369
Burbot	11,500	200			11,500	200
Carp, German	4,777	128			4,777	128
Ciscoes	75,339	1,368			75,339	1,368
Crappie	60	5			60	5
Goldeye and mooneye	1,639	29			1,639	29
Muskellunge	251	26			251	26
Pike	107,655	6,122			107,655	6,122
Pike perch (sauger)	41	7			41	7
Pike perch (wall-eyed or yellow pike)	333,623	30,821			333,623	30,821
Rock bass	1,150	80			1,150	80
Sturgeon	5,059	1,974			5,059	1,974
Suckers	51,087	800			51,087	800
Whitefish	75,906	4,395			75,906	4,395
Yellow perch	3,490	303			3,490	303
Total	677,877	46,627			677,877	46,627
Gill nets:						
Burbot	250	4			250	4
Cisco	22,079	221	54,565	$1,683	76,644	1,904
Crappie	378	37			378	37
Goldeye and mooneye	2,807	53			2,807	53
Pike	112,004	4,243	31,735	3,020	143,739	7,263
Pike perch (wall-eyed or yellow pike)	396,845	32,866	92,230	7,583	489,075	40,449
Rock bass			2,286	170	2,286	170
Suckers	28,865	446			28,865	446
Trout, lake	920	24			920	24
Whitefish—						
Common	12,789	944	51,814	3,020	64,603	3,964
Menominee	1,035	9			1,035	9
Yellow perch	1,622	85	7,755	578	9,377	663
Total	579,594	38,932	240,385	16,054	819,979	54,986
Fyke nets:						
Buffalofish	400	12			400	12
Bullheads	91,109	5,140			91,109	5,140
Carp, German	5,119	142			5,119	142
Crappie	2,926	251			2,926	251
Pike	54,494	2,089			54,494	2,089
Pike perch (wall-eyed or yellow pike)	8,819	484			8,819	484
Rock bass	188	12			188	12
Suckers	16,751	254			16,751	254
Yellow perch	337	25			337	25
Total	180,143	8,409			180,143	8,409
Grand total	1,437,614	93,968	240,385	16,054	1,677,999	110,022

NOTE.—There were, in 1922, three wholesale firms engaged in business on the above lakes. These firms used buildings, with accessories, valued at $41,150 and cash capital amounting to $26,500. There were 3 proprietors, or managers, 4 clerks, and 15 other employees engaged, the total wages paid amounting to $35,614.

Lightning Source UK Ltd.
Milton Keynes UK
UKHW011205051118
331792UK00006B/901/P